Evangelical Christianity
and Democracy
in Africa

EVANGELICAL CHRISTIANITY
AND DEMOCRACY
IN THE GLOBAL SOUTH

Series Editor
Timothy Samuel Shah

Evangelical Christianity and Democracy in Latin America
Edited by Paul Freston

Evangelical Christianity and Democracy in Africa
Edited by Terence O. Ranger

Evangelical Christianity and Democracy in Asia
Edited by David H. Lumsdaine

Evangelical Christianity and Democracy in Global Perspective
Edited by Timothy Samuel Shah

Evangelical Christianity and Democracy in Africa

Edited by
TERENCE O. RANGER

OXFORD
UNIVERSITY PRESS
2008

OXFORD
UNIVERSITY PRESS

Oxford University Press, Inc., publishes works that further
Oxford University's objective of excellence
in research, scholarship, and education.

Oxford   New York
Auckland   Cape Town   Dar es Salaam   Hong Kong   Karachi
Kuala Lumpur   Madrid   Melbourne   Mexico City   Nairobi
New Delhi   Shanghai   Taipei   Toronto

With offices in
Argentina   Austria   Brazil   Chile   Czech Republic   France   Greece
Guatemala   Hungary   Italy   Japan   Poland   Portugal   Singapore
South Korea   Switzerland   Thailand   Turkey   Ukraine   Vietnam

Library of Congress Cataloging-in-Publication Data
Evangelical Christianity and democracy in Africa /
edited by Terence O. Ranger.
    p. cm.—(Evangelical Christianity and democracy in the Global South)
Includes bibliographical references and index.
ISBN 978-0-19-517477-9; 978-0-19-530802-0 (pbk.)
1. Evangelicalism—Political aspects—Africa, Sub-Saharan.
2. Democracy—Religious aspects—Christianity.
3. Christianity and politics—Africa, Sub-Saharan.
I. Ranger, T. O. (Terence O.).   II. Series.
BR1642.A35E93 2006
322'.10967—dc22   2005031888

9 8 7 6 5 4 3 2 1

Printed in the United States of America
on acid-free paper

For
Vinay Kumar Samuel,
on the fortieth anniversary of his ordination to ministry
in the Church of South India
(1967–2007)

And for all the churches of Asia, Africa, and Latin America
it remains his joy to serve

Preface

The research project that generated this volume began as an effort in evangelical self-understanding. The globally minded and globally active International Fellowship of Evangelical Mission Theologians (INFEMIT), together with its research and study arm, the Oxford Centre for Mission Studies (OCMS), based in Oxford, England, undertook numerous efforts in the 1980s and 1990s to develop sophisticated evangelical analyses of a host of global issues, including modernity and modernization, market economics, population growth, and human disability.[1] Toward the end of the 1990s it occurred to INFEMIT's director, Indian theologian Vinay Samuel, that international evangelicalism itself merited a critical analysis, particularly because of its growing social and political prominence in the developing countries of the "global South" (i.e., Africa, Asia, and Latin America).

Evangelical politics merited analysis, Samuel believed, not only because evangelical political efforts were increasingly organized and consequential but also because their impact on global South politics seemed so varied and ambivalent. After all, some of the best known instances of evangelical politics include the military dictatorship of Efraín Ríos Montt in Guatemala in the early 1980s as well as the support many white evangelicals gave to apartheid in South Africa until the early 1990s. On the other hand, the evangelical wing of Kenya's Anglican Church proved to be authoritarian president Daniel arap Moi's most vocal critic in the 1980s and 1990s.

In this variety and ambiguity global South evangelicals are not unlike their evangelical counterparts in the United States. Major political figures (such as former president Jimmy Carter, former senator Mark Hatfield, and former attorney general John Ashcroft) and movements (such as the Moral Majority and the Christian Coalition) suggest the enormous growth and influence of American evangelical political activism during the last thirty years. But they also underscore evangelicals' deep differences in political philosophy, their divergent policy goals, and the uncertainty of their long-term political achievements.[2] The fact that American evangelicals have remained consistent and enthusiastic supporters of George W. Bush—a president otherwise deeply and increasingly unpopular both inside and outside the United States—only deepens the sense that global evangelicalism has bequeathed an ambiguous political legacy that evangelicals bear a special responsibility to scrutinize.[3]

To launch this project of critical self-understanding, Vinay Samuel gathered a small team of evangelical scholars, including myself, in 1997. For the necessary funding, we turned to The Pew Charitable Trusts, which had an impressive track record of supporting scholarship on, and by, evangelicals. Luis Lugo, head of Pew's Religion Program at the time, and Susan Billington Harper, program officer with the Religion Program, provided indispensable encouragement and guidance at this early stage. As a first step in Pew's support, they provided a seed grant to conduct a preliminary "mapping" of the basic patterns of evangelical political activism across the global South as well as the most promising avenues for long-term research on the subject. Paul Freston, an outstanding sociologist specializing in the study of pentecostalism in Brazil and a member of our team, agreed to produce this mapping, and in a few short months performed the major miracle of writing a booklength overview of evangelical politics in nearly thirty countries in Africa, Asia, and Latin America, complete with an exhaustive bibliography. Freston's study, first in manuscript form and later as a published monograph, became a constant point of reference as we designed the project and, later, as we conducted the research.[4] It also made a compelling case to our prospective funders that the subject deserved more systematic and sustained examination. So in June 1999, The Pew Charitable Trusts provided our INFEMIT research team with a generous grant to conduct field research on politically engaged evangelicals on three continents—Asia, Africa, and Latin America—over three years.

We focused our critical analysis of evangelical politics in these regions of the global South in two ways. First, we identified what seemed to be the most significant cases of evangelical political mobilization and influence in each region's most significant countries: Brazil, Mexico, Guatemala, Nicaragua, Chile, and Peru in Latin America; Nigeria, Kenya, South Africa, Mozambique, Zambia, and Zimbabwe in Africa; and China, India, Indonesia, South Korea, and the Philippines in Asia.

Second, to give our research a sharper analytical and evaluative edge, we decided to pay special attention to the relationship between evangelical politics

and democracy in each region. How has the overall trend toward democratization in all the regions of the global South, especially during the "third wave"
of democratization (1974–1991), given evangelicals new incentives and opportunities for political mobilization and influence?[5] And, more important for
our critical purposes, what has been the impact of politically engaged evangelicalism on democratization? To what extent has it contributed to the in-
auguration and consolidation of democratic regimes? And in countries where
democratic transitions have not occurred, to what extent have evangelicals
promoted the norms and practices of democratic politics, whether at the local,
regional, or national level? Conversely, to what extent have politically engaged
evangelicals blocked, slowed, or otherwise undermined democratization in the
global South?

Evangelicalism's impact on democratization compelled our attention not
only because of our interest in assessing the level and quality of evangelical
political activism. It also seemed worthy of study because democratization in
the global South, despite dramatic advances, remained so limited and fragile—
particularly insofar as democracy in its most robust and valid form requires
not only free and fair elections but also effective respect for basic human
rights and freedoms. Democracy in Asia, Africa, and Latin America needed all
the help it could get, and we wanted to know how much help, if any, evangelicals were giving. Since the start of our research, just how much the overall
social and economic development of the global South requires the establishment of more effective, transparent, and democratic governance has become
even more painfully obvious. Yet in Asia and Africa in particular, according to
a 2007 Freedom House report, democratization has stagnated or even reversed
since 2005.[6]

Furthermore, recent studies of religion and democratization had included
almost no broad, comparative treatment of evangelical influences. Numerous
scholars noted the important roles Catholic and mainline Protestant churches
played in democratic transitions throughout the global South during the "third
wave" of democratization, particularly in the 1980s and early 1990s. Indeed,
the pro-democratic activism of such churches continues to provoke scholarly
and journalistic interest. The vocal opposition of Zimbabwe's Catholic bishops
to the increasingly repressive regime of Robert Mugabe, for example, received
considerable attention in the press in early 2007, notably in *The Economist*.[7]
But mainstream scholarship on religion and democratization, whether focused
on Africa, Asia, or Latin America, tended to ignore or downplay the burgeoning evangelical sector of global South Christianity.[8] Granted that bishops and
archbishops, clergy and laity, as well as a globe-trotting pope mobilized Catholic and mainline Protestant churches to battle authoritarian regimes and support democratic transitions throughout the global South, what about evangelical churches, denominations, and political parties? What about evangelical
movements within mainline churches? After all, many of these churches in

the global South, if not in their counterpart churches in Europe and North America, remain animated by the biblicist theology and missionary activism that are the hallmarks of evangelicalism.[9] Finally, we were eager to investigate the political contributions of the pentecostal subsector of evangelicalism in particular, which has become the most dynamic and demographically dominant force not only in global South evangelicalism but in global South Protestantism as a whole.

In addition, demographic trends recommended a focus on evangelical contributions to global South democratization. Whereas throughout the 1950s and 1960s leading scholars and other observers, such as Indian historian and diplomat K. M. Panikkar, predicted with breathtaking confidence and uniformity that Christianity in Asia and Africa would collapse once the coercive pressures of Western colonialism were removed, Christianity and especially Protestantism saw continuing expansion, not contraction, in the last decades of the twentieth century.[10] In Africa, for example, according to religion demographers David Barrett and Todd Johnson, Christians numbered 10 million in 1900 and 30 million in 1945, but then jumped to 144 million by 1970 and further to 411 million by 2005.[11] Africa's most dramatic Christian growth, in other words, occurred *after* decolonization. Protestantism in particular has seen significant postcolonial growth across the global South, more than doubling from about 4 percent of the overall global South population in 1970 to about 10 percent by 2000. In comparison, Roman Catholicism saw its overall share of the global South population increase by only a little more than one percentage point during the same thirty-year period, from 13 percent to 14 percent, and Islam's share also grew rather modestly, from 19 percent to 23 percent. As a result of this exponential growth, the Protestant proportion of the population in Latin America was six times greater at the end of the twentieth century than at the beginning of the twentieth century, in Asia ten times greater, and in Africa thirteen times greater.[12] No other major religious group came close to experiencing such a dramatic, sustained, and extensive demographic expansion across the global South during this period.

The most important driver and beneficiary of Protestantism's demographic expansion across the global South has clearly been evangelicalism—particularly, in recent years, in its pentecostal expressions. Within most of the global South's thriving mainline Protestant churches, evangelicalism is the dominant, driving element, which of course is what increasingly separates Protestants from fellow Anglicans, Episcopalians, Methodists, Lutherans, and Presbyterians in Europe and North America, among whom, to put it plainly, a gospel of political inclusion has increasingly displaced a gospel of spiritual conversion. Evangelicalism is thus not a denominational category, as our research takes pains to emphasize. Evangelical Methodists in Mozambique may have far more in common with evangelical Presbyterians in South Korea or with evangelical pentecostals in Brazil than with fellow Methodists in Maine or Minnesota.

Evangelicalism in its Spirit-filled pentecostal form has proven particularly contagious, constantly spreading across otherwise well-defended ecclesiastical borders. Numerous Protestant churches in the global South, not to mention the Roman Catholic Church, have succumbed to pervasive "pentecostalization" in the form of highly successful charismatic movements, even as pentecostal denominations such as the Assemblies of God expand and multiply with remarkable velocity in virtually every corner of Asia, Africa, and Latin America. A ten-country public opinion survey of global pentecostalism conducted by the Pew Forum on Religion and Public Life in 2006 found that nearly half or more of all Protestants interviewed in Brazil, Chile, Guatemala, Nigeria, and Kenya were members of pentecostal churches, while more than a quarter of Protestants interviewed in South Africa, South Korea, Guatemala, and the Philippines were Protestant charismatics (i.e., people who identified with the pentecostal label or with pentecostal practice such as speaking in tongues but remained members of nonpentecostal churches).[13] In Africa, for example, according to 2006 figures from the World Christian Database, pentecostals and charismatics now represent nearly 17 percent, or about 150 million, of the population of nearly 890 million people, whereas they represented less than 5 percent in 1970.[14] When one considers that both pentecostal and nonpentecostal evangelicals generally have higher rates of religious observance than other Christians, the conclusion that evangelicalism has become the dominant form of Christian practice in much of the global South is inescapable.

Further arguing in favor of a focus on evangelicalism's contributions to democracy is an impressive body of recent research on the democratic potential of this burgeoning form of Protestantism. Distinguished sociologist David Martin and a number of other scholars have painted a picture of global South evangelicals in the late twentieth century reminiscent of Alexis de Tocqueville's picture of American Christians in the early nineteenth century: voluntarist, independent of the state, and assiduous practitioners of the "art of association."[15] In their churches and small prayer and Bible study groups, evangelicals carve out what Martin terms "autonomous social spaces" within which believers receive Word and Spirit directly, without priestly mediation, and are empowered to share them with others. Amid degradation and exploitation, they experience stability, dignity, and equality.[16] In addition, Martin and others document how conversion to evangelicalism involves the acquisition of a "Protestant ethic" that transforms drunken and indolent men into sober and responsible householders, which in turn provides their families with a modicum of economic stability.[17] As the pioneering sociologist of religion Peter Berger likes to say, "Max Weber is alive and well and living in Guatemala."[18]

In documenting these cultural, social, moral, and economic transformations, Martin and other scholars argue that they may well suggest that evangelicalism enjoys an intrinsic tendency to promote both the kind of moral and purpose-ful individualism and the kind of robust associational life that are conducive to democratization. But these somewhat tentative claims concerning evan-gelicalism's long-term democratic potential could and should be empirically tested, it seemed to us, against the actual political activism and performance of evangelicals across the global South. If the "evangelical ethic" really does promote the spirit of capitalism through microlevel moral and cultural change, does it also promote the spirit of democracy through macrolevel political change? The increasing number of cases of evangelical political activism in Asia, Africa, and Latin America enabled us to investigate whether evangelicals were living up to their democratic potential.

To direct the research on African evangelicals and democracy that gener-ated this volume, we turned to Terence O. Ranger, an eminent British scholar of southern Africa and an emeritus professor of race relations at Oxford, who has sensitively explored the interconnections between African religion, culture, and politics over a long career. Professor Ranger helped us assemble an out-standing team of African scholars to conduct intensive field research in the key countries we had selected: Anglican scholar Cyril Imo on Nigeria, church historian John Karanja on Kenya, theologian Anthony Balcomb on South Africa, religion scholar Isabel Phiri on Zambia, theologian Isabel Mukonyora on Zimbabwe, and sociologist Teresa Cruz e Silva on Mozambique.

The perceptive studies of these scholars reveal an African evangelical com-munity that is increasingly exchanging political passivity for faith-based civic engagement. The studies also reveal a growing democratic ferment *within* evan-gelicalism: evangelical leaders and laity are engaging in fierce debate among themselves about the most appropriate level and form of political participa-tion. Through their intensifying internal debates as well as their accumulat-ing stocks of social and moral capital, evangelical churches often function as "schools of democracy" even where they eschew direct political action. Such schools of democracy ground evangelical believers in participatory norms and practices; they also ground African social and political discourse in an in-creasingly evangelical religious culture.

At the same time, Ranger's scholars demonstrate that evangelical leaders, organizations, and churches are also participating in "high politics"—running candidates for national elections, lobbying for and against legislation, pro-testing against authoritarian governments—in all the countries they studied. In many cases, such political activism has contributed to democratization by drawing previously marginalized and quiescent groups into national politics and widening the boundaries of effective political participation. It has also often contributed to democratization by weakening the hegemony of authori-tarian rulers and increasing the competitiveness of political systems.

However, it is also true that the contributors document numerous in-stances in which evangelical leaders and their constituencies have been all too willing to offer their fervent prayers and praise for dictators they deem "godly"—a designation dictators usually earn by their adoption of biblical rhetoric and sponsorship of religious functions, particularly the ubiquitous evangelistic crusade. In so doing, some evangelicals reproduce and indeed reinforce the corrupt clientelist politics rife in the region: a pattern that perhaps no scholar has analyzed more widely and perceptively than Paul Gifford, who has honored this volume with an acute postscript.[19] But the authors are careful to note that the legitimation some African evangelicals offer authoritarian leaders is almost always challenged by at least some other evangelicals, and this kind of dissent seems to be increasingly vigorous as evangelicalism grows in internal diversity and as its adherents develop greater political sophistication and achieve higher social and economic status.

Though this research has in many ways been an exercise in evangelical self-criticism, it is important to note that many of the researchers who have been involved in it do not identify with evangelical Christianity. With respect to the world and worldview of evangelicalism, Terence Ranger himself reminded us—ever so gently—that he is an outsider, though a sympathetic one. To conduct field research and produce the country case studies, we sought scholars who were based in the countries they were studying and who had ample experience investigating evangelicalism in these countries, regardless of whether they were "card-carrying" evangelicals, as it were. In a number of cases, the most impressive scholars we could find *were* evangelicals. But that was not the point. Precisely because we wanted to offer the evangelical world a nondistortive picture of evangelical politics in the global South, warts and all, our overriding criterion in selecting our research team was not theological correctness but a proven ability to provide intelligent access to the phenomenon at hand.

Just as our research was produced by a religiously diverse team of scholars, however, we expect that it will be of interest to a religiously diverse audience. Evangelicals and nonevangelicals alike have a stake in understanding the political intentions and influences of this burgeoning, global movement, especially when a growing number of studies are sounding the alarm about the political dangers of religion in general and evangelical religion in particular.[20] The politics of global evangelicalism can be understood at the most basic level, however, only if one pays close attention to the politics of global South evangelicalism, which accounts for the vast majority of the world's evangelicals. At the same time, our research is an essential starting point even for those with no particular interest in global evangelical politics per se but who seek a deeper understanding of, say, American or Canadian or British evangelical political activism. For one cannot distinguish the constant and characteristically evangelical features of any of these movements from contingent features arising from the accidents of time, place, and political opportunity without systematically comparing them with forms of evangelical activism prevalent elsewhere.

"And what should they know of England who only England know?"[21] Understanding evangelical politics anywhere requires at least some familiarity with
evangelical politics everywhere.

Our somewhat fanatical insistence on the cardinal importance of broad
and comparative inquiry leads us to believe that this volume is best read in
conjunction with its companion volumes on Asia and Latin America. These
three volumes were not generated by three separate projects, after all, but by
one project motivated from the start by a common set of concerns and questions about the adequacy of evangelicalism's "political witness"—to use an
evangelical phrase—in the countries of the global South. We developed common approaches to our key concepts, particularly evangelicalism and democracy, and we immersed ourselves in a common body of literature on religion
and democratization. In the course of the project, there was significant interaction between the directors of the regional research teams, which encouraged
significant intellectual cross-fertilization. And in June 2002, all the project
participants gathered in Potomac, Maryland, to present our research to a distinguished gathering of scholars from around the world. The answers to the
questions that launched our project lie in the totality of this cross-regional
research and should not be inferred from any one volume or case study.

When seen in its totality, this body of research not only provides a broad
survey of evangelical politics in nearly twenty countries but also offers insights
into the wider trend that Peter Berger aptly terms the "desecularization of the
world": the process whereby all the major religious communities—Islam,
Hinduism, Buddhism, and Christianity—have surged in vitality and political
influence from the early 1970s right up to the present, thus weakening the
hold of secularist political regimes and ideologies throughout the world and
filling otherwise secular public spaces everywhere with religious voices.[22] Just
as no case of evangelical politics can be properly studied in isolation from
other cases, no case of religion's global political resurgence can be properly
understood apart from this broad spectrum of politically mobilized religions.
Any minimally adequate understanding of the causes and consequences of
the Islamic political resurgence, for example, requires rigorous comparison
with other cases of religion's political resurgence. And perhaps no case provides a more apt comparison than the worldwide evangelical political upsurge.
Evangelical Protestantism, like Islam, is an egalitarian, scripture-based religion without a central hierarchy that has achieved impressive global expansion and political influence largely through grassroots mobilization. Yet I am
aware of no systematic and sustained attempt to compare these powerful
forms of religious political activism, despite the fresh insights into both movements such a study would be bound to generate. Perhaps our research can
facilitate this and other potentially fruitful comparisons between the world's
politically resurgent religions.

In coordinating such a massive project over so many years, I have incurred almost innumerable and certainly unrepayable debts. David Battrick, Darin Hamlin, Matthew Fesak, and Anne Fontenau provided crucial support as the project was launched in 1999 and early 2000. David Fabrycky, Laura Fabrycky, Scott Bond, and particularly Dawn Haglund offered various forms of assistance, with Dawn Haglund taking on the monumental task of organizing numerous research workshops throughout the world as well as the project's large international conference in June 2002. In this massive undertaking, Eric Naus and Cara Farr were a tremendous and cheerful help. At a later stage, Sarah Mehta and Stephen Joyce offered invaluable assistance. Abey George helped coordinate the arduous task of organizing and cleaning up the bibliographies of all three volumes, assisted admirably by Laura Fabrycky.

In the last two years, no single person has contributed more to the seemingly endless task of preparing the volumes for publication than Rachel Mumford. She happily immersed herself in the minutiae of each volume to an extent that would have driven lesser mortals insane. I can explain this only by her repeated affirmation that she made the project her own. I cannot thank her enough. Working closely with Rachel Mumford, Patricia Barreiro contributed her tremendous skills as a copyeditor and in the process gave up more tears and sweat than our meager recompense could justify. Without this dynamic duo, the volumes might never have seen publication.

Several institutions provided crucial support at points. The Ethics and Public Policy Center (EPPC) offered me and the project an extremely happy and hospitable base of operations from the moment The Pew Charitable Trusts decided to fund our research in June 1999 until I left the Center in July 2004. Elliott Abrams took a personal interest in the project and saw to it that I received all the help EPPC could muster. Markus Österlund was an unexpected and enormously delightful and stimulating intellectual companion. Above all, EPPC vice president Michael Cromartie gave me the warmest possible welcome and made himself an instant and continuing friend of this project with his characteristic combination of sharp advice and strong encouragement. Fieldstead and Company gave valuable financial support, enabling us to considerably expand our June 2002 conference, thus helping to make it a great success.

In his new capacity as director of the Pew Forum on Religion and Public Life, Luis Lugo offered me and the project generous support when I joined the Forum in August 2004. Thanks to his remarkable generosity and consistent belief in the importance of the subject matter, I enjoyed tremendous freedom to work on the project as well as outstanding assistance from Forum staff. Among Forum staff, the most notable assistance came from Julia Kirby, who worked closely with Rachel Mumford in the summer of 2005 to prepare the manuscripts for their original review by Oxford University Press. Most recently, Boston University's Institute on Culture, Religion and World Affairs (CURA) and the Council on Foreign Relations have provided the perfect institutional settings for thinking through the long-term significance and geopolitical consequences of evangelical expansion in the global South. My friends at these institutions, Peter Berger at CURA and Walter Mead at the Council, are the most perceptive, encouraging, and stimulating interlocutors on the issues addressed by this project that one could possibly hope for.

Numerous other individuals offered incisive commentary and valuable guidance at various stages of the project: Philip Jenkins, David Martin, Samuel Huntington, Mark Noll, Robert Woodberry, Paul Gifford, Daniel Levine, Susanne Rudolph, Christian Smith, Christopher Sugden, Haddon Willmer, Richard John Neuhaus, Virginia Garrard-Burnett, Jeffrey Klaiber, David Maxwell, Lamin Sanneh, Daniel Philpott, Ken Woodward, Paul Marshall, Ron Sider, Jim Skillen, Keith Pavlischek, Oliver O'Donovan, Joan Lockwood O'Donovan, N. J. Demerath, José Míguez Bonino, Paul Sigmund, Timothy Steigenga, Hannah Stewart-Gambino, John Green, Dennis Hoover, Ruth Melkonian-Hoover, Hillel Fradkin, Daniel Bays, Marc Plattner, Carol Hamrin, David Aikman, Rosalind Hackett, John Wolffe, Matthews Ojo, Uwe Siemon-Netto, John Wilson, and Phil Costopoulos.

At Oxford University Press, Cynthia Read has been marvelously encouraging and unfailingly patient at every stage, despite the fact that the process of seeing the volumes to publication proved much more time-consuming and difficult than she ever dreamed possible. Christine Dahlin handled the volumes in the final stages with extraordinary efficiency and professionalism. We are also grateful for Theodore Calderara's and Julia TerMaat's assistance.

There would of course be no project and no volumes without our dedicated team of scholars. It has been a particular honor to work with our abundantly talented regional research directors: Paul Freston, director of the Latin American research; Vikram Chand, the first director of the Asian research, who had to give up his responsibilities with the project when he assumed a senior position with the World Bank in New Delhi in 2000; David Lumsdaine, who succeeded Dr. Chand as the director of the Asian research; and, as I have already noted, Terence Ranger, director of the African research. Each of these outstanding scholars contributed immeasurably to the project as a whole and not merely to his own piece of it. Above all, however, the chapter authors have been the heart and soul of this project. They have all produced rich and insightful case studies, and many braved considerable danger and difficulty in conducting their fieldwork. In addition to the Africa scholars already mentioned, our Asia scholars were Sushil Aaron, Sujatha Fernandes, Kim-Kwong Chan, Young-gi Hong, David Lim, and Bambang Budijanto; and our Latin America scholars were Alexandre Brasil Fonseca, Felipe Vázquez Palacios, Darío López Rodriguez, Clay Matthew Samson, Roberto Zub, and David

Muñoz Condell. In addition, University of Michigan political scientist Daniel Levine, a long-time student of religion and politics in Latin America, contributed a highly readable, personal, and illuminating set of observations on evangelicals and politics to the Latin America volume.

This project has had its highs and lows, with many of the lows falling thickly in the last two years prior to publication. Through it all, no one has been a more constant and energetic encouragement than my wife, Becky. Though she has had every right to be exasperated by a project that I have been working on longer than we have been married, she has instead been consistently herself: ferociously loyal and supportive and adamantly uncomplaining about the additional psychic burdens this project placed on me and therefore on her. I am deeply grateful.

Finally, let me reiterate that this ambitious project began as an idea in the fertile and deeply evangelical mind of Vinay Samuel. Without his leadership, at once visionary and practical, no such project would have been organized, funded, or even imagined. On behalf of all those who have participated in the project, I therefore gratefully dedicate the project volumes to the Rev. Dr. Vinay Kumar Samuel and to the simultaneously struggling and thriving churches of the global South he intended the volumes to serve.

—Timothy Samuel Shah
Council on Foreign Relations
Boston University
August 15, 2007

NOTES

1. Philip Sampson, Vinay Samuel, and Chris Sugden, eds., *Faith and Modernity* (Oxford: Regnum, 1994); Herbert Schlossberg, Vinay Samuel, and Ronald J. Sider, eds., *Christianity and Economics in the Post–Cold War Era: The Oxford Declaration and Beyond* (Grand Rapids, Mich.: Eerdmans, 1994); and D. G. R. Belshaw, Robert Calderisi, and Chris Sugden, eds., *Faith in Development: Partnership between the World Bank and the Churches of Africa* (Oxford: Regnum, 2001). Major INFEMIT-sponsored analyses also appeared in the international evangelical journal *Transformation: An International Journal of Holistic Mission Studies*, started in 1984, including a special 1998 issue on human disability edited by Rebecca Samuel Shah (October–December 1998; volume 15, number 4).

2. For an outstanding collection of sympathetic yet critical appraisals of the political activism of American evangelicals in recent years, see Michael Cromartie, ed., *A Public Faith: Evangelicals and Civic Engagement* (Lanham, Md.: Rowman & Littlefield, 2003). See also Christian Smith's powerful analysis in *American Evangelicalism: Embattled and Thriving* (Chicago: University of Chicago Press, 1998).

3. Seventy-eight percent of white evangelical voters supported Bush in 2004, giving him 40 percent of his winning vote share, and in the 2006 congressional

elections, 72 percent of white evangelicals voted Republican in races for the U.S. House nationwide. See John C. Green, Corwin E. Smidt, James L. Guth, and Lyman A. Kellstedt, "The American Religious Landscape and the 2004 Presidential Vote: Increased Polarization," available at http://pewforum.org/publications/surveys/postelection.pdf, last accessed on August 14, 2007; and the Pew Forum on Religion and Public Life, "Religion and the 2006 Elections," available at http://pewforum.org/docs/?DocID=174, last accessed on August 14, 2007.

4. Freston (2001).

5. Huntington (1991).

6. Arch Puddington, "Freedom in the World 2007: Freedom Stagnation amid Pushback against Democracy," January 2007, available at http://www.freedomhouse.org/template.cfm?page=130&year=2007, last accessed on August 9, 2007.

7. *The Economist*, "The Hogwash of Quiet Diplomacy," April 4, 2007.

8. See, for example, Paul Gifford, ed., *The Christian Churches and the Democratisation of Africa* (1995), in which independent evangelicals and pentecostals receive relatively little attention, as Terence Ranger notes in the volume's conclusion.

9. "As products of Evangelical enterprise, mainline churches in Africa uphold basic Evangelical doctrine with varying degrees of consciousness and conformity," notes Jehu J. Hanciles, in "Conversion and Social Change: A Review of the 'Unfinished Task' in West Africa," in Donald M. Lewis, ed., *Christianity Reborn: The Global Expansion of Evangelicalism in the Twentieth Century* (Grand Rapids, Mich.: Eerdmans, 2004), 171. On the evangelical and even fundamentalist tendencies of many mainline churches in other parts of the global South, see Lionel Caplan, *Class and Culture in Urban India: Fundamentalism in a Christian Community* (Oxford: Clarendon Press, 1987), and Philip Jenkins, *The New Faces of Christianity: Believing the Bible in the Global South* (Oxford: Oxford University Press, 2006).

10. K. M. Panikkar, *Asia and Western Dominance: A Survey of the Vasco Da Gama Epoch of Asian History, 1498–1945* (London: Allen & Unwin, 1959). Paul Gifford notes the predominance of this view among scholars of Africa during the era of decolonization in his introduction to *The Christian Churches and the Democratisation of Africa* (1995), 2.

11. David B. Barrett and Todd M. Johnson, "Annual Statistical Table on Global Mission: 2004," *International Bulletin of Missionary Research*28 (January 2004): 25. However, the figures in the text for 1900, 1970, and 2005 reflect revised and updated statistics accessed from the World Christian Database, directed by Todd M. Johnson, as quoted in The Pew Forum on Religion and Public Life, "Overview: Pentecostalism in Africa," available at http://pewforum.org/surveys/pentecostal/africa, last accessed on August 9, 2007.

12. Barrett, Kurian, and Johnson (2001), 4, 13–15; Robert Dudley Woodberry and Timothy Samuel Shah, "The Pioneering Protestants," *Journal of Democracy* 15 (2): 49.

13. The Pew Forum on Religion and Public Life, "Spirit and Power: A Ten-Country Survey of Pentecostals," October 2006, p. 3; available at http://pewforum.org/publications/surveys/pentecostals-06.pdf, last accessed on August 9, 2007.

14. Quoted in The Pew Forum on Religion and Public Life, "Overview: Pentecostalism in Africa," available at http://pewforum.org/surveys/pentecostal/africa, last accessed on August 14, 2007.

15. Alexis de Tocqueville, *Democracy in America*, translated by Harvey Mansfield and Delba Winthrop (Chicago: University of Chicago Press, 2000).

16. David Martin, *Tongues of Fire: The Explosion of Protestantism in Latin America* (Oxford: Blackwell, 1990); Martin (2001).

17. Cecília Mariz, *Coping with Poverty: Pentecostals and Christian Base Communities in Brazil* (Philadelphia: Temple University Press, 1994).

18. Peter L. Berger, "The Desecularization of the World: A Global Overview," in Berger (1999), 16.

19. See, for example, Gifford (1998).

20. For a few recent examples, see Christopher Hitchens, *God Is Not Great: How Religion Has Poisoned Everything* (New York: Twelve, 2007); Sam Harris, *Letter to a Christian Nation*(New York: Knopf, 2006); and Randall Balmer, *Thy Kingdom Come: How the Religious Right Distorts the Faith and Threatens America, an Evangelical's Lament* (New York: Basic Books, 2006).

21. Rudyard Kipling, "The English Flag," 1891.

22. Berger (1999).

NOTES

Contents

Contributors

Anthony Balcomb teaches theology at the School of Religion and Theology of the University of KwaZulu-Natal in South Africa. His research focuses on political theologies within the South African context as well as on the interface between African and Western theologies. He is the author of *Third Way Theology: Reconciliation, Revolution, and Reform in the South African Church during the 1980s* (1993), as well as the articles "Left, Right, and Centre: Evangelicals and the Struggle for Liberation in South Africa" (2004) and "Nicholas Bhengu: The Impact of an African Pentecostal on South African Society" (2005).

Teresa Cruz e Silva is a senior lecturer at Eduardo Mondlane University in Maputo, Mozambique. She studies the social history of Mozambique and has published on nationalism, social networks, religion, cooperatives, informal markets, HIV/AIDS, and women's rights. She is the author of *Protestant Churches and the Formation of Political Consciousness in Southern Mozambique, 1930–1974* (2001).

Paul Gifford is a professor of African Christianity at the School of Oriental and African Studies of the University of London. He has written extensively on the public role of Christianity in Africa, most recently *Ghana's New Christianity: Pentecostalism in a Globalising African Economy* (2004). Among his other books are *African Christianity: Its Public Role* (1998), *The New Crusaders: Christianity and the New Right in Southern Africa* (1991), and the edited volumes *New Dimensions in African Christianity* (1993) and *The Christian Churches and the Democratisation of Africa* (1995).

Cyril Imo is a professor of sociology and ethics at the University of Jos in Nigeria and teaches courses in the sociology of religion, ethics, and religious studies. He also teaches at the West Africa Theological Seminary. He has lectured in Africa, North America, Europe, and Japan. Among his publications is *Religion and the Unity of the Nigerian Nation* (1995). Dr. Imo was born in Umuahia in Abia State in Nigeria. He received his undergraduate degree at the University of Jos and his Ph.D. from the University of Ibadan.

John Karanja is an associate professor of church history and African studies at Trinity Lutheran Seminary in Columbus, Ohio. He was born and raised in central Kenya. After his studies at St. Paul's United Theological College in Limuru, Kenya, he was ordained in the Anglican Church of Kenya and served as a parish priest for four years. He received an M.A. in applied theology from Leeds University and a Ph.D. in history from Cambridge University. He taught at St. Paul's and later at Nairobi University. He has authored *Founding an African Faith: Kikuyu Anglican Christianity, 1900–1945* (1999) and *Rabai to Mumias: A Short History of the Church of the Province of Kenya, 1844–1994* (1994).

Isabel Mukonyora is an assistant professor in the department of philosophy and religion at Western Kentucky University. She teaches courses in Christianity, women and religion, and methods for the study of religion in a global society. She is the author of *Wandering a Gendered Wilderness: Suffering and Healing in an African Initiated Church* (2007), as well as numerous articles on African religions, the new religious movements, and social change in Africa. She received her Ph.D. from the University of Oxford.

Isabel Apawo Phiri is a professor of African theology and head of the School of Religion and Theology at the University of KwaZulu-Natal in South Africa. She is the general coordinator of the Circle of Concerned African Women Theologians. She is the author of *Women, Presbyterianism, and Patriarchy: Religious Experiences of Chewa Women in Central Malawi* (1997) and is coeditor of *Her-Story: The Histories of Women of Faith in Africa* (2002); *African Women, HIV/AIDS, and Faith Communities* (2003); *On Being Church: African Women's Voices and Visions* (2005); and *African Women, Religion, and Health: Essays in Honour of Mercy Amba Oduyoye* (2006). Dr. Phiri is a Presbyterian from Malawi. She has a B.Ed. from the University of Malawi; an M.A. from the University of Lancaster, England; and a Ph.D. from the University of Cape Town, South Africa.

Terence O. Ranger is emeritus professor at St. Antony's College, University of Oxford, where he held the Rhodes Chair of Race Relations, and he is an honorary fellow of the Oxford Centre for Mission Studies. He has published widely on the history of African religion, mission Christianity, and African initiated churches, as well as on the historiography of East Africa, with a particular interest in Zimbabwe. He is the author of *Are We Not Also Men? The Samkange*

Family and African Politics in Zimbabwe, 1920–64 (1995) and *Voices from the Rocks: Nature, Culture, and History in the Matopos Hills of Zimbabwe* (1999). He is also an editor of *The Historical Study of African Religion* (1972), *The Invention of Tradition* (1983), and the series *The Historical Dimensions of Democracy and Human Rights in Zimbabwe* (2001, 2003).

Timothy Samuel Shah is senior research scholar at the Institute on Culture, Religion, and World Affairs at Boston University; adjunct senior fellow for religion and foreign policy at the Council on Foreign Relations; and formerly senior fellow in religion and world affairs at the Pew Forum on Religion and Public Life. He also serves as a principal researcher for the Religion in Global Politics research project at Harvard University. Shah's work on religion and politics has appeared in the *Journal of Democracy, SAIS Review of International Affairs, Political Quarterly,* and *Foreign Policy.*

Abbreviations

OPC   Odua Peoples Congress
PDP   Peoples Democratic Party
PFN   Pentecostal Fellowship of Nigeria

Chapter 2 (Kenya)

AACC   All Africa Conference of Churches
ACK   Anglican Church of Kenya
AICs   African Instituted Churches
AIPCA   African Independent Pentecostal Church of Africa
CCK   Christian Council of Kenya (former name of NCCK)
CMS   Church Missionary Society
DC   Deliverance Church
EFK   Evangelical Fellowship of Kenya
GSU   General Service Unit
KADU   Kenya African Democratic Union
KANU   Kenya African National Union
KSCF   Kenya Students Christian Fellowship
MCK   Methodist Church in Kenya
MRA   Moral Re-Armament
NCCK   National Council of Churches of Kenya
NDP   National Development Party
PCEA   Presbyterian Church of East Africa
WCC   World Council of Churches

Chapter 3 (Zambia)

AICs   African Initiated Churches
CCIA   Commission of Churches in International Affairs
CCZ   Christian Council of Zambia
ECZ   Episcopal Conference of Zambia
EFZ   Evangelical Fellowship of Zambia
ICASA   International Conference on AIDS and Sexually
                Transmitted Infections in Africa
IFES   International Fellowship of Evangelical Students
IMF   International Monetary Fund
MMD   Movement for Multiparty Democracy
NCC   National Citizens' Coalition
NGOs   Nongovernmental organizations
OAU   Organisation of African Unity
PACWA   Pan African Christian Women Alliance
SAP   Structural Adjustment Programme
SDP   Social Democratic Party
UCZ   United Church of Zambia
UNIP   United National Independency Party

UNZASU	University of Zambia Students' Union
UPND	United Party for National Development
ZAFES	Zambian Fellowship of Evangelical Students
ZAP	Zambia Alliance for Progress
ZCTU	Zambian Congress of Trade Unions

Chapter 4 (Zimbabwe)

AICs	African Initiated Churches (also African Independent Churches)
EFZ	Evangelical Fellowship of Zimbabwe
MDC	Movement for Democratic Change
NACLA	National Association for Christian Leadership Assembly
ZANU/PF	Zimbabwe African National Union—Patriotic Front
ZAOGA	Zimbabwe Assemblies of God Africa
ZCC	Zimbabwe Council of Churches

Chapter 5 (Mozambique)

AEM	Evangelical Association of Mozambique (*Associação Evangélica de Moçambique*)
AICs	African Initiated Churches
CCM	Christian Council of Mozambique
COPAPEMO	Council of the Pentecostal Patriarchs of Mozambique (*Conselho dos Patriarcas Pentecostais de Moçambique*)
FRELIMO	Mozambique Liberation Front (*Frente de Libertação de Moçambique*)
INE	Instituto Nacional de Estatística
MNR/RENAMO	Mozambique National Resistance (*Resistencia Nacional Moçambicana*)
NGOs	Nongovernmental organizations
TVM	Mozambique Television
UCKG	Universal Church of the Kingdom of God
UMCM	United Methodist Church in Mozambique
UNDP	United Nations Development Program

Chapter 6 (South Africa)

ACDP	African Christian Democratic Party
AE	African Enterprise
AFM	Apostolic Faith Mission
AICs	African Initiated Churches
ANC	African National Congress
CESA	Church of England in South Africa
COSATU	Congress of South African Trade Unions
CPSA	Church of the Province of South Africa

EFSA	Evangelical Fellowship of South Africa
ICT	Institute for Contextual Theology
SACC	South African Council of Churches
SACP	South African Communist Party
SCM	Students Christian Movement
TEASA	The Evangelical Alliance of South Africa
TRC	Truth and Reconciliation Commission

Evangelical Christianity
and Democracy
in Africa

Introduction: Evangelical Christianity and Democracy in Africa

Terence O. Ranger

This volume is the product of an enlightened piece of academic encouragement. It emerges from the International Fellowship of Evangelical Mission Theologians (INFEMIT) project for a three-continent study of evangelical Christianity and democracy. The project covers Asia, Latin America, and Africa, comprising seventeen case studies. I myself am not an evangelical and still less a theologian, but when I was asked to be the research advisor to the six African postdoctoral scholars, I agreed at once because the topic is an increasingly important one. Moreover, it was an excellent idea to offer to African postdoctoral scholars research funding, guaranteed publication, and provision of scarce books and articles. All too often, African academics virtually end their research careers with their doctoral thesis and their publication careers with a revision of their thesis. African academic salaries are low, little research funding is available, and it is difficult to publish scholarly work. It is also rare for African academics in one part of Africa to be in contact with scholars in other parts of the continent. The project's funding of three workshops involving all the African researchers struck me as potentially very valuable.

So the research team was assembled: three women and three men, representing six different African nations. They came from varied religious backgrounds—Anglican, Catholic, humanist, pentecostal, and Presbyterian. They came from varying disciplines. But at the workshops they came together as a team, and discussions at these workshops were among the most intense, demanding, and rewarding of my academic life. These scholars are not propagandists for evangelical Christianity, though Cyril Imo, writing from northern Nigeria at a time of grave crisis for Christianity, strikes an understandably committed note. In general, however, the commitment all six researchers share is to democracy. They are not inclined to do evangelical Christianity any favors or to pull any punches. Cyril Imo himself is just as critical of an evangelical head of state as he is of a Muslim governor. The strongest impression given by these chapters is one of involvement in national aspirations for democracy.

This personal involvement emerges especially if, like me, one knows something of the researchers' backgrounds. One is aware of Teresa Cruz e Silva in Maputo, unable to research because of the tragedy of the floods or anxiously enduring months of tension after disputed elections. One is aware that Isabel Apawo Phiri's treatment of evangelicalism and gender is shaped partly by her own harsh experiences of Malawian patriarchy (Phiri 1997), and that her treatment of the declaration of the Zambian Christian nation is shaped partly by the excitement in her own Durban evangelical congregation when Zambian evangelicals visited it to show videos of the event. One is very aware that Cyril Imo's research has been carried out at much personal risk, as he visited the hot spots of the continuing northern Nigerian Sharia crisis and narrowly survived the religious riots in Jos in September 2001. Deeply buried within Anthony Balcomb's analysis is his own experience of having to leave a South African Pentecostal ministry because of his political activism (Balcomb 1993). Behind John Karanja's insistence on the evangelical character of Kenya's "historic" churches and on their active participation in the struggle for democracy lies his research on the development of Kenyan Anglicanism as a fully African church and his contemporary position as a radical Anglican democrat. In the first draft of Isabel Mukonyora's chapter, a reader is able to accompany her from 1979 to 2000 as she explores the realities of Zimbabwean Christianity and politics as a journalist, scholar, and citizen. The studies of these scholars thus emerge from a series of typical contemporary African emergencies—car crashes, floods, riots, university closures, and intense political strife. The six authors have continued undauntedly with their research and writing. Knowledge so painfully gained is worth having.

In other words, this is very much an African book, springing out of commitment and involvement, rather than a collection by expatriate scholars, however sympathetic. Readers will find some explicitly African responses to the general literature on evangelicalism, and especially on democracy. Evangelicalism is seen here as mainly an indigenized and African movement rather than as an external and missionary one. As for democracy, too many of the currently available analyses emerge from a Western secular tradition. Some of the scholars in this book have reacted against the secularity of the literature made available to them. If Western scholars want to join in African discussions of democracy, they caution, it will be necessary to make religion central to the analysis. Moreover, they argue that in the long term an African holism, which inseparably unites the "secular" and the "religious," always prevails. In the end, old-style evangelical theologies of the separation of the "two kingdoms" stand little chance in Africa. The question for these African scholars is not *whether* evangelical Christianity has been, is, and will be intensely "political," but *how*.

Some Definitions

This book adopts a generously open definition of "evangelical Christianity." In his magisterial survey of evangelicals and politics in Asia, Africa, and Latin America, Paul Freston remarks that "the definition of 'evangelical' is hotly debated in historical and sociological literature," and notes that some South African scholars have denied that the category "evangelical" has any utility (Freston 2001, 2).[1] Freston himself refers to the "working definition" outlined by Bebbington (1989), which "consists of four constant characteristics":

> Conversion (emphasis on the need for change of life), activism (emphasis on evangelistic and missionary efforts), biblicism (a special importance attached to the Bible...) and crucicentrism (emphasis on the centrality of Christ's sacrifice on the cross). (Freston 2001, 2)

This book adopts Bebbington's four defining characteristics, enabling its authors, like Freston, to "cast their net broadly." Like Freston, they insist on the evangelical tradition of many "mainline" missionary churches. They are even more concerned than he is to regard southern African Apostolic and Zionist movements as evangelical. As John Wolffe recently remarked, "arguments as to whether [the term "evangelical"] can be applied to the African Initiated Churches are ultimately likely to be as much political as intellectual." Isabel Mukonyora and Teresa Cruz e Silva, who write about Apostolics and Zionists in this book, argue that these movements meet Freston's four criteria. And in a book about evangelical Christianity and democracy, it has been necessary for us also to take a political position. Without the Apostolics and the Zionists the book would leave out huge numbers of the impoverished and marginalized men and women whose participation—or lack of it—will be the real test of African democracy (Wolffe 2002, 89–93).[2] In David Martin's words, "we have in Pentecostalism and all its associated movements the religious mobilization of the culturally despised, above all in the non-western world" (Martin 2002, 167).[3] A crucial question for democracy in Africa is whether its practice can extend beyond literate "modern" Christians to those who have previously been "culturally despised," which especially includes members of African Initiated Churches (AICs), pentecostals, and other evangelicals outside of the historic mainline denominations (Raison-Jourde 1995).[4]

Indeed, this book treats the term "democracy" in much the same way as it treats the term "evangelical." That is to say, it is concerned with practice rather than with structure or dogma. As David Beetham warned assembled churchmen at a 1993 Leeds conference on "The Christian Churches and Africa's Democratization," the successful establishment of democracy in Africa involves more than the overthrow of dictatorship and more than the introduction of multiparty electoral systems. Above all, it means the achievement of *participation* in voting, in discussion, in self-assertion and self-help, in the establishment of a democratic culture both within church and state. The chapters in this book necessarily spend much time on constitutions, elections, and referenda, but they spend even more on the creation of civil society (Beetham 1995).[5]

History and Contemporary History

At the initial workshop in October 1999, it was agreed that the African chapters should be historical in character. This decision seemed to be necessitated by definitions, which emphasized practice and process rather than dogma and structure. It was argued that it was impossible to understand contemporary evangelical Christianity in Africa without understanding how firmly—and correctly—nineteenth-century Protestant missionaries defined themselves as evangelicals (Comaroff and Comaroff 1991).[6] The churches that have descended from them must be counted among the evangelicals of today. Indeed, anyone who has participated in the revivals and prayer-meetings and consultations and exorcisms of the United Methodist churches in Zimbabwe and Mozambique, which are addressed in the chapters by Mukonyora and Cruz e Silva, will know how very evangelical they are.

It was argued also that it was essential to understand the history of the evangel itself: the dynamics of the translation of the Bible into the African vernaculars, and its assimilation into an oral prophetic culture.[7] It was important to understand that the first African-initiated Spirit Churches took over and intensified missionary evangelicalism, seeking to Christianize African tradition yet more profoundly than the missionaries and their catechists had been able to do (Ranger 1999).[8] Such African churches have to be defined as evangelical even if many of them possess an oral rather than a textual biblical tradition (West 1999).[9] Moreover, they provide a long ancestry for contemporary pentecostal movements that are often thought of as imports from North America.

History was essential, therefore, in order to define evangelicalism and to define democracy. At the initial meeting it was agreed that it was crucially important to problematize *transition*—not only transition within the churches but also political transition. It was agreed that the chapters needed to trace the passage from settler to majority rule in Zimbabwe and South Africa and the transition from independence to nationalist authoritarianism in Zambia, Kenya, and elsewhere. They needed to narrate "the second democratic revolution" and the establishment of multipartyism, followed in turn by the development of the current authoritarian regimes. They needed to analyze the transition from war to democracy in Mozambique, and from military government to democracy in Nigeria. The role of the churches, it was argued, was very different during the three stages of transition: the anticolonial struggle; the struggle against one-partyism; and today, the struggle against "third-termism." Once the need had been to challenge dictatorship and to demand democratic forms; now the need is often to move beyond democratic forms to democratic practice. Some churches were better at the first, and others better at the second.

Moreover, it was argued that the chapters should be historical in method and in content. Researchers should make extensive use of archival materials; they should employ open-ended interviews rather than questionnaires; they should not seek to impose large theoretical constructs for comparative purposes but should instead respond to the particularities of their own case study. What were aimed at above all were studies that retained all the complexity of each country, region, or city.

A good deal of all this, of course, has been retained. Readers will discover that every chapter draws on open-ended interviews, and that living evangelical voices are heard throughout the book. Definitions of both "evangelical" and "democratic" are situational rather than standard. Each author has made his or her own decision on which churches, movements, and leaders to include among the representative evangelicals; each has made his or her own decision on what issues are critical to democracy. The authors vary in discipline, representing theologians, church historians, students of comparative religions, and social historians. But there is a strong common identity to the book as a whole. There is a sense that this is a collective effort, a team spirit created by the two intense and intensely stimulating workshops in which the researchers encountered each other. There is, too, a common style, and this remains in a sense historical. Nevertheless, there has been a large change since the initial workshop. The common historical approach now focuses very much on what Isabel Phiri calls "contemporary history."

The emphasis of these chapters has come to be very heavily focused on the last few years—the last twenty in John Karanja's Kenyan case; the last fifteen in Isabel Phiri's Zambian case; the last ten in Tony Balcomb's South African case; and the last ten in the case studies of Zimbabwe, Mozambique, and northern Nigeria by Isabel Mukonyora, Teresa Cruz e Silva, and Cyril Imo. The latter three studies offer a brief historical background, but their emphasis is on the present and the recent past.

This emphasis has two major advantages. First, it means that the chapters bring us up to date, carrying on from where Gifford's and Freston's major surveys of the African and general field have left off (Freston 2001; Gifford 1998). In these chapters there is a sense of a desire to "go beyond" Gifford; in chronological terms at least, they certainly all do so. But there is more to it than that. The focus of this book is not on the recent past merely because it is necessary to add something. The focus is on the recent past because during the last few years the "public role" of evangelical Christianity has become more and more open and significant. Developments that have taken place since the research project began have compelled the researchers to work as "contemporary historians." This book is essentially about the new prominence of evangelicals in African politics and about the new importance of the "earthly kingdom" in evangelical theology.

What does all this mean for the purposes of this introduction? It means, in the first place, that I need to offer some general sketch of the historical background. I need to describe the major transitions in the African democratic process and in the relations between African churches and the state.

In the second place, I need to draw on the case studies in this book to explain why evangelical Christianity has recently taken so significant a role in democratic politics. In the process, I shall seek to bring out themes that are raised in some of the case studies but not in others, though they are relevant to all. Such themes include the role of African Initiated Churches, or AICs, which are taken as evangelical case studies by Cruz e Silva and Mukonyora but left unaddressed in the other chapters. There is a need to focus more directly on the effect of war and violence on religious change, a topic that in this book is only centrally dealt with in Cyril Imo's chapter. More needs to be said about gender and morality.

In the third place, I need to discuss topics that can best be dealt with comparatively rather than in a case study, an obvious example being evangelical transnationalism. And in the fourth place, I shall seek to raise some questions that are not raised in any of the chapters but that seem to me to be important in the contemporary history of democracy and the relationship of evangelical Christianity to it. One of these is the role of African "traditional" religion and the attitude of evangelical Christianity toward it.

Religion and Democracy: Some Transitions

It is conventional and useful to divide (as I have done above) Africa's democratic history into three "revolutionary" phases. The "first democratic revolution" was the anticolonial struggle that brought independence and "majority rule." In most of Africa, this effort was completed by the 1960s, though it was of course significantly delayed in three of our case studies: South Africa, Zimbabwe, and Mozambique. It is clear that this first revolution was democratic in intention. It is equally clear that it was not democratic in result

(Ranger 2003). From the beginning the new independent states were "commandist," espousing a theory of "general will" democracy in which the state was held to represent the interests of the population as a whole. In all too many places this authoritarian "modernizing" state gave way to mere autocracy.

The "second democratic revolution" of the late 1980s was the challenge to one-partyism and to military rule, both of which had arisen in many parts of Africa. In many countries this challenge led to the collapse of one-party regimes and the introduction of a competitive electoral system. But if the principle of "majority rule" did not ensure democracy in the 1970s and 1980s, neither did the concept of multipartyism in the 1990s. Movements originally committed to pluralism themselves became in effect one-party regimes; democratically elected presidents (and their clients) had too much to lose from yielding power. In many countries networks of corruption replaced outright military repression, but popular democracy seemed as far away as ever. Hence, what is being attempted at the beginning of the twenty-first century is a "third democratic revolution": the struggle against presidential third termism; the struggle for incorrupt "transparency"; the struggle not only to develop electoral institutions but also to achieve a democratic culture and practice (Ake 1991; Nherere and D'Engelbronner-Kolf 1993; Nyong'o 1987; Sachikonye 1995).

The churches have played a different role in each of the three stages. During the first anticolonial revolution the churches played an ambiguous part. Most of the white missionary clergy were implicated in one way or another in the colonial order and feared that a successful nationalism would usher in either a revived "paganism" or communism or both. These fears were especially strongly felt by churches of the evangelical tradition (Ranger 1978). AICs, though co-opted into the narrative of anticolonial "resistance history," were usually aloof from, and sometimes actively at odds with, the secular nationalist movements.[10] The Christian churches played only the most marginal role in histories of African nationalism (Hastings 1995).[11]

Yet there was, of course, another dimension. Lamin Sanneh has recently emphasized that the spread of evangelical Christianity in nineteenth- and twentieth-century Africa was quite distinct from, and in some ways antithetical, to that of colonialism:

> Europe's ascendancy in no way explains Christianity's successful spread and expansion in Africa. It was not European surrogates such as kept kings, paramount chiefs, trading clients, and coastal mulatto populations that carried the Gospel into the heart of Africa, but African preachers, evangelists, catechists, schoolteachers, lay readers, nurses, petty traders, women of note, their dependents.... The great promise of Christianity lay in the interior, not on the coast with its compromising European cultural climate. In African custom, the ancestors were venerated and male elders revered, whereas in

Christianity, by contrast, the young men were embraced and women enfranchised. So the religion irrupted in Africa as a mass youth movement in significant discontinuity with custom and usage. Similarly, what justified establishing the church in Africa was not late nineteenth-century classic colonialism but rather the drive a century earlier to abolish the slave trade and to create free settlements. (Sanneh 2001, 113)

Under the compromised surfaces of official colonial Christianity, this gospel of emancipation persisted (Sanneh 2001, 113).

Chapters in this book give some glimpses of the emancipatory and democratic potential of evangelical mission Christianity. Isabel Mukonyora describes the paradoxes of Rhodesian colonialism. It encouraged the growth of a Christianity that taught Africans to be submissive but that also taught "love for one another, justice and self-respect as equals before God, and a belief in the redemptive power of the Holy Spirit" (Ranger 2003). She describes Bishop Abel Muzorewa—heir to this tradition—as "an evangelical democrat." Teresa Cruz e Silva shows that in Mozambique, evangelical missionary Christianity, even while proclaiming an apolitical theology, inevitably took on more and more the role of an opposition to the colonial state. The Protestant churches "Africanized" their leadership; these African clergy "used the Bible as the foundation for their public statements, demanding independence, justice and freedom" (Cruz e Silva 1996). John Karanja argues that the "mainline Protestant churches" in contemporary Kenya—the main advocates of political democracy—"see themselves as the heirs to an evangelical tradition founded by the early Protestant missionaries" (Githiga 2001; Karanja 1999).

South Africa, as always, is different. In some ways South Africa combined both the first and the second revolutions, that is, the tropical African fight against "colonialism" taking in South Africa the form of a fight against settler authoritarianism. With the striking exception of Beyers Naude, Afrikaner theologians who had developed an anti-imperial theology found it impossibly difficult to develop an anti-authoritarian one. Meanwhile what Peter Walshe has memorably called the "phlegmatic churches"—the mainstream Protestants, as distinct from the charismatics—found it much easier than English-speaking mission churches elsewhere to develop theological critiques of white minority rule (Walshe 1995). As Tony Balcomb writes in his chapter in this book:

The role that Christianity has played in the democratization of South African society has been significant...from the earliest rumblings of democracy in the nineteenth century to its final culmination on April 27, 1994. That many of the early movers and shakers for genuine political democracy in South Africa were evangelical...is quite clear. (191–192)

None of the scholars in this book are making this surviving emancipatory radicalism the main feature of their analysis of twentieth-century Protestant evangelicalism. Tony Balcomb immediately goes on to add that "obviously this is not the whole story. The role of evangelicals in the democratization of South Africa has been ambivalent." But at least in South Africa the emancipatory strain was open and visible. Elsewhere in Africa during the first anticolonial revolution it ran much more underground.

If the Protestant churches were not at the forefront of the revolution that ushered in African independence, still less did they emerge as the theoreticians and guarantors of democratic practice in the new African states. Adrian Hastings notes that the churches approached the new African state in much the same way as they had the old colonial one. There was

> an anxiety on the part of church leadership to give the state the
> benefit of almost every possible doubt; a certain touchiness on the
> part of the state if and when church leaders did say anything verging
> on the political. In most cases church leaders were aware of a con-
> siderable weakness in their own position. If white, they could very
> easily be branded as interfering neo-colonialists. If black, their edu-
> cation and experience was generally far less than that of the political
> leadership. Moreover, black archbishops of the 1960s had, for the
> most part, few African clergy to back them up and no reliably orga-
> nized cohorts of the laity. (Hastings 1995, 43)

Black clergymen might sometimes appear in leading ceremonial positions in the new states, as the Reverend Canaan Banana did when he assumed the presidency of Zimbabwe. But Banana's role was not to speak for the church to the state. It was to speak for the state to the church. Liberation theology, he told the Christian Council of Zimbabwe, meant in independent Africa complete support for the sole agency capable of liberation—the state. The churches must unequivocally support state development programmes. And many Christian councils did just that (Maxwell 1995).[12]

Sanneh writes more trenchantly:

> The missionary compromise with the colonial state was seen as a
> betrayal not only of Africans but also of Christianity's message of
> liberation, justice and hope. Sadly for African church leaders, how-
> ever, with little political catechism about how to reposition the
> churches vis-à-vis the post-colonial state, they engaged in social crit-
> icism with not much more than a rhetorical flourish, and their
> own ambition for power and office weakened their moral authority.
> They behaved with the same authoritarian intolerance as the political
> leaders they criticized. Corruption and despotic rule despoiled

countries, divided society, and failed the national cause, but they did
succeed in uniting with the exploiters of the people. (Sanneh 2001, 115)

Even when "the Protestant bodies, organized under national Christian councils, stepped into the breach created by the weakness or collapse of the state,"
their enterprises were, in Sanneh's view, merely "a distraction from the real
problems of Africa at a time when distractions were the norm of political
practice. Contextual theology flourished in this setting...equally plausibly,
anything and nothing would help." In Sanneh's analysis, contextual theology
was thus as much discredited in independent Africa as liberation theology. No
other political theology, still less a theology of democratic practice, arose to take
their place (Sanneh 2001, 115).

All this intolerance, corruption, and authoritarianism were bound sooner
or later to give rise to the second democratic revolution. But it did not look as
if the churches would play any more of a role in this than they had done in
the first. As Paul Gifford remarked, "that the churches played such a role is
remarkable....This crucial involvement of the Christian churches in Africa's
political changes came as a surprise" (1995, 2).

Yet, as Paul Gifford's own edited volume shows more clearly than anything else, the churches *did* play a central part in the second African democratic
revolution. That volume—*The Christian Churches and the Democratisation of
Africa*—emerged from a conference in Leeds in September 1993. The conference was attended by a cardinal, an archbishop, three bishops, the general
secretary of a Presbyterian synod, the president of a Reformed church, two
leaders of national Christian Councils, and other African priests and clergy
engaged in processes of constitutional change. All had come hot from democratic politics. Some had been chairing national constitutional conventions;
some had been leading protest marches; some had been issuing prophetic
pastoral letters; yet others had been helping to end civil wars and to lay the
foundations for civil democracy. As Gifford wrote in his introduction to the
subsequent volume:

> In the late 1980s, at the time of the end of the cold war, Africa
> experienced the beginning of a second liberation, as the peoples of
> Africa tried to throw off the political systems that had increasingly
> oppressed and beggared them. The struggle was not the same ev-
> erywhere, but one of its common features was the significant role
> played by the churches. (Gifford 1995, 1)

Gifford described the Francophone national conferences, "at which a wide
range of groups debated the nation's future," and "the way in which Catholic
bishops were asked to preside over them." He described episcopal denunciations of authoritarianism in Kenya, pastoral letters in Malawi, support of
an opposition in Zambia: "In Kenya during the 1980s, when all opposition

activity was banned, the leaders of the opposition were effectively churchmen. Examples like these could be taken from many other countries too—like Togo, Malawi and Zambia" (Gifford 1995, 1–5).

Under the surface of quietism or of collaboration with the one-party regimes, the historic churches had been gathering strength, multiplying their adherents, recruiting their clergy, and setting up their structures. They offered the only alternative networks to those of the dominant party. Despite their complicity with the first generation of nationalist leaders, the churchmen still retained enough moral authority to act as arbiters and judges. The "relatively human and moderate autocracy" of the early post-independence regimes had given way to excesses that it needed no theological sophistication to denounce. For their part, the historic churches had largely outlived their connection with colonialism. They were able now to appeal to the subterranean tradition of emancipation. As Gifford wrote, "In general it is the mainline churches that have challenged Africa's dictators" (Gifford 1995, 5).

But where did that leave evangelical Christianity? In terms of the definitions adopted in the chapters of this book, it left it divided. Some of the "mainline churches" had always seen themselves as evangelical. Gifford says Kenyan Anglican bishops were the most active opponents of the Moi regime; in this book John Karanja describes their opposition as part of evangelical Christianity's interaction with democracy (Githiga 2001). The Reformed Church of Zambia was represented at the Leeds conference by the Reverend Foston Sakala, the chairman of the Foundation for Democratic Process. Sakala was part of that broad evangelical backing for Chiluba's challenge to Kaunda, which Isabel Phiri discusses in her chapter. As Teresa Cruz e Silva shows in her chapter, the historic but also evangelical United Methodist Church played an important part in the peace process in Mozambique.

In short, some members of the broad evangelical tradition that is discussed in this book did indeed participate in the second African democratic revolution. But at Leeds things seemed very different so far as other members of that tradition were concerned. "The mainline churches have challenged Africa's dictators," writes Gifford. "The newer evangelical and pentecostal churches have provided the[ir] support." As for members of AICs—the Zionists and Apostolics, whom Isabel Mukonyora and Teresa Cruz e Silva include both among their evangelicals and their democrats—they barely rated a mention at the Leeds conference at all.

In my own summary of the proceedings I noted that many people "got left out" of the Leeds conference and hence, apparently out of African democratic politics:

Virtually all the African Christians present were male clergy of the mainline churches—women, laymen, African independents, Pentecostals, were all conspicuous by their absence. Some of those present argued that this did not matter. It had been the male leaders of the mainline churches, after all, who had been playing the prophetic role; chairing the constitutional conferences; issuing the pastoral letters and pamphlets. . . . The assembled mainline clergy expressed themselves baffled by that broad spectrum of Christianity represented by the evangelicals, the African Independent Churches and the Pentecostals. As Bishop Diggs of Liberia exclaimed, "We don't know why they won't join us." (Gifford 1995, 24–25)

The assembled leaders of the historic churches had good reasons for their bewilderment at the political division of Christianity. Time after time, they were able to give examples of the newer evangelical and pentecostal churches rallying to the support of state authority; AICs, meanwhile, were seen as apathetically on the sidelines. It was left to young academic researchers to explore the potentialities of pentecostalism (Marshall 1995).

In the 1995 volume that emerged from the Leeds discussions, Paul Gifford and I tried to assess the democratic potential of the charismatic and pentecostal wing of evangelical Christianity. In both cases we were assessing future possibilities rather than current achievements.

Drawing on Latin American rather than African case studies, Gifford remarked:

Although the newer (mainly Pentecostal) churches may today support or at least fail to challenge oppressive political structures, they may in the long run do more for political reform than the mainline churches and [than] any "liberation theology." For in the circumstances of today's Africa, these Pentecostal churches are something new and important: voluntary associations of true brothers and sisters with a new organizational style. This new community provides free social space. Here members find shelter, psychological security, and solidarity. . . . In this new world they can forge a new notion of self, for here they can begin to make personal decisions. In the small area they have marked out for themselves, they can be free agents, responsible beings. They interact as equals. Here they learn patterns of discipline and independence . . . some even find leadership and responsibility. In this narrow sphere [of the world of personal behavior] an individual can bring control, order, and dignity. Having taken control here, individuals can then combine to exert control in the wider sphere. (Gifford 1995, 6)

Readers of this book will find some African case studies that illustrate these arguments; but these case studies were not available to Gifford in 1993. Nor were they available to me. Indeed, drawing on the African material submitted

to the conference, I contented myself merely with emphasizing the great range
of possibilities within the new evangelical and pentecostal tradition:

> Some were conservative, not to say reactionary, in their connections
> with American right-wing fundamentalism; others comforted the
> poor and powerless by giving them a place in sacred history; yet
> others had radical implications as they subverted hierarchies of sta-
> tus, gender, and generation.

I emphasized the growing numbers of the new evangelicals and pentecostals:
"Already in some African countries their membership was greater than that of
the mainline churches. If the latter had been important in the initial challenge
to regimes, the former seemed likely to be critical to the sustainability of
democracy." But in what ways they were going to be critical I left for the future
to reveal (Gifford 1995, 30–31).

The Third Democratic Revolution and the Crisis
of the Historic Churches

More than a decade after 1993 the future revealed quite a lot. The third African Democratic Revolution is essentially about "the sustainability of democracy." Hence the possibilities discussed by Gifford are being tested on the
African ground.[13] Just as I did in 1993, the chapters in this book certainly
emphasize the *variety* of evangelical political theologies and practice—indeed,
Tony Balcomb's, Isabel Mukonyora's, and John Karanja's chapters are essentially an examination of the contrasting implications for democratic politics
of contrasting evangelical styles. But collectively the chapters go far beyond
this. It becomes possible to discern the complex ways in which evangelical
Christianity, in all its variations, *is* being critical to democratic sustainability. It
is also possible to discern that the historic churches have been in danger of
losing their way in an era of democratic practice rather than of prophetic
challenge.

In April 2000, after I had attended the first project workshop and received
the first research reports, I gave a public lecture at the Jesuit Arrupe College of
Philosophy in Harare on "Religion and Democracy in Africa."[14] In it I offered a
version of the history of the previous seven years, which had the advantage of
being simple, if somewhat oversimplified. I stressed that the historic churches,
so central to the second African democratic revolution, had become less relevant to the third. Hierarchy and authority had given them great advantages in
denouncing dictatorial regimes, but they were obstacles to a genuine mani-
festation of democratic practice. However, the various evangelical churches,
largely marginal to the second revolution, had become central to the third:

How different things look now [I said] less than seven years after the Leeds conference. . . . In Malawi, neither the Catholic bishops nor any other heads of the historic churches seem to be sure how to continue to play a prophetic role within a multiparty democracy. In Mozambique, now that both parties have to appeal to mass constituencies, it is not the Catholic and Anglican churches who are important, but the burgeoning evangelicals, Pentecostals and Zionists. The era of the episcopally chaired Constitutional Assembly is over. And most striking of all there is the case of South Africa.

Even at the Leeds conference in 1993 Archbishop Desmond Tutu confessed:

We had a common position, our stand against apartheid. I now realize what I did not previously, that it is a great deal easier to be against. . . . Now that apartheid is being dismantled we are finding that it is not quite so simple to define what we are for. . . . We no longer meet regularly as church leaders because the tyranny is over. . . . We knew what we were against and we opposed that fairly effectively. It is not nearly so easy to say what we are for and we appear to be dithering, not quite knowing where we want to go or how to get there. (Tutu 1995, 96)

By the end of 1999, the crisis of the South African historic churches was being more forcibly expressed. At a conference in Uppsala entitled "Quo Vadis for South African Churches? Justice, Peace, and Reconciliation in Post-Apartheid South Africa," several of the participants referred to a striking paradox. Under apartheid the historic churches had been the voice of the voiceless. Now they were struggling to be heard. The Reverend Charity Majiza, general secretary of the South African Council of Churches, said that "for decades the liberal churches were at the core of the anti-apartheid movement, but in the 1990s they have become marginalized." The churches, she said, were "determined to speak out" on poverty, violence, gender, and race. But they had not discovered how to do so effectively.

In my Arrupe lecture I drew upon an early presentation by Tony Balcomb in which he discussed the South African transition more extensively than he does in this book. I summarized his argument:

Everything has changed since 1990. The radical churchmen who were the enemies of apartheid are mostly now part of a new establishment. It is difficult for them to escape some part of the blame for the co-existence of much greater freedom with much greater poverty. The Kairos Document has proved to be too "theologically thin" to provide guidance on how to go on being prophetic in majority rule South Africa. The initiative now lies with the charismatic rather than with the phlegmatic churches. These charismatic churches, which in the past have been quietist and conservative, now constitute a moral opposition to the new nationalist order. By so doing they make possible the *operation* of democracy.

In my Arrupe lecture I quoted one South African charismatic example, that of Pastor Ray McCauley. During the apartheid years, his Rhema church held that "the government was a Christian government, and that church leaders should not be in politics." In 1990, however, McCauley publicly confessed that "our silence in these areas was in fact sin." In January 2000 the Rhema church announced its participation with Roelf Meyer, former leader of the United Democratic Movement, to form Civil Society, "an organization aiming to change the moral tone of South Africa." McCauley claimed that it would be "a mechanism to encourage civil society [and] to make democracy real in the eyes of the people now" (Belinda Beresford, "Building Up the Body of Christ," *Mail and Guardian* [Cape Town, South Africa], January 21, 2000).

A similar story, I told my Arrupe audience, could be set out for Malawi. In his splendid account of the confrontation between the Catholic Church and the Malawi state between 1960 and 1994, Matthew Schoffeleers remarks how even the Leeds conference was "a somewhat sobering experience" for the Malawi participants. Bishop Alan Changwera of Zomba was quoted to the effect that

> the [Catholic] bishops, after the publication of their pastoral letter, were at a loss as to what to do, as this situation was totally new to them. The church had put out half a million booklets on "What is democracy?" ... The feeling of the conference was that before it could be determined what the church should do to further democratic sustainability, it needed to be discovered first whether the church was for democracy or merely against tyranny. Were the Malawian bishops themselves qualified to answer the question "What is Democracy"? When they spoke out against an intolerable regime this did not mean that they favored democracy rather than some more benevolent paternalism. (Schoffeleers 1999, 308)

As in South Africa, the questions posed here by Matthew Schoffeleers have turned out to be all too pertinent in Malawi. "With the advent of pluralism," asks Malawian pastor Felix Chingota, "are the churches now irrelevant?" (Chingota 2001).[15] In a recent "stock-taking" of democracy in Malawi there is an interesting chapter on churches and political life in Malawi's post-authoritarian era. The author, Peter von Doepp, finds that the contribution of the churches has been "ambiguous."

> On the one hand, the churches have continued to be visible in post-Banda Malawi: As the new political dispensation dawned in Malawi, the churches were quick to indicate that they would continue to play an active role in the politics of the country. The lessons of the

past had been learned. Silence and inaction on matters of public interest was not only bad for the country, but also contrary to the church's
understanding of its mission in the world. (von Doepp 1998)

During the 1990s, the historic churches have acted as "watchdogs" by means
of their Public Affairs Committee (PAC), which has raised questions concerning structural adjustment, corruption, and factionalism.[16] The PAC has
sponsored roundtable conferences on transparency, political tolerance, and
reconciliation, and it has run a public education campaign.

Yet von Doepp has serious reservations. The PAC limits itself to government corruption and is silent on "more fundamental matters concerning the
accumulation and distribution of wealth in the country." When it comments
on poverty, it merely rebukes "the spirit of laziness." In April 1996 the *Nation*
newspaper declared the PAC irrelevant:

> Small political differences have no impact on people's daily lives,
> whereas failure to improve their well being is truly a mat-
> ter of grave concern. . . . These priests, pastors and God-fearing
> men in that committee have no sense of sympathy for the suffer-
> ing masses.

Moreover, the churches themselves are seen to mirror Malawi's elite political
society. In the same *Nation* article, it is stated that "corruption is perhaps the
most widely perceived abuse of clerical authority": an Anglican bishop is accused
of embezzling huge sums of donor money; relief maize for the poor is sold off to
food processing companies; Sunday collections finance business ventures. Accounts of promiscuity also abound; women are said to be obtained and used as
symbols of status and power. Parishioners perceive the clergy as part of the same
"neopatrimonial" system they purport to monitor and regulate.

In such a situation charismatic Christians begin to be seen in a different
light. Von Doepp describes the emergence of the "born-agains" within the
Presbyterian Church. They deserve attention, he insists:

> Their religious message eschews "politics" and focuses instead
> on the need for a personal process of conversion that can bring sal-
> vation. The "born-agains" in many ways spearhead a movement to
> restore civil integrity. (von Doepp 1998)

He gives an example from a Presbyterian rural congregation "wrought by
financial scandal and organizational decay." Within a year the professed
pentecostal, the Reverend Dzina, had rebuilt the integrity of the parish. The
Women's Guild, previously nonexistent because local men feared sending
their wives to the manse, was in full operation. Financial accountability was
gradually reinstated. "The political importance of these seeming 'a-political'
matters should not be discounted," concludes von Doepp. "The minister in
question is helping to build a viable organization where men and women can

learn leadership skills, develop habits of co-operation and appreciate the benefits of civil (as opposed to mercantile) behavior. This is an important component of the democratization process" (von Doepp 1998, 109–125).[17]

Drawing on these South African and Malawian examples, and on a more
general discussion of the "strengths and weaknesses of hierarchy," I concluded
in my Arrupe lecture that

> it seems likely that cardinals, archbishops, bishops, moderators, and
> the rest have already made their contribution to the (third) African
> democratic revolution. They took the essential first step and challenged
> tyranny. The problem now lies with the second, third, and fourth steps.
> Democracy is a complicated business. The ground has to be cleared for
> it. Its machinery has to be set up. And most important of all, it has to
> run. The focus shifts from the leaders to the people.
>
> In the first stage, one needs grand ecclesiastical prophets to
> challenge tyrants [but] then one needs "professors of morality,"
> teaching good civic conduct more by example than by exhortation,
> like the rural Pentecostal Presbyterian minister in Malawi.... The
> values needed are civic as well as personal.... Moral leadership by
> means of high ecclesiastical injunction rarely does anyone any good
> and certainly rarely any democracy any good. For to make a democ-
> racy "run," the people have not to obey but to *participate*.... There
> has been no democratization of the church itself. The homily, the
> pastoral letter, instruction remain the norm rather than participation.
> This lies at the heart of the historic churches' marginalisation since
> 1993. [On the other hand], the charismatic tradition seems to be
> strong on participation.[18]

Toward a Richer Analysis of the Role of the Churches
in the Third Democratic Revolution

This oversimplified contrast was useful for stimulating a Jesuit audience, and
it revealed some basic and important facts. It also represented my response to
the early research reports of the scholars represented in this book. But two
things have made me realize that it *was* oversimplified. The first is that there
have been significant developments recently. The second is that the final
chapters of the project researchers are much richer and more complicated than
my sketch of the transitions could do justice to.

Recent developments have shown that I was premature in writing off the
democratic role of the historic churches. What has come to be called "third-
termism"—the attempt by elected presidents to change party and national
constitutions so that they can again stand for office—has offered another

opportunity for the prophetic challenge to authoritarian leadership that the historic churches can do best. At the same time there are signs of significantly new thinking. Once again, the case of Malawi is suggestive.

In Malawi, both the Catholics and the Presbyterians have issued pastoral letters warning against any attempt by President Muluzi to stand for a third term. There has been a pamphlet war on the streets of Lilongwe, with some anonymous leaflets urging citizens to show support for the churches, and others demanding that the churches stay out of politics. We are fortunate to have been given an insider account of the Presbyterian pastoral letter by one of those who initiated and drafted it, the Right Reverend Dr. Felix L. Chingota. The letter arose out of a fear that Malawi was in danger of becoming a one-party state again. It is entitled "Some Worrisome Trends Which Undermine the Nurturing of Our Young Democratic Culture." It seems in many ways a repeat of the famous church denunciations of Dr. Banda.

But in fact the drafters of the Presbyterian pastoral letter were self-consciously making a break with the past. As we have seen, earlier church de-nunciations of dictatorship had given rise to the PAC, designed to play a medi-ating role in the multiparty system and hence to end forever the need for prophetic condemnation. The PAC has attacked "partisan clergy" who want to denounce an elected government in a multiparty state. So the Presbyterian pastoral letter defied the PAC. Moreover, it springs out of theological rethink-ing. Chingota notes that

> after the 1972 pastoral letter, which was prophetic, the Malawi
> churches had to learn a lesson. Their role in the new democratic
> society is quite different from the one in times of oppression. The
> words of the Bible in a literal understanding do not apply to emerg-
> ing problems in constructing a nation and are not a cure for each and
> every social and political disease. And—unfortunately—the Bible
> provides a lot of examples of how to act in times of distress, but its
> advice for calmer political times is rather vague.

Nevertheless, "the spoken word must be made incarnate." This has to begin, says Chingota, *within* the churches. After 1972 they were not transformed. Now they have to be remodeled on the basis of a theology of the "people of God." Pastoral letters "must be rooted in a life lived in solidarity with the poor and powerless" (Ross 1996).

Finally, this time around the historic Presbyterian Church—perhaps influ-enced by the work of born-agains within it—has tried not to exclude the char-ismatic and pentecostal movements. Its pastoral letter was endorsed by the Charismatic and Pentecostal Association of Malawi (CHAPEL) (Chingota 2001).

One can perhaps see something of the same pattern of rethinking and rededication to the democratic project elsewhere in Africa, with this new emphasis on participation and interaction with the charismatic and pente-costal evangelicals. John Karanja's chapter in this volume reveals that even the days of episcopal participation in constitutional conferences are not over. Isabel Phiri (who has contributed significantly to Presbyterian theological re-thinking in Malawi) describes in this volume how Zambian charismatic Chris-tians have broken ranks to condemn Chiluba's attempt at a third term, but the historic churches have also been outspoken in their condemnation. Cyril Imo's chapter in this volume quotes prophetic statements by Catholic and Anglican bishops, making common cause with evangelicals in northern Nigeria.

In Zimbabwe, after a long period of indecision and inaction, the historic churches as members of the Christian Council recently (and after Isabel Mu-konyora completed her chapter) confronted government ministers face to face, denouncing them for lies and violence.[19] Interestingly enough, in their efforts to form a common front, the Zimbabwe Council of Churches sent "fraternal" delegates to "convert" the president of the Zimbabwe Evangelical Alliance, Andrew Watawanushe, whose attempts to Christianize the Zim-babwean state from within are described in Mukonyora's chapter.[20] Interest-ingly enough also, the Association of Evangelicals, representing national evan-gelical fellowships in forty-six African countries, has chosen Zimbabwe to be the seat of its Ethics, Peace, and Justice Commission. Its executive secretary, Patson Netha, says that the new commission would set out "to complement work covered by the Zimbabwe Council of Churches":

> People need to look seriously at issues of morality and ethical codes, for instance in tackling corruption. We believe that if all of us in Africa speak out against injustice we will make an impact. The need to promote justice has always been there, but we have not all been rising to that challenge. We will endeavor to do our best in Zimbabwe to ensure that justice prevails for all faiths and for those who do not belong to any faith. (Zimbabwe *Independent*, "Ethics, Peace, and Jus-tice Body to Set Up Base in Zimbabwe," July 27, 2001)

Most striking of all, perhaps, as a sign of a new collaborative thinking—and even theology—is the joint statement issued by more than forty churches in Zimbabwe's eastern Manicaland Province. Firmly biblical, unflinchingly crit-ical of violence and corruption, the statement is endorsed by historic churches, charismatic/pentecostal churches, and African Initiated Churches.[21]

It is in this new context, rather than in the context of structural opposition to the historic churches, that one must now see the increasing importance of evangelical Christianity in democratic politics. But if the political visibility of charismatic evangelical Christianity is not due solely to the withdrawal of the historic churches, what then are some of the factors of contemporary Africa that help to explain it? David Martin writes:

The broad background is the weakness of the African state, vast in-debtedness, and a corrupt clientelism, which means that churches become the main mediating institutions, and Christian appeals count as major arbiters of political legitimacy. Churches become alternative communities wielding power through non-governmental organiza-tions, and Pentecostals may sometimes act as alternative oppositions, picking up the sentiments of the excluded. (Martin 2002, 133–134)

But African states are not merely experienced as weak. They are increasingly experienced by their citizens as violent, bankrupt, and immoral. Each of these characteristics does something to explain the development of an evangelical democratic culture.

The Crisis of Violence

Most chapters in this volume say relatively little about violence. Yet violence is almost always present for most of them: the guerrilla wars in Mozambique and Zimbabwe; the post-independence war with Renamo in Mozambique; the post-independent repression in Matabeleland in the 1980s; anti-apartheid urban political violence in South Africa, followed by criminal urban violence today; military coups and religious faction fights in Nigeria; and state-backed ethnic violence in Kenya. Often violence functions as a catalyst for religious change and for theological rethinking.

Sometimes violence compels churchmen to take sides and to justify doing so. An example comes from Ngwabi Bhebe's study of the Evangelical Lutheran Church in Zimbabwe's guerrilla war. Historically, evangelical Lutherans had adopted Two Kingdom theology. During the war, however, black Lutheran clergy in the rural areas chose to support the guerrillas and to express theo-logical reasons for doing so. Bhebe writes:

Clearly in so far as the Evangelical Lutheran Church followers and their Church leaders were concerned, their relationship with and responses to the plight of the peasants and vis-à-vis the liberation struggle were not cast in the mould of the two kingdoms. . . . Soderstrom's suggested scenario of a Christian being a citizen of two worlds—the secular and the spiritual—may have applied in some churches elsewhere in Zimbabwe, but certainly not in the Evan-gelical Lutheran Church. The Church through its followers and leaders was simply part of the one kingdom, the impoverished and suffering rural kingdom. (Bhebe 1999, 152)

Bhebe describes how guerrillas accused Lutheran pastors of preaching a white man's God of pacifism and quietism. He also describes how the clergy drew on black theology and on ideas of the just war and sacrificial love to counter such accusations. The guerrillas were often astonished, and the Lutheran church changed. The last missionary bishop of the church, Sigfrid Strandvik, tried to persuade his pastors to stop their political activities. Elias Masiane of Shashe, who was later arrested, tortured, and imprisoned by the Smith regime, reacted "almost emotionally":

> My people are suffering economic disadvantages at the hands of Rhodesian whites. Do you want me to stop my involvement in politics and leave my people to continue to suffer? Then I quoted Romans 12, which says that the church must suffer with those who suffer and must rejoice with those who rejoice. I also said that if I was going to be arrested and suffer with my people, I did not mind. (Bhebe 1999, 162)

Such deep involvement with the guerrillas meant, of course, that the Lutheran pastors gave full-hearted support to the majority rule regime after 1980. But the western Lutheran dioceses suffered from brutal repressions in the 1980s, and their clergy once again suffered with those who suffered. Such continuous theological rethinking in this historic evangelical church has meant that it can now once again, in the third democratic revolution, respond to the need to take part in democratic politics. It is no accident that the Christian Council of Zimbabwe has begun to confront the Zimbabwean state under the presidency of Bishop Ambrose Moyo of the Evangelical Lutheran Church.

Violence can compel people to create their own institutions so that they can express their own agency and sustain the morale and sense of identity of their kin and clients. This happened during the Renamo/Frelimo war in Mozambique. Mozambican refugees in the camps created innumerable little Apostolic and Zionist churches, so that the camps were honeycombed with "democratic" cells. This was the politics of the personal. But it was to these charismatic cells that Christian Care's voter education was addressed, as refugees returned from the camps to take part in Mozambique's first election. This provides some background to Teresa Cruz e Silva's account of Zionist "democracy" in contemporary peri-urban Maputo.[22]

Sometimes violence demands that those involved in it, whether as participants or as victims, find some way of applying a moral code that will help them determine how they can legitimately conduct themselves. The spread of the Zionist churches in Mozambique from the 1950s did not affect only refugees in Malawi or Zimbabwe or in Mozambique's peri-urban areas. Many participants in the war in the rural areas also became Zionists and drew upon their new faith for moral guidance and justification.

Sometimes violence compels churches to unite. This requires the development of both an ecumenical and an activist theology. It is the situation described by Cyril Imo in his chapter in this book, in which he quotes Catholic and Anglican bishops in northern Nigeria as joining to articulate a general "evangelical" position (Sanneh 2001, 44).[23] Such bishops have approved of taking up arms in "self-defense"; and Christians in Kano, "including evangelicals" have used guns to repel attacks on their area, killing many Muslims. Imo tells us that while retaining "their views of the secularity of the state," evangelicals have reinterpreted the scriptural text "Give unto Caesar what is his and to God what is his":

> The new interpretation saw "Caesar" not as the "world," "worldliness," or even the "devil." . . . But many evangelicals now began to see "Caesar" in a new light, as an entity with a capacity for good, thus concluding that a "believer" should identify with politics and political leadership and at the same time remain faithful to God. . . . Many Christians in these areas have become even more politically conscious. . . . Few evangelicals believe that engaging in politics is "satanic." (60)

Not only in northern Nigeria but also in many other parts of Africa people fear a revival of violence, whether religious, criminal, or political. Ensuring peace by any means, including politics, seems work unequivocally approved by God.[24] Ruth Marshall, writing about Pentecostalism in southern Nigeria, speaks of "the omni-present reality of state violence," whether expressed in police shootings or the razing of slums. She adds:

> It is little wonder that popular discourse centers on themes of decline, disintegration, and unleashing of forces over which they have no control. Violence is the idiom which best expresses the often arbitrary and unreasonable quality of quotidian struggles. . . . That stories of conversion focus on the contrast between the hopefulness, sinfulness and destructiveness of one's own past and the security, hope and empowerment that new life in Christ brings is typical of the born-again experience wherever it is found, yet it takes on added poignancy and significance in the above context. This new hope and empowerment is not simply a case of false consciousness, and what is being created is not some unreal world of atavistic escapism, but rather an expressive act of individual and collective reconstruction. (1993, 223)

The Crisis of Poverty

There is a crisis of poverty, as well as a crisis of violence, in contemporary Africa. Charismatic evangelicals are centrally concerned with poverty. It is often asserted that the new evangelical and Pentecostal movements in Africa lay excessive emphasis on "the Gospel of Prosperity." There have been many pictures presented of grossly rich leaders flamboyantly displaying their wealth, and happy to benefit from patrimonial corruption. Their followers, meanwhile, live in a fantasy world, expecting prosperity to come almost magically. The chapters in this book present a wider and more sympathetic view. As both Isabel Mukonyora and Teresa Cruz e Silva emphasize, Zionist and Apostolic churches are certainly concerned with prosperity, but for most of their adherents "prosperity" means survival or, if possible, a little more. Nor is there anything magical about their expectations. The churches stress self-reliance and hard work. As David Maxwell has emphasized, pentecostalism encourages its followers to engage in what he calls "penny capitalism"—small-scale, local entrepreneurism (Maxwell 1998).

This emphasis can be described as "democratic" in so far as it encourages individual agency and participation, but it need not necessarily result in formal political activity (Maxwell 2000). Nevertheless, as it becomes more and more apparent that it is the African regimes that are largely responsible for frustrating hopes for advancement and even for threatening survival, it is possible to detect increasing pentecostal criticism of the state.

As long ago as 1997, the Reverend Njeru Wambugu, acting general secretary of the Organisation of African Instituted Churches (OAIC), argued that "the power of political and social change in Africa lies in the church and not in politicians." During colonialism, he argued, it had been the AICs that "protested against oppression." But in independent Africa things have all too often been different: "I don't know whether to place the AICs in the category of 'tamed' churches. But the paradox in Africa is that today most vocal opponents of dictatorship and other ills are members of the mainline churches." Yet the AICs ought to be in the vanguard of protest. In independent Africa "the vision of uplifting themselves socially, morally, and economically has been doomed." Yet still the AICs have left politics to the prosperous and influential ex-mission churches:

> Like thousands of others in Africa, members of [these churches]
> suffer in silence. They remain among disadvantaged groups of
> Christians the world over.... The OAIC general secretary does not
> spare the leaders of Independent churches. He alleges that they
> are today propping up dictators in power or watching injustice in
> its stampede.... Rev. Wambugu challenges the AICs to come out of
> their silence. He wonders [about] the essence of the independent
> churches' fight against the oppressive colonial governments if
> they cannot champion a similar struggle against prevailing unjust
> governments.... "I am challenging them to tell me what they con-
> sider to be evil. I am demanding to know whether poverty, lawless-
> ness, dictatorship, misrule, oppression, suppression, detention,
> corruption and violence are not evil."

The AICs must enter politics (Wambugu 1997).

Several years after Wambugu's challenge, there are indeed signs that charismatic churches are not merely demonizing poverty but also politicizing it. Maxwell has depicted the Zimbabwe Assemblies of God in Africa (ZAOGA) as democratic at the level of the local congregation and autocratic at the level of Bishop Guti's leadership. Until recently, Guti was happy to try to seek advantage through closeness to the Zimbabwean state. He agreed to serve on Robert Mugabe's 1999 Constitutional Commission; Mugabe's wife, Grace, is a member of ZAOGA. Yet now the "democratic" township congregations are applying effective pressure on the leadership. ZAOGA's strength lies in the townships, and it cannot remain indifferent when inflation and unemployment destroy any chance of modest prosperity and threaten family survival. The leadership cannot be seen as being identified with a state that is sending in its army to beat up township voters. In the June 2000 election the townships voted overwhelmingly for the Movement for Democratic Change (MDC); and in March 2002 they voted overwhelmingly for the opposition presidential candidate. Now the church leadership is beginning to change its tune. In July 2001 the second most influential man in the church called publicly for ZAOGA members to support the opposition MDC.[25]

The Crisis of Morality

Today in Africa there is a perceived crisis of morality, though even within the evangelical churches there are divisions about the nature of that crisis. None of the churches, whether evangelical or not, disputes the immorality of theft, fraud, adultery, rape, and murder. Some churches, though, view the whole "liberal" agenda as immoral. They consider it unacceptable to legalize abortion or homosexuality. I recently read an article by an extreme white evangelical in Cape Town who maintained that the South African constitution breaks every one of the Ten Commandments. But the liberalism of the South African constitution is exceptional. In many African countries, it has been possible for regimes to divide evangelicals by appealing for support for their repressive sexual policies. The issue at stake, therefore, is whether immorality is seen as something repressed by the state or as something that characterizes the state. Increasingly, it seems, the latter view is triumphing.

The chapters that follow reveal a range of ideas about how to moralize the state. Some represent a continuance of the old missionary separation of the private and the public sphere, and the old missionary assumption that a change in private morality will gradually transform society. At the other extreme is the Zambian case—so well discussed by Isabel Phiri in this book— where a real attempt has been made by evangelicals to achieve a "Christian state." Phiri shows all the ambiguities and dangers of this attempt, but she also shows that the vision of the Christian state has become the criterion by which

Zambian leaders and parties are judged. Between these two extremes are many other evangelical attempts to moralize the individual, the society, and the state.

The West African literature, inadequately represented in this book, has placed particular emphasis on evangelical and Pentecostal representations of morality and immorality. Ruth Marshall has analyzed the Nigerian Pentecostal churches. David Martin has offered a useful summary of her work:

> The background for the growth of the poorer churches is not merely economic decline and the increasingly abrasive struggle for survival, but the use of power and influence at every level for personal pillage, so that subordinate groups are burdened with a sense of forces out of control.... People find in these churches an equality and sense of worth outside the categories of worldly success or the hierarchies of age and wealth, and also a rudimentary social security.... Ethical discipline ensures that appetite for mammon is under control and "goods" keep circulating in not too hurtful a manner. Those living triumphantly "in the power of Jesus" have to abide by the rules or face ruin.... The reorganization of a chaotic moral field enables Pentecostals to participate in popular discontent with government. Most born-again Christians do not bribe officials or even tolerate such behavior, and they also articulate an indirect critique of state-sponsored violence and the operations of the fraternities. They wrestle against principalities and powers, and that means spiritual and satanic wickedness in high places.... There are signs that this spiritual contest with corruption and with the violence and lack of accountability of the powerful may grow into a more institutional participation in politics. (Martin 2002, 139–141)[26]

Marshall herself has cautioned that pentecostal participation in politics may very well not be democratic in its underlying ideology. We have seen that while the historic churches challenged dictatorships, their authoritarian structures limited their capacity to contribute to democratic practice. The pentecostal challenge to regime immorality is more profound, but the divine authority on which it is based may make even less allowance for democratic dissent. Marshall writes that "the Pentecostal discourse involves a critique which deligitimates the authoritarian use of power." But she goes on to quote the then president of the Pentecostal Fellowship of Nigeria (PFN), Pastor Adeboye, comparing his organisation to God's army:

> Everybody must take orders from the commander-in-chief. No arguments, no debates. I told you last time you came, I said, God is not a democrat.... I want PFN to become an invading army. I don't want it to become a social club. I want to see a PFN by the grace of God

that when the devil hears "P" he will begin to shake. That cannot happen if we go about it democratically. Because when God has spoken and we say this is the way we shall go, someone will say, let us vote. I can tell you, whenever you go to vote, the majority will vote for the devil. (1995, 257)

However, even where new evangelical ideology is authoritarian, the church and the domestic life of new evangelical churches may be democratic in their effects. Particularly important in evangelical discussions of morality are questions of gender. The "headship" of men is proclaimed, but the selfish promiscuity of men, especially of powerful men, is criticized. Many southern African evangelical churches have women's organizations that teach married women sexual techniques and emphasize their sexual rights. Marshall shows that Nigerian born-again doctrine transforms the practice of marriage, family, and sexuality in ways that are "highly attractive to young urban women." Manifestly, no democracy can succeed unless women participate as much as men do as voters and as citizens. Greater domestic and sexual equality will contribute to such participation. In this book, gender is discussed in the chapters by Mukonyora, Cruz e Silva, and Phiri, in the first two mainly with reference to Apostolic and Zionist churches. We need to explore further what is happening to ideas and practices concerning gender in other evangelical churches, as well as study, as Isabel Phiri does, the entry of evangelical women into electoral politics.[27]

At least what we can say is that in many places in Africa, and not only in relation to gender, the personal has become the political, and the moral has become the democratic. Evangelical Christians have taken the lead in making this so.

Evangelical Transnationalism

These, then, are some of the features of contemporary Africa that have propelled charismatic evangelicals into democratic politics. They are clear in the chapters of this book. What cannot come out clearly in a series of case studies is the transnational character of evangelicalism that ensures an exchange of ideas and institutional forms that strengthens its democratic contribution in Africa. By this I do not mean the much-discussed impact of North American evangelical missionaries and of the links between African and American churches. I mean transnationalism within Africa and across African boundaries (Maxwell 2001).

The case studies in this book are focused especially in southern Africa. To have chapters on South Africa, Mozambique, Zimbabwe, and Zambia overrepresents one region of Africa and one set of types of evangelicalism. Obviously

West Africa—and especially Francophone West Africa—is inadequately re-presented, and this introduction has made matters worse by deliberately draw-ing on supplementary literature for the countries included in this book, and particularly on very recent material from my own research area, Zimbabwe.

But there are advantages as well as disadvantages to this concentration. The main advantage is that the book deals with four geographically contiguous nation-states, across whose borders ideas and people have flowed for at least one hundred fifty years. Protestant missionaries moved across these borders in the nineteenth century—from South Africa into the Rhodesias, and from Southern Rhodesia into Mozambique. African labor migrants moved across these borders in the opposite direction in the late nineteenth and twentieth centuries and brought back new religious ideas. Charismatic and evangelical forms of Christianity and their missionaries are still moving across those borders today. Isabel Mukonyora's Masowe Apostles are members of a great pan-African church with congregations over the whole of southern and central Africa; Teresa Cruz e Silva's Zionists sprang originally from Zimbabwe and South Africa. David Maxwell's ZAOGA is an outstanding example of what he calls "Transnational Pentecostalism." Zionism—or Apostolic Pentecostalism—is significantly different in each place it establishes itself. The pattern of Zion-ist churches in Maputo, for instance, is unlike the pattern in South African or Zimbabwean cities. The role Zionism plays in each place depends upon the needs of the people. Yet there is a perceived commonality from which all its congregations draw strength. Not only states are allied in Southern Africa, but also those churches whose emphasis on the private sphere is profoundly af-fecting democratic politics.

Conclusion

I have said many positive things about the actual and potential contribution of both types of evangelical Christianity—the historic and the charismatic—to contemporary Africa. The time has come perhaps to make one very important modification that is not directly discussed in any of the case studies in this book. Cyril Imo's chapter raises directly the problem of democratic politics where there are two conflicting faith claims. He deals, of course, with Islam and Christianity. But no one in this book, and few others writing on evangelical Christianity, has dealt with another conflicting faith claim: between Islam and every form of Christianity on the one hand and African "traditional" religion on the other. And the central question that arises here is this: Are tradition-alists to be thought of as capable of democracy?

Leaders of AICs, like Wambugu, protest that African states have ignored or repressed them. African states, dominated by bureaucrats who were edu-cated in mission schools, still represent the values of missionary modernity

(Wambugu 1997). Adherents of African traditional religions, though, have much more to complain about. Kenyan scholar Makau Mutua quotes Ali Mazrui to the effect that "no African country has officially allocated a national holiday in honor of the gods of indigenous religions. The Semitic religions (Christianity and Islam) are nationally honored in much of Africa; the indigenous religious festivals are at best ethnic rather than national occasions" (Mazrui 1991). But Mutua argues that discrimination against traditional religion goes much further than this:

> The modern African state, right from its inception, has relentlessly engaged in a campaign of the marginalization, at best, or eradication, at worst, of African religion.... The destruction and delegitimation of African religion have been actively effected at the urging, or with the collusion and for the benefit of, either or both Islam and Christianity.... [T]he conscious, willful and planned displacement of African religion goes beyond any legitimate bounds of religious advocacy and violates the human rights of Africans:... it is in fact a repudiation... of the humanity of African culture. (Mutua 1999, 170)

It is by definition profoundly undemocratic (Mutua 1999).

Mutua, an academic lawyer, shows that the constitutions of independent African states—Kenya, Malawi, Nigeria, Zambia, the Congo, etc.—guarantee "liberal generic protection of religious freedoms." But these are defined in such a way that they refer exclusively to Islam and Christianity. At the same time the constitutions continue to espouse exceptions to that protection first introduced by colonialists on the grounds of "public morality" and "public health," which are plainly aimed at traditional religion. Mutua writes of "constitutional silence and the absolute refusal to acknowledge the existence of African religions" and gives examples of action taken against them since independence. He criticizes both Zambia and North African states for privileging "Semitic religions" by declaring themselves either Christian or Islamic and thereby depriving adherents of African religions of their national identity (Mutua 1999, 177–179).[28]

Mutua makes only passing reference to evangelical Christianity. But we must confront the fact that evangelicals of all kinds "demonize" African religion and seek to expel it both from the private and the public sphere. Let me take the example of Zimbabwe for one last time. Isabel Mukonyora shows that the Masowe Vapostori are profoundly democratic in the equality they establish in the wilderness between people of all ranks and especially between men and women. But this equality depends on the rejection and virtual exorcism of ancestral spirits. The Vapostori are more effectively hostile to African religion than any of the historic churches, whether evangelical or Catholic.[29] David Maxwell has argued for the democratic agency shown in the township congregations of the ZAOGA. But ZAOGA appeals to students by promising to "save" them from ancestral religion. The ancestors, who were poor, cannot help bring prosperity.

Other Zimbabwean evangelicals are as much concerned to expel traditional religion from public life. It is widely believed that Robert Mugabe derives his power from the blessing of the spirit mediums that represent great rain spirits or dead kings. In evangelical parlance these are "demons." The Reverend Tim Neill, an evangelical Anglican who figures largely in Isabel Mukonyora's paper, has set up a network of "Deborah" women's prayer-groups. These regularly pray for Zimbabwe to become democratic; they also regularly pray for it to be liberated from "demonic" spirits. The great heroes and heroines of Zimbabwe's first anticolonial resistance in 1896 were the senior spirit mediums, Kagubi and Nehanda. Their statues stand in parliament, and the Deborah women pray for their removal. In early June, during a televised debate on religion and the state, a black woman evangelical dismissed pleas for respect to be shown to Nehanda as a national heroine by telling her interviewer: "At this very moment Mbuya Nehanda is burning in hell. And unless you change your ways you will burn in hell, too."

Not surprisingly, such attitudes have given rise to controversy. During the discussions on a new Zimbabwean constitution in 1999, the Evangelical Alliance pressed for Zimbabwe to be declared a Christian nation. By contrast, in virtually every rural area the visiting constitutional commissioners were told that African religion must be respected. Rural respondents demanded democratic liberalism at the level of the state: they endorsed private moral and social conservatism with equal vigor.[30]

Members of the University of Zimbabwe's Religious Studies Department have taken up this issue. Dr. Paul Gundani is the founder and president of a multifaith movement. In May 2001 he told a public audience that evangelical prejudice against African religious adherents would make democracy impossible in Zimbabwe. In late June 2001 a two-day *festschrift* workshop was organized for me where various aspects of my work were examined by Zimbabwean scholars from different disciplines. Ezra Chitando from the Religious Studies Department made a "critical review of T. Ranger's portrayal of Christianity as an aspect of African identity." He concluded:

> Ranger and the translatability school may want to readily identify Christianity with African identity, but many Africans are hesitant to do so. As it associates itself with modernity, sophistication and globalization Christianity has been experienced as domineering. In its extreme evangelical expression, where progressive Africans are "delivered from the spirit of poverty" (Maxwell 1998), Christianity has in fact meant denying one's very own Africanness. (Chitando 2001)[31]

One of the works circulated to the scholars involved in this book was a November 1999 conference paper by Robert Woodberry in which he attempted correlations between Protestantism, Catholicism, and Islam on the one hand, and democracy on the other. Woodberry found "a strong positive association between the percentage of Protestantism in a society and the level of democratization"; there was "a negative relationship between Islam and democracy"; "the relationship between Catholicism and democracy is more complex." But Woodberry found that societies with indigenous religions "are the least likely to be democratic" (Woodberry 1999). This seems to me to raise a dreadful spectre. Is democracy in Africa just a Christian project, designed to legitimate the power of Christians—and especially Protestants—who alone understand it? Or, can there develop an African understanding of democracy that effectively draws on the communal values expressed in African traditional religion as well as on the moral and spiritual transformations wrought by evangelicals?

NOTES

1. On the South African debate, Freston cites Hale (1993) and Walker (1994).

2. Wolffe (2002, 89–93) has a discussion of South African evangelicalism. The politics to which he refers is rather different from our own focus on democracy. In his view, people call African Initiated Churches "evangelical" if they want to insist on their universal Christian character; and refuse to apply that name if they wish to insist on a uniquely African inspiration. He concludes that it is not sensible to impose rigid definitions—"there are no firm limits to religious movements."

3. In this global survey, Martin has a section on Africa in which he discusses Apostolic and Zionist churches (2002, 132–152).

4. Françoise Raison-Jourde, in a chapter on political change in Madagascar, asks whether it should be "normal that democracy should always be the business only of Christians, who nowadays represent no more than half the population?" This is a question that might well be asked of Mozambique also. In countries like South Africa, Zimbabwe, and Zambia—where Christians of various kinds constitute the great majority of citizens—it would have to be rephrased as I have done.

5. David Beetham, "Problems of Democratic Consolidation," in Gifford (1995).

6. For recent profound analyses of the theology and practice of nineteenth-century evangelical Protestantism, see Comaroff and Comaroff (1991); Peel (2000). In a fascinating discussion of evangelical missionaries, van Rooden (1996) emphasizes the modernity of Protestant missionaries and their innovation of a distinction between private and public spheres, which transformed Christianity in Europe and installed itself in Africa. Previously the norm in Europe had been established state churches. By "locating Christianity within a private sphere, expecting it to effect societal change indirectly, the missionary effort was both an indication and a cause of a fundamental discursive shift between religion and politics in the West" (van Rooden 1996, 84). A wide-ranging discussion can be found in Hutchinson and Kalu (1998).

7. For two important recent studies see West and Dube (2000) and Kurewa (2000). See also Wimbush (2000).

8. For South Africa, see Anderson (2000). Also, Sanneh argues that the vernacular Bible "had explosive consequences" within mission Christianity; that it was "the pulse" of revival movements; and that in the 1930s "translatability was a consistent force in transferring authority from the culture of the European missionary translator to that of mother-tongue speakers in Africa, with missionaries sooner or later becoming victims of vernacularisation" (1994, 44).

9. Gerald West writes that "the Bible plays an important role in the lives of many [Africans], particularly the poor and marginalized. The Bible is a symbol of the presence of the God of life with them and a resource in their struggle for survival, liberation, and life. This is true for a whole range of readers, including largely illiterate 'readers' in the townships and informal shack settlements ... who listen to, retell and remake the Bible." West argues that if scholars tell African Initiated Church members that they are theologians, no discussion is possible. If they say they are seeking to understand the Bible, they can immediately take part in oral exegesis. See also Philpott (1993). There are discussions of the oral Bible in Africa by N. Ndungu, Z. Nthamburi, and D. Waruta in Kinoti and Waliggo (1997).

10. For a discussion of the changing understanding of the "political" significance of African Initiated Churches, see Ranger (1986).

11. "Missionary clergy were even less temperamentally interested in politics than clergy at home in Europe and America," writes Hastings. "The gospel most sought to preach was in intention unambiguously other-worldly.... Missionaries were prone to think extremely well of colonialism, though not so often of colonialists." Yet most missionaries accepted that democracy was coming to Africa and should be prepared for. "From the 1920s to the 1950s, the principal secular contribution of the churches to black Africa was ... this training for democracy of a tiny elite" (Hastings 1995, 42).

12. For Banana's most recent reflections, see his book (1996).

13. Five years after the Leeds conference volume, Gifford himself has analyzed these questions further in his book *African Christianity: Its Public Role* (1998); and Paul Freston responds to Gifford in his *Evangelicals and Politics in Asia, Africa and Latin America* (2001). As is evident in the notes, the chapters in this book have been written with Gifford and Freston very much in mind.

14. The lecture was given on April 3, 2000. It was published in the 2001 issue of Arrupe's magazine, *Chiedza*.

15. Chingota cites an open letter to the Presbyterian General Synod in April 2001 by a Mr. Likambale objecting to its criticisms of the United Democratic Front government. "The current government under the UDF has committed no human rights abuses: there have been no political killings. Furthermore, now there are several political parties the Church should leave any political criticism to opposition parties. The Church should not act as another opposition party. Rather it should now concentrate on spiritual matters."

16. In September 1996, the Catholic Episcopal Conference of Malawi issued a pastoral letter condemning corruption.

17. There is lively literature on "born-again" preachers operating outside the Malawian historic churches (van Dijk 1992, Werbner 1998). Van Dijk argues that these young preachers and their "small fellowships and ministries" were more profoundly subversive of Banda's regime and its "democratic" successors than any other

religious movement. They showed contempt for political gerontocracy, for political appeals to "tradition," and for the pursuit of power, patronage, and profit. "If someone from within the Born-Again groups was appointed, even involuntarily, to one of the many political organisations (for men, women, youth, or whatever), that person was perceived forthwith as an outcast: someone who, for access to power, defiled the treasure of being born again" (van Dijk 1992, 174–175).

18. I drew here on the material that is presented in this book by Isabel Mukonyora and Teresa Cruz e Silva.

19. The South African Council of Churches has also found its voice in support of its Zimbabwean colleagues. Its secretary-general, Molefe Tsele, attended the Victoria Falls meeting of the Zimbabwe Council, and subsequently issued a statement: "We support the ZCC for its stance against misrule and we have no apologies for that. We don't expect these people (government) to voluntarily see logic but at one point they will be forced to. I have no doubt that ultimately the will of the people of Zimbabwe will prevail. You may delay it, but it is inevitable. One day Zimbabweans will have their legitimate representatives."

20. "What the ZCC is trying to achieve," one Anglican bishop is quoted as saying, "is nice brotherly love. We don't want voices that divide us. We are God's messengers and we should not allow ourselves to be used by these politicians. God will punish us heavily."

21. "Life in Abundance," Pastoral Statement of the Churches in Manicaland, March 2001. The forty churches, which had been meeting together since May 2000, included not only the Catholic, Anglican, and Lutheran churches but also the African Catholic Church, the Apostolic Church of Pentecost, the Elim Pentecostal Church, the Pentecostal Assemblies of God, the United Apostolic Faith Church, and the Zimbabwe Assemblies of God (ZAOGA). The scope of the statement did not, however, extend to all the evangelicals discussed in this book. The Vapostori churches, discussed by Mukonyora in her chapter, were not participants.

22. I owe this information to Shirley de Wolf, who represented Christian Care in the Mozambican refugee camps.

23. Revivalist and charismatic evangelical churches had played their own role in the Christian/Muslim polarization. Lamin Sanneh, discussing the Christian use of the vernacular in the presentation of the Scriptures and the Muslim repudiation of it, sees radical Islam and radical Christianity confronting each other in Nigeria: "According to a popular teaching of the Christ Apostolic Church—considered an elite among the charismatic churches—prayer is likened to gunpowder; and the Holy Spirit, that terror of the invisible enemy, is regarded as the gun, with the Bible as the ramrod. This is perhaps the closest that Christian revival came to the sphere of the sword of the Muslim reformers. . . . The Muslim 'sword of truth' identified them as the unerring target" (Sanneh 2001, 44).

24. When the Christian Council of Zimbabwe demanded a promise of nonviolence from Zimbabwe's minister of justice in December 2001, the minister of justice replied that he could not give such a pledge because violence was inseparable from revolution. For the doctrine of the "third revolution" in Zimbabwe, see Ranger (2002). Both mainline churches and evangelical/pentecostals have been divided in their

response to the official "revolution," some condemning its destructive violence, and others praising its redistributive justice.

25. Personal communication from David Maxwell.

26. He is drawing especially on Marshall (1991), and he also cites Meyer (1999).

27. The leading Zambian woman scholar, Dr. Mutumba Mainga Bull, has written a lengthy analysis of the gender dimensions of the 2001 elections in Zambia, which took place after Isabel Phiri had completed her chapter (M. M. Bull, "Gender Dimensions of Multiparty Politics: Elections 2001 in Zambia," Workshop on the Political Process in Zambia, January 2002). Dr. Bull notes that the Evangelical Fellowship of Zambia joined with the Zambia Episcopal Conference and the Christian Council of Zambia to work with the Women's NGO umbrella body so as to give women "space to air their view on whether President Chiluba should run for a third term." The Evangelical Fellowship also participated in a Conflict Management Committee to monitor voter registration and training. In the elections two women stood as presidential candidates. One hundred eighty-two women candidates stood for twelve different parties, some standing on an overtly evangelical program; sixteen were successful for six different parties. In March 2001 the National Women's Lobby Group brought together women members from eight parties and issued a joint Zambia Women's Manifesto. In mid-September 2001 a Women in Politics National Conference was held, which included delegates from the Zambian churches. Women candidates in the election were endorsed by the Women's Movement if they were "humble and [did] not give false promises." Women candidates were urged "to transform the male mainstream and make it conducive to both men and women of all categories and status."

28. An-Na'im's collection contains other chapters relevant to this book. Farid Esack, Lamin Sanneh, Benjamin Soares, and Chabha Bouslimani write on Muslim proselytization; Rosalind Hackett writes on radical Christian revivalism in Nigeria and Ghana.

29. This does not seem to be so much the case for Maputo Zionism. I was fascinated when visiting Teresa Cruz e Silva to go to the beach early on a Sunday morning. It was a positive theatre of possession and healing—Zionist healers and baptizers using the sea alongside exorcisers of Ndau spirits and invokers of the female spirits of the sea.

30. Matthew Schoffeleers, whose accounts of the Malawian Catholic church and democratic politics I have quoted above, has also insisted that "Catholics were not the only ones calling for reform. . . . [In] the early months of 1995 African Traditional Religion made its own contribution in the form of the massive Mchape pilgrimage." Schoffeleers insists on "the need to study local perceptions of Demokalasi" (1999).

31. At the workshop Paul Gundani made an oral presentation entitled "Saint Kagubi and Saint Nehanda." He pointed out that the spirit medium Kagubi had been baptized a Catholic the night before he was hanged in 1897, and given the name of the good thief, Dismas. Had Zimbabwean Christianity been like the early church, Gundani suggested, it would have seized the opportunity to connect itself to the once-dominant old tradition by sanctifying Kagubi and even Nehanda. But Zimbabwean Christianity had always been too evangelical—and modernizing—to contemplate any such thing.

I

Evangelicals, Muslims, and Democracy: With Particular Reference to the Declaration of Sharia in Northern Nigeria

Cyril Imo

The contest between evangelicalism and Islamic revivalism in Nigeria has intensified greatly within recent years, significantly affecting the country's politics. The form of Islam that first came to northern Nigeria was brought by the Sufis in the eleventh and twelfth centuries, while Protestant missionaries from the West were the first to effectively evangelize the region in the nineteenth century. Before Christianity came to the north, the Muslims had begun to attempt to gain dominance over the whole region. This began in 1804 when Uthman Dan Fodio carried out a series of radical religious reforms. He then sought the complete Islamization of Nigeria, especially the north. When Christianity spread, Muslims clashed with Christians. For a long time this confrontation was a silent one, not taking openly political, still less violent, forms. Most evangelicals in northern Nigeria took a pious, apolitical stance and were obliged to coexist with Islam even while competing with it for converts.

However, the intensity of this struggle has increased since Nigeria's independence in 1960, when Saudi Arabia began to float "its austere interpretation of Islam to the discomfort of the Sufi groups" (Hunwick 1992, 143). Much later, many Muslim youths in Nigeria began to admire the Iranian kind of Islam, giving way to a political militancy that has been commonly referred to as "fundamentalism." The rise of this form of Islam has intensified the push for the

Islamization of the country and has a close connection with the demand for full application of Sharia law. In response to this development, evangelicals have altered their apolitical attitude toward Muslim assertion. Since the rise of these forms of religious rivalry in the country, there has been tension and political violence with religious dimensions, as representatives of the Nigerian state have had to negotiate increasing pressures from these religious groups. All this has brought an increasingly close and increasingly vexed relationship between religion and politics.

The past few decades in particular have witnessed a tremendous involvement of religion in Nigerian politics. This involvement has taken several forms, including the use of religion to produce citizens who substantially abide by the norms of democracy and civility, the manipulation of religion to reinforce power, and the use of religion as an instrument to produce disruptive tension and conflict. Each of the two major religions, Islam and Christianity, has sought to control government. This has been clearest in the northern part of Nigeria where Islam has a stronger hold, especially in the core north. Because of the large population of Muslims in the north, Muslims have tried to exert greater control over the non-Muslim population of the area. But the non-Muslims have so far done their best to resist domination by the ruling Muslim class.

In 1999 the struggle for Islamic domination of Nigeria assumed a more drastic dimension, as the Islamic legal system and its criminal penalties were declared state law in some states in the north. This declaration came shortly after the installation of a democratic government in Nigeria, after many years of military rule and at a time when evangelical Christianity, including in the north of the country, was experiencing dramatic expansion. Evangelicals themselves are becoming more actively involved in politics. Northern Nigeria illustrates many of the most important dynamics and challenges associated with the contest between evangelicalism and Islamic revivalism within a religiously pluralistic society. Hence this chapter uses northern Nigeria as a case study of evangelical political involvement in the incipient democratic experiment in Nigeria. It is concerned with analyzing the extent to which evangelical political involvement has helped or hindered the development of democratic ideals and the realization of the goals of democracy in the face of Islamic "fundamentalism."

The issues discussed in this chapter are thus different from those discussed in other chapters; I focus on the evangelical attitude toward Muslim activism in a section of Nigeria that is predominantly Muslim. If I were writing a chapter on evangelical Christianity in Nigeria as a whole, I would need to address many issues similar to those explored in other chapters. These chapters set out the many different positions on democracy adopted by different kinds of evangelicals; they discuss debates about morality and accountability within the evangelical churches themselves as well as between the churches and the state; they emphasize the contrast between the "historic" types of evangelical Christianity and pentecostal and charismatic movements. All these topics are relevant to Nigeria. The country comprises many different kinds of evangelicals, as theology and lifestyle interact with ethnicity to create a bewildering variety of churches and sects. Scholars such as Ruth Marshall have written extensively about the variety of pentecostal churches in southern Nigeria, and their particular relation to democracy.

But my concern is to write about one part of Nigeria—the north; and to write about one topic—the confrontation of Christianity and Islam. None of the other chapters in this book is compelled to address this issue. For instance, clashes between Muslims and Christians have occurred in Nairobi in recent years, but, as John Karanja shows, these have not nullified a combined Christian/Muslim position on democracy and good government. The situation is very different in northern Nigeria where the mobilization of Islamic power is pervasive and inescapable. Thus, there are certainly different sorts of evangelicals in the north, including many pentecostals. Christian moral conduct is as far from Christian principles as it is everywhere else. But the perceived threat of Islam has the effect of uniting Christians and particularly evangelicals. It also has the effect of making debates about democracy focus on politics and law rather than on morality and personal conduct.

To pursue the main purpose of this study, this chapter has been divided into five broad sections. The next section seeks to clarify key terms for the Nigerian context. After that, the following section provides background on northern Nigeria, considering the relationship of Islam, Christianity, and politics; a brief history of Sharia in northern Nigeria; and the status of the Sharia in the national constitution and the penal code in the north. A subsequent section analyzes the evangelical tradition, Sharia, and the political democratic traditions, particularly the nature of democracy in the Fourth Republic. This section also examines how evangelical traditions have affected the present democratic process in Nigeria, how the declaration of the Sharia has led to the development of evangelical theological innovations, and the implications of the full implementation of Sharia as a state religion for evangelicals in the north. The fifth and concluding section examines the prospects of the relationship between evangelicals and Muslims in northern Nigeria in the twenty-first century.

Clarification of Terms

The key terms that must be clarified here are "evangelical," "democracy," and "Sharia." Even though these terms are relatively common, it is essential to capture the way they are understood in Nigeria today, especially to appreciate the dynamics of these phenomena in Nigeria.

"Evangelical" has been used variously by scholars. Acknowledging the lack of a generally accepted definition of the word, Paul Freston, in his publication *Evangelicals and Politics in Asia, Africa, and Latin America*, says that "the

definition of 'evangelical' is hotly debated in historical and sociological literature" (Freston 2001, 2). However, he found Bebbington's four-dimensional
measure of evangelicalism to have value as a working definition. In this study,
I identify with Freston's view of evangelicalism as most applicable to the Third
World. I will therefore not use the word "evangelical" strictly to designate
specific denominational categories, but to refer to denominations, wings of
denominations, and persons even in mainline Protestant churches that exhibit
the criteria outlined by Bebbington (1989) and used by Freston: conversionism, activism, biblicism, and crucicentrism.

It is important to emphasize that due to the ongoing wave of evangelical revival and awakening in different denominations in Nigeria, it is difficult
to simply classify a particular church or churches as evangelical or nonevangelical. Today, there is hardly any denomination in Nigeria that does not
have some members (no matter how few they may be) who emphasize conversionism, activism, biblicism, and crucicentrism. In the mainline churches,
which were not considered to be evangelical in the past, groups have emerged
that practice and emphasize just those beliefs and practices classically emphasized by evangelicals. In effect, I shall use the term "evangelicals" to represent individuals and groups who hold these beliefs and act in the ways
already described, irrespective of their denominations.

Perhaps there is no place where the definition of "democracy" faces more
problems than in Africa. This is a result of the particular historical development and transformation of the social and political organizations of the societies in the continent, from the precolonial period to modern times. This
history needs to be taken into consideration if a sustainable democracy is to be
built in Africa (Lopes 1996, 139). However, this is not to say that Africans
should define democracy in their own way. Democracy has certain universal
ideals that cannot be dispensed with if it is to have any meaning. These include representation, freedom, equality, justice, consultation, accountability,
rule of law, and civil liberty. Democracy implies that form of government in
which the poorer class, which is almost always the more numerous, is allowed
free and equal participation in all political processes. There is no doubt that in
precolonial Africa there were certain basic values that could support this kind
of democracy, often described as liberal democracy (Lopes 1996, 146; Bashir
1999, 16). In this study the term "democracy" will be used to refer to liberal
democracy, which involves periodic election of political leadership; popular
participation of all adults in the electoral process; a relatively high degree of
openness in the conduct of government; accountability of elected public officials to the rule of law; transparency of government; political freedoms; and
respect for fundamental human rights.

To assess the extent to which evangelicals are involved in the democratization of Nigeria, I shall examine the degree to which these liberal democratic
values and procedures are being promoted by evangelicals in the Nigerian state

administration, which was led by an evangelical until 2007, and how other evangelicals have contributed to the protection and entrenchment of such values.

Sharia is generally known to be an Islamic code of life, the legal articulation of all aspects of human endeavors and culture. It is often described as an Islamic way of life. But the understanding of what constitutes this "way of life" varies from place to place and sometimes from person to person, even among Muslims themselves. To understand Sharia as it is conceived by the majority of Muslims in Nigeria, one must consider the definition formulated by Sayyid Abul Ala Maududi, one of the greatest Islamic thinkers of the twentieth century, who has exerted an overwhelming influence on Muslim political culture in Nigeria. According to his view, Sharia represents the broad principles on which the system of human life should be based, as stated in the Book of God and the authoritative interpretation and exemplification of the Book of God by the prophet, through his words and deeds in his capacity as God's representative (Maududi 1967, 37).

For Muslims, therefore, Sharia is the legal system that is given by God alone and can be modified by no one. This is because God alone is sovereign, whose law is above all human and national laws. For Muslims in Nigeria, Sharia is above the constitution and can only be implemented by God's vicegerents. God's vicegerents are "the totality of Muslim believers who submit to the one sovereign and his laws received through the prophet, having repudiated all previous national, ethnic or cultural norms" (Singh 2000, 7). The implication of this is that the implementation of Sharia is only possible in an Islamic state and cannot be carried out nor practiced by non-Muslims.

However, since the declaration of Sharia as the official legal system in some northern Nigerian states, a difference between the theory and practice of Sharia has emerged. While in theory Nigerian Muslims emphasize that the Sharia system means Islam, and that Islam is an all-embracing system—a way of life for all aspects of life (political, economic, social, and cultural)—in practice they tend to limit Sharia to a set of criminal codes. Those codes have to be administered by courts of law where punishment will be prescribed for offenders. Thus, immediately after proclaiming Sharia, Sani Yerima, the governor of Zamfara state of Nigeria, who was the first to make the declaration on Sharia, appointed Sharia judges to try accused persons and set up a special police squad composed of Muslims to enforce Sharia. As evidence that total Sharia was in operation, a thief's right hand was amputated and the action was widely publicized (*The Punch* [Ikeja], February 25, 2000).

Background

Since the early part of the twentieth century, the crucial political issue in the relationship between evangelicals and Muslims in the predominantly Muslim north has been competition for dominance. Before the amalgamation of three southern and northern protectorates that took place after the British conquest of northern Nigeria in 1902–1903, Islam had enjoyed full control of the lives of the peoples of the area in the far north. The cultures of the people were Islamized in the legal sphere as well as in other areas. Before English jurisprudence was introduced to the area in 1904, there was a fairly systematized and sophisticated system of law based on the *Maliki* school of Islamic jurisprudence (Ofori-Amankwah 1986, 53; Anderson 1976, 27–28; Ostien 2000, 1–2). Even after the British conquest of northern Nigeria, the emirs still exercised a considerable degree of power and continued to be respected by their subjects (Hunwick 1992, 146). Under Lord Lugard, the colonial administration permitted a system of indirect rule, allowing the emirs to maintain some authority under Islamic law. When Christian missionaries came into the region later on the heels of the colonial officers, the Hausa and Fulani Muslims saw them as encroaching on an area where Islamic law was considered sovereign. The efforts of evangelical missionaries and the corresponding resistance of the Hausa and Fulani produced constant and intense religious competition in the north.

African Christians and European missionaries found it less difficult to convert the people in those areas of the north not controlled by Fulani Muslims (Kastfelt 1994, 2; Hunwick 1992, 145). The bulk of this area fell within the region that has often been referred to as the "Middle Belt." There was a significant Christian presence in this area by the early twentieth century. The activities of present-day evangelicals have led to the establishment of a greater Christian presence in these areas and also in some parts of what used to be Islamic states. With these developments and the present wave of evangelical activity and expansion in the country, there have been more frequent conflicts in northern Nigeria.

After the British conquest of northern Nigeria and Lord Lugard's introduction of indirect rule, the co-existence of English and Islamic laws produced contradictions. Over many years, several committees and commissions were set up to investigate them and to make recommendations. One result was the 1933 Native Courts ordinance. In 1955, further strategic changes were made that "marked the beginning of the integration of the judicial system through appeals" (Kumo 1972, 41). An appeals court was established to consider cases from the English law courts and those from the Muslim courts on the basis of the common law. But the emirs became suspicious of the British and felt that their power was being undermined (Anderson 1959, 442).

In order to appease the emirs, the British established a Muslim Court of Appeal in 1956. As independence was approaching, the British discerned that the existing criminal code in the north was not adequate for the exigencies of democracy. It became clear to them that the existing criminal code needed to be reformed to reflect the diverse religious and cultural values in the north, taking into account the existence of Christians and other non-Muslims in the area. Under the chairmanship of Abu Rannat Mini, then chief justice of Sudan, a panel of jurists drew up a compromise penal code that amalgamated the Islamic and English criminal laws. The criminal code was enacted into law as the Penal Code Law No. 18 of 1959, and has remained the penal code law of northern Nigeria to this day (Ofori-Amankwah 1986, 57). On October 1, 1960, a Sharia Court of Appeal was established in Kaduna.

Although the provision of the penal code and the Sharia Court of Appeal assuaged Muslim dissatisfaction to some extent, further protests occurred in subsequent years. Muslims began to feel that the Sharia had become subjugated to mere human law. These latent concerns came to the surface in 1976 when the nation experienced an acrimonious debate on Sharia. The debate concerned whether or not there should be a federal Sharia court of appeal that would be an intermediate court of appeal between the states' Sharia courts of appeal and the supreme court of Nigeria. In October and November 1988, when the time came for the nation to revise its constitution, there was another serious debate over the status of the Sharia. During a national conference in 1994, the debate arose again and was checked by the government of General Sani Abacha.

In the current 1999 Constitution of the Federal Republic of Nigeria, sections 275–279 deal with matters relating to the "Sharia Court of Appeal of a State." Section 275, the main section that provides for the establishment of "Sharia Court of Appeal of a State," reads as follows:

1. There shall be for any state that requires it a Sharia Court of Appeal for the State;
2. The Sharia Court of Appeal of the State shall consist of—
    (a) a Grand Kadi of the Sharia Court of Appeal, and
    (b) such a number of kadis of the Sharia Court of Appeal as may be prescribed by the House of Assembly of the State.

The subsequent sections spell out the qualifications of the Grand Kadi, his job descriptions, conditions of service, and so forth. It is specifically stated within this section that the Sharia courts will only be concerned with Islamic personal law.

The constitution is clear about the practice of Sharia law in the states of the federation that desire the legal system. But after his election and swearing-in, Governor Ahmed Sani Yerima decided to declare Sharia as the official legal system in his state, Zamfara. When he first made his intentions on this matter known to the public, many non-Muslims and Muslims insisted on the unconstitutionality of his proposed action. Even the federal government tried to dissuade him, but all warnings fell on deaf ears. On October 27, 1999, he made a public declaration of Sharia as the source of the guiding principles and law of his state. This date marked a turning point in the social and political history of Nigeria.

Today, the northern states of the Federation in which state governments have declared Sharia as the official legal system include Zamfara, Sokoto,

Kebbi, Katsina, Kano, Niger, Jigawa, Yobe, Borno, Bauchi, and Kaduna. The other northern states where such a declaration has not been made are Plateau, Adamawa, Gombe, Taraba, Nasarawa, Kogi, Benue, and Kwara.

Nigeria: Thirty-Six States of the Federation and the Sharia States

Since Governor Ahmed Sani Yerima proposed the idea of declaring Sharia as the official legal system of the state, the reactions and counterreactions have been numerous and intense. Before the declaration was made, opposition mounted from different quarters, including a federal high court injunction in Lagos. In spite of the opposition, Yerima made the proclamation during an official launching ceremony at the Ali Akilu Square in Gusau, the state capital of Zamfara.

Since then, many Nigerians have mounted vehement protests, some violent, shaking the unity of the nation and the viability of the nascent democracy. Ethnic militias were formed, such as the Odua Peoples Congress (OPC) in the west and the Movement for the Actualization of the Sovereign State of Biafra (MASSOB) in the east. The Middle Belt states have disassociated themselves from northern Nigeria. Some have called for states that are predominantly Christian to be declared Christian states and to adopt ecclesiastical courts. Others have called for a national conference to discuss the basis for continued national unity. The eastern governors have also demanded that the fiscal derivation formula be reviewed, as some of these governors did not want the revenue derived from mineral oil produced in their states to be used to run the Sharia states. Even the National Youth Service Corps, established to foster the unity of the Nigerian nation, was threatened as non-Muslims youths from the southern part of the country, with the support of their parents, refused to serve in the Sharia states when posted there. All this has called into question the sustainability of the country's present democratic experiment as well as the integrity of Nigeria as a nation.

How have evangelicals responded to problems posed by the declaration of Sharia in some northern states? In the next section I examine how evangelicals have responded so far to the challenges of Shariaization within the modern and pluralistic Nigerian nation.

Evangelicals, Sharia, and Democracy

In analyzing the evangelical response to Sharia, it is easy to fall into the kind of "political reductionism" found in "elite politics" (Marshall 1995). From such a perspective, discussion of the church's role in political change narrowly focuses on the interaction between the state and church leaders, "analyzed in terms of leaders' public statements concerning government actions, public and political morality" (Marshall 1995, 241). Such a discussion would be concerned only with "inclusionary democracies," which tend to collapse as a result of intrigue among the political elite (Bratton and van de Walle 1997, 546). I shall try to avoid such political reductionism by not only examining the roles of evangelical politicians and church leaders but also the involvement of evangelical laypeople and evangelicals of lower socioeconomic status in the political process.

Before I discuss the level of involvement of the different evangelical strata in the process of democratization, however, I must describe the overall Christian attitude to politics in Nigeria. This is necessary because it has been established that a particular historical dynamic underlies the religious and political changes currently occurring in Nigeria (Imo 1995, 15).

Evangelicals in Nigeria, like those in other developing countries, have become increasingly politically conscious in modern democratic situations. In the past, Nigerian evangelicals saw politics as a dirty game, as something that was unchristian (Ilesanmi 1995, 310). This, of course, was a result of the kind of theology they inherited from the early Western missionaries who sharply dichotomized human activities into the spiritual and the unspiritual. Politics fell under the unspiritual dimension of life. Any person involved in politics was therefore seen as being an unserious, unspiritual Christian. The evangelicals believed that serious Christians should place emphasis on things in heaven and not on the things that go on in this life, which they believed would be passing away soon. For a long time this made many evangelicals preoccupied with prayer, preaching, and awaiting the return of Christ.

As far as they were concerned, the only way a "true believer" could be involved in politics was to pray for the nation and for God to guide the rulers. Such prayers were offered regularly. Several "prayer for the nation" seminars, with prayers for good governance, were organized by those in political leadership. Evangelicals quoted the popular passage of Scripture, Proverbs 29:18, which reads in part, "Where there is no vision, the people perish"; and they offered prayers that God would give vision to the nation's political leaders. As justification, evangelicals also quoted 1 Timothy 2:2, which admonishes believers to pray for kings and "all that are in authority." (If they felt that a particular leader was wicked, some even prayed for the leader to die!) This attitude toward politics was prevalent among Nigerian Christians, including evangelicals, until the 1980s. With the rise of Muslim political activism in northern Nigeria and the Sharia controversies, evangelicals began to change their attitude toward politics (Marshall 1995).

The Role of Evangelical Politicians in Nigeria's Ongoing Democracy

Few evangelicals serve in government positions in northern Nigeria, where the states are predominantly Muslim and have adopted Sharia as the legal system.

In Zamfara, Kebbi, and Bauchi, even when evangelicals have succeeded in being appointed to the government, they have not been able to make any reasonable impact because of their minority position. However, the situation is different in the Middle Belt states and in Kaduna where Christians and Muslims share political positions. In Kaduna, for example, the deputy governor, Engineer Stephen Shekari, was an evangelical. When the state governor Ahmed Markafi and the Muslims in the state House of Assembly attempted to introduce Sharia in the state, Shekari and other Christians in the House strongly opposed this move. Their main weapons were spiritual. Supported by the members of the Kaduna state branch of the Christian Association of Nigeria, Shekari and other Christians joined together in fervent prayer sessions during this period of struggle.

This arrangement, in which ordinary evangelicals come together to pray with evangelical politicians, is common in the northern states. The governor of Plateau state, Chief Joshua Dariye, is an evangelical, and members of his church, the Church of Christ in Nigeria (COCIN), visit him regularly and pray with him. His wife has organized biweekly prayer vigils for select evangelicals from different denominations in the government House. Even though Plateau is not a Sharia state, during the initial stage of the Sharia controversy, some Muslims marched to the government House to demand full implementation of Sharia. The state House of Assembly had to deliberate on the matter and produced a public statement rejecting the institution of the Sharia legal system as part of state law.

Many evangelical politicians who relate closely with fellow evangelicals outside politics attempt to integrate their evangelical beliefs into their practice of politics. They strive to be truthful and not to take bribes or engage in other forms of corruption. Professor Jerry Gana, a renowned evangelical politician who served as federal information minister, demonstrates this approach. Although he was in the government, he was still involved in preaching at gatherings of evangelicals. In 2001 he preached at the Synod service of the Anglican Diocese of Jos at the invitation of the Right Reverend Benjamin Kwashi, also an evangelical. During his sermon, the minister shared how he had served in different governments and yet did not own his own house. According to him, this has attracted many critical comments, which do not bother him because he wants to do the will of God even while in government. This level of commitment is rare among politicians, many of whom are involved in the "politics of the belly" and its gross corruption (Bayart 1993; Gifford 1998, 5). Another example of an evangelical in government who has notably used his beliefs and practices to make an impact on the process of democratization is Justice Londji, who is currently the commissioner for Justice and Chief Justice of Plateau state. He was a member of the Full Gospel Business Men's Fellowship before he joined the government, and he has remained active in the Fellowship while in office. He has a reputation for insisting on truth, honesty, justice, and fairness. Standing on these principles, he has attempted to instill discipline in the state judiciary, and he has made it known that he is prepared to punish any of his subordinates who do not adhere to the values of democracy and integrity.

In considering the contributions of evangelical politicians to democracy, one cannot overlook the former president, Chief Matthew Aremu Olusegun Obasanjo. Obasanjo, a Baptist, became a born-again evangelical during his time in prison for his alleged involvement in a coup plot during the Abacha regime. In spite of the intricacies of Nigerian politics, he has struggled to be guided by the ideals of transparency and accountability in public office. Although various accusations have been leveled against him, none of these has been reliably confirmed or proved. On ascending to the office of the presidency, he promised to live above corruption and fight against it. It was not long after he was sworn into office that he introduced an anticorruption bill. Within a short time the bill was enacted into law as the "Anti-corruption Law of the Federal Republic of Nigeria 2000." On June 13, 2000, at the formal signing of the bill into law, Obasanjo said:

> It gives me great pleasure to welcome you all to this very impor-
> tant and indeed historic moment in the life of our nation. It is our
> firm hope and belief that the signing into law of the Anti-Corruption
> Bill will mark a turning point in all the major aspects of our lives,
> individually and collectively, politically and socially. During our
> campaign we promised total war against corruption. Corruption was
> identified as the number one enemy of development and prog-
> ress. Combating corruption was easily the number one priority action
> for Administration. Thus no sooner than we got into office, this
> Bill became the number one piece of legislation to be promptly sent
> to the National Assembly. (Obasanjo 2000)

The president convened the first retreat of all chief executives and chairpersons of boards of parastatals in the federation in Abuja, from October 7–8, 2000, to emphasize the need for government officials to be accountable and transparent in all their transactions. At the retreat, he presented a copy of the anticorruption law to each of the participants. Afterward, he tried to ensure that all department heads in government ministries and parastatals received the document. The widely respected Senate president, Anyim Pius Anyim, a member of the Assemblies of God Church (who stepped down as Senate president in 2003), and a few others like him appeared to make a serious effort to comply with the demands of the law. In fact, by 2005 Nigeria registered a slight improvement on Transparency International's Corruption Perceptions Index (Transparency International 2005).

There have also been attempts by the government to pursue programs of political liberalization and to allow some level of participation by the public in the process of establishing public policies. This effort was evident in the review of the constitution and during the human rights violation investigation panel headed by Justice Chukwudifu Oputa.

By identifying some of the pro-democratic features of President Oba-sanjo's policy making, I do not imply that he was free of failures. In fact, the president diverted from the path of democratization in ways that even prompt some people to question his evangelicalism. He exhibited authoritarian ten-dencies and often rejected consultation in making public policies. And in early 2006 he sought an unconstitutional third term in office. Genuine democracy includes the institutionalization of certain values and norms that promote equity, peace, and prosperity. But the lack of some basic elements of democ-racy tends to frustrate even its genuine achievements. One example of the president's authoritarian tendencies is the massacre of the people of Odi in Bayelsa State. The Odi crisis is one of the cases in the Niger-Delta area (where most Nigerian oil is produced) of protest by an underdeveloped community that the federal government has neglected. The crisis came to a climax on No-vember 19, 1999, when fifty army trucks rolled into the Kolokuma/Opokuma villages of Bayelsa State. The number of soldiers involved in this siege has been unofficially estimated at between three thousand and six thousand (*The News* 1999, 15). The army was ordered to invade the area in response to the killing of twelve policemen by area youths. The troops deployed to quell the Odi crisis were said to have been given the instruction by the president "to shoot, kill, especially every male found in Odi, old, young, infirm" (*The News* 1999, 20). This directive was carried out to the letter. All the houses in the village were pulled down, the males were shot to death, and there were many cases of rape.

It is obvious that the posture of the president on this matter was more military than civilian, not to talk of being undemocratic. It is a glaring case of blatant disregard for fundamental human rights. Some critics have seen the action as a hangover from the president's military past. Others feel that the administration is just an extension of the military regime. In all this, one thing is sure: The formal demilitarization of Nigeria has been no guarantee of its democratization (Ifidon 1996).

On several occasions, the executive and the legislature have had face-offs. One case concerned the president's declaration of May 29 as Democracy Day, ironically enacted without consultation with the legislature. The action caused much tension between the two arms of government. In another case, the House of Assembly accused the president in 1999 of not consulting with them before the approval of an extra budget for the year. Several other problems have arisen between the executive and the legislature, caused by the lack of due consultation. However, what gives some credit to the evangelicals in govern-ment is that during Senate President Pius Anyim's time in office, there was a relatively harmonious relationship between the presidency and the legisla-ture. This suggests that evangelicals have contributed to democratization by encouraging consultation and accountability, with hopes of producing a more stable democratic process.

Another indication of the lack of democratic freedom, however, is the absence of genuine popular participation in making public policies. An example of this was the president's announcement of a major increase in the price of petrol, a matter with great implications for workers and other citizens in Nigeria. Yet labor unions were not consulted, and they displayed their displeasure by marching in the streets. In addition, there have been numerous cases where government appointments have not been made on the basis of transparent and democratic criteria.

However, it should be noted that some of the worst problems took place within the first two years of the Obasanjo government and that the nation has been under military leadership almost since its independence. Seen from this background, it was hoped that there might be some improvement in the performance of the president and other evangelicals in government in a later phase of the ongoing democratization process. As these individuals and the entire government became more familiar with the operations of democracy, they have overcome some of the cumulative effects of military rule by institutionalizing basic democratic values and norms. To be successful, however, this process requires the personal internalization of democratic values and norms by both the government and the governed.

The Role of the Evangelical Ministers in Democratization Since October 1999

Since October 1999, when Zamfara state in northern Nigeria first incorporated Sharia into the state legal code, evangelical ministers from various Christian denominations have sensitized their congregations to the implications of Sharia through various means. Some have organized seminars, and others have incorporated words of civic instruction into their sermons. For many of the ministers, such action became necessary after the Christians in Kaduna were attacked on two different occasions in February and May 2000. Most of the activities of the ministers were carried out jointly under the umbrella of the Christian Association of Nigeria (CAN), as the hostile relationship between Muslims and Christians in the country made it necessary for Christian denominations to make common cause against their increasingly radicalized Muslim counterparts. Thus, a good number of the activities of evangelicals, in their contribution to democracy in Nigeria, have been subsumed under CAN's activities. However, some evangelical ministers have made independent statements and taken independent action to respond to the declaration of Sharia and its consequences. In order to document such views and actions, evangelical ministers from various denominational backgrounds were interviewed for this chapter. In this section I analyze both the activities of the evangelical ministers through CAN and those carried out by different denominational groups of evangelicals and individual evangelical ministers.

Before the declaration of Sharia by the Zamfara state governor, CAN had been involved in educating its members throughout the country about the radical Muslim agenda of Islamicization. This role of CAN came into prominence in 1986 and 1988–1989 during the fulmination over Nigeria's membership in the Organization of the Islamic Conference (OIC) and during an acrimonious debate on Sharia, respectively (Falola 1997, 268–280). Falola (1997) offers a critical analysis of the political activities of CAN and the implications of the group for the democratic process. In his conclusion, Falola regards CAN's role as ambivalent because it tries to build a solid ecumenism, distancing itself from direct attacks on the government on the one hand and making radical statements to satisfy those who want it to check the excesses of government on the other. He observes that "both positions create a problem of identity, one that generates mistrust from time to time in different quarters" (Falola 1997, 279).

Of all the branches of CAN, those in northern Nigeria, especially in Kaduna state, seem to be the most radical. The radicalism of the Kaduna state branch can be explained in two ways. First, the state is very volatile because of its highly pluralistic ethnic and religious composition. Second, the state is central to the political life of northern Nigeria. It served as the capital of the former northern Nigeria and has remained a rallying point for Muslims, especially those in the north. These qualities have made Kaduna the north's religious and political hot spot. The strategic position it occupies for the Muslims has made the Kaduna branch of the Christian Association of Nigeria particularly active and militant. The level of its activism is shown by the number of publications and activities that have been organized in the city (CAN 1989). As the rumored plans of the Muslim governors to launch Sharia began to spread, both the state branch of CAN and the Pentecostal Fellowship of Nigeria (PFN) Kaduna branch issued several press releases to enlighten Nigerian Christians on Sharia. Christian ministers organized many meetings, seminars, and workshops on Sharia in Kaduna beginning in 1999. Although CAN is an association that brings all Christians in Nigeria together, evangelical ministers are often more actively involved, and they hold key positions in the organization. Evangelical ministers seek to persuade CAN's members to contend for the faith as a mark of obedience to God. When the ministers do this, they try to bring their knowledge of Scripture and Christian beliefs to bear on the association's policies. Thus, when we speak of CAN's activities in relation to the democratic process, we are essentially talking about the role of evangelical ministers, who play a disproportionate role in the organization.

At the national level, one of CAN's leaders, Archbishop Anthony Olubunmi Okogie, readily comes to mind when it comes to political radicalism. Okogie became the president of the association in 1987 (Tomori 1991). During his regime, CAN became so active that the Muslims accused him of being another head of state. They asked the government why he should not be arrested and whether he was some kind of a sacred cow. However, because Okogie is a Catholic, and as such cannot be classed among the evangelical ministers being considered here, I will not discuss his contributions in detail.

However, many overtly evangelical ministers involved in CAN have been outspoken in defense of the ideals of democracy at the national level. One such minister is the former bishop of the Anglican Diocese of Akure, the Right Reverend Emmanuel B. Gbonigi, who has also served as both the national chairman of the Nigerian Evangelical Fellowship in the Anglican Communion (EFAC) and the organization's international chairman. He challenged General Abacha by openly opposing his authoritarian regime on various occasions through the media (Yemi Olowolabi, "Abacha Is Thoroughly Wicked—Bishop Ghonigi," *Tell: Nigeria's Independent Weekly*, May 25, 1998). The present Anglican bishop of Enugu, the Right Reverend Emmanuel O. Chukwuma, is another evangelical prelate who has insisted that democratic principles must be followed in administering the religiously pluralistic Nigerian state. He fiercely contended with the hostility of the Muslims when he was the Anglican bishop of Bauchi before he was transferred to Enugu. Another Nigerian evangelical clergyman worthy of mention is the Reverend James Ukaegbu, a leading Nigerian Presbyterian, who outspokenly denounced the tendency of Nigerian politicians to use religion to reinforce power and politics even to the point of fomenting religious crises, especially when canvassing for votes. In making his denunciation, he vigorously condemned both Muslims and Christians:

> The hands of our leaders are blood stained, blood thirsty, and have intentionally brutalized fellow Nigerians in a bid to keep political power ... oppression of the poor, perversion of justice, ostentatious lifestyle, desecration of the sanctity of life, religious bigotry and fanaticism and the hypocrisy of both the church (which is divided and commercialized) and the mosque (which has become the rallying point for fanaticism, and in many cases [a] ... hide out armory for religious fanatics and fundamentalists). (*New Africa* 1988, 19)

Many Anglican evangelical bishops in the north have participated in protests against the adoption of Sharia as a state law. From the interviews I had with nearly all the Anglican bishops in northern Nigeria, it is evident that each of them has at one time or another made a public statement in the media to reject the action of the Muslim governors of the core north. The Right Reverend Simon Bala, the bishop of Gusau, the capital of Zamfara, where Sharia was first declared as state law, led a delegation of Christian ministers to Alhaji Ahmed Sani Yerima and confronted him about his actions. They challenged him for using government money to finance the propagation of a particular religion, since he had created a separate government ministry charged with the propagation of Islam. The ministry is called the Ministry of Religious (Islam) Affairs, and it has a budgetary allocation like all other state ministries. The governor's reply to the bishop's challenge was that he did not regret his actions, as Allah will hold him responsible on the last day if he does not use his present office to pursue Allah's course. When the implementation of Sharia started on January 21, 2000, the Muslims intensified their discrimination against the Christians. As the bishop reported, the teaching of Christian religious studies was banned in the primary and secondary schools, not only in government schools but also in Christian-owned schools.

The bishop gave the example of the Fatima Nursery and Primary School in Gusau, which belongs to the Roman Catholic Church. The school was prohibited from teaching Christian religious knowledge. Christian women were discriminated against, because the law prohibited men and women from riding in the same vehicle. In order to enforce this rule, special vehicles were provided for the women, even though the vehicles were driven by men. However, Christian women were not allowed to enter the buses meant for Muslim women. Women were also banned from mounting motorcycles, so that parts of their bodies should not be exposed. This meant that Christian women had to walk on foot, no matter the distance. According to Bishop Bala, the CAN Gusau branch mounted fierce protests until the decision was rescinded. (Apart from CAN's protest, the law could not be enforced, as there were other attendant obstacles to it, including the very low patronage the professional motorcyclists experienced). Several other aspects of Islamic law are presently being enforced in Zamfara state that amount to a violation of the fundamental rights of Christians. Bishop Simon Bala is one of the youngest Anglican bishops in Nigeria, but he has openly confronted the Sarduana of Gusau. Together with other ministers and under the auspices of CAN Gusau chapter, he wrote to President Obasanjo and to the National CAN chairman in Abuja, describing their ordeals on the eve of the inauguration of Sharia in the state. Up to the time of this writing, he had not received any reply from the government.

The other northern bishops of the Anglican Church communicated their feelings about the declaration of Sharia through the media, public gatherings such as synods and ordination services. In a communiqué released at the end of their meeting held at the Cathedral Church of St John Jimeta, Yola, Adamawa State from January 24–26, 2001, the bishops of Province III of the Church of Nigeria, most of whom are evangelicals, made the following resolutions while addressing the issue of the declaration and implementation of Sharia in some northern states:

> The Council reiterated that while it is the duty of religious institutions to sanitize the society of moral decadence, the sanctity of the Nigerian constitution should be protected.

That continued implementation and operation of the Sharia Legal system in some States has put into question the Federal Government position that the controversy will fizzle out with time.

We call on state governors who are implementing Sharia system to know that they are unfair to their electorates, as it did not form part of the campaign manifestoes upon which they are elected.

It should be noted that Sharia practice contrary to the claim of the proprietors affect all and not Muslims alone. Its practice also facilitates violence and disharmony which is not only opposed to democracy and humanity but God's sovereign will that we should live in peace and love with one another. We strongly appeal to proponents of Sharia to consider the reckless loss of dear lives recorded in some Sharia spots and leave Sharia to God Almighty. (Church of Nigeria, Anglican Communion, Province III 2001, 1–2)

These resolutions show the concern of the evangelically oriented Anglican Communion to promote democratic ideals and the entrenchment of democratic values and norms in the Fourth Republic. It also goes some way toward revealing the consequences of the declaration of Sharia and its implementation for democracy in Nigeria and how a good number of Christians in Nigeria perceive it, since the Anglican Church represents a significant proportion of Nigerian Christians, including evangelicals.

The various Anglican bishops in northern Nigeria expressed their feelings and attitudes both about the declaration of Sharia and about the violence that accompanied it. For example, the Anglican bishop of Kaduna, the Right Reverend Josiah Idowu Fearon, former national chairman of EFAC, says that ordinarily he would not oppose Sharia as a system. According to him, this is because "the Sharia is basically part of what is contained in the books of law of the Old Testament, for example Deuteronomy 22–25." He feels that Sharia is supposed to set a good example of how even a Christian ought to live. "For me Sharia is a call to shape up." However, he lamented the process of implementing Sharia. He does not support the kind of Sharia implemented after the declaration because it is simply legislative, calling it "political Sharia." He says it also restricts the church's freedom even in carrying out evangelism in the rural areas.

The Anglican bishop of Kano Diocese in Kano State, Right Reverend Zakka Lalleh Nyam, writing in the popular northern paper *New Nigerian*, warned about the negative implications of establishing Sharia in a pluralistic setting. As Kolawole Dada reported, Bishop Nyam "explained that the governors [who were yet to introduce Sharia] should be aware that they are elected into offices with the votes of Christians and Muslims, and that if they wanted to introduce Sharia, the best thing was for them to honourably step down for emirs and other traditional rulers" ("Bishop Warns on Sharia Application," *New*

Nigerian [Kaduna], November 1999, 21). The Right Reverend Bishop Benjamin A. Kwashi, the Anglican bishop of Jos, in his address to the Third Session of the Seventh Synod in Jos on May 26, 2000, berated those who perpetrate violence in the name of Sharia: "Let me assure everyone that these crimes and evil will never go unpunished by God. The day of judgement is coming. Even if the people escape the law of man, God is a just God" (Kwashi 2000, 26).

His words exemplify the reaction of the evangelical bishops in northern Nigeria to violence. When interviewed independently, most of the northern Anglican bishops took the same position. However, they did not hesitate to add that under critical conditions, and particularly when the lives of their members are threatened, they would ask them to defend themselves and not to rely only on the ultimate judgment of God.

Another group of evangelicals that has made public statements about the declaration of Sharia in some northern states is the Evangelical Church of West Africa (ECWA). Shortly after the proclamation of Sharia law in Zamfara state, but before its formal launching, the General Council of ECWA held a consultative meeting at the ECWA headquarters in Jos, Plateau state, during October 20–22, 1999. At this meeting, the council declared that it was called to "blow the trumpet." Declaring its position, the council stated: "We, the evangelicals of the Evangelical Church of West Africa (ECWA) cannot and will not keep quiet in the face of this ominous danger that threatens the roots of our country. Rather we will blow the trumpet in Zion and send a danger alert to the whole Nation on the matter." At the end of the meeting, the council adopted a resolution that was then communicated to all ECWA churches in Nigeria and also released a public communiqué on its position. The following is part of the resolution, entitled "The Stand of ECWA":

> Without mincing words, the Proclamation of Sharia Legal System and by extension the declaration of Zamfara State by Governor Ahmed Sani as an Islamic State is a reckless transgression of Sections 10 and 271 of the Constitution of the Federal Republic of Nigeria. What Ahmed Sani has done is worse than a declaration of secession. It is a gross violation of his oath of office. It is a declaration of war against the Christian Faith and Nigeria as a Nation.... We equally believe that what is happening in Zamfara State is a manifestation of a hidden agenda aided and abetted by disgruntled looters of the economy to destabilize the Nigerian State and plunge the nation into a diversionary religious crisis. This is a very sad anticlimax and a deliberate sabotage of the re-assuring achievements of President Olusegun Obasanjo. It threatens the very foundation of our fledgling democracy. The trend is unacceptable to ECWA.... We must warn that any attempt to harass our members and indeed any

Christians in Zamfara will not be taken lightly. (ECWA General Secretary 1999, 5–6)

In their recommendations the council called on all members of ECWA in Zamfara state to "ignore the Law in question and go about their normal business as the same is invalid and fatally flawed." Many Nigerians share ECWA's view that the declaration of Sharia by the governor of Zamfara was an attempt to incite a "diversionary religious crisis." It is widely believed that some members of the political elites in the north felt deep disappointment when Obasanjo, a Christian and a southerner, became president. They hoped that because they helped Obasanjo come to power, he would submit to the Hausa and Fulani rulers, some of whom have come to see ruling Nigeria as their *bona fide* right. But after becoming president, Obasanjo demonstrated considerable independence (Dan Agbese, "Babangida: The Sharia Controversy." *Newswatch* [Ikeja], July 10, 2000). As a result, some prominent northern political elites raised the cry of marginalization and believed that the best thing to do was to create a crisis that would challenge the president and weaken the nascent democratic system.

I also interviewed a number of pentecostal evangelical ministers about their reaction to the declaration of Sharia and its aftermath, and about their contributions to democratic governance in Nigeria. One person I interviewed was the Reverend Dr. Bright O. Ndu, president of the Pentecostal Fellowship of Nigeria (Plateau state) and the president and general overseer of Footprints of Jesus Mission. He believes that the adoption of Sharia as an official legal system in some Nigerian states undermines the secularity of Nigeria and will infringe on fundamental human rights as enshrined in the Nigerian constitution. Answering questions on the contributions of the PFN to promoting democracy in Nigeria he said, "Usually, as evangelicals, the PFN members go out for evangelism even in these states where Sharia has been declared; and when they go there they help in providing some basic amenities like clinics, schools, and establishments that help to foster democracy." He also added that through the preaching of the gospel, Nigerian citizens—especially those in rural areas—are educated and admonished to comply with the demands of democracy. The Reverend Ndu described how they work under CAN to make suggestions to the government and are called upon to look into matters affecting PFN members or members of their congregations. All these actions, he says, help enhance peace, harmony, and political accountability in the state and the nation.

Other PFN members expressed similar views. These members include the Reverend Kenneth Ononeze, senior pastor and general superintendent of Winners Celebration Chapel in Jos, and treasurer of the Plateau state branch of CAN; and the Reverend Dr. Wilson Ezefor, one-time president of PFN of Plateau state. The Reverend Ezefor describes the implementation of Sharia as "a time-bomb which has given rise to the different religious crises we have experienced in the northern Nigeria in the last few months." He warned that those in authority should ensure that every Nigerian is given a sense of belonging in all parts of the country. Failure to do so would spell doom for the country, as religious wars are always very dangerous. He said that the work the PFN planned to provide has been hindered since many Nigerians, including pentecostal ministers, who were living in the Sharia states have had to flee for their lives. As he put it, this does not augur well for democracy, as it has undermined the social and peaceful interaction between citizens of Nigeria from other states and those in the northern Muslim states. With increased religious homogeneity in the north, according to Ezefor, religious freedom would inevitably suffer.

The Evangelical Low-Status Group and the Democratic Process

Apart from looking at the political attitudes of the evangelical Christian elite, it is essential to examine the role of low-status evangelicals in the democratization process, with "low-status" referring to lower socioeconomic status. We are specifically concerned with outlining how these groups activate their evangelical traditions to promote democratic ideas and values. Do they adhere to democratic principles in their political behavior? How do they do this in a hostile and conflictual legal environment? To answer these questions, it is necessary to isolate and examine the various forms of evangelical political behavior that we find on the ground in the Sharia states of northern Nigeria. This discussion, then, will exclude the bulk of the Middle Belt states. This inquiry has particular importance because this group of evangelicals directly faces the implementation of Sharia in their daily lives.

Consider first the attitudes of lower-status evangelicals to violence. Those charged with the responsibility of enforcing the observance of Sharia often do so coercively. In nearly all the Sharia states, one of the immediate steps taken to enforce the law is to isolate women from men in public. So, for example, when commercial vehicles carrying passengers approach a roadblock mounted by the Sharia enforcement agents, they are stopped and all men in the vehicle are asked to disembark, no matter the distance they are traveling. Ordinarily, one would be provoked to protest or fight. But typically evangelicals quietly get down, without biting the bait. In Kano city, the Muslims planned the commencement of the enforcement exercise to fall on a Sunday. Early in the morning the Sharia policemen made roadblocks. Just as Christians were traveling to their various places of worship, they were confronted with this provocation. Even though the intent seemed to be to intimidate the Christian men, evangelicals tended to adopt a course of self-restraint.

In Zamfara state, single ladies were asked to marry or leave the state. Many young ladies had to leave the state, even leaving their parents or relations behind before the rule was later relaxed. In places where public preaching was allowed before the declaration of Sharia, all forms of Christian public gatherings and preaching were banned. For example, in Sokoto, some members of the Great Commission Movement (GCM) were preparing to preach and show an evangelistic film when a group of young men came and shouted, "Sharia! Sharia! Sharia!" and they called on other Muslims to fight. The members of the GCM simply dismantled their equipment and left. In several cases, evangelicals and other Christians have been denied the right either to purchase land or to build a place of worship on land that had already been purchased. Some Christians have handled such situations by drawing on evangelical theology and conforming to a basic biblical ethic of peaceableness and self-restraint.

However, there have also been occasions when Christians fought back when their lives were threatened. One example was in Kaduna on two occasions of religious riots: February 21, 2000, and May 22, 2000. During the fighting in February 2000, many Christians were killed. But in May 2000, many Christians—including evangelicals—fought back, even to the point of organizing and arming themselves to shoot and kill Muslims who came to fight them. Many Nigerian evangelicals, including Anglican bishops, do not feel that anything was wrong with their actions, maintaining that the killing was in self-defense.

However, in general, evangelicals are not known to have flagrantly violated the moral dictates of Sharia. Some Christians have been punished by the Sharia courts for flouting Sharia laws, but none of these people were known to be members of evangelical churches or groups. This is perhaps not surprising because many Islamic rules are not contradictory to evangelical doctrines, such as refraining from consuming alcoholic beverages and avoiding prostitution and gambling. What many evangelicals object to, however, is the use of force and the lack of respect for human rights displayed in the punishment of people who are seen to break the laws as well as the restrictions on Christian religious activity. The evangelical ethic of love and personal responsibility does not agree with the coercive and punitive approach of radical Sharia and evangelicals do not hesitate to condemn it. It was in this spirit that the spiritual leader of the Anglican Church worldwide, the Archbishop of Canterbury, The Most Reverend George Carey, politely disagreed with the Zamfara state governor, Alhaji Ahmed Sani Yerima on February 3, 2001, when he visited Zamfara state. When he held talks with Alhaji Yerima, the Archbishop expressed concern about the rights of Christians in the state and said that he felt the Islamic legal punishments such as amputation and flogging were wrong (*This Day*, February 5, 2001, 1; *The Punch*, February 5, 2001, 1).

Another area where lower-status evangelicals have been able to use evangelical traditions to support and promote democratic ideas is in their political language. In Nigeria, when you are not able to fight back for whatever reason, the usual reaction is to curse your enemy or oppressor. This was what happened during the dictatorial governments of General Babangida and Abacha. Many poor people cursed them during their regimes because of the level of hardship and oppression to which they were subjected. But the evangelicals, holding firmly to the Scriptural teaching "Love your enemies, bless them that curse you, do good to them that hate you, and pray for them which despitefully use you, and persecute you" (Matthew 5:44), publicly committed to pray for all the Sharia governors. The church men, women, and youths, with or without bishops or clergy, organized prayers and night vigils frequently to pray for the Sharia areas and their governors.

Before the implementation of Sharia, when various forms of religious discrimination were already in place, evangelicals often voted without sectarian bias. In Nigeria both ethnic and religious politics are very strong. But for the evangelicals in Zamfara state, truth and sincerity were important civic virtues. In Zamfara where the All Peoples Party (APP) and the Peoples Democratic Party (PDP) keenly contested, the votes of the Christians gave an edge to the APP. This is because of the strong APP base in the eastern states, where the party is still the ruling party. In other words, those residing in Zamfara who are from these eastern states, most of whom are Christians, probably voted for the popular party in their home states and thus voted for Sani Yerima, the Sharia governor.

Although the level of involvement of low-status evangelicals in the actualization of democracy may not be prominent or high profile, it is nonetheless important. The experiences and reactions of these evangelicals affect the political stability of the areas concerned and the country at large. What happens to a group of religious people in any part of the country affects all the other members of that religion. Usually, retaliation by members of that religion follows in different parts of the country. The fact that low-status evangelicals have generally abided by evangelical teachings and norms directly or indirectly affects the march toward the realization of social harmony, political stability, and liberal democracy.

The Declaration of Sharia, Evangelical Theological Innovation, and Democratization

New religious ideas or the reinterpretation of existing ones often arise from political and social crisis (O'Dea 1966, 55–66). Given the tensions generated by the introduction of Sharia law in some northern states of Nigeria, new theological views have emerged in response to the imposition of the law. In this section I describe and analyze how such new theologies have developed, the nature of the innovations, and how they have contributed to the promotion of democratic values.

Throughout Nigeria's history Christians have maintained the belief that the solution to the problem of religious pluralism can only come through maintaining the secularity of the state. From the early stage of the Sharia controversy in 1977–1978, Christians held to this position. During the Sharia debate in the Constituent Assembly around the same time, the Christians advocated a secular state while Muslims at the Assembly protested against it (Kukah 1993, 121). The Muslims equated the word "secular" with "God-lessness."

A commonly cited basis for the Christian position is the statement of Jesus Christ in Matthew 22:21, "Render therefore unto Caesar the things which are Caesar's; and unto God the things that are God's." Drawing on this text, many Nigerian Christians believed up to the 1980s that religion should be kept separate from politics. But Mohammed Marwa, leader of the Muslim sect known as Maitatsine, used violence in 1980 to advance his cause, and this was followed by several other religious disturbances in which Muslim fundamentalists attacked and killed innocent Christians. Evangelicals began to rethink their position. They began to wonder how they could fold their arms and watch people who did not have the "mind of Christ" or the "fear of God" handle the affairs of state. They distrusted not only Muslim politicians but also corrupt Christians. As Marshall observed, "The Ogbonis and Freemasons have always been associated in Nigeria with high politics and powerful elite networks, and thus a reference to politicization makes the link between church leadership and an illegitimate form of state politics which oppresses the people" (1995, 246). The evangelicals Marshall refers to as the "born-agains" reasoned that even those who called themselves Christians and who campaigned for political positions under that banner were really cult members who were not able to represent them satisfactorily. These nominal Christian politicians were also believed to be guilty of vices that are frequently associated with Nigerian politics, including bribery and corruption, self-aggrandizement, self-perpetration, accumulation of interest, "politics of the belly," and moral decadence.

This "rethinking" brought many evangelicals to a realization that "born-again" Christians needed to be involved in active politics. They came to the conclusion that they needed not only to pray but to organize. At this point various groups, especially CAN, organized conferences, workshops, symposia, and seminars that emphasized the need for committed Christians, regardless of denominational affiliation, to change their attitude toward politics. This kind of teaching is illustrated in the words of Bishop Onaiyakan, a Roman Catholic bishop and one of the most outspoken Nigerian priests, now the Archbishop of Abuja, the federal capital territory:

> We can no longer avoid the question of the relationship between our Christian faith and politics. We must evolve a suitable popular theology of political engagement in the country. Never again should good Christians run away from politics as a dirty job to be left for crooks and rogues. Political leadership as a form of Christian

stewardship whose reward is great in heaven must now become a main feature of our Christian teaching and exhortation to the faithful. We should even go further to identify and encourage good gifted Christians to vie for public office, so as to ensure a good Christian component in the leadership corps of our country.... The aim would not be to achieve Christian domination of the nation, but rather to ensure a valid Christian contribution towards good and just government. (Onaiyakan 1989–1990, 28)

As evangelicals became increasingly involved in CAN, they adopted this kind of politically engaged posture with greater frequency and intensity.

While evangelicals retained the idea of the secularity of the state, they tried to reinterpret key scriptural texts. The new interpretation saw "Caesar" not as the "world," "worldliness," or even the "devil." When evangelicals commonly quoted this text in the past, they seemed to have the idea that "Caesar" was "something devilish." (The quotation was often used, for example, when a believer in traditional religion asked his evangelical brother to join in offering a sacrifice to appease the gods or their ancestors, and the evangelical brother refused. The traditionalist reminded him that Jesus commanded that you should give to the devil what is his and to God what is God's!) But many evangelicals now began to see "Caesar" in a new light, as an entity with a capacity for good, thus concluding that a "believer" should identify with politics and political leadership and at the same time remain faithful to God. To disseminate this new theology, evangelicals organized symposia, seminars, and teachings on "The Christian and Politics," "The Christian and Business," and "The Christian and the State"; the aim of each was to develop a more politically engaged Christian orientation and value system. These efforts began to yield results before the declaration of Sharia as the official legal system in some northern states in 1999.

However, since the declaration on October 27, 1999, a favorable attitude to political participation has been even more deeply entrenched in modern evangelical theology, especially in the northern states that have witnessed the operation of Sharia. Many Christians in these areas have become even more politically conscious. CAN and other evangelical groups publish books, magazines, and tracts and organize periodic symposia, seminars, and workshops to create political awareness. Now both Christians and Muslims observe CAN's political discourse and interventions with keen interest. Few evangelicals believe that engaging in politics is "satanic."

This greater evangelical openness to politics has led not only to increased evangelical activism in politics but also to increased evangelical attempts to "sanctify" politics. As evangelicals participate in politics, they seek to bring their demonstrative forms of spirituality with them. In many government offices, they ensure that on resumption of work each day their fellow employees gather together for "morning devotion" before work is started. During the devotion the Bible is read, prayers are made, and in some places choruses are sung. Those evangelicals who sell wares in the market usually come together in small groups in someone's store to pray at noon. Regular prayers are said for evangelicals who hold political positions, so that they remain faithful and "allow their lights to shine." These public office holders will themselves sometimes refer complex cases to some "Christian brothers and sisters" for their input. In these ways, evangelicals inject their characteristic emphases on prayer and spiritual accountability into modern Nigerian politics.

A particular issue evangelicals have addressed in their theology is that of vengeance or retaliation. Previously, Nigerian evangelicals believed that one should not fight back when someone slaps him on the cheek. For their justification of this principle, they often cited Matthew 5:38–47 from the Sermon on the Mount, with particular emphasis on verse 39, which reads: "But I say unto you, That ye resist not evil: but whosoever shall smite thee on thy right cheek, turn to him the other also" (KJV). In quoting this passage, they argued that there is no condition under which a "believer" should fight back. But recent developments concerning Sharia have forced them to reinterpret this text. Speaking comically, the retired bishop of the Anglican Diocese of Kaduna, the Right Reverend Ogboyemi, who called on the present bishop of the Anglican Diocese of Kano, the Right Reverend Nyam, during my interview with the latter, asked me, "As someone has asked, we have turned the other side of the cheek for the Muslims, and they have slapped us more than a second time; now which other cheek do we turn?" He thus supported the position of the bishop of Kano, an evangelical, who had just told me that he encouraged his members to fight back in self-defense. This new theological interpretation came about because Kano had become the most conflict-prone area, next to Kaduna, in the whole of the north. At one point, the Christians, including evangelicals, who reside in an area called "Sabon gari" ("strangers town") in Kano, mobilized and bought rifles and ammunition for self-defense. Once, when a group of young Muslims tried to provoke a religious conflict, thinking that the Christians would flee as they had done in the past, the latter opened fire on them and many Muslims were killed. Since then, "Sabon gari" has been secure and peaceful.

In other towns where Sharia is enforced, a similar retaliatory attitude is being practiced by evangelicals. Even in Jos, which is not a Sharia state, the evangelicals revised their theology of retaliation after the religious conflict that occurred in Jos during September 7–12, 2001. This religious crisis is widely believed to have arisen as a result of the declaration of Sharia in some northern states and to have been an attempt by some Islamic fundamentalists to destabilize Plateau state (which had become a hiding place for people escaping from Sharia states) even if they could not establish Sharia in the state itself. In a memorandum to the Commission of Inquiry into the crisis in Jos in

September 2001, the executive committee of CAN in Plateau state, under the chairmanship of the Right Reverend B. A. Kwashi, an Anglican evangelical bishop, stated:

> In this political dispensation, some faceless, disgruntled [people] are reacting in an attempt to make the democratic process impossible, so the military, who have been their benefactors may come back to power. They are doing this by declaring some Northern states to be Islamic States with Sharia laws to govern them, and so making it intolerable, and indeed impossible, for Christians to survive in such States. By this action they are bringing to the test the Constitution of the Federal Republic of Nigeria, and already some nations, like Iraq, Sudan, and Iran have endorsed the stance of such States in the Federal Republic of Nigeria. This is a clear signal for confusion and intolerance. Take for example, the events of 7th September 2001 in the city of Jos. . . . Contrary to the widely publicized claim that the immediate cause of the crisis was at the instance of a [Christian] woman who insisted to pass when the road bloc near a mosque at Congo Russia for Jummat prayer was in place; CAN has since discovered that this is false and a deliberate attempt to cover up a well-masterminded ploy by Muslims to strike against Christians. (CAN, Plateau State, 2001)

I interviewed evangelical ministers in Jos and asked them if they had any reason to change their attitude to retaliation since the widespread declaration of Sharia in the north and the increasing violence that has accompanied it. One respondent, the Reverend David Laje, who heads the ECWA Good News church located in the centre of Jos at a place called Terminus, said:

> Evangelicals are known to be people that follow the Bible. The Bible says if someone strikes you on one cheek turn the other cheek. . . . Ordinarily, I will enjoin that we be patient with the Muslims and by so doing practice the word of God. But I am also saying that God speaks to us according to circumstances. At some other time God will want you to retaliate; not for anything but for His name's sake. There is no way one can fold his hands and allow the Muslims to come and destroy our church property and kill our church or family members.

The Reverend Laje narrated how the crisis started on September 7, when his church was holding a Bible study. He asked his members to rush to their homes and bring weapons to safeguard the church building because he knew that, being in the center of Jos, the building was likely to attract the attention of Muslims. As he had feared, at midnight a group of Muslims came with petrol to burn the church buildings. The members keeping vigil in the church fought back and chased them away.

According to Laje the Muslims made another attempt at 3 A.M.; again, the Christians resisted. In this way, he believes, evangelicals in Nigeria should fight—but only in self-defense. In the same church the following Sunday, the assistant pastor preached a sermon entitled "Finding Peace Even in the Midst of Crisis." One of the instructions he passed to his congregation was that "those who do not have a sword [i.e., for war against the Muslims] should sell what they have to buy one," referring to Luke 22:36 to support the statement. Since it was still the peak of the crisis, the members of the congregation felt obligated to comply. The PFN president of Plateau state, the Reverend Bright O. Ndu, and another member of PFN who is both the treasurer of CAN Plateau state and the president and superintendent of the Winners Celebration Chapel of No. 9 Zaria Bye-pass, Jos, also quoted Luke 22:36 as they advocated retaliation and self-defense. All this was contrary to the views held earlier by these men, who had before believed that evangelicals ought to turn their cheek each time they were attacked. They confess that it is difficult for someone to fold his arms and watch his family be killed. All of my respondents, both ministers and nonministers, stated that wherever aggressive resistance and retaliation was made, the Muslims retreated and never did further harm in that area. The Reverend Ndu reported how his church buildings and everything in them, which were worth 3.2 million naira, were burnt by Muslims during the September crisis. But he admitted that Christians, including evangelicals, also burnt Muslim mosques, residential buildings, and Islamic schools.

What effect has this changing evangelical attitude had on democratization? Although increasing evangelical acceptance and practice of retaliation would appear to be a negative development, it arguably helped to put the militancy of some Muslims in check. Such militancy can often be deterred because frequently it is materially motivated criminal elements among the Muslims that spearhead the rampage, mainly for the opportunity to loot. But when religious disturbances are stirred up, for whatever reason, they undermine the sociopolitical and economic stability of the whole country because they often generate reprisals in other parts of the country. Such instability is certainly not healthy for democracy and democratization. Insofar as an increasing evangelical tough-mindedness helps deter aggression and bring a modicum of stability, then perhaps the conditions necessary for the long-term stabilization and deepening of Nigerian democracy are more likely to be established.

Yet there is another element of evangelical political theology that has been affected by the declaration of Sharia. This is the evangelical emphasis on submission to the political authorities, articulated in Romans 13:1–7. In the past the evangelicals understood from this passage that God had established all authority, and that civil rulers were his agents. In this interpretation, God controls and regulates the political structures and expects Christians to see their obedience to political leaders as a nonnegotiable divine obligation. The performance of civic duties was therefore an inescapable requirement for all Christians (Imo 1995, 57). However, since the declaration of Sharia in certain northern states, some evangelicals began to conclude that all political authorities are *not* necessarily from God, for they cannot understand how the governors of the Sharia states can be from God. For the evangelicals advancing this interpretation, God is good, and every good and perfect gift comes from God (James 1:17). Since the activities of these governors are not good, these evangelicals will say, they are not from God. To reinterpret the Romans text referred to above, these evangelicals feel that the text should be seen from the point of view of Ephesians 6:1, in which Paul enjoins children to obey their parents "in the Lord." They interpret the phrase "in the Lord" to mean that it is only when a parent is in the Lord should he or she be obeyed. Similarly, the meaning of the Romans passage is that only those rulers who rule according to the pattern of God require their loyalty and obedience. Such evangelicals will ask those who hold the older interpretation, "Do you mean you will do anything a political leader tells you to do, even if it is against the word of God?" The effect of this emerging political theology on democratization is arguably ambiguous. On the one hand, it spurs evangelicals to critically inspect and, if necessary, resist and check unjust political authority. On the other hand, it may give evangelicals an unwarranted excuse to exempt themselves from general civil obligations.

As I end this section, it is important to note that some of the political theologies developed by Nigerian evangelicals have not necessarily been formally promulgated or officially adopted by any evangelical body. They function implicitly and informally. They are coming into consideration because of the current religious crisis. However, some provocative theological reformulations and responses have been documented, such as those of Yusuf Turaki (2000, 12), the director of the International Bible Society, Enugu, when he called for the "legislation of Christian Human Rights Bills in all Sharia states"; or of John U. Gangwari, a Roman Catholic priest who lectures at St. Augustine's Major Seminary, in Jos, Plateau State, who argued, "If Sharia law and courts are allowed, then canon Law and Ecclesiastical courts or Tribunals should also be accorded constitutional and legal recognition" (Gangwari 2000, 7). Of course, these statements are responses to the declaration of Sharia in some states and illustrate how the challenges posed by the declaration of Sharia have led to new Christian political theologies and strategies, including evangelical ones. As more evangelicals consider and debate these theologies and strategies, they are likely to develop an even greater variety of reflective responses to the Sharia movement, and these responses, in turn, will have important long-term consequences for Nigeria's democratic development.

Conclusions and Prospects for the Twenty-First Century

In the mostly Muslim Sharia states of northern Nigeria, there have of course been very few evangelical politicians. As one would expect, in the various Sharia states, the governors' cabinets and the States' Houses of Assembly are overwhelmingly Muslim, which of course is why it was possible for Islamic law to be introduced in the first place. In the absence of evangelical political leadership, evangelical religious leaders in these states and evangelical "low-status" groups have made some significant attempts to integrate their religious traditions into the modern Nigerian political process. As for Obasanjo, the evangelical head of state, he seems not to have fully broken with the authoritarian style of governance he acquired in his military days, which became especially evident in his ultimately unsuccessful bid for a third presidential term in 2006. The political culture of corruption that characterized earlier governments remained despite the lofty rhetoric of politicians from the ruling People's Democratic Party (PDP).

Our findings further reveal the dramatic extent to which northern evangelicals, like other evangelicals in Nigeria, are increasingly becoming interested and active in politics. Of course, the dominant reason for such an increase in political participation is the challenge posed by the increasing militancy of Muslim radicals. We also observed that the declaration of Sharia in some northern states has led to the development of certain evangelical theological innovations that directly bear on the long-term prospects for democratic consolidation in Nigeria. Even though some of the new evangelical theological innovations may be ambiguous for democratic stability, most promote a more robust and democratic civic engagement. Some of the evangelical politicians in non-Sharia states, and those serving at the national level who are from the north, are making an effort in the nascent democratic process to bring their evangelical beliefs and practices to bear on their governance. The evangelical Anglican bishops in the north have made energetic and consistent contributions to the ongoing political process. Low-status evangelicals have made their own political contributions through prayers, nonresistance, and self-restraint. In these ways, they have sometimes succeeded in de-escalating tensions and have helped to check Muslim efforts to Islamicize the north.

The introduction of Sharia has borne profoundly negative consequences for the development of democracy in the country, as the crises and violence generated by the declaration of Sharia in these northern states have seriously undermined the kind of stable environment that is conducive to democratization. Despite these unfavorable circumstances, the prospects for evangelicals contributing to the Nigerian political arena in a way that enhances democracy are encouraging. Since they have largely repudiated a political theology that separates politics from religion, they have the potential to make a substantial impact. However, such an impact is not likely to be sustained or dramatic until the dust raised by the declaration of Sharia has time to settle. Radical Sharia is not likely to hold sway in northern Nigeria, as the people of the Middle Belt are not likely to yield to the political imperialism of the Hausa/Fulani any longer. Even in the core north where the declaration of Sharia was made, the flame of Sharia is dwindling. More Muslims are beginning to discover the hidden agenda of the Shariaists, and the economic base of these states is fast crumbling as many industrialists, traders, and people of money-yielding establishments have left the states for more stable Christian states like Plateau. Moreover, the distraction the Shariaists hoped to inflict on the Obasanjo-led government was largely neutralized by the posture of Obasanjo, who refused to allow the action of these states to rob him of his political energy or distract him from his political program. Already, certain aspects of Sharia law that were enforced at the early stage of the implementation have been relaxed. One of the major factors that has led to the relaxation of these laws has been the attitude of the evangelicals, whose overall response to the provocations of radical Sharia has been measured and even tolerant where possible but also resistant and even retaliatory where necessary.

Numerous factors are likely to play important roles in determining the pattern of relations between evangelicals and Muslims in northern Nigeria and the extent to which evangelicals will be able to mobilize their traditions to strengthen the democratic process. These factors include the outcome of the 2007 elections and the ultimate success of the anticorruption law of 2000 and the government's subsequent anticorruption campaign.

Above all, a peaceful and democratic handover of power from the evangelical and southern president Obasanjo to a Muslim president from the north, as required by the informal power-sharing arrangement in place since 1999, will go a long way toward defusing the tensions between Muslims and Christians brought on by the Sharia crisis. In fact, the 2007 elections produced a political outcome that large numbers of Nigerians judge was reasonably legitimate. Thus, the constructive political activism of evangelicals triggered by the Sharia crisis can now be channeled into the many other areas of fundamental importance for the consolidation and deepening of Nigerian democracy, including the crucial ongoing struggle against corruption in government.

2

Evangelical Attitudes toward Democracy in Kenya

John Karanja

In this chapter I attempt to describe and explain the diversity of political beliefs and attitudes among Kenyan evangelicals, focusing particularly on democracy and democratization. For evangelicals from mainstream churches, theological reflections, practical considerations of evangelism, and pastoral care inform these beliefs and attitudes.[1] However, the political involvement of evangelicals from less well-established churches has tended to be shaped by more narrow considerations, such as self-interest. The *terminus a quo* of the study is 1986, the year when the latent divisions among evangelicals on politics came into the open, following the government's introduction of queue voting for parliamentary and civic elections. Special emphasis will be given to the group of churches that form the Evangelical Fellowship of Kenya (EFK), together with other important independent and pentecostal churches not belonging to the EFK. These three categories of churches, which have generally allied themselves with the state, have not been fully researched before.

Broadly speaking, Kenyan evangelicals may be divided into two categories. First, there are the leaders of the mainstream Protestant churches who are also active in ecumenical bodies: the National Council of Churches of Kenya (NCCK), the All Africa Conference of Churches (AACC), and the World Council of Churches (WCC).[2] They are heirs to the evangelical tradition founded by the early Protestant missionaries.[3] Moreover, all mainstream Protestant churches are strongly influenced by the East African Revival, which has strong evangelical connections.[4] Second, there are those who constitute the EFK. With the exception of the Africa Inland Church, which has been in Kenya since 1895, these ministries arrived in Kenya within the last thirty-five years.[5] The most numerous component within this category is pentecostalism, which combines biblical orthodoxy with a charismatic form of worship and an emphasis on spiritual healing. Initially, there was a tendency to perceive the phenomenal expansion of the new evangelical ministries as a form of American cultural imperialism, supported by American money and spearheaded by American missionary personnel. However, a close examination of the new Kenyan pentecostal churches reveals that almost all of them are independent and indigenous in both personnel and finance (Berger 1999, 38). Since the founders of all Kenyan Protestant churches came from an evangelical background, this study adopts an inclusive definition of evangelicalism that embraces all Protestant Christians.

The Context

Kenya has a population of twenty-nine million with over forty distinct ethnic groups, of which the most numerous are the Kikuyu, the Luhya, the Luo, the Kalenjin, and the Akamba. Kenya obtained independence from Britain in 1963 under a multiparty system of government. At independence, the two main political parties were the Kenya African National Union (KANU) and the Kenya African Democratic Union (KADU). KANU was the largest political party. It drew the bulk of its membership from the Luo and the Kikuyu, then the largest and most politically conscious ethnic groups. KADU was the party of minority ethnic groups who feared the possibility of domination by the larger ethnic groups. The two parties also differed in political orientation. While KANU supported a strong central government and open competition for resources, KADU favored a policy of federal government or regional autonomy. Within one year of independence, KADU members of Parliament had crossed the floor of the National Assembly to join the ruling party in creating a government of national unity. Throup and Hornsby noted that "on the first anniversary of independence in December 1964, the opposition formally dissolved itself and its remaining members joined KANU, creating a *de facto* single-party state" (Throup and Hornsby 1998, 12). Jomo Kenyatta, the newly elected president, moved rapidly to consolidate his power by making it impossible for new political parties to thrive.[6] The only opposition party to be registered during his reign was the short-lived Kenya People's Union, founded in 1966 and banned in 1969.

   In 1982, Kenyatta's successor, Daniel arap Moi, took advantage of an abortive coup to declare the country a *de jure* one-party state.[7] At the same time, the government became increasingly authoritarian, imprisoning many of its political opponents on trumped-up charges. In 1986, it introduced queue voting for parliamentary and civic elections. The measure was intended to exclude from voting the most educated and professional sections of the population, a group that also happened to be critical of the political establishment. Such people would avoid queue voting for fear of possible reprisals in case their favorite candidates lost the elections. The 1988 general elections were the first to be held under the new voting system. They were rigged to ensure that only candidates favored by the government won. Following mounting pressure from civil society, the government scrapped queue voting. However, Kenya remained a one-party state until 1991, when domestic and international pressure forced the government to revert to a multiparty system. The introduction of a multiparty system did not mean that Kenya became fully democratic. As Paul Freston has noted, it was "concession without conversion," and KANU continued to manipulate the electoral process to ensure its victory (Freston 2001, 146; Throup and Hornsby 1998). The task of this research is to assess the role of evangelicals in these developments.

Kenya is a predominantly Christian country in which evangelicals number about 9.75 million, or 34 percent of the total population (Barrett, Kurian, and Johnson, 2001, 426).[8] Protestant evangelicalism is the oldest form of Christianity in the country. It is possible to identify five phases in its development. The first began in 1844 with the arrival of the Church Missionary Society, which was joined in 1862 by the Methodist Missionary Society. The activities of these missions were largely confined to the coast. The second phase ran from 1895 until 1914. It was characterized by a rapid expansion into the interior and a marked increase in the number of Protestant missions. Among the newcomers were the Africa Inland Mission (1895), the Church of Scotland Mission (1898), the Friends African Industrial Mission (1902), and the Seventh-Day Adventists (1906). The building of the Uganda railway and the establishment of colonial rule facilitated missionary expansion. During this period, however, missionary activity was confined to the coast, as well as Western and Central Kenya, and mainly consisted of preaching and provision of literacy. The third phase began after World War I and continued until the end of colonial rule in 1963. It was characterized by a phenomenal increase in the number of African Christians, devolution of church responsibilities to Africans, and the rise and growth of African Instituted Churches (AICs). The fourth phase began in 1963 and ended in 1985. During this period, church leadership was almost entirely in the hands of African Christians, who enjoyed a close relationship with the leaders of the new state. At the same time, many new faith missions arrived in Kenya mainly from the United States. They emphasized healing, speaking in tongues, prophecy, and prosperity through giving. They attracted many young people from mainstream churches. The fifth phase began in 1985 and is still in progress. It is characterized by a huge proliferation of new evangelical "ministries" and a polarization of evangelical Christians on the question of political participation.

Scope and Methodology

This is an in-depth study of the sociotheological character of the main evangelical institutions and how that character affects their political orientation. It also explores their participation in political developments since 1986. The institutions are classified into three categories:

1. "Activist" institutions, or those institutions that have openly criticized some state activities;
2. "Loyalist" institutions, or institutions that have allied themselves with the state;
3. "Apolitical" institutions, or those that have largely kept aloof from politics.

In this study, five evangelical institutions are examined, including one pan-church umbrella organization from each of the first two categories. From the "activist" institutions I chose the NCCK; from the "loyalist" ones, the EFK. The Anglican Church of Kenya (ACK) represents the "activist" churches, the African Independent Pentecostal Church of Africa (AIPCA) the "loyalist" churches, and the Deliverance Church (DC) the "apolitical" ones. These churches were selected because of their numerical strength and influence on society. For each of the churches, fieldwork was conducted in one of their dioceses, regions, or parishes and one particular congregation within it. Wherever possible, I interviewed at least two national-level leaders of the chosen institution.[9]

In studying the five institutions, attempts were made to establish the following:

1. The size of the institution in question, as well as the social and ethnic background of its membership;
2. The nature of the institution's decision-making structures;
3. The institution's autonomy from parent/umbrella organizations;
4. The essentials of the institution's theology.

The National Council of Churches of Kenya

The National Council of Churches of Kenya (NCCK) is the umbrella organization for most of the mainstream Protestant churches. It was founded in 1943 under the name Christian Council of Kenya (CCK) to promote cooperation among Protestant churches. After independence, its name was changed to the National Christian Council of Kenya in order to reflect national aspirations. The present name, National Council of Churches of Kenya, was adopted in 1988. Currently, the NCCK consists of thirty-nine churches and pan-church organizations with memberships of between ten thousand and three million each. The dominant church organizations within the NCCK remain those with colonial missionary roots, particularly the Anglican Church of Kenya and the Presbyterian Church of East Africa.[10]

Although the NCCK is not exclusively a Luo-Kikuyu organization, it is dominated by these two ethnic groups. This dominance has a historical explanation. The activities of the Church of Scotland missionaries and the founders of the Presbyterian Church of East Africa were confined to Kikuyu, Embu, and Meru areas during the colonial and immediate postcolonial period. Similarly, those of the Church Missionary Society—the founders of the Anglican Church of Kenya—were largely confined to Kikuyu, Luo, and coastal areas. These churches drew most of their African leaders from these areas.

In spite of this ethno-historical formation, the NCCK has shown a concern about issues of governance and democracy that transcends the ethnic constitution of its leadership. It displays a holistic theology that seeks to address the physical, spiritual, and intellectual needs of humanity. It emphasizes that God is concerned with every sphere of human life, including politics and economics, and that all systems of government are ultimately accountable to God.[11] This theological conviction is one important factor that motivates the NCCK to participate in the country's political process.

The Evangelical Fellowship of Kenya

The Evangelical Fellowship of Kenya (EFK) represents a feeble Luo-Kalenjin alliance in which the Kalenjin faction assumes a preponderant position. Although it was formed in 1976, "it only acquired organizational flesh and bones in 1980 when it established a secretariat to run its corporate activities" (Ngunyi 1995, 142). The EFK did not come into the limelight until 1990, when some defectors from the NCCK joined it, arguing that the council's political profile was incompatible with biblical teachings.[12] This was followed by a visit from the leadership of the EFK to the president, apparently resulting in its co-option by the regime for purposes of competing with the NCCK (Ngunyi 1995, 142–143). Currently, the EFK has sixteen church and parachurch members. The most prominent of these are the Africa Inland Church, the DC, the Redeemed Gospel Church, and a few emerging pentecostal churches.

In stark contrast to the NCCK, which has maintained a fairly consistent doctrinal position independent of the identity of its leaders, it is difficult to distinguish the theological position of the EFK as an organization from that of its leaders. However, the political theology of the EFK leadership has been consistent, at least to the extent that it is based on Romans 13:1–2 (KJV):

Let every soul be subject unto the higher powers. For there is no power but of God: the powers that be are ordained of God. Whosoever

therefore resisteth the power, resisteth the ordinance of God: and
they that resist shall receive to themselves damnation.

As will be shown in subsequent sections, this theology enables the EFK
leadership to bolster the present regime and keep politics beyond the reach
of ordinary Christians (Abuom 1994).

The Anglican Church of Kenya

The Anglican Church of Kenya (ACK), which was founded by the Church
Missionary Society (CMS), is the oldest Protestant church in Kenya. Today the
ACK has a membership of three million, making it the largest Protestant
church in the country. The relationship between the ACK and the colonial state
has been very close. Indeed, the Anglican Church was the official church of the
colonial regime, and the residence of its bishop was situated close to that of
the colonial governor. The membership of the ACK, which cuts across the
entire social, economic and intellectual spectrum, is drawn from all over Kenya,
especially the coast, central, and Nyanza provinces.[13] Consequently, no single
ethnic community dominates the church. The membership is also diverse in
terms of age. Although its mode of worship is noncharismatic, the ACK has
successfully attracted young adherents, partly through its development activities. The church's income-generating projects also account for its attractive-
ness to peasant and urban working-class households.

Doctrinally, the ACK is neither fully liberal nor fully conservative, though
it leans in a conservative direction. The fact that its dioceses are relatively
autonomous from the provincial synod allows for the coexistence of considerable variations in theological positions, pastoral styles, and political considerations. A diocesan bishop is free to pursue political activism based on his
understanding of Scripture, provided it does not contradict the church's basic
articles of faith. This doctrinal diversity accounts in part for the ACK's broad
appeal.

The historical heritage of the ACK seems to have contributed significantly
to its political activism. According to Dr. David Gitari, the church's archbishop:

> The early CMS missionaries were well grounded in their theology
> and did not refrain from commenting on sensitive political issues.
> Archdeacon W. E. Owen of Kavirondo (Western Kenya) helped to
> found the Kavirondo Taxpayers Welfare Association (KTWA) to ar-
> ticulate the political and economic interests of the Luo. Archdeacon
> (later Archbishop) Leonard Beecher represented the interests of in-
> digenous Kenyans in the Legislative Council. This spirit of political
> prophetic witness continued after independence through the Church
> leaders who took over from the missionaries.[14]

As Archbishop Gitari states, some of the early Anglican missionaries openly attacked the injustices of colonial rule. Walter Owen of Kavirondo was so outspoken that the colonial settlers nicknamed him "the Arch-demon of Kavirondo."[15] Leonard Beecher was appointed to Kenya's Legislative Council in 1943.[16] He made remarkable contributions to the council's deliberations. He staunchly defended and sought to advance African interests. The spirit Beecher brought to his new task was exemplified in an interview he had with the press, in which he said he had tried to avoid issuing any form of "manifesto," but announced that he looked forward to the day when Africans would sit along-side the nominated Europeans and would even replace them. He appealed for Africans to write to him; and before he resigned in 1947, he was receiving "an enormous mailbag" (Bennett 1963). In the mid-1950s, two young Anglican missionaries, Andrew Hake and Stanley Booth-Clibborn, arrived in Kenya to work for the CCK. They differed from older missionaries in that they were theologically more liberal and their gospel was as much social as individual. Their task was to help the churches of Kenya relate the fast-changing social, economic, and political conditions in the country to the Christian faith.[17] These two men played an important part in giving the Anglican Church a sense of prophetic mission. *Rock*, a monthly journal edited by Booth-Clibborn, became an important means of arousing African Christians' political consciousness. It was Booth-Clibborn who recruited Henry Okullu as editor of *Target* newspaper, the successor of *Rock* (Okullu 1997, 48–55).[18] Okullu was to become one of the most outspoken clerics on political issues.

The autonomy of the dioceses and the diverse ethnic backgrounds of the bishops allow each bishop to respond individually to the challenge of political pluralism. Consequently, although the ACK has generally criticized state extremism, some bishops enjoy such friendly relations with their local members of parliament that they are reluctant to criticize them in public.[19] Nonetheless, the ACK bishops consider it their primary duty to measure the state's actions by the standards of Scripture and to remind the state about its accountability to God (Benson 1995, 191). Personal interests tend to be subordinated to this goal, and the bishops nearly always take a common stand on national issues.

The African Independent Pentecostal Church of Africa

The African Independent Pentecostal Church of Africa (AIPCA) came into being in the 1930s following mass defections of Kikuyu Christians from mainstream Protestant churches over the issue of clitoridectomy (Murray 1974).[20] Its membership is therefore almost exclusively Kikuyu, Embu, and Meru. During the colonial period, the church was actively involved in nationalist politics because it believed that cultural liberation would be incomplete without political independence. In the 1950s, the AIPCA officially supported the

Mau Mau movement and encouraged its members to participate in armed struggle against colonial rule.[21] The Church also allowed the use of its buildings for the administration of Mau Mau oaths. In 1952, following the declaration of a state of emergency in Kenya, the colonial government closed down all AIPCA churches and schools, which the authorities viewed as recruitment grounds for the Mau Mau movement. These institutions were reopened after independence. The AIPCA has approximately one hundred thousand members, most of whom are old and poorly educated. Since independence, the church has been embroiled in leadership wrangles and each warring faction has sought to woo state support

The head of the AIPCA is Archbishop Samson Gaitho. He is assisted by twenty-two diocesan bishops. Each diocese is subdivided into archdeaconries under archdeacons. The archdeaconries are further divided into parishes, each under a pastor. The smallest unit of administration is a congregation, which is headed by a deacon. Thus the church's administrative structure is hierarchical. The AIPCA does not have a clearly defined doctrine, though it describes its mission in terms of "preaching the Gospel and devoutly observing the principles of salvation."[22] The church perceives itself as a "nonpolitical organization that seeks closer co-operation and collaboration with other churches and philanthropic societies all over the world."[23] It is also the church's stated goal to give African Christians a suitable environment to express their faith in their own cultural terms.

Several factors seem to explain the AIPCA's political transformation from agitator to collaborator. First, the church is still recovering from the trauma of its ban by the colonial government.[24] It therefore cannot risk another confrontation with the state. Second, the leadership of the AIPCA strongly believes that the church's lack of international connections means that they have nobody to turn to in the event of persecution by the state. Listen to Archdeacon Muchai:

> When anything happens to the Catholic Church or to the ACK,
> you hear a lot of noise from abroad; but if today the President de-
> clared the AIPCA Church closed, that will be all, and tomorrow we
> cannot get past these gates into this Cathedral.[25]

Muchai was referring to the international condemnation of the Kenyan government following the storming of the Anglican All Saints Cathedral, Nairobi, by paramilitary troops on July 7, 1997. Yet this fear of deregistration is probably misplaced. According to Archbishop Gitari:

> The government is fully aware of the possible repercussions of
> such a move and would therefore not dare to deregister a church.
> Indeed, despite its constant threats to do so, the state has not de-
> registered a single Church since independence.[26]

Third, and probably most importantly, the AIPCA supports the government for the benefits that it is able to provide. On February 9, 2001, while leading celebrations to mark the sixty-fifth anniversary of the AIPCA, Archbishop Gaitho accused the Bretton Woods institutions (the World Bank and the International Monetary Fund) of championing neocolonialism in Africa by imposing difficult conditions for the resumption of economic aid to Kenya. The chief guest at the ceremony was Kenya's Minister for Lands and Settlement. The archbishop appealed to him to give title deeds to the Church for its lands, and the minister announced that he would grant the request. The archbishop further announced that the church would soon hold a major fundraising event, which would be presided over by the head of state (*Daily Nation*, February 10, 2001).[27] It is therefore expedient for the AIPCA to be viewed as a government supporter in order to continue receiving such benefits.

On the other hand, the leadership of the AIPCA maintains that their support of the state is based on Paul's teaching in Romans 13. Paradoxically, the church did not feel bound to adhere to this teaching in the colonial period. The leadership of the AIPCA explains this paradox in terms of the changed political context. It argues that while the colonial government was illegitimate in that it did not enjoy the support of indigenous Kenyans, the Moi government is legitimate in that it has the mandate of Kenyans. In the words of Archdeacon Muchai, "We should not fight our own government."[28]

The Deliverance Church of Kenya

The Deliverance Church (DC), founded in Nairobi in 1970, is one of the fastest growing churches in Kenya. From a membership of fifty-six congregants at its inception, the church has a membership of about one hundred thousand and more than one thousand congregations countrywide.[29] In the urban areas, most of the congregations are situated in high-density areas, targeting the urban worker. Where such congregations are found in middle-class suburbs, their appeal seems to be confined to domestic workers. The main adherents of this church are the rural peasants, the urban poor, students, and unemployed youth. The small group of urban and rural middle-class members within its ranks occupies positions of leadership. The membership and leadership of the DC is drawn from nearly every ethnic group in Kenya, giving it a very cosmopolitan outlook.

The majority of members of the DC are young, and they are drawn to the "attractive" mode of worship that is employed in its services. Most of the Deliverance churches have modern musical equipment with talented singers. Worship is lively, and the congregation dances to contemporary music. The mode of prayer is intensely participatory. Each congregant says his or her prayer aloud, sometimes gesticulating, and when the noise subsides, the worship leader concludes with a single prayer, which is punctuated by exuberant agreements from the congregation. Because of the church's cosmopolitan nature, its services are conducted in English and Kiswahili throughout the country.

Regarding polity, the church is headed by a general overseer or bishop, who has no executive powers. The central decision-making organ is the governing council, which is chaired by the overseer. The whole country is divided into nine regions and each region is administered through a regional council. The regions are further divided into subregions, and the subregions into local churches. The governing council is made up of delegates elected from the nine regions. The executive committee of the council consists of the overseer, who is its chairman, the church's general secretary and his assistant, the treasurer, and three representatives. Members of the executive council are elected by the delegates to the governing council. The present composition of the executive council reflects the church's attempt to ensure a fair regional balance. But these organs of the church hardly meet, and each local church is left to run with little direction from above.

The DC adheres to a conservative evangelical theology. Its theology of the state is based on Romans 13. The church is fully aware of the ills plaguing the present government, as well as the ongoing political initiatives. But according to its leadership, such problems arise from corrupt human nature and can only be solved through prayer rather than confrontation. Its emphasis may be described as "social transformation through positive individual influence." This means that if each "born-again" Christian lived in accordance with Christian principles, the whole nation would be morally transformed.[30]

Like the AIPCA, the leadership of the DC concedes that a lack of strong international connections inhibits the church from being more outspoken on political issues. According to one senior pastor, the leadership of the DC "cannot afford to be seen on a constant warpath as it does not have the resources and does not have the international contacts to fall back to for support in case of deregistration."[31] The ethnic diversity of the DC has also contributed to its silence on political issues. According to the same pastor, the fear of driving away members of the church who hold different political views has prompted the pastors to be cautious and avoid raising sensitive political issues in their sermons. However, as will be seen later, some leaders of the DC have unsuccessfully attempted to use their positions to influence members to support the political parties of their choice.

Evangelicals and the Democratic Process: 1986 to the Present

In this section I shall explore the extent to which the sociotheological character of the three categories of evangelical institutions examined above has informed their involvement in recent political developments. There are three issues over which evangelical differences have emerged: the queue-voting controversy (1986–1990); the multiparty debate (1990–1991); and the constitutional review process (1999 to the present).

Evangelicals and the Queue-Voting Controversy, 1986–1990

On August 19, 1986, the national executive of the KANU proposed to the ruling party's annual delegates' conference that elections to the National Assembly should be reformed. According to this proposal, the elections should be divided into two parts: a formal KANU primary where only party members should be allowed to participate, and a second runoff among the three leading candidates. In the second phase, all adult Kenyans could participate in those constituencies where no one had secured more than 70 percent of the primary vote. The most contentious element of the proposal was to abolish the secret ballot in the first round, so that the voters would have to queue behind the candidate of their choice. The new voting method threatened to disenfranchise sections of the population who feared that an open ballot would jeopardize their careers.

The ruling party stated that it wished to adopt queue voting because it was faster and more straightforward than the secret ballot. However, observers of Kenya's political scene have noted that the new policy "was symptomatic of the growing authoritarianism of the Kenyan government" (Throup and Hornsby 1998, 39). Following the abortive coup of 1982, the Moi regime became increasingly paranoid, equating political dissent with subversion. The leadership believed that to ensure political stability, it was necessary to consolidate political power around the president and the ruling party, to reduce freedom of the press, and to crack down on political dissidence. The government favored queue voting because it gave the ruling party the opportunity to manipulate the electoral process and elect the candidates of its choice.

The KANU delegates' conference coincided with a regularly scheduled meeting of pastors, sponsored once every five years by the NCCK. Under the chairmanship of Bishop David Gitari, the gathering opposed the ruling party's decision. Gitari was mandated to draft a statement, which was signed by the General Secretary of the NCCK and released to the press. The statement asked the ruling party "to find an alternative method in which church leaders can exercise their democratic rights as members of this nation" (*Weekly Review*, August 29, 1986, 3). From this statement, it is clear that the church leaders initially joined the debate primarily because they felt their interests had been threatened by the new proposal. They feared that standing behind candidates of their choice would publicly reveal their political preferences and possibly alienate members of their flock who supported different candidates. Thus, the concern of the clergy was similar to that expressed by Kenya's public servants and other professionals. As the controversy progressed, however, the clergy were seen as the champions of the voiceless. In a country where freedom of expression was severely curtailed, the church was virtually the only means of expressing dissent. The pastors' courage in challenging the ruling party on this issue won them the support of most Kenyans. They were also vindicated by the widespread rigging that marked the 1988 parliamentary and civic elections (Githiga 1997, 165).

Predictably, the church's crusade against queue voting infuriated party stalwarts. The NCCK was accused of all manner of crimes. At the same time, the ruling party worked tirelessly to create a rift among the NCCK member churches, urging those that did not support the "politicization" of the organization to leave it. In response to this appeal, some less well-established churches left the NCCK for fear of deregistration. They included the Full Gospel Church, the Association of Baptist Churches in Nyeri, and the United Pentecostal Church. Other larger churches followed suit, among them the Africa Inland Church and the AIPCA. Why did the evangelical churches adopt different positions in the queue voting controversy?

The "activist" clergy seem to have been motivated by several factors in their struggle against queue voting. As we have seen, they were concerned about the potential of queue voting to alienate some members of their congregations. Theological considerations played an important part too. Archbishop Manasses Kuria of the ACK, in an address to a Kenya Anglican Youth conference, described queue voting as "unchristian."[32] Citing the election of Matthias to replace Judas (Acts 1:25–26), Kuria argued that the secret ballot was the electoral system supported by Scripture (*Weekly Review*, August 25, 1986; Musalia 2001, 99). Electoral rigging and cheating, a hallmark of the 1988 general elections, is viewed as unbiblical. Bishop Gitari often alluded to "new political mathematics in which a man with only five voters behind him is declared winner and his other contestant who has five hundred voters behind him is declared the loser" (Gitari 1996). Moreover, it was considered immoral for the state to adopt an electoral system that, by disenfranchising many of its citizens, denied them the opportunity to participate in shaping their destiny. But the episode also reveals an interesting interplay between principled leadership and local politics. This is especially evident in the experiences of Bishops Muge and Gitari.

Alexander Kipsang Muge was born in Nandi District in 1948.[33] He began his career as a policeman until he became a priest in the mid-1970s. After studying for a degree in theology at the London Bible College, he was stationed at the All Saints Cathedral, Nairobi, where he openly attacked tribalism within the ACK. In 1983, he was elected bishop of the newly created Diocese of Eldoret. There he soon fell out with the local party leaders for publicly exposing the vices of the Moi government. But his position was complicated by two other factors: internal Kalenjin politics and local denominational rivalry. Muge's arrival in Eldoret coincided with the 1983 general elections. Daniel arap Moi, Kenya's president since 1978, belonged to the Tugen subtribe of the Kalenjin.

He was unpopular among some Kalenjin politicians who accused him of serving the interests of the Kikuyu. Moi was determined to assert his authority over all the Kalenjin. The 1983 elections in Nandi were rigged to ensure the return of the president's supporters. Both the provincial administration and the General Service Unit (GSU), a paramilitary organization, were deployed to secure the victory of Moi's associates, including Stanley Metto in Mosop, Bishop Muge's home constituency. Appalled by the behavior of the GSU and the widespread intimidation of voters, Muge fiercely challenged the validity of Metto's election. Naturally, this reaction poisoned his relationship with local KANU leaders. Muge's relationship with Kalenjin politicians further deteriorated in August 1986 when, in his address to an Anglican youth conference, he warned that "the church could not compromise theological issues with secular or temporal matters." He urged the church to protest "when God-given rights and liberties are violated." Muge further challenged the church "to stand up against the pressures of totalitarianism in the name of one-party systems and against the detention of political opponents without trial" (*Weekly Review*, August 29, 1986, 5).

Besides internal Kalenjin politics, the conflict in Nandi was fuelled by a long-running rivalry between adherents of the Anglican Church of Kenya and those of the Africa Inland Church. The majority of Muge's opponents, including Stanley Metto, were members of the AIC, President Moi's church. The bishop and his supporters suspected that the AIC was attacking them and identifying the ACK as antigovernment in order to weaken Anglican influence in the area. Thus, Muge's attack on queue voting reveals both his brave and principled leadership and his concern about the electoral system's potential to weaken his church and undermine his ministry.

David Gitari was born in Kirinyaga District, Central Kenya, in 1937. He was educated at the Royal Technical College (1959–1964)—now the University of Nairobi—and Trinity Theological College, Bristol (1968–1971). From 1972 to 1975, he served as general secretary of the Bible Society of Kenya and chairman of Kenya Students Christian Fellowship (KSCF). He was bishop of the Diocese of Mount Kenya East from 1975 until 1990, and bishop of Kirinyaga Diocese from 1991 until 1996. In 1997, he was enthroned as the third archbishop of the Anglican Church of Kenya. Even before his consecration as bishop, Gitari had demonstrated his political courage by preaching sermons that implicated the Kenyatta government in the murder of Josiah Mwangi Kariuki, a prominent government critic.[34]

Like Muge, Gitari's principled and prophetic leadership antagonized local and national party leaders. But unlike Muge, whose local opponents were from the AIC, Gitari's local antagonists were senior lay leaders of his own church who also happened to be staunch KANU members. Since independence, the ruling party in Kirinyaga had been divided into two camps supporting two local rivals: James Njiru and Nahashon Njuno. Both leaders sought to manipulate the country's electoral system to gain political mileage. In the 1985 KANU grassroots elections, James Njiru's camp secured all the top positions in Kirinyaga District through rigging. This glaring abuse of justice caused widespread unrest and bitterness. It was against this background that on July 28, 1985, Gitari, then bishop of Mount Kenya East, preached a courageous sermon on the subject of justice and righteousness as the way of peace in a nation. In his sermon on Philippians 4:1–9, the bishop called upon the clergy to preach these virtues, and the national leaders to aspire to live by them. The luncheon following the service was boycotted by supporters of James Njiru and Geoffrey Kareithi, the winners of the rigged elections.[35] The losers, Nahashon Njuno and John Matere Keriri (a senior civil servant in the Kenyatta era), attended the luncheon and thanked the bishop for his sermon (Gitari 1996, 48–53).

This incident is striking in that it strongly suggests that for Gitari, theological convictions are the basis of unyielding political imperatives. For him, it seems, these theologically grounded political imperatives should not yield even to his own political self-interest. This becomes more apparent when one reflects on the prelate's immediate political context in Kirinyaga District. Geoffrey Kareithi was the chairman of the Kirinyaga Diocesan Development Programme. His connections were crucial to ensuring that the program was on a sound financial footing. But this consideration did not deter the bishop from exercising a bold and prophetic ministry. Ironically, three years later, Kareithi was deposed from his party position following rigged elections won by Njuno, who had now joined the camp of Njiru. Although Njuno and Gitari had previously supported one another, Gitari was the only person who publicly protested the rigging of the elections in Njuno's favor.

Gitari's political activism stems from his understanding of Scripture, especially his theology of God, creation, incarnation, and the kingdom of God.[36] According to him, God created humans in his own image and gave them the mandate to exercise stewardship over the earth. God gave this mandate to all humanity and not only to politicians. In his own words, "Creation left to politicians only ends up in 'Hiroshiman' experiences." Gitari maintains that Christ's incarnation challenges Christians to take this world seriously. By emptying himself and taking human form, Christ demonstrated the need for us to dedicate ourselves to the transformation of the world. While living on earth, Jesus' concern was not confined to spiritual matters. Rather, "he went to many villages in Galilee preaching, teaching, feeding, and healing. He came to heal the sick, free prisoners, and announce the acceptable year of the Lord." Gitari's theology of God's kingdom is both realized and futuristic. According to him, every healing act performed by Jesus was a foretaste of the kingdom, an indication that we too can experience the kingdom here on earth. Christians should participate in sociopolitical activities to give people a chance to experience the kingdom of God here on earth. The archbishop also pays a glowing tribute to the World Evangelical Conference at Lausanne in 1974 for opening his eyes to the relationship between the Gospel and social transformation. He admits that his hermeneutic is also greatly influenced by British evangelical theologian John Stott's expository preaching, whereby he expounds a passage of Scripture and applies it to a contemporary situation or circumstance.[37]

Gitari's theologically grounded approach to the issues of democracy differs somewhat from that of his Anglican counterparts, especially Bishops Muge and Okullu. Muge perceived himself in light of the Old Testament prophets who had to warn the state of looming danger. But his sermons were not based on a thorough exposition of biblical texts. Okullu's political activism was based on his theological understanding of justice. For him, justice is the chief characteristic of God's intervention in the world. This "justice" is not limited to retribution for wrongs. It entails actively promoting righteousness and human wellbeing. God's plan is that the church and the state should coexist as two institutions independent of one another, but sharing a common calling to promote justice (Benson 1995, 187).

However, it ought to be understood that Gitari is also a pragmatic cleric. Before 1990, he supported a one-party system of government, believing that KANU could be "cleaned from within." His conversion to a multiparty system of government was due to the realization that "KANU is beyond cleaning" (Okullu 1997, 129).

The member churches of the EFK were conspicuously silent during the queue voting controversy, choosing to leave politics to politicians. Citing Romans 13, they argued that in accepting queue voting, they were exercising their loyalty to the government of the day. By the same token, they maintained that objection to this method amounted to a rebellion against a divinely instituted authority and would lead to divine punishment; hence the withdrawal of some churches from the rebellious NCCK to join the EFK. But other motives seem to have played a part in their silence too, among them opportunism. For many years, many of these churches had envied the special relationship that existed between leaders of the mainstream churches and state leaders. They had seen the mainstream churches benefit from development projects patronized by state functionaries. The clash between mainstream churches and the Moi government gave the EFK member-churches access to the corridors of power. Because the government was keen to split the NCCK, it encouraged their move and readily sponsored their activities (Ngunyi 1995, 143). In the case of the AIC, ethnicity was a strong factor in its political orientation. Not only is the church strongest in Kalenjin-occupied areas, its leader at the time, Bishop Ezekiel Birech, was related to President Moi through marriage. In the eyes of the leadership, it would have been improper for the president's church to be seen as opposing him by remaining a part of the NCCK.

From the foregoing, it is clear that various factors contributed to the evangelical churches' decisions to support or oppose queue voting. Initially, the opponents of queue voting attacked it on the basis of its potential to divide the

church. Later, as the electoral process was implemented, its opponents discovered serious flaws that were deemed incompatible with biblical teachings.
These included vote rigging and intimidation of voters. Although the members
of the EFK cited Scripture in support of their position, it appears that non-
theological factors, such as fear of deregistration, ethnic considerations, and
the desire for state patronage, were crucial in their decision to support queue
voting.

Evangelicals and the Multiparty Debate, 1990–1992

Polarization among evangelicals became especially evident during the debate
over the reintroduction of a multiparty system of government. On the one hand,
the NCCK and its member-churches spearheaded the campaign for multipartyism. On the other hand, the EFK, the AIPCA, and the faith ministries
generally stayed out of the debate.

But some EFK leaders rendered invaluable support to the Moi regime and
openly attacked the campaign for political pluralism. One such leader was
Archbishop Arthur Kitonga of the Redeemed Gospel Church of Kenya who, at
the height of the clamor for multipartyism in 1991, uttered the often-quoted
words:

> In heaven it is just like Kenya has been for many years. There is only
> one party, and God never makes a mistake. . . . President Moi has
> been appointed by God to lead this country, and Kenyans should
> be grateful for the peace prevailing. . . . We have freedom of wor-
> ship; we can pray and sing in any way we want. What else do we
> need? That's all we need. (*Kenya Times*, February 2, 1991)[38]

Besides being one of the very few members of the EFK to publicly support
the one-party system, Kitonga is important for four other reasons. First, he was
the founder of the Redeemed Gospel Church, one of the largest indigenous
pentecostal churches in Kenya. Second, as an active member of the EFK,
Kitonga has been present in nearly all the fellowship's delegations to President
Moi. Therefore he has intimate knowledge of the confidential consultations
between the EFK and the head of state. Third, nearly all the emerging leaders
of faith ministries in Kenya regard him as their mentor. These leaders com-
mand devoted followings ranging from ten thousand to fifty thousand members. But unlike Kitonga, they have kept away from politics so far, choosing to
concentrate on preaching the word. The state has been making unsuccessful
attempts to reach them through Kitonga. Fourth, despite his support of the
government, Kitonga seems not to have full control over the clergy of his
church. One of his bishops, Allan Nyaga, ran for and won a parliamentary seat
on an opposition ticket in the 1992 general election.[39]

Although the leaders of the member-churches of the NCCK denounced corruption in high places, they were divided on the question of the suitability of multiparty rule. Their positions seem to have been informed by a combination of theological considerations and self-interest. This is demonstrated by the activities of three clerics—Dr. Timothy Njoya of the Presbyterian Church of East Africa, Bishop Okullu of the ACK, and Bishop Lawi Imathiu of the Methodist Church in Kenya. Njoya is the most outspoken government critic within the Presbyterian Church of East Africa. He was born in Nyeri, Central Kenya, and educated at St. Paul's United Theological College, Limuru (Kenya), and Princeton University in the United States. Njoya is a staunch member of the East African Revival and is often invited to conduct Bible expositions in Revival conventions. Indeed, his denunciatory sermons are congenial to the habit of members of the Revival to rebuke and correct one another in the biblical spirit of "speaking the truth in love." Above all, his support of a multiparty system of government is based on his understanding of Isaiah 1:18—"Come now, and let us reason together." This is a popular text within the East African Revival, and it has been a theme in several of their conventions. Citing this text, Njoya argues that far from being a dictator, God welcomes dialogue. From this observation, he concludes that a multiparty system of government is compatible with, even required, by God's nature and will.

Okullu's biblical hermeneutic was discussed in the previous section. He had established himself as a critic of one-party rule for nearly two decades before the advent of political pluralism in 1991. His views are well articulated in his sermons and writings, especially his book, *Church and Politics in East Africa* (Okullu 1974). He and Njoya were the first Kenyans to publicly predict the end of one-party rule. In December 1989, Okullu drew a sharp comparison between the events leading to the fall of Ceausescu's dictatorship in Romania and one-party dictatorships in Africa. He predicted that African dictators would experience a similar fate within five years. On January 1, 1990, Njoya repeated the same warning in a sermon at St. Andrew's Presbyterian Church, Nairobi (Okullu 1997, 127–128). Predictably, these utterances provoked a sharp reaction from KANU leaders. But they also set the scene for a prolonged political battle that finally resulted in the reintroduction of a multiparty system of government.

For many years, Imathiu was the presiding bishop of the Methodist Church in Kenya (MCK). Even after his retirement, he has continued to exercise great influence in the church. Unlike Njoya and Okullu, Imathiu defended one-party rule. At the height of the campaign for the reintroduction of multiparty democracy, Imathiu and Muge issued a joint statement in support of a one-party state. In their statement the two bishops argued that a multiparty system would merely fragment Kenya along ethnic lines. But both bishops acknowledged the need for powerful constitutional checks and balances to limit the power of the president and the ruling party (*Weekly Review*, May 4, 1990; Okullu 1997, 128–129; Hansen and Twaddle 1995, 163). While Muge's position raised eyebrows because it seemed to contradict his image as a radical political activist, Imathiu's orientation was viewed in terms of his moderate and nonconfrontational approach to politics (Okullu 1997, 128–129). This stance seems to derive from his close relationship with the political establishment in both the Kenyatta and the Moi eras. Under President Kenyatta, he had served a term (1974–1979) as a nominated member of Parliament. The MCK has benefited greatly from his closeness with President Moi through a number of fundraising events presided over by the head of state. The latest of these fundraisings was for the construction of the Methodist University in Meru, which is Imathiu's brainchild. It is also not inconceivable that Imathiu's close relationship with the president will expedite the accreditation of his university. It is not surprising, therefore, that in all the major controversies between the church and the state, Imathiu has either adopted a conciliatory line or openly supported the state.[40] But his successor as head of the MCK, Professor Zablon Nthamburi, has been outspoken and active on issues of good governance. As will be seen in the next section, Nthamburi is an active participant in the debate on constitutional review.

Like Zambia's former President Frederick Chiluba, former President Daniel arap Moi is himself an evangelical.[41] He is an active member of the theologically conservative Africa Inland Church. He strictly adheres to the disciplinary code of the church, which forbids smoking and consumption of alcohol. Kenya's state-controlled media portrays Moi as a God-fearing leader who is guided by Christian principles. Every Sunday, the state-run television, the Kenya Broadcasting Corporation, covered Moi's attendance at a church service.

In his 1986 book *Kenya African Nationalism*, Moi lays down the main principles of *Nyayo* philosophy, his administrative ideology.[42] According to him, Christian faith is one of the three main sources of *Nyayoism*. He argues that the three keywords of *Nyayo* philosophy—love, peace and unity—are derived from Scripture. Here is a quotation from the book:

> The central summation of all the commandments of Christian teaching is love: love of God above all things and of one's fellow man as of oneself. As a Christian, I have had to live a life of love. Our saving Lord Jesus Christ said, "Peace I leave with you . . ." thereby commanding His followers to propagate and live in peace. Then, on the eve of His sacrificial death for our redemption, He prayed fervently and devotedly that we should be united, as He and His Father are united. For this reason, then, as a Christian I would be wrong if I did not practice peace, love and unity. (Moi 1986, 21–22)

Moi then proceeds to apply these three biblical teachings to political life. He makes the following observations:

In political life, the practical management of a nation is a predictable
defeat unless human relations are governed by love. In the absence
of peace, consolidation of nationhood is impossible, let alone progress. Thus *love* begets *unity*, and the two create peace. These, I have
found, are the three essential ingredients in the consolidation of nationhood. From my African origins, through my Christian conversion
and then during my political profession, all three have recurred—
peace, love and unity. These are the principles by which I have lived
and acted all my life. I know no other trio: from them stem all else,
justice, equity, comradeship, parity of treatment, etc. (Moi 1986, 21–22)

But Moi's expressed political theology leaves no room for political pluralism.
Indeed, a close observation of the Moi regime indicates that for him, national
peace and unity can only be achieved through consolidation of power in him
and in KANU, the ruling party. Hence, before the introduction of political
pluralism in 1991, *Nyayoism* had come to mean suppression of political dissent
and enforcement of conformity.

Evangelicals and the Constitutional Review Process,
1999 to the Present

The period since 1999 has witnessed efforts to review Kenya's constitution. But
this exercise has been marked by deep polarization across Kenyan society.
On the one hand, KANU, the National Development Party (NDP), and a
handful of other opposition legislators have insisted that the process should be
directed by parliament, where KANU has a narrow majority. On the other hand,
most opposition legislators and civil society, including the main religious
groups (Christians, Muslims, and Hindus), have openly expressed their lack of
confidence in the legislators' ability and integrity. They have insisted that the
process should involve all stakeholders—members of parliament, nongovernmental organizations, religious leaders, and others. Early attempts to reconcile
these two groups proved futile, and they set up rival committees to review the
constitution. On December 15, 1999, KANU took advantage of the absence of
most opposition legislators from the National Assembly to set up a select
committee of twenty-seven members of parliament to review the constitution.
The committee consisted of fourteen KANU legislators and thirteen from the
opposition, thus giving the ruling party the numerical advantage.

The following day, at Ufungamano House near the University of Nairobi's
Halls of Residence, Kenya's main religious leaders, with the backing of most
opposition legislators and nongovernmental organizations, set up a parallel
council to spearhead talks on reform. The council consisted of leaders of the
major religious groups in Kenya—mainline church leaders, the head of the
Supreme Council of Kenya Muslims, and the chairman of the Hindu Council

of Kenya—and representatives of civil society. The steering council of the Ufungamano group consisted of fifteen members drawn from major religious groups. The representatives of mainstream evangelical churches included the Reverend Mutava Musyimi, the NCCK General Secretary; Archbishop David Gitari of the ACK; the Reverend Jesse Kamau, moderator of the Presbyterian Church of East Africa (PCEA); and Bishop Professor Zablon Nthamburi, presiding bishop of the MCK. Musyimi was the official spokesman of the steering council, and Archbishop Gitari served for a while as its chairman. Thus, the mainstream evangelicals had a strong voice in the council. The faiths-led group proceeded to appoint twenty commissioners, all of whom are professional lawyers. Immediately after their appointment, the commissioners began traversing the country collecting Kenyan views on the constitution. The commissioners would then submit the written proposals to the steering council.

The alliance of Kenyan Muslims and Christians in pursuit of good governance is significant, given the animosity displayed by the two groups elsewhere in the continent.[43] Unsuccessful attempts have been made to drive a wedge between them. The burning of churches and mosques in Nairobi in December 2000 was widely seen as the ruling party's attempt to stall the faiths-led initiative. But the religious leaders are fully aware of this ploy and have appealed for calm among their followers (*East African Standard*, December 2, 2000; *Daily Nation*, December 2, 2000).[44]

For a time, it seemed as if the two constitutional review councils would never come together. Although the KANU review committee had the necessary legislative backing, the faiths-led committee—popularly known as the Ufungamano initiative after its venue—enjoyed the backing of most Kenyans. KANU leadership was fully aware of this. On December 26, 1999, President Moi appealed to the minority Christian denominations, which traditionally support him, to come out openly and proclaim their stand on the review. In response to his appeal, on January 24, 2000, the EFK organized a rally at Uhuru Park, Nairobi, ostensibly to pray for reconciliation between the two "warring factions." Besides the EFK, the rally was also attended by the head of the AIPCA, Archbishop Samson Gaitho, and some members of his church. The master of ceremony, Bishop Tuimising of the DC, read Psalm 133 to remind the gathering about the need to live in harmony.[45] But other speakers were less cautious. Speaker after speaker reminded the crowd of twenty thousand that parliament and the president were the "custodians and watchdogs of the constitution." Archbishop Kitonga appealed to the opposition members of parliament supporting the faiths-led Ufungamano initiative to take up seats allocated to them on the parliamentary select committee. The speakers also declared, "We are here as a body of Christ; we speak for millions. Other religious and political parties should recognize us." Archbishop Kitonga declared, "We have been quiet for a long time and this should not be misunderstood for lack of a voice" (*Daily Nation*, January 25, 2000).[46]

But the EFK's effort to mobilize its membership in support of the government proved counterproductive. There were murmurs from Christians who felt they had been duped into attending the rally. Most of the people with whom I spoke confessed they attended the rally thinking it was a genuine prayer meeting for national unity, but were disappointed to discover that it was a political rally. They accused their leaders of misleading them and vowed never to attend similar gatherings in the future. Nearly half of the attendees left before Archbishop Gaitho, the main speaker, took the floor. Indeed, the rally revealed that the political views of the leadership of the EFK do not necessarily represent those of its ordinary members. In fact, immediately after the meeting, Bishop Tuimising was asked to resign from the leadership of his church.

Realizing the popularity of the Ufungamano group, the ruling party sought to persuade some of its leaders to withdraw from it. Early in May 2000, two senior cabinet ministers, also respected members of the Anglican Church of Kenya, were dispatched to Archbishop Gitari (*Daily Nation*, May 7, 2000). Although Gitari declined to divulge the contents of their discussion, it is generally believed that their mission was to ask him to withdraw his support from the Ufungamano group. The government targeted Archbishop Gitari because they knew he was a powerful and influential member of the group. But the archbishop remained a member of the group.

Soon after the Ufungamano commissioners began their work, the parliamentary group appointed fifteen commissioners, whom Parliament approved. They were sworn in to start the review process on November 26, 2000. But the commission's chairman, Professor Yash Pal Ghai, declined to take the oath of office until the two rival commissions were reconciled (*East African Standard*, November 29, 2000). Through his efforts, a compromise was gradually reached in which the Ufungamano group took twelve seats in the commission (*Daily Nation*, April 7, 2001). Following this breakthrough, Ghai agreed to be sworn in. But another problem resurfaced. The EFK team insisted that it should have the same number of representatives in the commission as the Ufungamano group. They filed a case in the High Court of Kenya seeking to halt the operations of the (joint) Kenya Review Commission. Although many Kenyans saw the EFK as innocent spoilers, some political pundits saw them as agents of the highest authorities in the land who stood to benefit if the constitutional review process stalled. Finally, realizing that stubborn insistence on representation was hurting its national reputation, the EFK withdrew its demand and allowed the constitutional review process to start.

Conclusion

It is clear that Kenyan evangelicals are likely to remain polarized for a long time to come. As long as some evangelical churches continue to hold a theology that renders uncritical support to the government of the day, there is little hope of evangelicals coming together over issues of governance. As long as ethnic considerations continue to determine Kenyans' political affiliations, some evangelicals are unlikely to question that governance. As long as the state continues providing incentives to the minority churches to dissent from the position held by the mainstream churches, this polarization will continue.

But the willingness of evangelicals from mainstream churches to forge political alliances with people of other faiths bodes well for the evangelical contribution to democracy for two reasons. First, democratic practice requires cooperation with people who do not share one's religious beliefs. Second, evangelicals are more likely to have a significant influence on the government in a democratic direction to the extent that they work in concert with other groups.

One group of evangelicals will probably have an important future role in Kenyan political life. It consists of churches led by young charismatic leaders who enjoy an intense, if not fanatical, following. These are the fastest growing ministries in Kenya. So far, the leaders of these ministries have shown no interest in political issues, preferring to concentrate instead on evangelistic crusades or missions and spiritually nurturing their followers. It is not clear whether they will take an interest in politics in the future and what form that interest will take. But judging from parallel developments in Latin America, their entry into politics is probably only a matter of time.[47]

What do ordinary Kenyans make of these political developments? Public interest in the constitutional debate remains high, as evidenced by the large number of people who turn up to present their views to the Kenya Review Commission. The birth of a new political movement, *Muungano wa Mageuzi* (Movement for Change), led by young radical politicians, has been key to ensuring that the question of constitutional review remains at the top of Kenya's political agenda. Amid strong resistance from the government, this group has been holding political rallies throughout the country, and Kenyans have been turning out in large numbers to listen to its leaders. The group's leadership has identified itself with the faiths-led initiative and urged Kenyans to support it. Leaders of *Muungano wa Mageuzi* are opposed to the merger of the two constitutional groups, fearing that the government will compromise the twelve commissioners appointed by the Ufungamano group.

But there are skeptics too. Geoffrey Ikinu, an employee of the Kikuyu town council near Nairobi, does not support any of the constitutional review groups. Asked why, he replied: "I personally cannot trust either group completely, since the parliamentary group will only serve [President] Moi and Raila's interests, while the Ufungamano group is only interested in removing Moi from power."[48] But Ikinu represents a very small section of the Kenyan population. Most Kenyans fully supported the Kenya Review Commission and believed its recommendations would have serious implications for their lives.

Evangelical contributions to Kenya's democratic development are highly diverse with respect to their causes and consequences. For mainstream evangelicals, theological considerations provide the paramount impulse for political participation, though practical considerations of evangelism and pastoral care are significant too. These considerations have yielded an intense political involvement designed to bring democratic reform. By contrast, although the AIPCA and the member-churches of the EFK cite Romans 13 as the basis of their support of the Moi regime, self-interest of one kind or another also seems to play an important role. For the Kalenjin-dominated AIC, ethnicity and desire for state patronage seem to be important factors. For the less well-established churches, such as the AIPCA, the Redeemed Gospel Church, and the DC, fear of deregistration and a desire for state favors are decisive. As for the emerging charismatic ministries that are currently busy consolidating themselves, the fear of deregistration may keep them away from publicly expressing their views on issues of governance for the time being.

NOTES

1. The only exception is the Africa Inland Church, which, as we shall see, has tended to support the political status quo. The product of an early round of American evangelism, the Africa Inland Church is the second largest Protestant church in Kenya, with a membership of about 2.5 million.

2. Mainstream Protestant churches in Kenya include the Anglican Church of Kenya, the Presbyterian Church of East Africa, the Methodist Church in Kenya, and the Africa Inland Church. The Africa Inland Church withdrew from the NCCK in the 1980s to join the Evangelical Fellowship of Kenya.

3. The pioneer Protestant missionaries in Kenya were evangelicals. Evangelical Christianity arose from the Christian revival in Europe and America in the eighteenth and nineteenth centuries. It emphasized plenary inspiration of Scripture, the doctrine of the original sin and human depravity, personal salvation by faith through Christ's death on the cross, public confession of sins, and the proclamation of the gospel to those who had never heard it. It was this form of Christianity that the pioneer Protestant missionaries introduced in Kenya.

4. The origins of the East African Revival date back to the 1920s, when the Church Missionary Society (CMS) set up its medical mission at Gahini in Rwanda. John E. (Joe) Church, who joined the Rwanda mission in 1927, provided the European inspiration and leadership of the movement. As a student in Cambridge, Church had been profoundly influenced by two movements: Keswick, an annual summer gathering of evangelicals at Keswick in the English Lake District, and Moral Re-Armament (MRA). Keswick, which originated in the Moody-Sankey Revival of 1875, emphasized prayer, reverent Bible study, and "practical holiness." MRA was founded by Frank Buchanan as a moral and spiritual force to transform society. It stressed conversion through confession, surrender, and sharing. These two movements gave Church the vital background that he came to transmit into the Revival movement. The Revival began in 1929, after "the renewing experience" of Church and Simeon

Nsimbabi, a civil servant from Uganda. Both men had retreated to Mengo in Uganda to seek the power of the Holy Spirit as they studied the Bible. After returning to Gahini, Church shared his experience with three African colleagues. The four worked, studied the Bible, prayed together, and formed the first of the many "teams" of the Revival. The primary aim of the Revival is not to evangelize new territories but to raise those who are already Christians to a new and higher level of Christian living. To this end, the movement emphasizes public confession of sins, acceptance of salvation from sin by the "blood of Christ," radical moral transformation, and regular fellowship meetings for mutual support. In April 1937, the movement reached Kenya, where it has exercised profound influence on the mainstream churches. Nearly all the clergy of these churches are members of the Revival.

5. The new evangelical churches and ministries are the fastest-growing Christian organizations in the country. The main ones are the Deliverance Church, the Redeemed Gospel Church, Faith Evangelistic Ministry, Jesus Is Alive Ministry, and Maximum Miracle Centre. The Deliverance Church will be covered in subsequent sections. The Redeemed Gospel Church was founded by Bishop Arthur Kitonga in 1974 and has about one hundred thousand members. Faith Evangelistic Ministry was founded by Evangelist Teresa Wairimu Nelson in the late 1980s and has a membership of about fifty thousand. Jesus Is Alive Ministry was founded by Evangelist Margaret Wanjiru in the early 1990s and has about twenty thousand members. Maximum Miracle Centre, which was founded by Pastor Pius Muiru in the mid-1990s, has a membership of about thirty thousand.

6. Jomo Kenyatta, Kenya's first president, was born in Kiambu District, Central Kenya, circa 1895. He died on August 14, 1978.

7. Daniel Toroitich arap Moi was born in 1924 in Baringo District, Rift Valley Province. After his primary education, he trained as a teacher, a career that he pursued until his entry into politics in 1955. Moi held several positions in the Kenyatta government, including the vice presidency (1967–1978).

8. The figure of 6.75 million, given in the World Christian Encyclopedia (second edition), does not include the three million Kenyan Anglicans as evangelicals.

9. I say "wherever possible" because some church leaders declined to be interviewed. Members of the congregation interviewed were introduced to me by the priest/pastor, but were not selected by the church leader. Rather, in most cases they were people who happened to be there when I visited the institution.

10. The Presbyterian Church of East Africa (PCEA) is the third largest Protestant church in Kenya, with a membership of about two million. Its history dates back to 1891, when the Imperial British East Africa Company invited a group of Scottish missionaries to Kenya. Operating as the East African Scottish Mission and later (1898) the Church of Scotland Mission, the church was initially established in Central and Eastern Kenya among the Kikuyu, Embu, and Meru peoples.

11. Interview with Dr. Peter Bisem, NCCK Deputy General Secretary, in Nairobi, March 15, 1998.

12. The most prominent entrant was the Africa Inland Church, which, as we shall see in subsequent sections, opposed the NCCK's objection to the government's introduction of queue voting in 1986 and the Council's campaign for the end of a one-party system of government.

13. For the purposes of administration, Kenya is divided into eight provinces: the Coast, Central, Nairobi, Nyanza, Eastern, Nairobi, Western, and the Rift Valley.

14. Interview with Archbishop David Gitari at Difatha, Kirinyaga District, February 19, 2001.

15. Interview with the Right Reverend Stanley Booth-Clibborn, Anglican bishop of Manchester, United Kingdom, August 22, 1986. I interviewed the bishop in his office in Manchester.

16. Born in England in 1906, Leonard J. Beecher arrived in Kenya in 1927 to teach at the Alliance High School, Kenya's first African secondary school. He represented African interests on the Legislative Council between 1943 and 1947, and on the executive council between 1947 and 1952. Between 1960 and 1970, Beecher served as the first archbishop of the Church of the Province of East Africa.

17. Interview with Bishop Booth-Clibborn, August 22, 1986.

18. Henry Okullu was born in Nyanza Province of Kenya in 1929. He was educated at Bishop Tucker Theological College, Uganda, and Virginia Theological Seminary, USA. He worked for *Target* newspaper from 1968 until 1971. Between 1971 and 1974 he was the Provost of All Saints Cathedral, Nairobi. In 1974 he was elected bishop of the newly created Diocese of Maseno South.

19. Interview with Archbishop Gitari, February 19, 2001.

20. The controversy arose from Protestant missionaries' attempt to force Kikuyu Christians to renounce clitoridectomy, an old Kikuyu cultural practice. Those Kikuyu who wished to remain Christians and still retain their cultural identity through the practice of clitoridectomy left mission-founded churches to start the African Independent Pentecostal Church.

21. The Mau Mau was a secret movement that operated in Central Kenya in the 1950s. Its main objective was to overthrow colonial rule. The Mau Mau used tribal oaths to bind its membership and rally it to the common cause. Detailed studies of the movement include Barnett (1966), Rosberg (1966), Lonsdale (1992).

22. Interview with Pastor Nene Gikonyo and Archdeacon Muchai in Nairobi, March 25, and April 6, 2001.

23. Interview with Pastor Gikonyo and Archdeacon Muchai, March 25 and April 6, 2001.

24. Interview with Pastor Gikonyo and Archdeacon Muchai, March 25 and April 6, 2001. During the interviews, Gikonyo and Muchai constantly lamented the setback experienced by their church as a result of its ban in 1952.

25. Interview with Archdeacon Muchai, April 6, 2001.

26. Interview with Archbishop Gitari, February 19, 2001.

27. On September 2, 2001, the *Daily Nation* reported a declaration by a senior cabinet minister that the government intended to transfer 328 primary and secondary schools in Central Kenya currently under the sponsorship of the mainstream churches to the AIPCA. The minister gave two reasons for this action. First, since the schools belonged to the AIPCA before the colonial government took them away in the 1950s, it was fair to return them to their original owner. Second, the transfer would enable the children to learn Kikuyu cultural values, which in turn would guard against the spread of school strikes. But the minister's argument seemed to have no merit. First, it is doubtful whether the tally of the schools taken away from the AIPCA was

anywhere near 328. Second, this desire to instill "Kikuyu cultural values" runs counter to the government's policy of building a strong nation through suppression of retrogressive institutions, movements, and tribal practices. Indeed the Moi government is committed to the eradication of clitoridectomy. The move is probably intended to reward the AIPCA for its loyalty to the government and to punish the mainstream churches for their oppositional stance.

28. Interview with Archdeacon Muchai, April 6, 2001.

29. Interview with Pastor James Thumbi at Eastleigh, Nairobi, September 26, 2000.

30. Ibid. For a similar view, see Gifford (1995, 5–6).

31. Ibid.

32. Manasses Kuria was the archbishop of the ACK from 1980 until 1994.

33. Muge was a Nandi, a Kalenjin subtribe.

34. See, for example, Gitari (1996, 13–21). Josiah Mwangi Kariuki was both a hero of resistance against colonial rule and a populist Member of Parliament. The discovery of his charred remains in Ngong Hills, southwest of Nairobi on March 3, 1975 sparked nationwide unrest. The government set up a commission of inquiry to investigate his murder. However, the commission's findings were never made public.

35. Geoffrey Kareithi was the head of Civil Service and secretary to the Cabinet during the Kenyatta era and the early years of Moi's rule. After his retirement from civil service, he became involved in local Kirinyaga politics, serving as a member of Parliament for the Gichugu constituency between 1983 and 1988. In the rigged party elections of 1985, he was elected chairman of KANU in Gichugu.

36. Interview with Archbishop Gitari, February 29, 2001.

37. Born in Britain in 1921, John Stott is a leading biblical expositor who seeks to relate the Christian faith to the contemporary social, economic, political, and cultural realities. He has mentored many African scholars and church leaders, including Mutava Musyimi, the current general secretary of the NCCK.

38. Also quoted in Gifford (1995, 4) and Freston (2001, 146).

39. Interview with Samuel Wanjohi, pastor of RGC Huruma Church, December 14, 2001. My efforts to interview archbishop Kitonga have proved unsuccessful.

40. As chairman of the NCCK during the queue voting controversy, Imathiu sought to mediate between the Council and KANU. For the NCCK statement on queuing, see *Weekly Review*, November 28, 1986.

41. For a detailed study of Frederick Chiluba's political theology, see Isabel Phiri's chapter.

42. "Nyayo" is a Kiswahili word meaning "footsteps." Moi first used the term at a political rally to mean that he would follow the footsteps of his predecessor, Jomo Kenyatta. But it later became obvious that Moi expected Kenyans to follow his own footsteps or, as he often put it, "to toe the line."

43. In Nigeria, for example, Muslim-Christian relations are marked by hostility. See Cyril Imo's essay (chapter 1).

44. My efforts to interview the secretary of the Supreme Council of Kenyan Muslims on this and other matters have failed.

45. Like President Moi, Bishop Tuimising is a Kalenjin. He is a close friend of the head of state.

46. I attended the "prayer" meeting.

47. See, for example, the Brazil case in Freston (2001), chapter 1.

48. Interview with Geoffrey Ikinu, February 26, 2001. Raila Odinga, son of the celebrated Luo nationalist, Jaramogi Oginga Odinga, is leader of the National Democratic Party that has forged a working alliance with KANU.

3

President Frederick Chiluba and Zambia: Evangelicals and Democracy in a "Christian Nation"

Isabel Apawo Phiri

The case of Zambia is central to a study of evangelical Christianity and democracy in Africa. President Frederick Chiluba, an evangelical, publicly declared the southern African country a "Christian nation" in December 1991. He also played a critical role in Zambia's democratic transition and published a book glorifying democracy. His presidency thus constitutes a critical test case of the relationship between evangelical faith and African democracy.

Chiluba's presidency, therefore, is the main theme of this chapter. It focuses on his career from his election as president in October 1991, to his decision not to contest for a third term in April 2001. Its argument is twofold. First, in his book on democracy and in his declaration of Zambia as a Christian nation, Chiluba established the criteria by which his presidency would be judged and ultimately found wanting. Second, Chiluba's "Christian nation" concept has had the inadvertent consequence of giving evangelicals a clear basis on which to judge Chiluba and the Zambian state, and hence has served as a catalyst for more energetic and extensive evangelical political engagement in Zambia.

Many churches denounced the Christian nation declaration at the time it was made. However, politics in Zambia has not fractured into two opposing camps on the issue: there is no dyadic pattern of one party that supports the Christian nation contesting another party that opposes it. Zambian politics is increasingly played out *among* supporters of the Christian nation idea. This chapter describes, for

example, how Pastor Nevers Mumba, an evangelical enthusiast for the declaration, nevertheless founded his own party to oppose Chiluba in the elections.
Mumba's case exemplifies how evangelicals could not help but have strong
opinions about the Christian nation concept, and how, once they started publicly
articulating these opinions, they soon acquired the habit of being politically
informed and engaged.

This chapter also describes how the split within Chiluba's party (the Movement for Democratic Change) over his intention to stand for a third term politically divided the very men who were responsible for the declaration in the first
place. Thus, Brigadier General Godfrey Miyanda, whom some people credit as
the originator of the idea of the Christian nation declaration, opposed a third
term for Chiluba. He was expelled by Chiluba from the party, sought to impeach
his old friend, went into opposition along with many other evangelicals, and
formed the Heritage Party, which also advocates the Christian nation concept.

As the foregoing already suggests, Christians in general and evangelicals
in particular have come to dominate Zambian politics. There are three reasons
for this. First, Chiluba's regime fell far short of the expectations of those—
particularly evangelicals—who supported the Christian nation idea at the beginning of his presidency. The argument among evangelicals came to be not
whether there should be a Christian nation, but what should be done to achieve
it. For many, this came to mean replacing Chiluba with someone who would
actually achieve a genuine Christian democracy in Zambia.

The second reason is that during Chiluba's presidency, once evangelicals
were provoked to speak out on the Christian nation declaration, a more vibrant
evangelical civil society emerged, which has been gaining confidence ever since
and growing increasingly ready to play a political role. This evangelical civil
society consists prominently of women and student groups, two key constituencies in Zambian politics.

The third reason is that the old "two-kingdom" theology of the evangelical
mission churches has come to be subverted by an African holism that makes
no effective distinction between the spiritual and the material worlds. This
theological development has paved the way for greater Christian involvement
in politics.

This chapter seeks to illustrate these general claims. It begins with a
consideration of Chiluba's writing on democracy and goes on to his election as
president, his spiritual "cleansing" of State House, his "anointing" as a godly
leader, and his declaration of Zambia as a Christian nation. After outlining
Chiluba's claims to be both a faithful Christian and a faithful democrat, the
chapter goes on to examine Zambia's economic decline, human rights abuses,
and lack of good governance. It was out of this context that Nevers Mumba's
challenge arose. The chapter then turns to the emergence of a stronger evangelical civil society, focusing first on women's organizations and then looking
at religious education and the formation of a student Christian Democratic

conscience. Finally, it narrates the dramatic events of early 2001, in which most of these factors came into play, and ends with some general conclusions. At the end of the chapter I have also added a postscript on Zambia's December 2001 presidential elections.

Motivation

The case of Zambia has generated intense interest on the part of scholars of religion and politics. Paul Gifford, for example, has written a detailed chapter concerning evangelicals and politics in Zambia in his book, *African Christianity: Its Public Role* (1998, 181–231). He has provided useful background on Zambia's churches by examining the mission churches, the African Initiated Churches (AICs), and the "born-again" movements that are founded by Zambians but have links with charismatic and pentecostal churches in the United States. He highlighted the churches' role in Zambia's political development by showing how the first president of Zambia, Kenneth Kaunda, used the platform of Christianity to advance his political position, yet attracted the churches' intense and decisive opposition when he appeared to stray from the Christian faith by linking himself to the Indian spiritual leaders Maharishi Mahesh Yogi and Dr. Raganathan.[1] Gifford also shows how Chiluba came to power through the Zambian Congress of Trade Unions (ZCTU) and later the Movement for Multiparty Democracy (hereafter MMD). He discusses the widespread support he initially received from the churches; how he surprised everyone by declaring Zambia "a Christian nation"; and yet, how he ultimately failed to stamp out corruption in government and civil society. Gifford successfully captures the feelings of most Zambians, who feel that Chiluba's Zambia is an "uncaring Christian nation" because poverty has been dramatically on the rise.

Gifford's research covers events in Zambia up to 1996 but before the second presidential elections. Paul Freston has argued that "the whole of Gifford's text at this point, even though it is the main work available on evangelical politics in Zambia, shows how little is really known about the role of the churches beyond the leadership of the mainline churches" (2001, 156). This is because Gifford's primary research mainly reflects the perspectives of middle-class Zambians. Very little is heard from the relatively marginalized sectors of Zambian society, which includes women, youth, and rural people. It is the aim of this chapter, as much as possible, to avoid repeating Gifford's valuable findings and at the same time provide a different social perspective and more recent information.

In addition, Gifford does not discuss President Chiluba's book on politics, which is entitled *Democracy: The Challenge of Change* (1995). It is crucial, however, to understand how African leaders themselves define democracy. In the book, Chiluba begins by defining democracy in terms of its key characteristics:

> Firstly, democracy values each individual person as a rational, moral unit, and recognizes the right to, and capacity for, a measure of self-government. Secondly, there is the idea of the supremacy of the people. Thirdly . . . democracy recognizes that consent of the people makes possible the formation of a government of the people. . . . A fourth important characteristic of democracy is accountability. . . . Finally, there is the rule of law. (1995, 4–5)

With respect to the purpose of politics, Chiluba argues that

> politics is about power. Its business is to manage and try to resolve conflict, not just over access to scarce resources, although that is a particularly notable feature in developing countries, especially in Africa, but also conflict of opinion about how society should be organized and about matters of life in general. The manner in which power is acquired is bound to influence the way in which it is exercised. (1995, 6)

Of special relevance to understanding Chiluba's conception of democracy is what he says about the rights of minorities. He argues that any democratic system ought to protect all minority groups through "a bill of rights, separation of powers, and institutional checks and balances, and an electoral arrangement, which necessitates a degree of power-sharing among parties in governments" (1995, 8). Thus, in the context of religion, as far as the constitution is concerned, minorities such as Muslims, who form about 1 percent of the Zambian population, have the same rights as the majority Christians. He thus favors not just democracy but *liberal* democracy. However, he also insists that individuals need to respect certain limits for the sake of the whole country. Individual responsibility must accompany individual rights. It is noteworthy that this understanding of democracy has the support of many Christians, especially the Roman Catholic Church in Zambia. In fact, one Catholic priest with whom I spoke, Father Nakoma, suggested that the president reread his book every night before going to bed to be reminded of what he stands for (interview, January 2000). Chiluba's elite critics who have read the book say that it is a useful way to judge his decision making as president.

Chiluba's book further suggests his understanding of democracy by arguing that although the colonial government of Northern Rhodesia (pre-independence Zambia) was not democratic, it practiced multiparty politics. When Zambia received independence on October 24, 1964, under the leadership of Kaunda and the United National Independency Party (UNIP), multiparty politics continued up to 1971. The period from 1964 to 1971 is described as the first republic. The period from 1972 to 1991 is the second republic, which is characterized as one-party democracy under the leadership of Kaunda. Chiluba argues that the creation of a one-party government at this point was the result of the declining Zambian economy.[2] It was assumed by the UNIP that "growing economic and financial difficulties would erode the ability of UNIP, the governing party, to win votes in competition with other parties" (Chiluba 1995, 27). He acknowledges the global events that effected changes in the politics of Zambia, and further discusses the campaign for democracy in the early 1990s that led to the establishment of the third republic under the MMD on October 31, 1991. He also discusses his international and economic development policies up to 1993.

In his book Chiluba says very little about the role of the church in ushering in democracy in Zambia. He discusses the church's role in one page (1995, 66). Furthermore, although the book covers Chiluba's political changes and policies up to 1993, he does not mention his 1991 declaration of Zambia as a Christian nation. The declaration is mentioned only in the "Chronology of Events 1988–1992," at the back of the book (1995, 162). Could it be that Chiluba felt that his declaration of Zambia as a Christian nation, or the way he declared it, stood in some tension with the very principles of democracy he articulated in his book and championed at the beginning of his presidency? Alternatively, did he consider the declaration a merely personal expression of his commitment to God and not a political act? What was the significance of Chiluba's Christian nation declaration for his presidency, for other evangelicals, and for Zambian democracy? These are the questions I address in this essay.

Methodology

The main approach I adopt in this study is contemporary history. Where past history is discussed, it will be to shed light on the current situation by providing background and context. It takes seriously the critical importance of the relationship between religion and politics in contemporary Zambia, with an emphasis on how those inside Zambia understand and evaluate this relationship.

The research is based on mixed sources: library research, documentary research (including church publications, newspapers, and the writings of Christian politicians and church leaders), and video recordings. Field research consisted of interviews with different church groups; these included church leaders, but I placed special emphasis on lay people—men and women, youth and adults. I also interviewed politicians. I interviewed evangelical Christians closely connected to President Chiluba or working at State House (the Zambian president's official residence). However, most people I interviewed were ordinary, active (regularly attending) members of churches affiliated with the Evangelical Fellowship of Zambia (EFZ), such as satellite churches of the

Northmead Assembly of God and the Rub Road Baptist Church. I attended a number of evangelical meetings/conferences for women, youth and mixed. I visited the EFZ offices. I also visited churches belonging to the Christian Council of Zambia (CCZ), such as the Anglican Church and the United Church of Zambia (UCZ), as well as the offices of the Episcopal Conference of Zambia (ECZ). In so doing, I contacted the three mother bodies of Zambian Christianity to gain a comparative perspective.

The Churches in Zambia

Even since Paul Gifford's research in the mid-1990s, there has been remarkable growth in the number of Christians in Zambia. In a population of more than nine million, the proportion has grown from 75 percent in 1995 to 85 percent in 2000. Most new converts to Christianity are coming from traditional religions, adherents of which constituted 24 percent of the population in 1995 but only 12.6 percent by 2000. The number of Muslims has also grown, from 1 percent in 1995 to 1.4 percent in 2000. But there has been a particularly significant increase in the number of evangelicals. By one estimate, there were 515,000 (9 percent) evangelicals in Zambia in 1980. This figure grew to 800,000 (12.6 percent) in 1990 and more than doubled to 2.2 million (25 percent) in 2000 (Johnstone 2001, 686). However, these figures do not include charismatics (18.9 percent) and pentecostals (10.2 percent). Since I include pentecostals in the evangelical category for the purposes of this chapter (as is the case with all the chapters in this volume and in the project as a whole), whether or not they are members of the EFZ, I estimate the number of evangelicals to be about 43 percent of Zambia's population.

Some Christians in Zambia attribute the tremendous evangelical growth in this period to Chiluba's Christian nation declaration in 1991. At the same time, economic hardship and the AIDS pandemic have also caused many Zambians to seek God in Protestant and African Initiated Churches. With the increase in evangelical Christianity in Zambia, the EFZ has become an important focal point of fellowship, cooperation, and collaboration for evangelical denominations and agencies (Johnstone 2001, 687).

Chiluba: Evangelical and President

Chiluba's background is not without controversy. According to official records, Frederick Jacob Titus Chiluba was born on April 30, 1943, in Kitwe on the Copperbelt. His highest education qualification is a Master's degree in Philosophy and Political Science from the University of Warwick in England. His leadership career began with his involvement with trade unionism on the

Copperbelt. His Christian commitment is traced back to his membership of the UCZ. He had a "born again" experience in 1981 while he was in prison, having been arrested by Kaunda's government. The person who led him to this conversion was evangelist Christopher Ngoma, who is now his principal private secretary at State House. Chiluba was also attached to charismatic fellowships within the UCZ and to the Northmead Assembly of God.

Gifford has argued that Chiluba did not come to political power in 1991 on a Christian ticket (1998, 197). However, it is also noteworthy that he had large church support because his faith commitment was being favorably compared with that of President Kaunda, who at this time was publicly associated with Eastern religion, which was unacceptable to Zambian Christians, as I noted earlier. Christian multimedia gave Chiluba extensive coverage that effectively introduced him to the masses. Christians also played a prominent role in promoting peaceful discussion among the different political parties, which led to the constitutional changes mandating multiparty elections in 1991. The churches also formed the Christian Churches Monitoring Group, which helped monitor the elections and ensure a free and fair voting process.

The Cleansing of State House

Chiluba was declared the president of Zambia on October 31, 1991. He left State House unoccupied for three months after the elections. Due to his charismatic theology, he did not wish to enter the president's residence until charismatic friends and associates had performed a "cleansing service." A group of fifty Christians from evangelical fellowships went to State House, which had just been vacated by Kaunda. Prayers were conducted in each room of State House with the intention of chasing out evil spirits associated with Eastern religion. A woman is said to have seen a vision of a sea horse leaving State House, which Kaunda had allegedly invited into the residence. Some of the State House guards confirmed that during the time of Kaunda, they were sometimes instructed to leave the gates to State House open at 3 A.M. They could then hear (but not see) a sea horse entering the residence (Peter Linthini, interview, January 2000).

The belief that we inhabit a spiritual world in which opponents can use spiritual powers to do harm motivated the cleansing ceremony. Such beliefs are not unique to charismatic or pentecostal Christians; they are also present in African Traditional Religion and are practiced by many people at the grassroots level. The significance of the ceremony is that it demonstrates that Chiluba was a person deeply influenced by his charismatic faith at the very time he assumed the presidency. Even though the cleansing ceremony was not organised by the EFZ, it had the support of the many Christians in Zambia who were scandalized by Eastern religion and its influence on Kaunda. It highlighted the deep difference between Kaunda and Chiluba in their faith commitment.

The Anointing Ceremony

The link between church and state was further strengthened when an "anointing" service was organised for President Chiluba by the three main Christian bodies: the Christian Council of Zambia (CCZ), the EFZ, and the ECZ. Significantly, while the charismatic and pentecostal groups initiated the event, it had the support of other churches. This is confirmed by the fact that the service was held in the Lusaka Anglican Cathedral and the Anglican archbishop personally conducted the anointing. The programme for the service was organised by Mbita Kabalika, a cousin of Chiluba. He claims that the inspiration for this service was the anointing of King David in the Old Testament. Kabalika argues that the Old Testament has a special place in his family history because they consider themselves Black Jews, like the Lemba people of South Africa (Mbita Kabalika, interview, Lusaka, January 2000). Members of the Northmead Assembly of God were also intimately involved in organizing the ceremony. As reported by Gifford, the Anglican archbishop gave Chiluba the following charge: "Be strong and show yourself a man, keep the charge of the Lord your God, walk in his ways, keep his statutes, his commandments, his precepts and his testimonies as it is written in the first and second testaments" (Gifford 1998, 197). Though Chiluba was Zambia's president, the anointing ceremony suggested that he was first of all God's servant.

Some Christians from pentecostal circles saw a specific and practical significance to the anointing of the president: because the president is the anointed one of God, nobody has the right to question or disagree with him. They believe the opposition represents the devil because they resist the will of God's chosen leader.

The Declaration of Zambia as a Christian Nation

On December 29, 1991, President Chiluba declared Zambia a Christian nation, yet with full religious freedom for all faiths (Johnstone 2001, 686). The declaration was made in a private ceremony held at State House. The arrangements for this ceremony were shrouded in secrecy because Chiluba knew it was going to be controversial. The motivation can be traced back to Chiluba's spiritual experiences before he became president. In the 1980s, Chiluba attended a Christian meeting during which a Swedish woman claimed to receive a prophecy about him. According to the prophecy, Chiluba was going to be a leader of his nation. He claims he did not take this prophecy seriously. In 1989, Kabalika had the same revelation, which he shared with him during a visit to the United Kingdom. Chiluba did not comment. In charismatic circles, the testimony of two people is said to confirm the divine origins of a revelation, and Chiluba began to think about it seriously. Privately, he then made a vow to God that if he was indeed chosen by God to lead the nation of Zambia, he was going to give the country to God. Therefore, when he became president, he asked Mbita Kambalika and Brigadier General Godfrey Miyanda to organise the declaration. This may explain why some people, as reported by Gifford, have argued that the declaration of Zambia as a Christian nation was the brainchild of Miyanda.

In contrast with the anointing ceremony, the planning for the declaration ceremony was entirely secret. A few friends from the charismatic churches were invited the night before the declaration for a night of prayer. The president himself came in and out of the prayer meeting. Invitations were sent by telephone and word-of-mouth to various church leaders to attend a private function at State House, along with fifty of their church members. Nobody who came to the function knew what was going to happen except the president and the small team that had conducted the prayer meeting the previous day. Cabinet ministers heard about it for the fist time on television; they were not invited because Chiluba did not consider it a "political" function.

Chiluba stood between two pillars at the State House. Gifford relates:

> He claimed that "the Bible, which is the Word of God, abounds with proof that a nation is blessed, whenever it enters into a covenant with God and obeys the word of God." He quoted 2 Chronicles 7:14: "If my people who are called by my name will humble themselves and pray and seek my face and turn from their wicked ways, then will I hear from heaven and forgive their sin and will heal their land." On behalf of the people of Zambia, he repented of "our wicked ways of idolatry, witchcraft, the occult, immorality, injustice and corruption." He then prayed for "healing, restoration, revival, blessing and prosperity" for Zambia. "On behalf of the nation, I have now entered into a covenant with the living God [...] I submit the Government and the entire nation of Zambia to the Lordship of Jesus Christ. I further declare that Zambia is a Christian Nation that will seek to be governed by the righteous principles of the Word of God. Righteousness and justice must prevail in all levels of authority, and then we shall see the righteousness of God exalting Zambia." (Gifford 1998, 197–198, quoting from *Times of Zambia*, February 20, 1994)

Christian Reaction to the Declaration

The declaration generated serious conflict among the three main Christian bodies and between the churches and politicians. Zambian Christians were deeply divided. On the one hand, the Roman Catholic Church and the Christian Council of Zambia, as well as some evangelical groups, who in principle supported the declaration, maintained that there should have been public consultations before the declaration because of Zambia's democratic nature. On the other hand, pentecostal circles, especially the Northmead Assembly of God, were delighted because they believed the rule of God was coming to Zambia through Chiluba. Furthermore, those who support the declaration see themselves as true Christians and those who do not as the enemies of God's government and therefore pseudo-Christians. For them, the manner or process whereby the declaration was made is irrelevant. What matters is putting God above everything.

As observed by Gifford, the churches' struggle for state recognition may also be a factor in explaining their reaction to the declaration. The pentecostals directly involved in the ceremony were no doubt gratified and delighted that they had effectively been brought into the president's inner circle (or so they believed). Other church bodies felt neglected, although they had been in the forefront of politics all along. The planning committee of the ceremony has argued that no church body was in fact neglected; it was only last-minute confusion that gave the impression that some church bodies were left out. Nevertheless, the damage caused in church circles was irreversible, for it planted seeds of disunity among the churches and a spirit of resistance from other Christian quarters.

Melu has argued that as far as the president was concerned, the declaration of Zambia as a Christian nation was not a political statement.[3] Chiluba was not asked to make the declaration by anyone; it was something he believed he needed to do as long as he was president. Melu believes that there was no need to consult the people about his decision. It was his personal conviction that he needed to make the declaration, and it was one for which he was prepared to lay down his presidency. According to Melu,

> Chiluba believes that King Josiah's mission to the nation of Israel is mirrored in him as president of Zambia. That is why he made the declaration while standing between two pillars at the State House. The declaration was not made to people; it was made to God. It was in a form of a prayer. He was basically saying that "I believe God, and I believe what God has told me to do, and my government will follow. Where we fail, the standard that will judge us is not our manifesto, it is not how well we perform human rights as such, it is on how well we follow the principles as laid down in the Scriptures." That is the declaration. (Melu, interview, January 2000)

This strengthens Gifford's claim that some Zambians have argued that the declaration of Zambia as a Christian nation could not have been debated because it was based on Chiluba's religious convictions. On the other hand, others argued that because it affected the nation and Zambia is a democratic country, the people should have discussed it. This, after all, would have been consistent with Chiluba's definition of democracy as set out in his book.

Chiluba's personal faith no doubt influenced his public policies as president. First, Zambia reestablished diplomatic links with Israel, which were cut during Kaunda's rule. The talk of the day was Christian Zionism, or the idea that Christians should have a special regard for Israel as a part of God's plan for history. Second, he cut ties with Iran and Iraq, because they supported Kaunda and were Muslim states. Third, some pastors were appointed as members of the cabinet. Fourth, relations between the Muslim minority and the Christian majority within Zambia soured, particularly because Muslims felt increasingly insecure about their position in a Christian nation. Fifth, there has been an influx of Christian missionaries into Zambia. New charismatic churches or church organisations have increased, with the encouragement of president Chiluba. For example, the president invited international church leaders to hold evangelistic crusades in Zambia at government expense. In April 2000, the deputy education minister, Dan Pule, was in Durban attending a Benny Hinn crusade (an American televangelist and international preacher) as a representative of the Zambian government. He issued an invitation to Hinn on behalf of the president to hold a crusade in Zambia in 2001. Sixth, a department of Christian Affairs was opened in the president's office with its own minister. Eighth, among other social organisations, churches that support the president receive presidential discretionary funding. For example, Chiluba gave ZK129 million to Dan Pule for the construction of his Dunamas International church, studio and offices (*The Post*, June 15, 2001).

The crucial question is: what did it mean to the people of Zambia that their country was declared a Christian nation? The fact that the disagreements among the churches on this issue have continued is itself a sign that Chiluba failed to clearly explain to the Zambian people the meaning of the declaration.

However, it is clear that some Christians see it as the first step toward the Christianization of the government. At a 1995 meeting of church representatives and politicians, the church representatives said they expected that all political leaders would subsequently be drawn from the church and that the church and state would be partners in running the government. As of now, a significant number of members of parliament and cabinet ministers are "born-again" Christians. Other Christians believe that a necessary step in Zambia's Christianization is that as many evangelists as possible be sent into the communities to teach people what it means to be a Christian and to intensify their prayers so that God would raise up good leaders in their local constituencies. If the people were well taught, it is assumed, it would not be difficult for them to choose good Christian leaders from among themselves. They would choose their parliamentary representatives based on Christian character rather then their status in the church. The president would then choose from these Christians to form a cabinet. Because this has not happened, the people of Zambia are blameworthy for having failed to catch Chiluba's vision of a

Christian nation (Chikumbi, Towani, Banda, and Chikontwe, interviews, December 1999). In any case, it is clear in pentecostal circles that Zambia has become a chosen nation of God. Consequently, the ruling party stands for everything that is good, and any opposition is from the devil.

Not all evangelicals share this vision, however. One voice representing those who oppose the Christian nation concept argues that

> you cannot declare a Christian nation in the same way you can declare an Islamic state; because when you declare an Islamic state, you have a top-down kind of giving the law on how the people should live. But you cannot do that with Christianity. You cannot make people Christians by legislation. If we insist that all ministers should be Christians, then we would become very similar to an Islamic state. It is also not accurate that every Christian can make a good politician. People can be very good Christians and make very good ministers in a congregation but not in the political arena. Personally, I think people should be chosen on merit and on how well they can deal with issues at hand. You can put standards as to what is ethical and what is exemplary leadership without insisting that everyone must have Christian conviction and faith. The reason why people should repent and become Christians is because they feel sinful, and not because they are seeking political posts. (Kuzipa Nalwamba, interview, December 2000)

In addition, the stand of the Roman Catholic church of Zambia is clear. "The church must endeavour to be seen as independent from political influence and challenge the nation morally as it did so well in the past. In other words, the separation of powers (church/state) must be seen in deed" (Catholic Commission for Justice and Peace 1998, 16).

The Christian Nation Declaration and the New Zambian Constitution

In 1996, the preamble to the Zambian constitution was amended to declare the Republic of Zambia a Christian nation, while upholding the right of every person to enjoy freedom of conscience and freedom of religion.

The constitutional amendment to include the Christian nation declaration had far-reaching consequences. The initial declaration of 1991 was said to be between God and Chiluba. When this was extended to the country's constitution, the declaration had profound legal and political implications that extended well beyond Chiluba's presidency. Therefore, there was a public outcry demanding that the new constitution be passed through a national referendum. The EFZ, CCZ, and ECZ commented on the proposed Zambian Constitution in a joint memorandum:

We, Church leaders, have listened to the people's apprehension about the Government's White paper, regarding the adoption
of the New Constitution. We wish to add our voice to the call of
how best the proposed constitution can be legitimised.

The constitution of the country is a national document of the
highest importance. As the supreme law of the land, it must
be recognised and respected, as embodying the sovereign will of
the majority of the people. The mode of adoption either facilitates or obstructs this popular acceptance and recognition.

We share the apprehension of the people for the following
reasons: (. . .) There are sections in the draft Constitution, which are
highly controversial and therefore deserving of widespread debate
that would contribute to decisions regarding the final wording. (*Times
of Zambia*, October 3, 1995)

Chiluba simply offered the constitution to Parliament to approve. The
controversial items were mainly two. Chiluba insisted that the constitution
should change to include a clause that requires that both parents of a presidential candidate should have been born in Zambia, which was interpreted as
an attempt to bar Kaunda from running as a presidential candidate for UNIP.
In the same vein, he overruled the opposition over the inclusion in the constitution of the Christian nation declaration. Arguably, both actions diverged
from his own conception of democracy because there was no popular participation whatsoever in these crucial decisions.

Economy and Good Governance in a Christian Nation

One reason Zambia was declared a Christian nation was the belief that a nation
whose leader fears God prospers economically. When Chiluba came to power
in a free and fair election, the international world supported him with financial aid. The International Monetary Fund (IMF) recommended that Zambia
should follow a structural adjustment programme and privatise the state-
owned copper mines, which contributed 80 percent of Zambia's foreign exchange. It also recommended that Zambia should develop its agricultural
industry.

In practice, however, Zambia's economy has declined even further. The
removal of government subsidies on food resulted in high inflation and the
suffering of many ordinary people. Privatization meant that many goods were
available, but there was no money to buy the goods. It has also meant that a
small number of Zambians grew wealthy at the expense of the majority of the
people. It is now estimated that more than 80 percent of Zambians live at
extreme poverty levels (*The Post*, May 22, 2001).

During the same period, there have been widespread accusations of corruption, especially among politicians. Drug trafficking among politicians is also said to have increased, which has led to the dismissal of some ministers and the resignation of others who felt the president was not doing enough to stop corruption. Due to the poor economy, investors are not inclined to invest in Zambia, and many small businesses have closed. This in turn has led to severe unemployment. Government employees also suffer due to delays in getting payment. Strikes also increased among professionals like doctors due to lower salaries and lack of medical facilities in government hospitals. When the mines were eventually sold in 2000, it was at a loss due to the poor timing of the sale.

Chiluba has also been accused of violating human rights. During his presidency, he faced two coup attempts. In the 1993 coup, Kaunda and other UNIP leaders were arrested. The October 1997 coup was codenamed, "Operation Born Again." The leader of the coup, Captain Solo, told Zambians that an angel had instructed him to mount the coup (*Africa Confidential*, November 7, 1997). In the case of both coups, Chiluba declared a state of emergency, which gave him powers to arrest his political opponents and detain them without trial. There is also evidence that his opponents were tortured while in custody. One case in point is Dean Mung'omba, the president of the Zambian Democratic Congress. Chiluba and the MMD have also been accused of masterminding car accidents that led to the death of opposition leaders. Kaunda is said to have survived three attempts on his life.

By the time the 1996 presidential elections were taking place, there was so much frustration with Chiluba's tactics that the major opposition parties decided to boycott the elections. The opposition wanted to make Zambia ungovernable if the elections continued. International donors suspended their aid to Zambia. Chiluba and his party were also accused of buying votes with public funds. Nevertheless, despite all the confusion, presidential elections went ahead and Chiluba got a majority vote of 70 percent, with 40 percent voter turnout.

Impact of Lack of Good Governance in Pentecostal Circles: The Case of Nevers Mumba

The main focus of this section is the relationship between Chiluba and Nevers Mumba. Nevers Mumba is the founder and president of Victory Ministries International, an evangelistic Ministry based in Kitwe, Zambia, which was founded in 1984. He is of the Bemba tribal group, like Chiluba himself. He is responsible for a number of Victory Bible churches in Africa and is the president of the Victory Bible College (now being upgraded to university status). He conducts gospel crusades, taking extended ministry trips each year into Europe and America. In 1990 he began a national television outreach campaign that brought him thousands of members in Zambia and Namibia. When Chiluba declared Zambia a Christian country, Mumba was one of his supporters. Mumba also invited Chiluba and his wife to a number of Victory conventions where he gave Chiluba a platform to get political support. The followers of Mumba believed that Nevers Mumba was becoming a very prominent voice for the church in political circles during the first term of Chiluba's presidency. However, as governance issues continued to deteriorate in Zambia, Mumba decided to enter politics. He therefore formed a National Christian Coalition in 1996, which was packaged much like the Christian Coalition in the United States. Its aim was to act as an independent voice in guiding the president in matters with which the church was concerned. However, he changed the name to National Citizens' Coalition (NCC) because he did not want to limit it to Christian participation. It then turned into a political party that seeks to nurture potential political leaders of integrity for national leadership. Here again one sees a link between the church and the state.

The question that one may ask is: why another party led by a Christian? What is the difference between Chiluba and Mumba? Mumba has capitalised on the issue of quality of leadership. In the NCC manifesto, Mumba has stated that

> Zambians and people worldwide have lost confidence in politics and politicians. The abuse of office, the high levels of selfishness and an overall lack of character in politicians has impeded economic growth in our nation. This is the reason why NCC was created to meet the challenges of a new and different world. Until a measure of faith is re-injected into our political system, Zambians will continue to be cynical and uninterested in supporting the efforts of government. This is evidenced by the current high voter apathy.

The above quotation can be seen as Mumba's evaluation of Chiluba's government, which he sees as lacking in integrity. He further elaborates on this point by describing the type of leader that Zambia should have:

> I believe the manifestos alone do not change nations, but rather, good people do. Bad people cannot achieve good governance. Good governance demands good governors. It takes a leadership of morality and integrity to bring healing to Zambia. The only hope for Zambia is to insist on putting into office leaders of proven morality whose values are faith-based and anchored in Godly values. NCC objective is that there will never be good governance without good governors. The delivery of goods and services to the citizens is dependent on the morality of its leaders.

Mumba has clearly connected good political leadership with belief in God, but he deliberately does not claim that only Christians should hold office. At the same time he upholds Chiluba's stand of declaring Zambia a Christian nation. He has argued that the

> NCC shall uphold the declaration of Zambia as a Christian nation, with the view of making it more practical. Love, tolerance and justice shall be the basis of the declaration and NCC shall establish points of reference to under gird it. NCC shall respect our citizens' freedom of association and assembly and will ensure the full rights of other religions to practice without intimidation.

Therefore, at face value, Mumba insists that people of faith besides Christians can and should occupy political positions in Zambia. This suggests a high level of tolerance coming from an evangelical politician who supports the Christian nation concept and at the same time respects the contribution of non-Christian religions. If Mumba has been interpreted correctly, it seems that he can happily accept and operate within a pluralistic democracy. Mumba's major reason for starting his own party is his frustration with the leadership of the present government.

Mumba went to the polls in 1996 but did not win a seat in parliament. His argument was that he had only just formed the party earlier in 1996 and did not have the resources or time to campaign. At the grassroots level, the pentecostals and charismatics did not give him the support that he had anticipated because they felt disappointed that he used a Christian ticket to get into politics. He had thought that his large support as an evangelist would translate into political support. But other Christians felt betrayed by Mumba because in his sermons he used to say that he was called to be a prophet and that this calling was higher even than that of president. His church members were confused when he then declared himself a founder of a political party and a presidential candidate. Some Christians asked why he was downgrading himself from the high calling of an international evangelist to seek to be a state president. In the process, Mumba seems to have lost many church followers.

Mumba's combination of politics and evangelism was visible at the 1997 "Victory" convention held in Namibia in August 1997. The main message of this meeting was that God calls some people to full-time political leadership while he calls others to full-time church leadership. Mumba in particular encouraged Christians to take up political leadership positions if that is what God is calling them to do. His change in emphasis did not seem to alienate the other evangelical leaders at the convention, who included Mensa Otabil from Ghana; Enoch Sitima, a Malawian based in Botswana; David Newburry of the United States; Ezekiel Guti of Zimbabwe; and Mushoe, the leader of the Christian Democratic Party in South Africa. The "Faith Gospel" was combined with politics. (Despite being warned by his American friends not to invite Mensa Otabil to his conventions because of his radical gospel on racial and other issues [Gifford 1998], Mumba showed that he had an independent mind and invited him.)

With at least the tacit support of some evangelical leaders, Mumba prepared to compete in the 2001 presidential elections. Forty political parties registered to contest the presidential elections. However, the major political parties that posed a challenge to Chiluba's MMD were only three: the UNIP, which is also going through leadership crisis after the resignation of Kaunda as its leader and the death of his son Wezi Kaunda in November 1999; The United Party for National Development (UPND); and the Zambia Alliance for Progress (ZAP), which consists of six parties, one of which is Nevers Mumba's NCC. Mumba hoped to become the presidential candidate for the ZAP. Regardless, he helped make it fashionable for political party leaders to declare themselves to be Christians in order to seek the votes of the Christian community. In addition, Mumba tried to make the advancement of Chiluba's Christian nation idea a "draw card" to attract the support of the masses.

Evangelical Women in a Christian Nation

Interestingly, with the declaration of Zambia as a Christian nation, evangelical women seized the opportunity to voice their views on politics. The politics of the Pan African Christian Women Alliance offers a striking example.

In September 1987, toward the end of Kaunda's era, the general assembly of the Association of Evangelicals of Africa and Madagascar was held in Lusaka. The women delegates to this assembly agreed to establish a continental Pan African Christian Women Alliance (PACWA). The actual launching of PACWA took place in Nairobi, Kenya, in 1989, under the leadership of Judy Mbugua from Kenya. At the first meeting, it was agreed that every African nation should have a national PACWA. The aims of PACWA were

- To stop the tide of ungodly liberalism and secularism with its resultant materialism.
- To assert the true dignity of women as found in Jesus Christ and contained in the Bible.
- To inject into African society biblical morals and values through women, who are the mothers of any society.
- To deliver Africa from decadence and ultimate collapse.
- To make disciples of African Nations for Christ in the Continent of Africa. (PACWA covenant, Commission of the Association of Evangelicals of Africa and Madagascar on Women Affairs, 1990, 2)

The theme of this conference was "Our Time Has Come," implying that the time had come for Christian women with an evangelical character to make a definite contribution in the affairs of the African continent both in the church and society. Their areas of concern included: women in the image of God; Christian character formation; Christian home and family; women's ministries; evangelisation and discipleship; social justice and economic development; and what they called "ungodly practices." With respect to social justice and economic development, the PACWA covenant declared:

> We are appalled therefore that in many African nations women are discriminated against in matters of social justice; barred from highest levels of leadership both in church and society; and often denied access to economic sources of production. In all matters of social justice and economic development, we strongly advocate equal treatment of men and women. (in Mbugua 1994, 147)

As a challenge to the missionary definition of the roles of women, one of PACWA's resolutions stated that, "whereas in the past the tendency of society has been to limit women to the roles of wife and mother, we recommend a change in approach which will give women equal opportunities to develop their educational abilities and talents to the maximum" (Mbugua 1994, 9).

At the same assembly, Christian women were challenged to get involved in politics. In the paper presented by Ruth Yaneko Romba, entitled "Women and Society," she argued that "today Christian women should not hesitate to take up positions at social, economic and political levels, to such an extent, that they can fulfill their commitment to serve and not to be served" (Mbugua 1994, 108). This was a radical statement coming from women who were brought up with the notion that church and political leadership belong to men only.

In February 1993, PACWA organized a consultation on Christian Women and Politics. Fifty leading women politicians from fifteen African countries, including ministers of governments, ambassadors, and mayors, attended the consultation (Mbugua 1997, 9). All Christian women were challenged to get involved in politics to promote honesty in the practice of true democracy.

In Zambia, PACWA leadership has been associated with Eva Sanderson (née Namulwanda), from the Copperbelt. Charged with developing PACWA's message for the Zambian context, she was involved in campaigning for Chiluba in the 1991 elections. She also became the first woman mayor of Kitwe. One of Sanderson's major roles has also been to educate the community about HIV/AIDS. She has mobilized resource persons to go into schools, communities, and churches to teach about the epidemic, which has exacted a massive human cost in Zambia. She has also initiated projects advancing the basic education of women at the grassroots level.

The contribution of Inonge Mbikusita-Lewanika from the Zambian PACWA has also been important. She became involved in politics in 1991 when she joined the campaign for political change from a one-party government to a multiparty government as a member of the MMD. Concern about poverty motivated her to go into politics. She says: "As a Christian, too, I saw my Christian response to the suffering in fulfilment of the Scripture that says 'give sight to the blind, release the captive, mend the broken hearts, and proclaim freedom to the people' " (Mbikusita-Lewanika 1998, 150). Mbikusita-Lewanika was elected to parliament in 1991.

However, she was one of eleven members of parliament who became highly critical of the MMD government and who opposed the state of emergency in 1992. Her argument was that a state of emergency was as bad under Chiluba as under Kaunda. "In addition we were opposed to a lot of things that were going on: corruption, nepotism, treachery, dictatorial tendencies and insensitivity to the suffering of the people" (Mbikusita-Lewanika 1998, 151).

In 1993 she resigned from the MMD, together with ten other MMD members of parliament. They formed a new party called the National Party, and she was elected to be its first interim chairperson. Thus she became the first Zambian woman to be head of a political party. When the MMD declared the eleven MP seats vacant and called for by-elections, she won back her seat as MP of the National Party. However, when the convention of the National Party met in May 1994 to elect its leaders, she lost the chair of the party. In fact, the new party itself developed undemocratic tendencies that made it difficult for her to continue as a member. As the 1996 national presidential and parliament elections were approaching, both men and women who wanted her to stand as a national presidential candidate approached her. "I realized that people were attracted by my experiences and qualifications; my insistence on integrity, honesty and hard work; my emphasis on spiritual development, my character and personality" (Mbikusita-Lewanika 1998, 153). However, she was sufficiently concerned about the direction of the National Party that she turned down their request.

In 1996 she campaigned as a candidate for the Mongu constituency as a member of a new party called Agenda for Zambia, instead of the Senanga constituency as a member of the National Party. She enjoyed strong rural support and won the election. She claimed: "I won the seat without bribing a single person. I am living proof that elections can be won, and not bought. My victory also strengthened my faith in rural people. They displayed great courage and were not moved by threats, intimidation or gifts" (Mbikusita-Lewanika 1998, 154).

Nevertheless, she admits that being in opposition has its own challenges. The greatest challenges that she faces include the ruling government withholding financial support for projects that are in the opposition constituencies; the people who voted for her expecting her to provide them with social services that only the government can; the donors being reluctant to finance projects run by the opposition because they are already funding the government; and withdrawal of support from Christians who are stubbornly loyal to the ruling party. She says when she joined politics she had the support of most members of the Church of God. However, the attitude of some Christians quickly changed.

> After resigning from the MMD I encountered hostility among some of my fellow Christians. Some Christians have stopped talking to me. They feel that MMD is a God-given Christian organisation, and anyone opposed to its style of government is in the devil's camp.... I resigned from the MMD because my conscience would not allow me to close my eyes to corruption, nepotism and lack of commitment around me.... I am not afraid to stand alone as long as I am still convinced that I am doing God's will.

In the paper that she presented at the 1993 PACWA meeting, entitled "The Role of Christian Women in Multiparty Politics," she said that joining politics was a response to a call from God. As an evangelical in particular, she seeks to ensure that her political service testifies to God by virtue of its purity and integrity.

> Christian women in politics should not lose themselves but hold on to the Lord. They have to be persistent and consistent. Their "yes" should be "yes" and their "no" should be "no" always. Christian women politicians should be people of their word. Their thoughts, words, and actions should testify to the goodness of the Lord. Christian women politicians should embody pure good thoughts, which lead into positive action. (Mbikusita-Lewanika 1997, 23)

Once in politics, the spirit of caring that animates Christian women should motivate them to steer government's policies toward social and economic justice.

> Christian women are a rare spice that has been missing for a very long time in politics. At last the time has come. With more Christian women in politics, we are more likely to see relevant human betterment issues being raised and addressed. More useful policies to the majority of the people will be formulated. The poor, marginalized, weak youth and young children will move up the priority list to the top of the agenda. May God bless us with Christian women in politics and in government so that defense budgets can come down as the budgets for people's basic services move up. (Mbikusita-Lewanika 1997, 23)

At the time, Zambian newspapers (such as *The Post*) echoed the views of Inonge Mbikusita-Lewanika and other Zambian women that Chiluba's government was not gender sensitive.

TABLE 3.1. Representation in Parliament and High Political Office by Gender, 1988 and 1992

Gender	Members of Parliament	Cabinet Members	Deputy Cabinet Members	Permanent Secretaries
January 1988				
Women	5	2	0	3
Men	120	19	0	31
Total	**125**	**21**	**0**	**34**
January 1992				
Women	6	0	3	5
Men	144	25	31	30
Total	**150**	**25**	**34**	**35**

Constraints on the Participation of Women in Politics

In fact, there was a strong outcry among women in Zambia that Chiluba was not gender sensitive, and some women wondered whether this was related to his Christian nation declaration. Table 3.1, from Bornwell Chikulo (1996, 47), shows that there has not been much change in the inclusion of women in leadership positions in President Chiluba's government.

It is worth noting that no woman was appointed to the first MMD 1991 cabinet. The National Women's Lobby Group also compiled data to highlight gender inequalities in Zambian politics. Table 3.2 shows the composition of cabinet ministers and members of parliament by gender (1995–1998). The small number of women in parliament certainly suggests that the voice of women in Zambian politics remains weak. Princess Nakatindi Wina is quoted as saying, "Watching the political scenario from childhood to date, I can safely conclude that women's participation in politics is basically forcing matters. Men do not want to accept women within the political mainstream" (in Nalumango and Sifuniso 1998).

TABLE 3.2. Representation in Parliament and High Political Office by Gender, 1995 to 1998

Decision-Making Positions	1995			1996			1997			1998		
	M	F	Total	M	F	Total	M	F	Total	M	F	Total
Cabinet Ministers	20	2	22	20	2	22	23	1	24	22	2	24
Deputy Ministers	37	1	38	42	1	43	37	4	41	38	2	40
Members of Parliament	149	6	155	149	6	155	140	15	155	142	16	158

In order to force common strategies to strengthen the political voice of Zambian women, all the women members of parliament are also members of the women's caucus, which is under the leadership of Dr. Inonge Mbikusita-Lewanika. The aim of the group is to encourage unity among women politicians on policies that affect women and children.

In response, the MMD government refused to institute any affirmative action for women. In August 2000, on the International Day of Women, President Chiluba declared that in Zambia women will not be given special favors and they must compete in politics just like anyone else. However, Zambian women protest that the competition in politics between men and women cannot be equal because the ground has never been level. Politics in Zambia, like the rest of the world, has favored men. The National Women's Lobby Group is particularly concerned with the way President Chiluba used his presidential prerogative to appoint eight members of parliament. While in office, he failed to use his presidential prerogative to appoint even a single woman to parliament. However, the National Women's Lobby Group believes that this failure is not rooted in Chiluba's evangelical Christian beliefs but in his patriarchal upbringing, which has made him unable to see politics as a woman's place.

At the same time, I would argue that neither evangelical Christian teachings nor African culture have actively promoted women's involvement in leadership positions in church and society. In particular, the proclamation of Zambia as a Christian nation has had ambiguous effects. It has allowed evangelical women to claim that unless they take part in politics as Christians it will not be possible to make Zambia a truly moral and Christian nation. However, Zambian male evangelicals have not abandoned their assumptions about the need for male "headship." And Chiluba has arguably failed to put into practice his own principles of liberal democracy and equality as far as women's involvement in politics is concerned.

The National Women's Lobby Group has embarked on a program to campaign for any woman who wants to stand for political elections. It helps women candidates develop self-confidence and present themselves effectively in public. The group also works with selection committees of each political party to persuade them to nominate women candidates to stand for constituency elections. Finally, it provides civic education to the general public so that the Zambian people as a whole accept the leadership of women.

For example, the National Women's Lobby Group campaigned for Gwendoline Chomba Konie, who is the president of a new party, the Social Democratic Party (SDP), which was launched at the Pamodzi Hotel on September 28, 2000. Konie is best known as a pioneer Zambian woman legislator who became a member of the Legislative Council in 1962 when the country was still Northern Rhodesia. When Zambia become independent in 1964, she wanted to campaign for a seat in parliament but was advised against it by Kaunda, who preferred that she should go into the Foreign Service. Since the period of Kaunda up to 1996, she worked at the ambassadorial level, achieving the posts of ambassador to the UN and ambassador to Germany. Of special interest to this essay is the Christian commitment that has motivated Konie's political service. She served as the president of the Lusaka Young Women Christian Association for two terms. Then she also served as president of the Zambia Young Christian Women Association for two terms. She served in various capacities at the Christian Council of Zambia. She was a member of the Board of Governors of the Mindolo Ecumenical Foundation in Zambia. At an international level, she served as commissioner on the Commission of Churches in International Affairs (CCIA) of the World Council of Churches. She was also a commissioner on the Commission of International Affairs of the All Africa Conference of Churches. Konie is well known in local and international church and community circles. However, both Konie's SDP and Mbikusita-Lewanika's Agenda for Zambia failed to win enough votes in the 2001 elections even to get parliamentary representation (Selolwane 2006, 19).

PACWA and HIV/AIDS

Another major contribution of PACWA in Zambia has been its active fight against the HIV/AIDS pandemic. PACWA in Zambia is now housed in the EFZ under the women's commission. The HIV/AIDS pandemic was declared a national disaster at the XI International Conference on AIDS and Sexually Transmitted Infections in Africa (ICASA) held in September 1999. The church has been working toward the prevention of further infection and for the promotion of home-based care for patients and care for orphans. In 2000 it was believed that 20 percent of the Zambian population is infected with the HIV virus and that there are three hundred new infections every day. Life expectancy was reduced to forty-five. The number of orphans increased to half a million by 2000. In that same period, the World Bank reported that 80 percent of Zambia's population is living below poverty levels of less than $1 (U.S.) per day. The AIDS situation is considerably worsened by the high level of poverty and high unemployment. Chiluba and many Zambians identified the imposition of structural adjustment programs (SAPs) by the World Bank and the IMF as the cause of the economic suffering of the people (*The Post*, February 9, 2000). However, the IMF representative in Lusaka argued that

> the standing arrangement between Zambia and the IMF, like all other countries, is voluntary and not imposed on the government. It is voluntary and if an individual government is not happy with the programme, why should they make the commitment that they will pursue it? (Kenneth Meyer, *The Post*, February 10, 2000)

Nevertheless, Benjamin K. Acquah has echoed the sentiments of Chiluba in his evaluation of the SAPs. He states that

implementation of SAPs in many African countries has caused political difficulties, social problems and economic stress. These have
come to be appreciated by the proponents of SAPs. According to FAO
[the Food and Agriculture Organization of the United Nations], it is
now recognised that SAPs have had negative impact on the 'chroni-
cally poor' and created a 'new' power sector. (Kinoti and Kimuyu
1997, 54)

On the issue of poverty, the churches in Zambia were remarkably unified
in their condemnation of Chiluba's government. An example is the case of the
Roman Catholic Church's Association of Sisterhood who highlighted the issue
of poverty in December of 1999. The police prevented the association's planned demonstration against the government on issues regarding health, education, and prevailing poverty levels. This led to a further souring of the relationship between the church and the government at the beginning of 2000.
The mother bodies of the major churches united to condemn the action of
the government toward the Roman Catholic sisters. (For the response of the
Evangelical Fellowship of Zambia, see *The Post*, February 11, 2000.)

With respect to HIV/AIDS, the high levels of poverty in Zambia have
meant that extended families are not able to care for the orphans resulting from
the HIV/AIDS epidemic. Children are often moved from one relative to another as parents and other family members die of AIDS. The Roman Catholic
Church in Zambia is the leader in the provision of orphanages. However, the
demand for orphanages is well beyond the capacity of the Catholic Church.

Given the overwhelming need, the PACWA office of the EFZ embarked
on a number of projects to educate the most affected communities and train
church-based women volunteers in orphan care support. In 1997, PACWA
organized conferences, seminars and workshops with the intention of training
and equipping women leaders to deal with the complexities of AIDS; challenging the women participants to go back to their communities to train other
women and equip them to reach out to widows and orphans. The goal of
PACWA was to identify and recruit ninety volunteers from the churches for the
purpose of establishing community-based orphan care programmes.

The Christian Council of Zambia also asked its nineteen member denominations and its fourteen associate members to start programs for the care
of orphans in their communities. At the same time, the churches accused
Chiluba's government of not doing enough to show that it takes the issue of the
HIV/AIDS pandemic seriously.

Zambian Fellowship of Evangelical Students (ZAFES) and Politics

Nonevangelical university students played an important role in the challenge
to the Zambian one-party state. Owen B. Sichone, a student activist in the

Kaunda period, writes that "university student politics provided a training ground for many of Zambia's younger politicians. The democratic movement had been growing during the years of one-party rule in various social groups but university students were especially active" (1999, 152).

From 1976 there were confrontations between the University of Zambia Students' Union (UNZASU) and the government of Kenneth Kaunda. According to Sichone,

> the University of Zambia enjoyed the unique position of being a sort of "one-party state within a one-party state" where criticism of the government was the norm and participation in republican rituals seriously discouraged. Even the singing of the national anthem, one of the symbols of independence was more or less banned on campus. Although student activists were always a minority, we managed to give the student body a left-wing radicalism which other students supported and which even the government respected. (1999, 155)

Chiluba agrees with Sichone's assessment of university students' power in the transformation of Zambia from a one-party to multiparty politics. He says "the students certainly made a useful contribution to the momentum for democratisation, by sparking off more widespread public demands for reform, even though they were not normally natural allies of the business community, which was to provide another and very important focus of opposition to the one-party state" (Chiluba 1995, 65).

During the same period, however, Christian university students were quiet about politics. Among evangelical students, a theology of separation between one's faith and political involvement was the norm. But this began to change in the period after Chiluba's Christian nation declaration. The current General Secretary of Zambian Fellowship of Evangelical Students (ZAFES), Kuzipa Nalwamba, makes the following observation:

> In the last few years we have had a number of our members participating in student politics, which was not the case in the 1980s. Most of us [as] students shunned student politics. Only a minority were involved. We now have cases whereby a good number of leaders in student politics are drawn from our fellowship. The chairperson of ZAFES National Executive of last year was also a chairman of his student union of his college. (interview, December 2000)

The teaching of the International Fellowship of Evangelical Students (IFES) has also changed on the issue of Christian involvement in politics. At the IFES Africa regional staff conference held in Mozambique in 1993, the discussion centered on how to prepare Christian university students to take Christ into the society where they will be working. The following year, at an IFES meeting held in Kampala, Uganda, topics for further study were assigned to the various national student fellowships, and the topic assigned to the ZAFES was "A Christian in Politics." ZAFES was given this task because Zambia had already been declared a Christian nation by Chiluba. In 1997 IFES published a Bible study book, *The Christian in Politics*. In the introduction to the book, evangelical lawyer Charles Owor outlines his belief that God called him to politics in his home country of Uganda. The major thrust of his contribution is a presentation of why and how a Christian should get involved in politics. This introduction is followed by seven Bible studies that examine why a Christian should get involved in politics and provide biblical examples of people who were called by God for political transformation. It is aimed at helping students to see that being called by God is not limited to full time Christian work. God also calls people to secular works, including nation building and political reform. Interestingly, the book is used in Zambia every year during leadership training of the National Executive Committee of ZAFES. It is presented as an example of how evangelical leaders should integrate their faith and work. Some leaders have used the book in their weekly Bible studies on university campuses. The students have found this Bible study to be effective in changing their thinking about what is secular and what is holy. In effect, their evangelical faith is being brought into line with an African worldview that looks at life holistically.

ZAFES feels proud that there are some Zambian politicians who are former members of ZAFES. One who stands out, and who has maintained links with ZAFES, is Ernest Mwase, who served as Deputy Minister of Health under Chiluba. On the whole, however, ZAFES members feel less pride than anger on account of their belief that Chiluba's government has not given education its rightful place. The university has suffered frequent closures, which in turn undermines the university's credibility as an educational institution. The general feeling is that there has not been a strong political will to work with the university to find constructive solutions. In particular, ZAFES members mention the brain-drain issue, a problem that has not only been ignored by Chiluba's government but has also been exacerbated by it insofar as it continues to provide money to send young people overseas to study.

Evangelical Zambian youth, like evangelical Zambian women, have developed a holistic theology of political participation during the period of the "Christian nation," and have prepared themselves to serve. But, like the women, their potential has been neglected.

The 2001 Presidential Elections

The Zambian constitution, which came into effect in 1996, adopted a two-term limit for the president. In his book *Democracy: The Challenge of Change*, Chiluba himself praised his party, the MMD, for limiting the presidential office to two five-year terms. Chiluba also emphasized the MMD's demand that anyone participating in presidential elections must observe the two-term limitation and that a referendum must be held before any major amendments are made to the constitution (May 7, 2001).

On a number of occasions when Chiluba was with international dignitaries, he promised that he was going to allow democracy to run its course by ending his political life at the end of his second term in office. Furthermore, Chiluba said the same to the Zambian nation on January 15, 2000:

> When I was defending my thesis at Warwick University, one question I received was, "What makes you think you will be different from other leaders, you are African and you want power, and especially at your age, don't you think you will continue?" I said No! It is not only Africans who want to stay on … we must never be sorry to go, because if we are happy to come in, we must be equally happy when we are going out. (*The East African*, May 7, 2001)

However, as the presidential elections drew closer, Chiluba changed his position. He submitted to pressure from some people within the MMD to seek reelection in the 2001 elections. Their argument was that the current constitution of the government only became valid in 1996. Therefore, according to this constitution, he had completed only one term in office. However, according to the MMD party constitution, he had completed his two terms of office as head of the party. Thus Chiluba's bid to return to the presidency in 2001 required a change of the party constitution as well as a possible change in Zambia's constitution to accommodate a third term in office.

Chiluba therefore initiated a debate instead of a referendum on the third term issue. He argued that he initiated the debate simply to gauge the mood of the country. He organized a group of people to campaign for him to stay in power for a third term, and he went further by arranging a special MMD party conference in Kabwe on April 27, 2001, where he proposed a change in the party constitution to allow him to run for a third term. The party constitution was changed, and he was reelected as the party's president. A group of pentecostal and charismatic pastors went to offer him their support for a third term.

The change of the party constitution was not without strong opposition. On 10 April 2001, at a prayer meeting held at the Cathedral of the Holy Cross, the three main church bodies, some nongovernmental organizations (NGOs), and representatives of political parties initiated a declaration to oppose the change of the constitution. Fifty-nine members of parliament, of whom forty-three were members of the MMD party, signed the declaration. The Minister of Education, Brigadier Godfrey Miyanda, and Vice President Christon Tembo were some of the signatories (*The Post*, April 12, 2001). The opposition was extended to college and university students who staged massive demonstrations across the country. Eight international donor countries also pressed Chiluba not to proceed with the third-term bid.

Chiluba reacted undemocratically by expelling twenty-two senior members of the MMD party who opposed him, including Miyanda. Soon after that Chiluba dissolved his entire cabinet, and a new team of ministers loyal to him was appointed. He instructed the police to prevent the expelled MPs from holding public meetings. This was extended to any and all anti-third-term campaigners. In fact any group of people that was thought to constitute a political gathering was dispersed by the use of tear gas. This was true even when Vera, the estranged wife of Chiluba, was going to hold a meeting in Kitwe for her Hope Foundation (*The Post*, June 11, 2001). Chiluba also accused the churches of being partisan and therefore promoting hatred and division among the people (*Pan African News Agency*, May 10, 2001). This allegation was challenged by some church leaders, including evangelical Pastor Nevers Mumba, who accused the state of manipulating the churches, for the president did not condemn the partisanship of the pastors who supported his third-term bid.

The expelled ministers and MPs initiated a petition to impeach Chiluba on seven counts of violating the constitution. The motion to impeach the president was brought to parliament on May 3, 2001, by Ackson Sejani and Mike Mulongoti. The motion was supported by more than half of Zambia's 158 members of Parliament. According to the Law Association of Zambia, the National Assembly speaker, Amusaa Mwanamwamba, should have convened the National Assembly within twenty-one days of receiving the motion. However he decided to wait for a court ruling to end the dispute (UN Integrated Regional Information Network, May 2001).

In addition, in the High Court an injunction was initiated by the expelled ministers and MPs to stop their expulsion from the MMD party because there was already a court injunction prohibiting the party from taking any disciplinary action against them. They also went further to ask for an injunction to deny Chiluba unrestricted use of party machinery. The lawyers of the MMD party applied to the High Court to overturn the injunctions so that the parliamentary seats of the expelled MMD party members could be declared vacant. At the beginning of May the High Court rejected the MMD party attempt to remove the court injunction that prohibited the expulsion, which meant that the expelled MMD MPs were still members of the party. And on May 4, Chiluba bowed to pressure from civil society and the international Western donor nations. He announced, "I will leave office at the end of my term. Let's take national interests into consideration. This is in the best interest of the nation."

President Chiluba's announcement was not assumed to be his last word, for he had come to be seen as a person who violates his word. It was expected in fact that he would still come back to fight for a third term (*The Post*, May 9, 2001). Confirming this expectation was the fact that the MMD delayed nominating its presidential candidate. The opposition noted with caution that the MMD current vice president, Enoch Kavindele, was not being chosen as the automatic MMD republican presidential candidate. The suspicion was heightened when the MMD party spokesperson, Venon Mwaanga, announced on May 31 that the party had launched a search for presidential candidate. The fact that Chiluba had remained the president of the MMD meant that he still had time to change his mind again and run for the presidential elections.

In the end, however, Chiluba stuck to his decision and did not contest the elections. Despite this, his leadership of Zambia as a "Christian nation" ended with his dual reputation as a Christian and a democrat in ruins. Chiluba's change of heart, after all, was compelled and more than anything was a powerful sign that civil society in Zambia is strong and can overrule even the president. Such a sign of civic health was not evident in the case of Namibia when President Sam Nujoma changed the constitution and ran for a third term in November 1998. (At the time of this writing, Nujoma was already testing the waters to change the constitution again so that he can run for a fourth term. President Muluzi of Malawi was also testing the waters by encouraging his supporters to initiate a third-term bid, but opposition from the churches was very strong.) South African President Mbeki, among others, commended Chiluba for resisting a third term because the image of African leaders, who are already seen as bent on lifetime presidencies, would otherwise have been further damaged (U.N. Integrated Regional Information Network, May 2001). Zambian civil society's successful opposition to Chiluba's "third-termism" will be of great importance to politics throughout Southern Africa.

Conclusion

Zambians like to believe that they are the champions of multiparty democracy in Africa, since Zambia was the first English-speaking African country to undergo a smooth transition to multiparty politics. However, the principles of liberal democracy as understood by Zambia's first democratically elected president, Frederick Chiluba, were in fact not applied when he declared the country a "Christian nation" in 1991. His faith convictions could not by themselves serve as an adequate guide to running a country democratically because the source of authority in democratic politics is different from the source of authority in evangelical faith. Democracy gives power to the people, while Chiluba's evangelical theology views God as the only source of power and authority. From a democratic point of view, the idea of a Christian nation—while it may have been good for the growth of the church—was imposed on the people without their consent. Similarly, the Christian nation declaration was added to the preamble of the 1996 constitution in a nondemocratic fashion.

Nevertheless, the idea of a Christian nation will shape Zambian politics for years to come. For example, a burning issue will continue to be *how* a president should govern a Christian nation that is also democratic. Furthermore, by making this issue so salient, and with it the larger issue of the relationship between evangelical faith and Zambian democracy, one can argue that Chiluba's presidency has managed to make the country's evangelical Christians much more interested in politics. Many evangelical Christians voted in the 2001 elections and will vote in future elections because they seek a Christian leader who will help them emerge from poverty and improve the quality of life for the average Zambian. Chiluba has thus managed to make politics a live issue for evangelicals. Consequently, Zambia has witnessed a definite shift among evangelicals, from an apolitical position to a position of intense involvement. Secular and church newspapers now abound with argument and commentary on what it means or does not mean to be a Christian nation.

Dictatorship and corruption are enemies of democracy, and they are much of the reason for the economic and social crisis of sub-Saharan Africa. Chiluba's presidency saw many dictatorial tendencies, perhaps the most obvious being the change of the national constitution to bar Kaunda, the president of UNIP, from competing in the 1996 elections. The Organisation of African Unity (OAU) found Zambia guilty of violating the provisions of the African Charter for Human and People's Rights following this 1996 constitutional amendment (*The Post*, June 12, 2001). In addition, Chiluba denied Zambians the right to hold dissenting views concerning his proposed third term. Student leaders, who were in the forefront of the opposition, were detained. Churches were accused of "contaminating the atmosphere with hate, bitterness and vice." The international community was accused of fuelling the spirit of uncooperativeness among Zambians. The opposition parties were not given permits to hold meetings.

Chiluba's ten-year presidency failed to improve Zambia's economic situation, even though prosperity was one blessing that evangelicals believed would follow the declaration of Zambia as a Christian nation. In addition, as a Christian leader, Chiluba failed to stamp out corruption among his fellow leaders. Even as the structural adjustment programs helped worsen the economic conditions of 80 percent of Zambians, Chiluba did not stop the corruption that helped drain public funds and enrich a tiny minority. For example, Chingola Baptist Pastor Choolwe strongly argued that much of Zambia's poverty in fact stems from corruption. The Roman Catholic sisters echoed this argument when they demonstrated in January 2000.

During the Kaunda period, the churches were united against so-called scientific socialism as government policy. Toward the end of Kaunda's rule, the churches united to support the opposition and help usher in a multiparty democracy. In the ten years of Chiluba's rule, the role of the churches in relation to the state has expanded. The churches, representing the poor and the marginalized, have been increasingly outspoken in public. This is especially true of the Roman Catholic Church of Zambia. The formation of the NCC by Nevers Mumba and of other parties by other evangelical Christians should also be considered a protest against bad governance and is a strong sign of the vibrancy of Zambian democracy and civil society.

At the same time, the evangelical church has been divided in its political stand. Some have decided to be silent in the midst of corruption because of the belief that the president is "a brother in the Lord" and chosen by God to be the leader of Zambia. A letter by Alex Mulume of Livingstone, published in *The Post* on January 4, 2000, illustrates the point:

> Even Israel, which was declared God's chosen people by God Himself, did not live up to the name of the chosen nation. They also had crime like we have. They had all sorts of vice like we do. That is why the book of Deuteronomy was written. In case you did not know, they even rejected the Son of God. Yes the one man of God, Frederick, on behalf of us all who are willing and proud to be citizens of a "Christian Nation," made the declaration.... May I remind you that when Moses went up Mt. Sinai to receive the Ten Commandments, did they not worship the golden calf? Did they not forget their God? Did Israel cease to be called God's chosen people as a result of sin?

Recently, however, evangelical Christians have spoken with one voice in condemnation of Chiluba's separation from his wife, and an overwhelming majority opposed his quest for a third term in office.

In addition, the marginalization of women during Chiluba's presidency is difficult to justify. A few brave evangelical Christian women have stood out, the most prominent being Dr. Inonge Mbikusita-Lewanika. If democracy means equality of gender, one wonders why Chiluba made no effort to increase the participation of women in the Parliament through a quota system or at least through presidential prerogative powers that give him the right to appoint eight members of parliament. Some women believe that when a country is at peace with its neighbors, women have a greater chance to participate in politics. Zambia has not been subjected to war with its neighbors or to civil war, even though it has received refugees from Angola, Congo, Burundi, and Rwanda. Yet ten years of Christian nationhood, democracy, and peace have not changed the patriarchal nature of politics. Worse still, even though civil society in Zambia lobbied hard for Inonge Mbikusita-Lewanika—a powerful evangelical leader, in addition to being a woman—to become the secretary general of the OAU, Chiluba has refused to endorse the nomination (*The Post*, June 14, 2001).

The churchwomen of PACWA have made HIV/AIDS a high priority. With 80 percent of all hospital beds occupied by AIDS patients, the epidemic is having a devastating effect on the country's population and on government health services. Though Chiluba's evangelical faith raised the expectation that the plight of the masses would become a major concern to the government, this devastating problem was not a political priority under Chiluba.

University students continued to be an active force in civil society during Chiluba's presidency. The declaration of Zambia as a Christian nation motivated evangelical university students to participate in politics both at the campus and the national level, while some of Zambia's political leaders emerged from the Christian student movement.

The presidency of Frederick Chiluba is thus a compelling case study of the interaction of evangelical faith and democratic governance and how this interaction has influenced the relationship between evangelicals and democracy in Zambia as a whole. In sum, what does Zambia's recent history show about the relationship between evangelicalism and democracy?

Some Western experience and thinking suggest that Christianity and democracy are highly compatible. European countries, like Germany and Britain, have shown that a country can be officially "Christian" and democratic. And it was a Western evangelical publication presumably friendly to democracy that observed that "the Chiluba government began well in freeing up the economy and outlawing abortion, pornography and prostitution" (Johnstone 2001, 685). It might be argued that the Chiluba government also created an atmosphere that encouraged the dramatic growth of evangelical Christianity. However, its failure to maintain democratic freedoms and improve the status of the majority of the people fell far short of the promises and ideals implied in Chiluba's Christian nation declaration. At the same time, the problems facing Zambia during the Chiluba period are common throughout the region, in both "Christian" and "non-Christian" nations. In spite of Chiluba, and in some ways because of him, Zambian evangelicals over the last ten years seem to have developed a definite view that evangelicalism is compatible with democracy, as well as a significantly heightened political activism. Most hope and pray for a Zambia that is both more evangelical and more democratic, with an evangelical president firmly at the helm.

Postscript

On December 27, 2001, Zambians went to the polls to elect a new president. Levy Mwanawasa, who is from the MMD and is also a Jehovah's Witness, won the elections amidst strong protest from the opposition parties that the results were rigged. Particularly important for this essay is that Chiluba handpicked Levy Mwanawasa to be the MMD presidential candidate. When he accepted, the Jehovah's Witnesses excommunicated Mwanawasa because they do not permit their members to participate in politics. Strikingly, Mwanawasa promised to uphold Zambia's status as a Christian nation, but he has also said that he will no longer make financial contributions to the churches, as Chiluba did.

The 2001 elections divided the church much more than previous ones because there were twelve presidential candidates, many with a Christian base. The evangelical Christian presidential candidates were Nevers Mumba, president of the National Citizen Coalition Party; Inonge Mbikusita-Lewanika, president of the Agenda for Zambia; Godfrey Miyanda, president of the Heritage Party; and Levy Mwanawasa, who was being promoted by Chiluba (*National Mirror*, January 26–February 1, 2002). The evangelical community asked Mumba and Miyanda to form a coalition and present one candidate, but they both refused because of differences in political views (Daniel Ngulube, interview, February 2002).

After the elections, churches in Zambia faced the difficult question of whether to accept Levy Mwanawasa as from God or not. Miyanda was among the three party leaders who petitioned the High Court to refuse to accept Mwanawasa as the new president of Zambia. The Independent Churches Association, which is evangelical, was pro-Chiluba and is now pro-Mwanawasa. The OASIS forum—which consists of the EFZ, EZC, CCZ, the Law Association of Zambia, and the Non-Governmental Organizations Coordinating Committee—joined with the opposition parties to reject the results of the presidential elections because of evidence of rigging. The CCZ followed with a pastoral letter to confirm their refusal to recognize the president. However, the EFZ issued a pastoral letter saying that while it believes that there were electoral inconsistencies, their belief in the authority of God and the Bible requires that they accept the results until and unless the High Court ruled otherwise. The full text of the letter is as follows:

EFZ PASTORAL LETTER ON THE PRESIDENCY (2002)
Fellow Zambian Citizens,
We as the EFZ would like to give an extended response to the question of the presidency. We have felt it necessary to respond at length in this pastoral letter, because we need to reflect on this issue in view of the biblical principles we stand for (and believe generally speaking most Zambians believe in) and our role as Church. We also address the issue within the context of the electoral process as we witnessed it in the months running up to the tripartite elections held on 27th December 2001. We as a fellowship would therefore like to reiterate that we are committed to:
   • Our role to be a prophetic voice in the nation to uphold righteousness, integrity, peace and justice in all matters, in accordance with the Word of God—siding with God's Word and rising above partisan politics in these matters.
   • Serve the Zambian people, to speak for the voiceless and to challenge structures and policies, which infringe on the freedoms and rights of Zambian people.

- Work in partnership with any legitimate government of the day in the cause of nation building and development for the welfare and dignity of the Zambian people.

In view of the question of the presidency, we are concerned that the 2001 polls were marred by serious flaws and irregularities. We note the following:

Pre-election

- Un-moderated presidential powers which led to use of national resources for [the] campaign for the ruling MMD presidential candidate.
- Unjust use of the public order act, which favoured the ruling party.
- The role of the Electoral Commission, which was not truly non-partisan because it was appointed by the executive and depended on the government for its function.
- Electoral monitoring (especially by Zambian NGOs) was impeded by the ECZ's (late) introduction of monitoring fees.
- There was fear of conflict and spurts of violence, and not enough public condemnation of the same by the ruling president and the (many) presidential candidates.
- There was confusion in the electorate because of lack of essential unity among parties in order to narrow down the number of candidates, which resulted in vote splitting, and a consequent minority-elected presidential winner (we appeal for constitutional review in regard to this question).

At Polling

- The extension of polling time was not uniformly done. Some polling stations extended voting time to the 28th morning while others closed at the end of the day on 27 December.
- Late opening of polling stations.
- Announcement of results while polling was still in progress in some stations.
- Inconsistencies in the counting (e.g., large numbers of spoilt ballots or the lack thereof in some stations).
- Examples of other irregularities noted by observers are as follows:

After Polls

- The ruling against the recount of presidential votes.
- Observation that [a] recount for parliamentary candidates was sanctioned in some constituencies.
- The constitutional fourteen-day period within which to contest results favours the declared winner who has access to government

machinery during the litigation process. (We urge review of [the] constitutional clause pertaining to this.)

Final Statement of the Presidency

We as EFZ acknowledge the following concerning the presidency:

a. The republican president, Mr Levy Mwanawasa, was sworn in on 2nd January 2002, according to the laws of Zambia.

b. The opposition has filed in a petition to challenge the results of the presidential (and parliamentary) polls.

c. Parliament convened to start the statutory process of governance. We as a Fellowship are therefore legally bound to acknowledge the presidency until the courts of law rule otherwise. In the matter of the impending ruling, we urge [the] independence of the Judiciary. We further appeal that there be a constitutional review to make the Judiciary (and other government wings) independent of the Executive.

"The Lord foils the plans of the nations; he thwarts the purposes of the peoples. But the plans of the LORD *stand firm forever, the purposes of his heart through all generations." Psalm 33:10–11 [NIV]*

The pastoral letter from the EFZ caused some divisions within that body because some of the members did not agree even with its tentative acceptance of Mwanawasa as president.

For one month, Nevers Mumba served as the spokesperson of the opposition parties but stopped doing so after a private meeting with Levy Mwanawasa (*The Post*, January 31, 2002). Thus, the battle over whether Mwanawasa was a valid president made it difficult for him to settle into the work of leading the country. It also brought conflict, even within the MMD, between the supporters of Chiluba (who felt they needed more prominent positions in government) and those of Mwanawasa (who felt that Chiluba should no longer be president of the party).

NOTES

1. Kenneth Kaunda was a son of a Presbyterian minister. During his presidency, Christianity played a significant role as he also claimed to have been a lay preacher of the African Methodist Episcopal Church before he became a politician.

2. The copper mines earned 80 percent of Zambia's foreign exchange. When the copper prices declined in the mid-1970s, the Zambian economy was hit very hard. The structural adjustment program was introduced in 1986. The people of Zambia responded to the SAP with riots, which made Kaunda very unpopular.

3. At the time of the interview, Melu was the director of World Vision International in Zambia. He was one of the members of the planning committee for the declaration ceremony.

4

Foundations for Democracy in Zimbabwean Evangelical Christianity

Isabel Mukonyora

Context and Aim

It is difficult to write about evangelical Christianity and democracy in Zimbabwe when much of what is happening in the country portends the continuing and dramatic decline of democracy. In the last several years Zimbabwe has been characterized by problems of growing authoritarianism, corruption, lack of freedom of expression, violence, a rapidly declining economy, and thousands of young people left unemployed. Investors from abroad and international aid agencies have long been advised by European and American governments to withdraw their resources because Zimbabwe has become too volatile for international trade and development (Rotberg 2000). Particularly disturbing for outsiders are regular reports of human rights violations, including threats to the lives and livelihood, and sometimes murder, of white commercial farmers and their black workers, who have been victims of the violent repossession of land by war veterans. The latter, working under the authorization of President Robert Mugabe, believe they are implementing the aims of the liberation war of the 1960s and 1970s, which was centered on regaining control of the land on behalf of the masses. The war itself ended with the installation of the Mugabe regime, which has remained in place for more than twenty-five years. As corruption continued to take its toll and the government faced ongoing criticisms from the Zimbabwean people for failing to relieve poverty, President Mugabe finally decided that the forcible takeover of white-owned farms should proceed in order to enhance his dwindling legitimacy.

Pleas for a more just and peaceful redistribution of land repeatedly voiced by opposition parties, a wide array of churches, and the former colonial master, Britain, have gone unheeded. According to Rotberg, President Mugabe has joined the list of authoritarian heads of state whose preoccupation with staying in power explains much of the current mayhem in Africa (Rotberg 2000).

Under these difficult circumstances, it is a challenge to describe how evangelicals—or anyone else—are contributing to democracy and democratization. It is particularly challenging to write about one select group of Christians in a country where Christianity is the dominant religion, with at least 80 percent of the population confessing many of the same basic theological ideas that evangelicals espouse (Barrett, Kurian, and Johnson 2001, 821). For example, the Catholic Justice and Peace Commission speaks for an estimated 3.5 million Zimbabwean Catholics when it challenges the state on a regular basis. Representing more than a third of Zimbabwe's nine million people, Zimbabwe's Catholic Church is arguably well ahead of any other Christian community in championing the causes of democracy, justice, peace, and economic prosperity. Indeed, it would be fair to say that the Catholic Church in general and the Catholic Commission in particular represent the most widely influential advocates of democracy that Zimbabwe has known since its independence in 1980.

When it comes to the Protestant segments of Zimbabwe's Christian community, it is important to note that evangelicals are not imprisoned within structures that bear the "evangelical" label. While there is an Evangelical Fellowship of Zimbabwe (EFZ), it does not tell us everything about the thinking of evangelicals and democracy. For example, the Zimbabwe Council of Churches (ZCC) contains many evangelicals in mainline denominations who work alongside nonevangelicals to promote political democracy and justice. The ZCC is a mixed pressure group in which one finds representatives of churches founded by Europeans from the evangelical traditions of Europe and America, such as the Lutheran, United and Zimbabwe (formerly called British) Methodists, the Reformed and Brethren in Christ (Weinrich 1982, 8), and also representatives of African Independent Churches who have passed the test for membership in matters of doctrine and structure (Turner 1978). I have visited many congregations whose leaders are part of the ZCC and who are evangelical because they are the fruit and the bearers of evangelical missionary teaching and emphases. They stress the authority of the scriptures in arriving at knowledge about God, salvation through Christ alone, personal conversion and prayer. However, they do not happen to use the term "evangelical" to describe their churches nor do they join the EFZ. This chapter includes a discussion of how such members of the ZCC have pressed for justice and democracy and pressured the government to stop using violence on the same grounds as groups of Christians from the Evangelical Fellowship of Zimbabwe.

To complicate matters further, I take up Freston's admonition that scholars of evangelicalism pay more serious attention to the African Independent Churches (Freston 2001, 110). Freston's challenge creates a special problem of definition. African Independent Churches, nowadays called African Initiated Churches (AICs), are treated with suspicion by some other Christians because they are believed to adapt Christianity to African culture in ways that transgress Christian orthodoxy (Daneel 1971). Because of worry that they depart from the norms of belief and practice inherited from European missionaries, many AICs are excluded from important ecumenical meetings, including those organized by the Zimbabwe Council of Churches. For example, despite Pobee and Ositelu's attempt to draw attention to the importance of AICs (Pobee and Ositelu 1998), the World Council of Churches held in Harare in December 1999 ruled (not for the first time) that many AICs failed to meet the doctrinal criteria for membership.[1] Groups such as the Masowe Apostles, which I examine below, were excluded. Notwithstanding the fact that most churches in Africa now adapt Christianity to local cultures in various ways and do so with minimal and sometimes no interference from European mother churches (Walls 1996, 111–118), and despite the much discussed shift of the main demographic base for Christianity from the north to the global south countries of Asia, Latin America, and Africa, the term "independent church" continues to be used to suggest that millions of Africans belong to churches that fail the standards of orthodoxy (Barrett 1968).

Independent churches are often called "sects" in order to draw attention to the suspicion that Christian truths are distorted, especially in cases where believers are semi-literate. Even more difficult for Western observers is the common fear that AICs allow for polygamy and therefore breach norms of monogamy derived from the New Testament. Despite or perhaps because of such perceptions and misperceptions, I am pleased to have this opportunity to highlight the increasingly popular independent church of the Masowe Apostles (Dillon-Malone 1978; Mukonyora 1998, 2000b/2001a). Ranger has characterized the Masowe as "radical" Christians influenced by American Methodism during a wave of Pentecostalism in Makoni District, the home area of the founder Shonhiwa Mtunyane (Ranger 1999). Although anyone familiar with nineteenth- and early twentieth-century American Methodism will know that evangelical ideas are foundational to whatever teaching the founder of the Masowe Apostles received, I proceed in the full knowledge that the inclusion of the Masowe Apostles in a discussion of Zimbabwean evangelical Christianity is bound to be controversial. In this essay I bring into the open some of the major differences between the Masowe Apostles and more "mainstream" evangelicals, but nevertheless insist on the inclusion of the former in any reasonably complete discussion of how evangelical Christianity has made an impact on politics and democracy in Zimbabwe.

I highlight as particularly relevant to the subject of this essay the extent to which Masowe Apostles function as "schools of democracy"—that is, vehicles for the education of otherwise voiceless Zimbabweans in the norms and practices of participatory politics. In short, I am in agreement with Freston in arguing that there are lessons to draw from AICs on the subject of evangelical Christianity and democracy. I have chosen the Masowe Apostles as my example because this is the AIC group with which I am most familiar (Mukonyora 1998a, 1998b, 2000b/2001a).

Because the chapter on Mozambique in this volume justifies the attention it pays to independent churches on similar grounds, I must clarify that the key question is not the normative theological issue of whether Masowe Apostles and other AICs are "heretical." It is about whether democracy in Zimbabwe is being strengthened or weakened by the ideas and institutions characteristic of the broad spectrum of churches with roots in the evangelical tradition. The material collected from key leaders of the evangelical community who represent "mainstream" evangelicalism in Zimbabwe certainly provides an important part of the story. But in my opinion an equally important part of the story comes from the Masowe Apostles, who help to widen the scope of this inquiry to include the millions of poor and often illiterate Christians who are a huge proportion of Zimbabwe's population.

In its various forms, Zimbabwean evangelicalism is experiencing rapid growth (Maxwell 2007). The use of the mass media by local television evangelists and gospel singers from evangelical churches partly explains the fast growth of this movement. According to Noah Pashapa, widely known in Zimbabwe for using radio to promote the idea that Zimbabwean society should draw its ideals on good living from the Bible, the number of evangelicals in Zimbabwe today exceeds one million and continues to grow (interview with author, May 15, 2000, Harare, University of Zimbabwe). That figure means that at least 10 percent of the population follows evangelical teaching (interview with author, May 25, 2000). Another evangelical claims that there are at least three million evangelical Christians in Zimbabwe, or 30 percent of the population (Roy Musasiwa, interview with author, September 2, 2000, Pietermaritzburg, South Africa). Pashapa and Musasiwa argue that evangelical ideas have made a strong impact on the nation, hence the importance of an inquiry of this kind, focusing on how evangelical beliefs contribute to politics. Particularly in a study of democracy, it is important to encompass as wide a spectrum of evangelicals as possible even if some members of the Evangelical Fellowship of Zimbabwe find such an inclusive study of their movement unsettling.

My aim, therefore, is not to restrict my study to evangelicals who belong to official groups and their leaders, but to reflect on the broad range of ideas and groups associated with evangelical faith and how they shape attitudes to politics and promote active participation in the quest for democracy. In view of the contribution of other Christians in the same grim political context of contemporary Zimbabwe, it has to be acknowledged from the start that the vast majority of all Christians agree that it would be better if Zimbabwe transformed itself into a peaceful nation where justice and peace prevail. The political role of the evangelical Christian in Zimbabwe should therefore not be overstated. Nevertheless, the Evangelical Fellowship of Zimbabwe and other religious communities influenced by evangelical teaching are a dynamic and increasingly consequential and mobilized segment of the country's civil society.

Definition

This essay begins with a discussion of the beliefs of what could be called "other-worldly Christians" or those individuals reluctant to reflect on the way their beliefs shape their politics and who reinforce the status quo, believing they are avoiding politics altogether. The idea that politics is "this-worldly" and therefore inappropriate for evangelical Christian involvement is so common that Paul Gifford argued that evangelical Christians cannot be said to function as anything approximating a "school of democracy" (Gifford 1988). Yet this essay presents examples of evangelical Christians who understand their role in society as the "salt of the earth" and therefore necessarily political. Others see themselves as prophets whose ministry is to challenge others, to honor God, and to promote love and justice without contradicting the terms of faith in the evangelical tradition. In other words, there are several different schools of biblically informed political thought among evangelical Christians. Even if one trend seems to stand in the way of enhancing democratic practice, other trends provide different avenues for strengthening democracy.

Evangelical Zimbabweans are different from other Zimbabwean Christians by several key characteristics. I carried out extensive interviews with church leaders who use the label "evangelical" to describe themselves, and I also circulated more than five hundred questionnaires among ordinary adherents of evangelical faith between January and June 2000. Based on this research, I concluded that evangelicals in Zimbabwe are distinguished from other Christians by their consistent attachment to all of the following beliefs:

a. God as the creator of the world, and humanity as created in the image of God, though now corrupted by sin;

b. Christ as the personal Savior of the converted believer, who must be able to testify about an encounter with him;

c. The Holy Spirit as an important sign of God's power in the world; and,

d. The Scriptures as the authoritative text in all matters of faith, including, in this case, providing answers to questions about politics.

Although these characteristics are derived from my research on Zimbabwean Christians, I note with interest that they are consistent with Freston's working definition of evangelical Christianity, which he developed from a global perspective as well as from the definition of David Bebbington and other scholars (Freston 2001).

From the interviews it is possible to identify three distinct patterns of thinking about the world that explain the way evangelical Christians address politics in Zimbabwe. One group confirms Gifford's thesis that there are evangelicals in Zimbabwe who hold to beliefs that impede political participation. They focus on the spiritual aspect of Christian living in a way that excludes the issues of how to live in an unjust society (Gifford 1988). Space does not permit me to revisit Gifford's evidence in detail, although many evangelical Christians dispute his main contention that rather than serving their own interests by avoiding politics, they actually further the political interests of American "right wing" groups (see, for example, the statement by the former director of World Vision, Gary Strong, below). The dominant characteristic of other-worldly Christians is their refusal to engage in politics and their criticism of those Christians who do engage in politics as "this-worldly." They may emphasize prayer over political action, i.e., invoking God to intervene supernaturally through the power of the Holy Spirit. The interviews I conducted with Christians of this kind lasted only a few minutes because they considered democracy a function of "this world." Because preachers of this sort address matters of faith in a way that does not further understanding of social issues, church services rarely evinced useful information for this study. More helpful information came from the questionnaires, in which believers made explicit and sometimes elaborate statements shunning politics.

The second group of evangelical Christians acknowledges the power of God and the work of the Holy Spirit that the other-worldly Christians affirm, but they seek to function as a "school of democracy" in the sense that they emphasize Christian ideals of love, peace, and harmony and seek to oppose political injustice. I call this group "the salt of the earth" school of democracy. It emerges especially from evangelicals in the Council of Churches and in the special Evangelical Fellowship. The Masowe Apostles can be included in this "salt-of-the-earth" group. Within this community, there is a focus on a God who works through the Holy Spirit to confront evil spirits, and where believers are continually learning to challenge the authoritarianism of their own prophets and healers, to set aside class divisions and even sexism by appealing to the idea of a loving God who cares for all believers and freely blesses children, women, and men with gifts of the Holy Spirit. In these respects, they represent a "school of democracy." Although the late Border Gezi, a leader of one sector of the movement, added to the negative image of the Masowe Apostles among other churches by showing support for Mugabe's policies for the repossession of land (*The Daily News*, February 2001), it does not follow that many Masowe

Apostles held this view or failed to promote grassroots democracy in a wide variety of ways.

The third school of democracy promotes the idea of making Zimbabwe a "Christian nation." This idea has not managed to take root, but I nonetheless came across evangelical Christians who believe that biblical principles for good governance can be identified as a basis for defining and organizing Zimbabwe as a Christian nation. Andrew Wutaunashe, the former president of the Evangelical Fellowship of Zimbabwe, is one church leader whose "salt of the earth" politics led him to seek a nation-state united by the adherence of the majority of Zimbabwe's population to Christianity.

As the essay progresses, I describe the religious concerns of the Masowe Apostles in a way that demonstrates that certain important differences notwithstanding, significant common ground exists between them and mainstream evangelicals. Hence it is possible to trace among some Masowe Apostles the same pattern of thought found among some evangelicals, whose concentration on the "other world" is so strong that they ignore politics almost completely. I shall argue, however, that other-worldly Christians in Masowe communities differ from the others because they are radical believers, not because of serious differences in matters of belief. I shall also indicate the ways in which Masowe Apostles follow the logic of their quest for equity to limits that one does not find in other evangelical churches, which is partly because of the poverty experienced by so many Apostles. Again, I maintain that Masowe Apostles have beliefs that are found in evangelical Christianity but behave rather differently in large part because their religious fears and aspirations reflect their profound poverty and social marginality. Mainstream evangelical Christians should consider this fact more carefully before they close their doctrinal door to Masowe Apostles.

Toward the end of the essay I discuss how gender influences the quest for democracy. Gender issues need to be considered because, from my experiences with the Masowe Apostles and other evangelicals, whose churches typically draw many women and children, the meaning of "the people" must be extended in any serious discussion of democracy to those on the underside of history. I have chosen to focus particularly on women among the Apostles because they come from even lower ranks of society than many women found in the mainstream evangelical churches and thus broaden the scope of this inquiry still further.

Methodology

I have done much fieldwork among Masowe Apostles. My Oxford doctoral thesis explored the relevance of gender in the imagery and theological ideas of a group that previously had received little attention (Mukonyora 1998a). I used this inquiry to open a debate on the way orthodox Christians react against Masowe Apostles. Newer to me, therefore, are the evangelical Christians in mainstream Zimbabwean society with whom I have had nothing more than informal links through friends and students at the University of Zimbabwe. In undertaking this chapter, I learned the key theological concepts that provided my evangelical friends and students their goals and direction in politics. The conversations I had with devout evangelicals whom I already knew (e.g., Noah Pashapa, Phineas Dube, and Roy Musasiwa) helped to orient my thinking on key issues, especially the definition of evangelicalism.

In addition, I closely tracked newspaper articles from evangelical church leaders and other evangelicals who work in the media. As a well-known exponent of evangelical ideas in Zimbabwe, Pius Wakatama appeared in print many times, giving advice to fellow evangelicals on how best to respond to threats to life, poverty and injustice. Also widely reported in general letters to the editor of *The Herald* were the views of Andrew Wutaunashe, the former president of the EFZ, who argued that since the majority of Zimbabweans (80 percent of the total population) confess to be Christians, the country should become a Christian state. This assertion led other evangelicals to make public statements challenging his interpretation of evangelical Christianity. This public dialogue was helpful in that it drew from many evangelical churches and groups, representing different views on how best to bring about a democracy in Zimbabwe and on the way evangelical Christians perceived their role in society.

The newspapers did not always feature evangelical Christians discussing politics, so I relied on extensive interviews with well-known evangelicals such as Phineas Dube and Noah Pashapa (mentioned above). Timothy Tavaziva, John Bell, and other key figures mentioned below are individuals I had to make special arrangements to meet. Unfortunately, the then-president of the EFZ was not available during these investigations. For his views and those of the EFZ, I relied on information from fifty questionnaires circulated among the members of his church, the Family of God, by research assistants belonging to his congregation, as well as on media reports and some fellow evangelicals in the EFZ.

In addition, with a team of four students from the University of Zimbabwe, I visited at least twenty different churches in Harare to carry out interviews and circulate among rank-and-file believers a carefully structured questionnaire focusing on the extent and nature of Christian witness in the current political situation. Among these were Baptists, Methodists, Anglicans, Lutherans, Brethren in Christ, members of the Zimbabwe Assemblies of God Africa (ZAOGA), and, as stated above, the Family of God Church led by the then-president of the EFZ, Andrew Wutaunashe.

These methods of inquiry made it possible to interrogate a wide range of evangelical Christians. Accordingly, the answers to my questions reflected a wide range of opinion. In fact, church leaders often held opinions with which the rank-and-file members disagreed, especially on the role that Christians should play in politics. This means that the "schools of democracy" discussed in this essay can assume highly divergent forms, confirming an opinion I have held as a theologian that many of the statements of faith made by Christians are not as straightforward as they seem. Even evangelical Christians in the same national context who enjoy a shared and reasonably clear definition of themselves produce quite different responses to questions about their role in society. The politics of evangelicals in Zimbabwe, like everywhere else, cannot be assumed a priori; they must be probed and interpreted on a case-by-case basis, as this essay attempts.

The Other World Christians

Paul Gifford has written widely about the way some biblical ideas found among evangelicals have undermined the power of Africans to address their chronic poverty and oppression (Gifford 1988 and 1990). He summarized the problem in a small document entitled "Christianity: To Save or Enslave" (Gifford 1990). He asks:

> Whose interests are served by a Christianity that diverts attention from social conditions and says you can prosper under the present system if you believe?
> - Claims sickness has nothing to do with deteriorating health services but with one's own faith?
> - Believes God decreed the miseries of the poor?
> - Expects things to get worse, because God has foretold this?
> - Teaches one should not expect any rights or contentment here and that only in heaven will one find peace and justice?
> - Says a government's sole task is to allow unrestricted evangelizing, and to such a government obedience is a Christian duty?
> - Asserts this world is not our concern, so something like deforestation is of no importance?
> - Believes any changes God wishes to bring about He will accomplish miraculously?
> - Teaches morality concerns only personal and private issues?
> - Says politics and Christianity are completely different things, to the extent that if you concern yourself with the former, you have renounced the latter? (Gifford 1990, 24)

Gifford asserts that this apoliticism is desperately shortsighted and that the Western evangelicals who promote it are blatantly hypocritical. Why? "Because," maintains Gifford, "foreigners from the First World who promote this way of viewing reality through crusades and television evangelism such as the Evangelist Billy Graham" are not themselves apolitical (Gifford 1990). According to Gifford, they are interested in seeing capitalism flourish as a global economy, with Third World countries providing cheap labor and America and Europe sure to extract material wealth from Third World countries filled with people who spend their time thinking about heaven (Gifford 1990). There is no scope for a longer discussion about these foreign "crusaders" in this essay (Gifford 1988). What is interesting for our purposes is the fact that there are many Christians in Zimbabwe who adopt such an evangelical apoliticism: they are either reluctant to make explicit what they think politically, thus giving the impression that they are only concerned with matters of heaven, or make it plain that they are not interested in politics because they are evangelical Christians following what the Scriptures say.

The interviews and questionnaires in particular showed that the majority (at least 60 percent) of the rank-and-file evangelical Christians we encountered were reluctant to discuss politics and gave reasons comparable to the views listed above about the need to focus on the spiritual self rather than "the things of this world." Out of the thirty questionnaires circulated among the members of the Family of God Church, for instance, where I expected the believers to agree with their founder and leader Andrew Wutaunashe, twenty Christians asked to remain anonymous and maintained that they were uncomfortable with the idea of evangelical Christians being as directly involved in politics as their leader. They believed that heaven comes first.

On Sunday morning, April 8, 2000, the BBC World Service announced that the British government was prepared to provide homes for any white families considering migrating to the U.K. following displacement from farms forcibly expropriated by "war veterans." The same day, the preacher at the Evangelical Northside Community Church addressed a group of about one hundred believers, among whom were many whites directly affected by the random takeover of farms that had been owned by their relations. Still, the pastor neither expressed concern about this matter, nor consoled members of his congregation by drawing attention to this major news of the day, the U.K.'s offer of hospitality to white victims of social displacement in Zimbabwe. The preacher stressed instead that Christians should always remember that prayer to the almighty God is the most important weapon in this world, where the forces of evil have always prevailed since "the fall of Adam and Eve." "Standing firm in Christ" through prayer, said the preacher, was the lesson for the day. At the conclusion of this service, it was difficult to know how to engage the members of this congregation on the news from the British government. The only two people willing to talk to me on this subject commented laconically that "it was interesting news" and went home.

Another Sunday morning, April 23, 2000, the day after a bomb exploded in the vicinity of *The Daily News*, a newspaper that quickly gained popularity for voicing fierce criticism of the current government's corruption and use of violence to suppress opposition, I chose to visit three evangelical churches within an eight-kilometer radius of the explosion. To a multiracial group of Anglicans at Holy Trinity in Eastlea, Harare, the Reverend Mundamawo preached about repentance from sin and the meaning of conversion to Christ, the importance of knowing the Bible, and continual prayer. Mundamawo called for "prayers for our nation, which clearly needs direction from God at the moment." Following the same pattern as the sermon at Northside two weeks earlier, besides prayer, there was no mention of social and political ways by which evangelical Christians could respond to the ongoing crisis in the country.

On Sunday, April 30, 2000, at Trinity Methodist Church in the heart of Harare, three kilometers away from the explosion, the circuit preacher talked about the need for personal salvation and stressed the importance of prayer by circulating information about a forthcoming National Day of Prayer to be held on May 25, 2000, in the National Sports Stadium. There was no mention of the explosion. At the same time, the congregation of approximately eight hundred believers was reminded of the power of God who raised Jesus from the dead, and asked to pray harder for peace and justice. Yet the congregational prayer was oblivious to the immediate political context. The preacher recited standard prayers for the leaders of the nation without mentioning the political crisis and directed the congregation to deal with the nation's future through prayers for God to intervene. The preacher did not provide any guidance on what believers could or should do besides pray; hence, in the interviews carried out after the service, the common answer to the question "What can an evangelical Christian do?" was "Prayer." To a question about the appropriateness of evangelical involvement in politics, all replied in the negative.

Evangelicals in other communities placed their hopes in God the same way. It was common to see in the daily newspapers announcements about "vigils"—all-night prayer meetings for the nation held in churches across the board. The questionnaires showed that there are evangelical Christians who believe that when one is leading a life of prayer, everything can be left to God. "Christians must pray to God about Zimbabwe and not get involved in politics" was a common answer to the question: "What do you think evangelical Christians should be doing to counter oppression?" Hence the cartoonist for *The Daily News* juxtaposed people being violently abused by the "party thugs" in one corner with three clergymen saying, "Hear no evil, See no evil, Speak no evil" (*The Daily News*, April 14, 2000).

Timothy Tavaziva, a senior worker for a well-known organization helping to spread evangelical Christianity in Zimbabwe, expressed his concern with evangelical Christian teaching. "I am now starting to wonder that many evangelicals associate politics with being worldly and would rather focus on repentance from sin and seek God's Kingdom first" (interview with author at

Scripture Union Office, Harare, May 27, 2000). Tavaziva, like many other evangelical Christians interviewed during the violent eruptions in the month leading up to the July 2000 elections, tended to view the "Kingdom of God" in other-worldly terms of heaven and the future. However, he agreed that the political situation had become so intolerable that evangelicals had to make it more clear that they could be role models for the construction of a well-ordered and just society: "The problem is determining the public role of Christians in worldly affairs" (Tavaziva, interview with author at Scripture Union Office, Harare, May 27, 2000).

In an answer to a questionnaire on the same matter, George Gagambira from the Zimbabwe Assemblies of God explained the dilemma: "Democracy is about material freedoms in this world . . . life on earth is temporal, my salvation takes me to heaven and for now I should live in obedience to the scriptures, not get mixed up with politics" (Gagambira, response to questionnaire, May 15, 2000). Gagambira was speaking for many evangelical Christians trained to think only about personal salvation, leaving the duty to actively work for justice on earth to non-Christians while they seek God through prayer first. Out of the five hundred questionnaires circulated in various evangelical congregations in Harare, about half showed either a reluctance to discuss politics or rejected openly the view that Christians need to actively promote democracy as a system of government. Emmanuel Tevera explained, "It is not the business of evangelical Christians to sort out the affairs of this world as some of our leaders are now starting to say, but to pray for God's will to prevail" (response to questionnaire, May 15, 2000, Central Baptist Church, Harare).

According to Tavaziva, Gagambira, Tevera, and other evangelical Christians, seeking God almost exclusively in prayer is part of a larger cosmology consisting of a dual reality whose lower half is this world where politicians seek to govern under the control of "principalities," which are evil forces, and an upper half from which people await a salvation in Christ that will empower them to transcend this world. And yet Tavaziva expressed misgivings about this dualism. "I am having to revisit the question of whether politics is a dirty game, as I was brought up to believe," said Tavaziva, expressing an ambivalence shared by many other evangelicals described here as other-worldly (interview, May 27, 2000).

Salt-of-the-Earth Evangelical Politics

Such is the spectrum of evangelical churches in Zimbabwe that there are groups of evangelicals who do more than pray for divine intervention. For example, a breakfast meeting was called by the Zimbabwe Council of Churches to encourage different political parties to reach a consensus on stopping the use of violence during the June 2000 election campaign. This was an important meeting because the Zimbabwe Council of Churches includes many evange-lically oriented Lutherans, Methodists, Baptists, and others. At the breakfast meeting, leaders from the United and Zimbabwe Methodist Churches and the Baptist Church made a joint public statement asking the government to ne-gotiate peaceful co-existence with opposition groups. The Movement for De-mocratic Change led by Morgan Tsvangirai and leaders of other small political parties standing in opposition to government attended this meeting to listen to what the churches had to say.

Half the time was spent in prayer and laying down the biblical foundations for the quest for peace (John 14:27), led by the well-known city administrator and Zimbabwe Methodist minister, the Reverend Griffiths Malaba. Concrete discussions on the political situation then began in small study groups with participation from the leaders of various political parties, including Morgan Tsvangirai. Frustrated by what he later described as the persistent talk about peace at a meeting intended to iron out the problem of government-sponsored violence, Morgan Tsvangirai walked out before the meeting ended. He ridi-culed church leaders on BBC World News for expecting his followers to close their eyes in prayer and to talk about peace when they were being brutally murdered (BBC Radio World News, April 27, 2000).

The Reverend Griffiths Malaba and the moderator of this meeting, Max Chigwida from the City Baptist Church, clearly did not understand their ac-tivities in the same way. Prayer, in this case, was not a way of focusing on the "other world," but given the agenda for the day—to negotiate a path for es-tablishing peace during elections—prayer was an essential part of the evan-gelical way of solving problems. Placing hope in a God who controls the affairs of humanity from beyond this world is thus not a substitute for confronting political problems using this-worldly means.

Noah Pashapa, a popular leader of a Baptist Church in Hatfield in Harare, is an evangelical Christian whose own church is not represented in the Zim-babwe Council of Churches. Following his studies at Spurgeon College, an evangelical institution of higher learning based in London, Pashapa undertook doctoral studies on evangelical Christianity in Zimbabwe. "It is part of my ministry to counsel individuals from all walks of life," he explains. "Politicians are no exception, especially when their decisions affect many people" (Pa-shapa, interview, May 20, 2000). During the 2000 elections, he says he ad-vised Professor Jonathan Moyo, the spokesman of the ruling party Zimbabwe African National Union–Patriotic Front (ZANU/PF), to show more tolerance for the opposition in his public statements—and the elections, it turned out, nearly tipped the balance of power away from the current rulers in favor of the Tsvangirai-led Movement for Democratic Change (MDC) (Pashapa, interview, May 20, 2000). At the time, incidents of violence in the city were becoming intolerable for everyone, and Mayo had incited more violence by deriding the opposition party and blaming them for disrupting peace. Noah Pashapa also responded to the challenge to engage in politics by creating a "think tank" of evangelical Christians who wanted to reflect more deeply on the political situation and plan paths of action to further democracy. Pashapa drew heavily from the vocabulary of civil society and civic mobilization—capacity building, consultancy, arbitration, advocacy, reconciliation, restoration, enlightenment, and empowerment—to describe the aims of the group, which he calls the "Concerned Christian Network Zimbabwe" ("Clean up Zimbabwean Politics Campaign," Hatfield Baptist Church circular, referenced by Reverend Noah Pashapa during our interview, May 1, 2000). Pashapa, it appears, has not merely offered an ad hoc response to a crisis situation but is seeking to sustain an evangelical presence as the "salt of the earth" in politics (Pashapa interview, May 1, 2000).

The evangelical Christianity that Pashapa represents is not blind to political issues. Frustrated by the "racist attitudes of white evangelical Christians at Central Baptist Church" in the 1980s, Pashapa became another "Ethiopian" by founding his own church group as a way of reacting against racism (Sundkler 1961a). Today Pashapa is the leader of a thriving community at Hatfield Baptist Church, known as "Life and Liberty Centre," where a black theology of self-empowerment can be heard from the pulpit. Pashapa has not only confronted racism by openly encouraging blacks to believe in themselves and their color, but also sees the role of the Christian in the world as that of "affirming, reinforcing and generating just and peaceable relationships and conditions which lead to prosperity for all." He writes:

> Current politics reflect contradictions to do with the Black Zimbabwean historical consciousness and struggle for politico-economic selfhood, the neo-colonial, international-capitalist-globalization and local white settler alliance as well as Black Zimbabwean demands for greater democratization of governance and its institution through transparency and accountability in the interest of efficiency and progress.

Additionally, he says, "Christianity has at its core, empowerment into a "fuller and more fulfilling 'image of God' life experience for those who believe" (Pashapa, interview, April 15, 2000).

On June 1, 2000, The National Constitutional Assembly organized a meeting in the Monomotapa Hotel called "Is the Church Part of the Problem or Part of the Solution?" Two evangelical Christian leaders—Tim Neill and Ngwiza Mkandla—debated before a public audience how Christians should respond to the breakdown of law and order in Zimbabwe. Neill, the evangelical Anglican priest of St. Luke's Greendale Parish Church, strongly voiced his opposition to the government: "The time to fear is coming to an end. All those who live by the truth will die for the truth and all those who live lies will die liars. So brothers, tell it as it is to the nation." Neill deplored Christians who remain passive in the face of injustice and made an appeal for the Church to become part of the solution so that justice and peace might prevail. "The Christian love for nonviolence must be fuelled by a desire for freedom" and a readiness to engage in "the politics of freedom, justice and peace" (Neill, *The Daily News*, March 30, 2000).

For Neill this means "standing up to evil with good" and not what he called "developing the skill for blame or avoiding politics altogether" merely because God is in heaven. Neill's speech ended with a proposal for Christians not to invest in government bonds but instead to invest in industry and the employment sector (public speech in Monomotapa Hotel, June 1, 2000). This type of evangelical Christian leadership on political matters was remarkably specific in elevating politics as a serious evangelical responsibility and in providing detailed directives concerning how evangelicals can best exercise that responsibility.

The Reverend Ngwiza Mkandla followed Neill's speech with a summary of the theological premises for the active participation of Christians in measures that promote democracy. Mkandla's views are important because he is widely known in Zimbabwe as the second president of the Evangelical Fellowship of Zimbabwe following its founder Chairman, Phineas Dube (Rev. Phineas Dube, interview with author, Harare, Domboshaua House, May 5, 2000). The Reverend Mkandla opened his speech with a criticism of those evangelicals who shun politics. He questioned the suggestion that politics is dirty: "The life of a city is the responsibility of the community. Jesus reorganized society by showing a respect for women and putting no boundaries between Jews and Greeks, showing a social concern by taking action against the evil enshrined in his society." Mkandla added, "It is bad theology not to understand the Christian God as a God of creation allowing us to think in terms of both the sacred and secular." For the Reverend Mkandla, God is concerned with the totality of human experiences; and when justice does not prevail and there is no love of one's neighbor, it angers the God whose son "became flesh and lived amongst us." This means that "the rule of God must prevail; one must be grounded in the community and be politically active, even if it means becoming a victim of injustice as Jesus did."

Being "salt and light" on earth does not mean "standing firm in faith" through prayers only. Christians have the responsibility to be knowledgeable and express their opinions as members of society by joining a march of protest against government or voting as necessary. As "members of the city," evangelical Christians must thus conduct themselves more proactively as Jesus did in the city of Jerusalem (Mkandla, speech in Monomotapa Hotel, June 1, 2000).

The theology that Neil and Mkandla espouse is not unique to them. During the years leading to the official independence of Zimbabwe, the veteran evangelical Christian and founder member of the Evangelical Fellowship of

Zimbabwe, Phineas Dube, addressed many audiences and helped many black African evangelical Christians develop a sense of self-worth and dignity in relation to whites. This political self-confidence was essential because of the imminence of independence. At the National Association for Christian Leadership Assembly (NACLA 1979), an international conference organized by Africa (Evangelical) Enterprise at the University of Zimbabwe, Dube challenged Africans to wake up to political realities (Mukonyora in audience, 1979). Dube still holds these views today: "Social ills arising from corruption and human greed had to be challenged and if people had to vote for a better society to be realized, well and good. Just as Christians have had to think about removing racism, they must also thing about the social ills arising from corruption and human greed" (Dube, interview, May 5, 2000).

Gary Strong, another outspoken Zimbabwean evangelical Christian, has stated that "intercession, prayer, the use of the spiritual realm is vital to Christian living." However, it does not follow from this that a Christian should avoid politics because it is necessary to vote against a government that is under the control of "a man causing national grief by his megalomania and paranoia about losing power" (the Reverend Gary Strong, interview with author, June 7, 2000, Harare, Hear the Word Ministries office). Strong is an evangelical whom Paul Gifford portrays as someone representing an organization (the evangelical development NGO, World Vision) that stands for the interests of Western outsiders in the global politics of the "right" (Gifford 1988). Strong likes to be remembered otherwise, as a man who supported the cause of blacks because, he says, "there is no denying that farmers were greedy, arrogant and needed to show more love" (Strong, interview, June 7, 2000). His challenge for Christians today is "to make political decisions that support the need for solving the problem of land acquisition, but under peaceful conditions, not tyranny" (Strong, interview, June 7, 2000).

The combination of a passion for political involvement and hope for divine intervention indicates how evangelical Christianity is multidimensional. It was not only Strong who emphasized the fact that there was a spiritual battle behind events in society. Pashapa and Dube were of the same opinion. Mkandla also returned to the matter of prayer and supplication before God. He went out of his way to stress the need for divine intervention in human affairs and the fact that humanity is tarnished by sin since the fall described in Genesis. It is not human beings who save themselves but God who saves people by his grace. Christians, then, must pray like warriors in this "spiritual battle between the forces of evil and good" stated Mkandla. The people of God, guided by the Holy Spirit, must triumph against political leaders guided by spirit mediums and n'angas (Mkandla, Monomotapa speech, June 1, 2000).

In other words, although the Reverend Mkandla is convinced that Christians should make political demands in favor of democracy, he recognizes that the problem at hand is beyond humanity's power. His speech ended by drawing attention to the transcendence of God through whose power change is possible, on one hand; and to "Principalities" that he saw as forces of evil that also influence humanity to perpetrate evil, on the other. Whether one belongs to the group of evangelicals that believe in stopping evil with prayer alone or to the "salt of the earth" school, hope for salvation depends on a God who defeats Satan through supernatural power.

In short, some political activists in evangelical Christianity also recognize the language of the victorious confrontation and conquest of evil through the power of the Holy Spirit. In addition, the lesson to draw from the "salt of the earth" trend in evangelical Christianity in Zimbabwe is that Christian beliefs—including "standing firm" in prayer—can inspire a sense of social and political responsibility. But, as shown above, there is also the danger that other-worldly evangelical Christianity undermines both the will and capacity of some evangelicals to influence political matters.

The Christian State

Andrew Wutaunashe was the president of the Evangelical Fellowship of Zimbabwe when he was among those Christian leaders invited to join the commission of inquiry established by the government to draft a new constitution for Zimbabwe in 1999. Although the phrase "Christian nation" did not receive mention in the final draft constitution that resulted from these consultations, an early draft constitution circulated for popular consideration in November 1999 began with a declaration that the nation should submit to the authority of God. In the end, 54 percent of the Zimbabwean electorate voted against the final draft because the head of state was given too much power to dictate proceedings in parliament. It was also unacceptable to the majority of Zimbabwean voters that the head of state had made himself immune from criminal and civil proceedings for human rights violations (*The Daily News*, February 18, 2000).

During this time Wutaunashe was reported to have argued in favor of Zimbabwe becoming a Christian nation. This argument drew the attention of many evangelical Christians because he was the president of the Evangelical Fellowship of Zimbabwe, which enjoys a large following. He is also a founder and leader of the Family of God Church, with a large urban middle-class clientele. Questionnaires distributed among this group revealed that not everyone was of the same opinion about Zimbabwe becoming a Christian nation, nor enjoyed having their leader involved in politics. In the wider evangelical community, however, Wutaunashe inspired an important debate on the role of Christians in society.

According to statistical evidence dating as far back as 1976, Christianity has been the dominant religion in Zimbabwe for at least the last thirty years

(Weinrich 1982, 8). If statistical evidence were all that mattered, a declaration of Zimbabwe as a Christian nation would have been uncontroversial. As indicated at the beginning of this essay, however, Zimbabwean Christianity is deeply divided denominationally and theologically, with some Christians even considered "false Christians" because of their beliefs about ancestors and witches. In this pluralistic religious context, Wutuanashe's proposal was criticized by other evangelical Christians.

For example, Phineas Dube, a former president of the EFZ, explained that it tarnished the image of evangelical Christianity in Zimbabwe to have the president of the Fellowship "muddled in politics" on account of his Christian nation proposal as well as other political interventions. Promoting the idea of a Christian nation in the current political circumstances could only work to legitimate an authoritarian regime that causes millions of people to live in poverty and suffer from arbitrary violence perpetrated by government forces. It was bad enough that Wutaunashe had been involved in consultations leading to a new draft constitution rejected by the people for failing to meet the standards of democracy (Dube, interview, May 6, 2000). Dube argued that an evangelically inspired Christian nation declaration would make it difficult to practice a politically prophetic ministry because it would associate evangelical Christians with the corruption and the inevitable mishaps in governance that the "salt of the earth" can challenge best from a position that is strictly independent of the government (Dube, interview, May 6, 2000).

Eddie Cross, well known in evangelical Christian circles in Zimbabwe as a prosperous economist, criticized Wutaunashe for "doing nothing to promote good governance by 'taking sides with the government'" (public statement on Web site at zimchurch.subscribe@cc.egroups.com, May 5, 2000). In the process of criticizing Wutaunashe, Cross articulates how his evangelical faith has led him to associate with the opposition Movement for Democratic Change:

> I stood with those who supported the struggle for the rights of Black Zimbabweans during the Smith era. I condemned the government for the Matebeleland genocide in 1985 to 1987 and was made persona non grata for this.... I sit on the National executive of the Movement for Democratic Change and am party to all the key decisions of the party. I can assure the Christian community that the MDC condemns violence in all its forms, stands for democratic principles and the rule of law, it stands for the full observance of basic human rights. (Cross, public statement, May 5, 2000)

In other words, in the eyes of Eddie Cross, Wutaunashe made a grave strategic error in promoting the Christian nation proposal, which the government could interpret as a kind of blessing from evangelicals. Furthermore, according to Phineas Dube, Wutaunashe was blunting the prophetic ministry of "salt of the earth" evangelicals by supporting a government-sponsored draft constitution that the majority of Zimbabweans ultimately rejected as undemocratic (Dube, interview, May 5, 2000).

During the same period, further fissures within Zimbabwean evangelicalism were revealed when veteran journalist and evangelical Christian, Pius Wakatama, wrote repeatedly to *The Daily News* attacking fellow evangelical Christians for compromising their Christian values by working for the government. One target of these attacks was the veteran politician and evangelical Olivia Muchena: "And you, beloved Mai Muchena, Zimbabwe knows you to be a brilliant academic and gentle and devout Christian woman. You just don't belong among those crooks and warmongers. . . . Get out of that Babylon" (Wakatama, *The Daily News*, April 24, 2000). Muchena was a member of the United Methodist Church, a group that enjoys a large membership among the Protestant churches of Zimbabwe, in part because of the Ruwadzano women's groups that boast more than three hundred thousand members (Hansson 1991). Interviews with members of the United Methodist Church during this time of crisis showed that the majority of believers supported the idea of Christians becoming involved in politics as a way of improving an increasingly desperate situation (UZ questionnaires, May–June 2000). Mai Muchena did not believe she was part of Babylon but instead served as a role model for other Christians (Mai Muchena, public speech at Bronte Hotel, July 2000). In any case, that this debate was even possible showed the extent to which evangelicals in Zimbabwe were increasingly taking for granted that they should be politically involved, even if they strongly disagreed about the most appropriate means of doing so.

Masowe Apostles as Radical Evangelicals

It is not an accurate portrayal of Masowe Apostles to refer to them as mostly rural people when they have always had a following in towns (see below). However, the reason for looking at Masowe Apostles, apart from the evidence suggesting that evangelical ideas strongly shape them, is that Masowe Apostles take us beyond the theologically and socially mainstream evangelicals discussed in the previous sections, who live fairly middle-class lifestyles in Zimbabwean terms, and extend our vision to the lower sectors of society where suffering is acute and adherence to Christianity strong. Masowe Apostles make it possible to include in a discussion on democracy the fears and aspirations of thousands of impoverished believers in the urban and rural areas. It is vital that such people develop a sense of self-worth and participate in realizing the ideals of equity, justice, and prosperity for themselves and others, if Zimbabwe is ever going to succeed in its quest for democracy.

Ranger traces the roots of the Masowe Apostles to American Methodism and particularly to the pentecostal revivalism that emerged from the Methodist and Holiness traditions. Whether this genesis is enough to justify calling them evangelical requires us to look more closely at the founder of the Apostles, Shonhiwa Mtunyane (born ca. 1920s, died 1973). Shonhiwa came from Gandanzara, a rural area in Makoni District (Ranger 1999). According to Shonhiwa's own testimony, he read the Bible continuously as a young man. He fell sick and had a conversion experience in which he heard the "voice" of God calling him to preach to *vanhu vatema* (black people). During the 1930s when Shonhiwa gained popularity under the religious name John the Baptist or the derivative Johane Masowe (John of the Wilderness), *vanhu vatema* meant victims of colonial oppression. The majority of them were still illiterate, with the semiliterate among them working in mines, factories and white households as domestic servants. Middle-class evangelical Christians were rare in this period. Johane's message of repentance and baptism in the Holy Spirit made sense as a translation of evangelical Christianity into a local and largely indigent culture (Mukonyora 2007). Shonhiwa was drawn to the Gospels and the Acts of the Apostles, and the title given to the followers of Jesus determined that his own followers should be called apostles. His religious call hinged on biblical figures such as Moses, John the Baptist and Jesus (Dillon-Malone 1978, 13).

Yet Shonhiwa was considered a heretic and was repeatedly arrested by colonial authorities during the 1930s. According to Dillon-Malone, Shonhiwa became widely known partly because of all the police questioning he was subjected to (1978, 11–12). An indicator of how committed he was to spreading the gospel is the way Johane Masowe traveled from his rural home in Gandanzara to various towns in Mashonaland: Norton, Headlands, Rusape, and the capital city then called Salisbury. Frustrated after being harassed by the police, Johane went south to Bulawayo, then out of the country to Francis town in Botswana. For fifteen years he lived surrounded by his white-robed followers in a shanty town called Korsten in Port Elizabeth in South Africa (Mukonyora 2000a). Following repatriation by the South African government, Johane Masowe permitted those of his followers who wished to return to Zimbabwe to do so and migrated north to Lusaka in Zambia, continuing his exodus to Malawi, Tanzania and Kenya. According to Dillon-Malone, Masowe Apostles can still be found in all these places. When the founder died, he left behind at least 1.5 million followers in southern and central Africa (Dillon-Malone 1978).

Today's Masowe Apostles are amorphous, including both those who read the Scriptures and others who insist on using the oral tradition of song and sermons that transmit the message of the gospel to people whether they can read or not. My own estimate is that in Zimbabwe alone, Masowe Apostles exceed half a million if all of their offshoot groups are taken into account, such as the Masowe Apostles weChishanu with at least three hundred thousand members in Zimbabwe today (Engelke 2002). Among these was Border Gezi, who rapidly rose to high rank in the ruling ZANU/PF party and who after his death in a car crash now lies buried in Heroes Acre. Gezi behaved as a prophet who drew the attention of the media by making political statements that gave support to the ruling party led by Robert Mugabe and rallying the support of other Masowe Apostles behind the current regime (Engelke 2002). The group has thousands of followers, but in no way represents the entire movement of the Masowe Apostles. With Border Gezi now deceased, it is especially important to learn about the very diverse ways the Masowe belief system shapes people's attitudes to themselves and their social and political world.

Given the focus of this essay on evangelical Christianity, let me provide a few clues on how best to interpret Masowe Apostles for the purpose of highlighting some of the issues that this essay has already raised and also other matters of interest in a discourse on democracy. One difficult issue is the authority given to the Scriptures in evangelical Christianity.

The Bible as the Word of God

The majority of evangelical Christians, especially those represented by the leaders referred to in preceding discussions, can read, write, and converse easily in English. All except one of the Church services that I attended used Shona, the language that prevails among Masowe Apostles. If the evangelical Christians did not walk into church holding personal copies of the Bible, they found Bibles in the pews to read during worship. Evangelical Christians thus insist that emphasis must be given to the authority of the Bible, which rightly or wrongly the majority access through the English language.

Masowe Apostles, called by others Wilderness Apostles, worship out of doors in white robes and without shoes (Werbner 1985; Mukonyora 2005). Some groups are known to bring their Bibles into the open air to read and instruct one another in matters of the faith (Dillon-Malone 1978; fieldwork with Engelke in Chitungwiza, Harare, October 1999). Many others do not bring Bibles into the open air or cite the Bible during worship, even those who know all about the Bible and would compare well with other evangelicals in reading, writing, and speaking English. Shona, observed Sundkler, is the language that the Masowe Apostles take pride in and insist upon for worship (Sundkler 1961a). With that insistence, I suggest they practice traditional Shona methods of transmitting ideas through songs, dance and carefully structured stories whose didactic value is obvious.

From the looks of things Masowe Apostles cannot be equated with evangelicals and, according to the definition of an evangelical provided above, it makes a mockery of the faith to compare Christians who respect the tradition of submitting themselves to the authority of the Scriptures with people who appear unprepared to do so. Yet, as stated above, Masowe Apostles use the name "Apostles" deliberately because of a high regard for the New Testament testimony to Jesus Christ (Dillon-Malone 1978, 13). So what is happening here? I am of the opinion that Masowe Apostles give authority to a set of ideas from the biblical religious heritage that the founder conveniently made part of an oral tradition in order to make his message accessible to everyone, especially the large proportion of believers who are either illiterate or barely able to read the Bible meaningfully. During my fieldwork between 1997 and 2000, I was struck by the use of songs, appropriately called "verses," and carefully constructed sermons in which "verses" were sung to inspire belief in God and build people's confidence in the power of the Holy Spirit. This means that while reading, writing, and speaking the English language may be characteristic of evangelical Christianity in postcolonial Zimbabwe, a lack of English and even basic literacy have not presented stumbling blocks for those seeking God in the vernacular and through a ministry of church leaders who hold that the gospel needs to touch thousands of people for whom an understanding of the world still requires oral traditions.

The majority of the evangelical Christians I know react strongly against Masowe Apostles' talk about the Bible as an ancient book that contains truths that they don't really need. Masowe Apostles, explained Madzimai Susan, are confident that God speaks to his children directly today as he did during the times spoken of in the Bible: "We are not afraid of contradicting the Bible because we don't. God is consistent; He transmits divine messages to all believers throughout time through the Holy Spirit. Holding the book in public itself and reading do not make people true children of God" (Madzimai Susan, interview with author, Lake Chimombe, Harare, July 14, 1993).

I asked Madzimai Susan whether she reads and writes. In this case, yes, the woman has in her possession an English and Shona Bible. She reads them and learns from them, but as "books telling stories about God in days gone by.... When I want to hear God's *izwi* [word] I kneel down and wait upon Mwari-Baba [God-the-Father] in prayer." This means she prioritizes knowing God directly through the Holy Spirit. Christians are meant to trust in the promise of the Holy Spirit to continue the work of Christ in the church. Of course, this is precisely what kept Christian communities going for decades before the New Testament appeared during the early church.

Jesus himself among his Aramaic-speaking friends had to use the vernacular and oral traditional idioms and parables to communicate the message of God. Even in the origins of evangelical Christianity as part of Protestantism in Europe, the vernacular was taken seriously as a way of ensuring that people understood the gospel for themselves. Consequently the language used by the Pope and the magisterium in the Roman Catholic Church, Latin, was challenged and replaced in evangelical communities with mother tongues throughout Europe.

"Other World and Culture"

Scholars have observed that Masowe Apostles are predominantly rural-based communities who "have consistently resisted development" as exemplified by "their rejection of schooling and biomedicine." This can be seen as a rejection of the Zimbabwean state's gospel of "development," which President Canaan Banana so urgently pressed upon the Zimbabwean churches in the 1980s (Maxwell 1999, 124). Together with the practice of polygamy, these tendencies can also be seen as slowness to accept modern values, including those of democracy (Weinrich 1982, 156–158). Thus, Weinrich argues that living in the rural areas and holding on to old traditions that fit in with an agrarian life style (such as polygamy) far removed from the city, hinders the acceptance of modern values in indigenous-led churches in general. In short, before we discuss the ways in which belief in the supernatural "other" impinges on the growth of a school of democracy among the Masowe Apostles, we must acknowledge that the background culture is not something these believers overcame and turned away from immediately, especially in rural areas where the capacity to create new identities around missionary-packaged Christianity was slow to take root.

The majority of evangelical Christians in Zimbabwe would object to the use of the "evangelical" label by Masowe Apostles on the grounds that illiteracy causes these believers to distort Christianity. At the World Council of Churches meeting held in Harare in December 1999, polygamy was ruled an important reason for keeping some independent churches out of the Council (Seminar on AICs, World Council of Churches, Harare, Zimbabwe, 1999).

I don't have to defend Masowe Apostles on all fronts, but I do invite more careful study of contemporary Masowe groups. Many Masowe Apostles are monogamous and accept Western medicine alongside services of prayer for healing. Over the last ten years of fieldwork among Apostles in suburban areas, I have found that, if nothing else, the living standards in domestic servant dwellings are too restrictive for domestic workers to keep many wives. In fact, having two of three wives complicates life as much in towns as in rural areas, where Weinrich places the majority of Masowe Apostles (1982, 156). Also, as Dillon-Malone observed, Masowe Apostles know more and more each day about the contents of the Bible with the rise in literacy among them. My own research in Harare shows that there is considerable ambivalence among Apostles concerning the relationship between tradition and modernity. Many Masowe believers are ready to adapt to the demands of living in a modern, changing society by rejecting polygamy and taking medicine when prayers have not sufficed. I would also say that Masowe Apostles are not uniform with respect to sexual morality anymore. Many communities favor monogamy and object strongly to the practice of sexual relations with more than one wife by calling it a form of adultery (Mukonyora 2007). In short the hold of traditional Shona culture on the Apostles is gradually loosening and in any case does not constitute a reason to ignore their contributions to democracy or to deny that they have much in common with mainstream evangelicals in the city.

More Other-Worldly Christians

With regard to the fact that some Masowe Apostles still find it difficult to adapt to the modern world to the extent other Christians do, it is important to understand that this has less to do with traditional Shona culture and more to do with their particular beliefs about "the other world." As I maintain in my entry in the *Encyclopedia of Religion and Nature*, Masowe Apostles treat *zvinhu zvechirungu* (i.e., material objects associated with the wealth and culture of Europeans), as evils that stand in the way of the faith of believers and as worldly temptations that cause immorality in society (Mukonyora 2005). Consequently, Masowe Apostles worship in the open air in white robes to remind the believer of the importance of sanctity and during worship prohibit any other clothing for those confirmed in the faith. Watches, shoes, and earrings are also removed and hair kept short; otherwise, one is suspected of immorality. Condemning *zvinhu zvechirungu* is really a way of cautioning believers and reminding them that they are children of God preparing for the other world called heaven. Masowe Apostles are radical Christians in this respect, but not necessarily anti-modern.

On the matter of spiritual healing, most evangelicals don't have to think twice about taking Western medicine. However, as stated above, many believe in the miraculous healing of diseases. Such beliefs show that Western medicine is not all that counts. The majority of testimonies offered by evangelical Christians refer to moments of struggle with either physical pain or misfortune, both of which God is believed to remove through prayer. My fieldwork shows that Masowe Apostles will not refuse medicine all the time and in many ways approach "biomedicine" like other evangelical Christians. The scandals of Masowe Apostles refusing medicine involve a few Apostles who have gone to uncharacteristic extremes with the belief in the healing power of God and did not arise from their basic belief in divine intervention, which is characteristic of Christianity and which evangelicals, especially those caught up in the recent wave of Pentecostalism, would readily accept.

Evil Spirits and Satan

Ancestors and witches frequently receive mention in Masowe prayers. In common talk about Masowe Apostles by Christians from the mainstream, these beliefs suggest a syncretistic "mixing" of religious beliefs, which ortho-dox Christians should refrain from doing. Much is overlooked in this way of talking, however, of which is useful to explore here.

Johane Masowe interpreted the ancestors and witches as evil and contin-ually referred to the need to exorcise them (Dillon-Malone 1978, 138). He described his own call as one in which God commanded that he preach against witches, and burning *machira avadzimu* (memorabilia of the ancestors) was Johane's way of dramatizing his opposition to beliefs in the ancestors and even to benevolent spirits (Dillon-Malone 1978, 143; Mukonyora 2000a). The people who claim to be possessed by ancestral spirits are seen as people in need of prayer that would chase these spirits away like Satan (Mukonyora 1998a). Johane Masowe did not contradict evangelical teaching in this respect but carried it through. European missionaries started the legacy of suppressing witchcraft and shunning the ancestors, with prayers often made to ward off evil spirits and remove the works of Satan. This is what one finds among evan-gelical Christians in Zimbabwe, where ancestors and witches may not receive direct mention but remain part of the background religious culture inherited from evangelical missionaries.

Masowe Apostles stand out in their talk about the ancestors and witches because, for them, mentioning such phenomena is the most appropriate way of confronting Satan and his evil forces. In a sense, we learn from Masowe Apostles about what lies on the opposite side of God and his angels in the view of the "other-worldly Christians." Zimbabwean evangelical Christians do not merely call upon God and the Holy Spirit to direct their lives. They also ask for protection from the same evil forces that they believe are at the heart of corrupt governments. Arguably, however, the preoccupation with ancestors, witches, and Satan undermines the power of believers to take responsibility for their own behavior and can thus make it difficult to engage in politics critically and effectively.

Freedom from Poverty School

It is widely assumed that the so-called gospel of prosperity only attracts the young educated evangelicals of the city. In evangelical Christianity there is room to consider a third "school of democracy" in which material well-being is just as important as the spiritual well-being of the believer.

As argued by Maxwell, among the characteristic expectations of a growing number of evangelicals is that they will be "freed from poverty." In Maxwell's analysis of the theological ideas underpinning the gospel of prosperity, poverty is associated as much with human folly as it is with Satan or evil spirits (Maxwell 1998). This view is based on Maxwell's research on ZAOGA, a church with a clientele that is accustomed to living in towns and earning incomes from the city as clerks, secretaries, managers and so on (Maxwell 1998, 2007). Among Masowe Apostles, the picture is different. From the early days of the founding of the Apostles in the 1930s, communities arose in which members contributed to each other's well-being through sharing information about employment and sometimes by creating cooperatives whereby profits from growing crops, making tins, clothes and baskets, and selling vegetables were used for the benefit of the whole community. According to Dillon-Malone, Johane Masowe wanted his followers to be economically self-sufficient so that they would not have to rely on employment by whites in the towns (Dillon-Malone 1978; cf. Kileff and Kileff 1979). Today, the fight for freedom from poverty is difficult to organize along such radical lines and, as a result, one comes across Masowe Apostles in various levels of employment in the city, just like everyone else (Engelke 2002). Still, it is part of Masowe thinking to offer mutual advice on how to alleviate suffering and how to empower individuals to feel integrated in society. That is what healing means beyond relieving pain in a physical sense among African Apostles in general (Dillon-Malone 1978).

Today Masowe Apostles are recognized transnational travelers, frequently crossing borders between Zimbabwe, Botswana, South Africa, Zambia, and even Mozambique, trading from one major city to another as a way of overcoming poverty (Mukonyora 2000b/2001a). Though prosperity cannot be achieved in the crumbled economy of Zimbabwe, it is important to note that Masowe Apostles believe in a God who provides for his children in a material sense too. So we can say that the "gospel of prosperity" attracts evangelicals among the more privileged class as well as evangelicals among Masowe believers.

Democratic Practices of Women Evangelicals

According to Barnes, although generally expected to remain in rural areas of Zimbabwe, women soon became a feature of life in the city during the colonial era. If these women were not subordinate to their husbands and male consorts in a system of life in the city known as *ruche mapoto*, they worked as domestic servants, nurses, and teachers (Barnes and Win 1992). They also started gathering in church-organized groups where they learned Western methods of cooking, sewing, knitting, looking after the home, living with husbands, reading the Bible and prayer. Most of these "deserters of culture," as colonial administrators came to characterize women who came to look for work in towns, struggled to survive as subordinates of an already oppressed group of male workers (McCulloch 2000).

Consequently, my discussion of women in evangelical Christianity in Zimbabwe starts with a recognition of Masowe Apostles as the community to which the many women trying to find a means to survive in towns, which were not initially designed to include women, could turn for religious schooling.

Just as women were not welcome in the towns, so the founder of the Masowe Apostles was arrested and rejected in the towns because of his preaching the gospel. Women in the towns identified with his plight and followed him (Mukonyora 2000b/2001a).

Across the spectrum of churches today, church leaders in Zimbabwe now applaud their women followers for being the "backbone of the church" because women participate in very large numbers. Throughout this inquiry I have found myself over and over again in congregations with 60 to 80 percent of the adherents composed of women and children. There is room here for further research on the reasons why women continue to be so actively interested in Christianity, despite the problematic legacy of colonialism (Mukonyora 2000b/2001a). Among the Masowe Apostles women are more than the backbone of the Church. Their marginality drives them to apostolic spirituality in such a forceful way that understanding Masowe beliefs depends crucially on understanding Masowe women (Mukonyora 2007). Of particular interest here is the extent to which democratic ideas are expressed by Masowe women at prayer meetings. Since this essay explores the various ways in which evangelical ideas either have been or can be translated into political praxis, here is a sketch of how Masowe ideas concerning women make the Apostles an effective school of democracy.

(1) Masowe believers talk about the Holy Spirit as a transcendent power working through whomever he wills across the gender divide and among believers of all ages. Women equal men in their chances to receive the blessing of the Holy Spirit. Children, too, are considered spiritually privileged, and the idea of a child is commonly used to describe the attitude with which all believers must address God. However, sexism of the male leadership, especially the insistence that only men can be called leaders of the movement, sits uncomfortably with the egalitarian beliefs and practices of the Apostles concerning gender.

(2) Education as a way of claiming authority among the Masowe is prohibited. As I was told at Lake Chimombe, salvation has nothing to do with education among the members of the wilderness church but is entirely the work of the Holy Spirit. The white robes symbolize the radical equality of all believers, and items of dress that might accentuate class differences are prohibited in the Masowe. The basis for election as leader has nothing to do therefore with class, material possessions, high levels of literacy acquired in school, or the ability to speak the official language, English. Instead, the ability to master the oral traditions of the movement and narrate them in the vernacular are important. As in the past, women are the custodians of important knowledge, including the ability to sing the movement's foundational "verses." With the large numbers of women deprived of education because of their sex, the Apostles enable these women to transcend this disadvantage and share the knowledge of God in songs to fellow believers. Again, however, the ruling that

only men can fulfill the role of leader can be questioned against the foundational Masowe idea of a wilderness in which the believers are meant to be able to transcend the divisions placed between them in formal society.

(3) Women have always sat separately from men among the Masowe. This is echoed in the background culture where there is often a separation according to gender in the use of space. Shona men generally like to sit in areas that are considered exclusively theirs when they eat food in the kitchens or talk about lineage matters and solve family problems. The carrying over of this practice by the male leaders of the Masowe Apostles explains the development of a male-oriented Masowe theology and hierarchy, which Western scholars focus on (Mukonyora 2000b/2001a). In my fieldwork I found that some women challenge this theology during public rituals by interrupting the sexism reflected in sermons through song or words of prophecy. Esther, a woman elder and healer in the Avondale community, explains the problem of sharing the sacred wilderness with men preoccupied with hierarchy and leadership:

> Men often show a sign of weakness by turning the sacred wilderness into a place for fighting for the control of the work of the Holy Spirit. The sowe as women understand it is a place for peaceful prayer and healing, not a venue for men to abuse women and solve their leadership squabbles. . . . Fortunately, we the elder women giving guidance to women in the movement know about this already and can intervene through prayer and words of prophecy when men go too far. The Holy Spirit teaches peace, harmony and love among believers who are equal before God, including children. We all come to the sowe because we are equal and love God. Anyone who says otherwise misrepresents Masowe teaching and will wake up one day to find the Spirit gone. (Madzimai Esther, interview with author, August 13, 1999)

Masowe women thus know that they deserve respect in the communities to which they belong, and in time they come to see themselves as deserving equal opportunities with men in the city and beyond.

As for women in the more formal evangelical churches, Hansson notes that the Ruwadzano movements of uniformed Christian women are the backbone of evangelicalism in Zimbabwe, especially as in the Methodist and Lutheran churches. Hansson observes that in the Lutheran church alone, there are three hundred thousand women who gather in groups under the banner of the Ruwadzano to read the Bible, pray, and share skills such as baking, sewing, and etiquette that help to make the modern home a happy and peaceful environment in which husbands get their full respect as heads of households (Hansson 1991). The same attitudes prevailed among the followers of the women's movement in the Methodist church led by Bishop Abel Muzorewa. There were so many Ruwadzano women cheering the bishop at his political rallies in Rufaro Stadium, Harare, in the months leading to the 1980 elections, that it became clear to the press that women had expectations of the demo-cratic state on the horizon that were just as high as those harbored by the young men of the liberation war (Mukonyora, Mambo Press trainee journalist, 1978–1980).

Unfortunately, the exclusivist mentality of Ruwadzano women hinders a democratic egalitarianism. As Hansson noted, there is such a high regard for marriage in the movement that divorced women, single parents, or anyone unable to prove that they are formally married and living with their husband cannot become full members of the Ruwadzano. Widows are the exception (Hansson 1991). However, in some evangelical churches there are single-parent groups, in which women whose husbands are deceased as a result of the AIDS pandemic meet with divorced women to discuss common problems and pray together (Pashapa, interview at Hatfield Baptist Church, May 20, 2000).

In the Masowe movement, there is no need to run special groups for women. A prostitute can stand up to publicly confess any number of illicit relationships formed in a lifetime without losing the respect of others. Single parents, divorced women, widows, and married women sit side by side in a community in which there are many reminders of egalitarian principles that extend the right to speak in the name of the Holy Spirit even to children (Mu-konyora, fieldwork observations, 1996–2000). In short, whatever needs to be said about sexism in Masowe theology, the spontaneous mutual tolerance of the white-robed women during prayer meetings presents a profound democratic challenge to the evangelical women belonging to the Ruwadzano group and many of Zimbabwe's other mainstream evangelical churches and fellowships.

Conclusion

This study is about the quest for democracy in a country that joins many others in Africa in seeing democratic advances subverted through corruption and the use of armies and prisons to silence opposition. Zimbabwe is a society in which Christianity plays a substantive and pervasive role in shaping the minds with which people address questions of modernity, authority, and the peaceful running of society. I have tried to show that evangelical Christianity provides an increasingly buoyant springboard for the discussion of important issues of justice and freedom. I have also identified ideas and tendencies found in evangelical Christianity that hinder democracy, such as an exclusive preoccu-pation with spiritual forces or the "other world"; the narrow class strata from which the main exponents of evangelicalism in Zimbabwe are drawn; the negative attitude toward the Masowe Apostles (and other AICs) as heretical when in fact they can be called evangelical; and, last but not least, woman-to-woman exclusion and oppression on account of marital status.

At the same time, evangelical Christians in Zimbabwe have an important role to play in promoting and internalizing a culture of democracy. They can and do help ordinary people cope with modernity in Zimbabwe while enabling them to appropriate the values that are crucial if democracy is to truly flourish, such as love for others, self-respect, a positive attitude to work, and a desire for justice. As shown in the other contributions to this volume, evangelical Christianity is so dominant in sub-Saharan Africa that it is an indispensable vehicle for promoting the values and practices that make democratic cultures possible. As hinted at in the opening remarks to this essay, many of the democratic patterns of thought and practice found among evangelicals are found elsewhere in the broad spectrum of churches found in Zimbabwe. And yet, because the only regime known to Zimbabwe since independence is the one responsible for the country's continuing oppression, democracy remains a distant dream for the people of Zimbabwe. Since I wrote this chapter, the political crisis in Zimbabwe has greatly worsened; prospects for democracy have deteriorated; the poor have become more and more desperate for change. If democracy is to have a chance, evangelicals and other Christians will have to find more dynamic and effective ways of turning their religious aspirations for freedom and equality into political reality.

NOTE

1. Mukonyora attended a workshop on AICs at the University of Zimbabwe, Harare, in December 1999.

5

Evangelicals and Democracy in Mozambique

Teresa Cruz e Silva

During the late 1970s and 1980s in newly independent Mozambique, there were many studies of the emergence and development of political consciousness and of the armed liberation struggle. However, study of the relationship between religion and politics was rare and difficult to undertake because of the impact of state ideology on the academic environment. Moreover, in the Mozambican educational tradition, theological and religious studies were undertaken mainly in Christian seminaries. University studies of religion were carried out under the umbrella of the social sciences, which in these years were themselves limited by a lack of resources and the need to concentrate on basic education and the production of general texts. Hence, little was known about religion in contemporary Mozambique and still less about its interaction with politics.

However, the impact of globalization and the important social and political changes that have occurred in Mozambique during the last quarter-century have had a profound impact in the fields of both religion and political culture. The role played by different religious denominations in peacemaking and development, as well as their more general political involvement, reshaped their relationship with the state and reinserted religion into political culture. This development necessitated new research on the interaction of religion and politics in Mozambique.

This chapter is part of such new research. It studies the dynamics of religious and political interaction in the context of rapid social and political change, focusing particularly on evangelical

Christianity. It seeks to do this by contrasting two case studies.[1] The first is of the United Methodist Church in Mozambique—a church whose history and political significance are increasingly well known. The second is of the Zionist churches in Maputo City and, in particular, in Luis Cabral suburb. The rise of the Zionists[2] is relatively recent; very little analysis has been done concerning their significance in Mozambique. The United Methodist Church is clearly part of evangelical Christianity, just as Isabel Mukonyora argues in another chapter of this volume concerning the Zimbabwean sister-church, led until recently by Bishop Muzorewa. These Methodist churches clearly have played political roles and expressed aspirations for democracy. In addition, just as Mukonyora argues for the *Masowe Vapostori*, so I maintain with respect to the Zionists that they are both evangelical and potentially democratic.

My research has focused not only on formal church declarations, nor only on the visible work of church leaders and congregations, but also on the wider evangelical contributions to democratic development and to new political forms. The focus is the contemporary period, particularly the 1980s and 1990s, though history will be used to put the current situation in context. This chapter will explore economic and political transitions since independence and the role of evangelical Christians in the peace process and in sustaining a democratic society. I shall argue that both Methodists and Zionists have played a key role in securing peace and enabling democracy.

I shall make generalizations about Mozambique as a whole, but the two case studies are set in the south, the most evangelical region in the country, and particularly in Maputo city, which has Mozambique's largest concentration of evangelicals (INE 1999). The chapter in general and the two case studies in particular are based on various sources: secondary and archival material; material in the Ministry of Justice's Religious Affairs National Department (Direcção Nacional de Assuntos Religiosos); analysis of media from press cuttings and television programmes, particularly those of TVM (Mozambique Television) and TV Miramar (Miramar Television, a channel from The Universal Church of Kingdom of God, in Mozambique); semistructured interviews; and, finally, personal observation.

Background and Context

The colonial boundaries of Mozambique were demarcated toward the end of the nineteenth century. By this period both Protestant and Catholic Missions had established themselves in different areas of the country. From the period of conquest, around 1895, until the transition to independence in 1974, however, Protestants had a very difficult relationship with the Portuguese authorities. They were suspected first of working for the political interests of their countries of origin against the Portuguese, and later of helping to form a nucleus of African opposition to colonial domination.

The Catholic Church enjoyed a very different relationship. The Concordat and Missionary Agreement in 1940 and the Missionary Statute in 1941 established collaboration between the Vatican and Portugal in the colonial undertaking. Government policy on social issues, education, and "assimilation" of the indigenous African population reflected the state's adoption of Catholic moral principles. Implementation of the statute resulted in the expansion of Catholic missions and their engagement in promoting the ideology of assimilation. It also resulted in the institutionalization and reinforcement of the already existing separate education for the African population, and in discrimination against Protestant institutions and severe restrictions on their mission activities (Helgesson 1994; Cruz e Silva 1992, 2001a, 2001b).

The 1940s and 1950s were difficult decades for Mozambique's Protestants. Under the umbrella of the Christian Council of Mozambique (CCM), founded in 1948 (Biber 1992), some Protestant denominations struggled to devise common strategies to respond to Portuguese colonial policies. At the same time, even relations between the Catholic Church and the colonial state became increasingly complex and difficult. During the 1960s and 1970s, a profound crisis developed within the Catholic Church in Mozambique as a result of growing opposition to the conservative wing of the Church and to its commitment to the state. As a result, the anti-conservative White Fathers were expelled from Mozambique in 1971, and in the next few years, priests were arrested, detained, or expelled (Hastings 1979, 1991; Ferreira 1987).

Relations with Protestants reached a crisis point in 1972 when the massive detention of Protestant leaders and believers by the Portuguese political police resulted in the death of Presbyterian religious leaders. The colonial state disliked Protestant efforts to "Africanize"[3] church leadership, the strong anticolonial position adopted by the African Presbyterian Church, and the participation of young black Protestants in the nationalist struggle. Only in 1974, with the end of the liberation war in Mozambique, did the conflict between colonial state and the Protestant churches come to an end.

After the Lusaka Agreements with Portugal on September 7, 1974, Mozambique began the transition to independence. A considerable number of nationalists had been educated in a Christian environment, and FRELIMO— the Mozambique Liberation Front—"appreciated the efforts which a minority of priests had made in the struggle for justice" (Hastings 1979, 213). But although during the transition period FRELIMO maintained a neutral attitude on Church issues (Morier-Genoud 1996), the collaboration of the Catholic Church hierarchy and the state during the colonial period led to an anti-Christian, and particularly an anti-Catholic, position by some FRELIMO leaders.

When Mozambique became independent in 1975, its Constitution established a secular state, providing for separation between state and church and recognizing religious freedom. The Catholic Church not only lost its special relationship with the state but also witnessed the erosion of the economic and social structures in which it had been involved. FRELIMO nationalized social services, land, and rented property (Hanlon 1991, 11–12). The Catholic Church lost most of its property. Most priests from the conservative wing left the country, and the subsequent indigenization of the priesthood occurred in this context of political marginalization and alienation.

Protestant churches were in a stronger position. They had already established African churches with many African pastors, rooted in African "communities" and in African culture. They were also affected by the new state's religious policy, but after independence they moved from opposition towards greater freedom, and "in contrast to part of the Catholic clergy, most Reformed churches and pastors remained positive towards the new government" (Morier-Genoud 1996, 38). After 1974, more churches joined the CCM and through this Council, they developed programmes of cooperation with the government for national reconstruction (Morier-Genoud 1996). Many Protestants, using private channels, managed to communicate and to establish a relationship with FRELIMO (Vines and Wilson 1995).[4]

In the first stage of independence, then, evangelical churches were closer to the state and to politics than Catholic churches. However, between 1977 and 1981, FRELIMO introduced new policies in order to "socialise and modernise the country." These were accompanied by open hostility to religion. The 1978 FRELIMO Ideological Work Department Conference declared that religion had to be combated (FRELIMO 1978). Church activities became hard to carry out. Between 1977 and 1979, both Catholics and Protestants (the latter under the CCM's umbrella) wrote pastoral letters and issued public statements protesting the position of the Church in Mozambique and criticising FRELIMO policies. During 1979, government hostility softened and the first signs of a new policy emerged.

After Zimbabwean independence in 1980, the rapid spread of MNR/RENAMO (Mozambique National Resistance), consequent destabilization, a long drought, and the decline of the national economy marked the next decade in Mozambique. Destabilization and dependence on external aid made Mozambique vulnerable to external influences, but it also led FRELIMO to establish internal "alliances" and to define partners with whom to face the crisis. The 1982 meeting between FRELIMO and religious institutions (FRELIMO 1983), the first in a series of meetings between church and state leaders and presided over by Samora Machel himself, initiated a new period of constructive dialogue.

Warfare and dislocation gave a new social role to the churches, which now directed their efforts to the distribution of food, clothing, seeds, and medicines in the countryside. The churches acted as pressure groups for socioeconomic and political change and as facilitators in the search for peace. The 1980s also brought a new wave of "Christian groups moving into Mozambique with money, expertise and personnel, often with their own particular aims as well" (Gifford 1993, 2). In the 1990s even more missionaries entered Mozambique.

The churches began to call for political dialogue between the warring parties. The Catholic Church undertook its first attempts in 1983, and in 1984, under the umbrella of CCM, the Protestants set up a Peace and Reconciliation Commission (Vines and Wilson 1995). The intense violence of 1987 led to more active initiatives. Between 1987 and 1992, the churches redoubled their efforts to facilitate dialogue and in October 1992, the General Peace Agreement was signed (Sengulane 1994; Raul Domingos, interviewed by T. Cruz e Silva, 2001). After the Agreement, the churches undertook important work to guarantee the peace process and played a role in the preparation of multiparty elections, in a substantial civic education programme, and in the supervision of the elections themselves.

The construction of the peace process and the building up of a democratic society not only benefited from the participation of churches but also contributed to new relationships among them, reinforcing the necessity for ecumenical work. From published studies on the role of the churches in the new situation in Mozambique, we note that since 1993 they have maintained direct contact with political parties and have often publicly articulated their positions on social change and the construction of democracy.

There are few published studies on the development and spread of Christianity in Mozambique, and those that exist concern the Catholic Church or the "historic" Protestant churches of mission origin. In Mozambique church history, the new evangelical movements—Zionists, Apostolics, Ethiopians, and in general, pentecostals—are more or less invisible. Their lack of presence reflects how marginal the sociopolitical leadership believed them to be during the colonial and postcolonial periods (Morier-Genoud 1998). Yet, they played a role in the opposition to the colonial system, and, more recently, in the construction of a democratic society. Moreover, they also represent an alternative social ideal.

In fact, there was a great expansion of evangelical churches in the 1980s and 1990s, particularly in the south and central areas of Mozambique. Some of this expansion was the work of the historic Protestant churches, but it also involved the newly arrived Assemblies of God, Baptists, various Ethiopian and Zionist churches, and, more recently, the Universal Church of the Kingdom of God (UCKG), which originated in Brazil. As pointed out by Gifford, these churches "take over on Sundays the schoolrooms, cinemas, [and] hotel conference rooms" (Gifford 1993, 2), and not only the large meeting places, but for the less organized churches, also many smaller spaces in the poorer suburbs of the major cities in the country. Their spread all over the country is becoming more and more visible (Roesch 1994, 45), as will be illustrated further in this chapter.

Some Religious and Political Definitions

Most scholars of African religion have felt difficulty and frustration when confronted with the need for classification and terminology (Chidester 1992; Chidester, Kwenda, Petty, Tobler, and Wratten 1997; Freston 2001; Balói 1995). Both theologians and social scientists experience similar difficulties in seeking to define evangelicalism.

Freston (2001, 2) refers to four characteristics used by Bebbington (1989) to define British evangelicalism, which can be made universally applicable: *conversionism*, or the need for a radical change of life; *activism*, or evangelistic and missionary effort; *biblicism*, or importance attached to the Bible; and *crucicentrism*, or emphasis on the centrality of Christ's sacrifice on the cross. From these four characteristics, we can derive a wide definition of evangelicalism, including some of the historic Protestant mission churches; the so-called African Initiated Churches; and the new pentecostal movements.

Like the United Methodist church in Zimbabwe, as described by Isabel Mukonyora in her chapter on Zimbabwe in this volume, historic Protestant mission churches in Mozambique came under African leadership during the colonial period and used the Bible as the foundation for their public statements, demanding independence, justice, and freedom in scriptural terms. This frequent appeal to the authority of biblical texts can be seen as characteristically (if not exclusively) evangelical. As Pastor Jamisse Taimo of the United Methodist Church in Mozambique told me, "The term 'Mission Churches' is a pejorative form of classification. They are dead.... The living churches are the ones such as the United Methodist Church, the Methodist Episcopal Church, the African Methodist Church, the Nazarene Church, the Free Methodist Church and many others."[5] I shall argue that the Zionist churches, despite all their differences in history, organization, and style, are equally evangelical.

The concept of democracy is equally difficult to define, especially in the African context. It is crucial to be aware that there are many forms and practices of democracy. For our purposes, considering that "democracy is about inclusion and exclusion, about access to power, about the privileges that go with inclusion and the penalties that accompany exclusion" (Horowitz 1994, 35), it is necessary to underline the crucial importance of "levels of citizen participation and their access to power" (Diamond and Plattner 1996, xi).

Considering the importance of elections in the democratic process, our case studies must highlight how and where the public role played by evangelicals in society relates to politics in general, and election processes in particular, and also how democracy impacts evangelicals (de Gruchy 1995). As Moyser says, "Politics is a process, a complex set of activities that form part of a 'group of people's' shared existence. The purpose of those activities is . . . essentially the making of collective decisions—the exercise of power" (Moyser 1991, 3). However, while elections involve citizens and the exercise of power, they are not necessarily synonymous with a democratic politics that is truly liberal and inclusive (Zakaria 2003).

Evangelical Trends

In its broader definition, the evangelical movement reached Mozambique towards the end of the nineteenth century by means of the "historic" mission churches (Helgesson 1994, Butselaar 1984, Gonçalves 1960, Morier-Genoud 1998). In the same period, there were already signs of emergent indigenous evangelicalism in Mozambique, spread by means of migrant workers and traders who had found their faith in South Africa, such as Robert Mashaba, who began to preach in Lourenço Marques (Maputo) as early as 1890, using Ronga (the Tsonga language) as a mean of communication (Helgesson 1994, 60).

Despite the colonial policy of preventing the growth of the "Native Religious Sects" (Figueira 1972), they spread particularly into southern and central Mozambique. Control over African pastors preaching in local languages was quite impossible for the Portuguese authorities (Helgesson 1994, 60). During the first two decades of the twentieth century, evangelicalism in the form of Ethiopianist, Zionist, and Apostolic churches (Figueira 1972) spread with more vigor and grew even more significantly in the 1950s and 1960s.

Marginalized and in some cases officially unrecognized by the colonial state, evangelicals experienced much the same from the postindependence administration (Morier-Genoud 1998). However, the rapid social and political change of the 1980s and 1990s, associated with military destabilization, natural disasters, and economic reform, contributed to the relative weakness of the state apparatus. The latter's incapacity to provide social welfare and basic services (water, electricity, sanitation, health, and education) displaced responsibility for much social management to so-called civil society, in the form of different associations, nongovernmental organizations (NGOs), churches, and social networks, such as those based on kinship, neighborhood, ethnicity, friendship, or religious identity (Cruz e Silva 2000b). Within this context, there occurred a "religious revitalization" (Roesch 1994, 45), including the significant growth of evangelicalism, which now enjoyed a wider space in which to develop its influence and activities.

The war drove people from the countryside into urban and peri-urban settings, such as district and provincial capital cities, gradually altering the human geography of most urban areas. The last two decades of the twentieth century were marked by the very rapid growth of urban areas (Ministério do Plano e Finanças 1996, 15). The major cities of Beira and Maputo offer the best examples of the process of urbanization by flight from the countryside, though drawing their migrants not from one particular district or province but from all over the country (Araújo 1990, 80).

This rapid process of urbanization coincided with the rapid growth of new evangelical movements, much as in South Africa, where the growing numbers of "African Indigenous Churches"[6] corresponded to urban development (Venter 1999). In particular, pentecostal churches mushroomed in the peri-urban areas, those grey zones between urban and rural environments.

Evangelical trends in Mozambique are poorly studied, especially when it comes to the "nonhistoric" churches. In particular, for the most recent period, there are many gaps in empirical knowledge. Unlike neighboring countries, Mozambique urgently needs a basic mapping of religious distribution. Here we offer a brief account of religious zonal distribution and analyze data collected from the Ministry of Justice, in the hope of depicting evangelical dynamics in contemporary Mozambique and particularly the flow to the urban areas.

Religious Zonal Distribution

The political history of precolonial, colonial, and postindependence Mozambique, and its differentiated insertion into the regional and international economy, shaped the heterogeneity of the country. Its strong cultural, linguistic, and religious diversity is a key factor in understanding the spread of Christianity and its response to political developments.

Although statistics are weak and have many gaps, they give us an idea of religious distribution in Mozambique, illustrating the various cultural influences and shifts that result from global and local forces. The 1980 census ignored data on religion. The first organized national collection of statistical data, which included religion, was produced in 1991 (Direcção Nacional de Estatística 1995, quoted by Balói 1995, 504–505). The last national census (1997), although showing the limitations of statistical experts in measuring religious affiliation, nevertheless made much more effort to map religious trends (UNDP 1999; INE 1999). However, apart from the fact that the 1991 information is only a projection, any attempt to compare statistical data from 1991 with 1997 information failed because of different definitions of religious denominations.

Statistical data from 1991 (Direcção Nacional de Estatística 1995, quoted by Balói 1995, 505) gave us the following zonal distribution:

- The Roman Catholic Church, the only religious institution organized at national level and covering all regions in the country, constituted 24.1 percent of the total population.
- Muslims, concentrated mostly in the North and coastal areas, amounted to 19.7 percent.

- Protestants, based predominantly in the South and in the capital city, Maputo, formed 21.5 percent, and in Maputo constituted 41.8 percent.
- Hindus amounted to 0.04 percent.
- The "Animists"—adherents of "African Traditional Religions"— present in all regions, account for 31.9 percent.

More recent information, published in 1999 and collected during the 1997 census (UNDP 1999; INE 1999), confirms the strength of the Roman Catholic Church nationally (23.8 percent) and the predominance of Muslims in the northern areas and the coastal plain (17.8 percent). It did not, however, use either the terms "Protestant" or "Animist," but introduced two new categories. Those with "no religion" amounted to 23.1 percent, and "Zionists," predominantly in the South and in Maputo, came to 17.5 percent.

The National Department of Religious Affairs Data

Apart from those evangelicals originating from the historic Mission churches, most others, and particularly the pentecostals, belong to churches that spread to the country via returning migrant workers, into the south from South Africa, and, to a lesser extent, into the center and the north from Zimbabwe, Malawi, and Zambia. Influence from neighboring countries, especially from South Africa, has continued into the most recent periods. There are many *Masowe Vapostori* in Mozambique, and many members of the Zimbabwe Assemblies of God, as well as many adherents of South African pentecostal churches. But most Mozambican evangelicals assumed very local characteristics. As David Martin says:

> The main upsurge is not in the older, more staid Evangelicalism, but in Pentecostalism. That means we are dealing with movements offering what are called the "gifts of the spirit," such as healing, prophecy, speaking in tongues. (Martin 1999, 38)

Given these origins of evangelicalism in Mozambique, and the restrictions imposed by colonialism, the movement mainly flourished in the rural areas. But the African churches that emerged from the Protestant "mission churches," though initially born and settled in the countryside, had urban links and strong bases in the main cities even before national independence in 1975. Most of the Christian-educated elite are a product of their activity.

The recent spread of evangelicalism in the 1980s and 1990s, however, is characterized by a strong relationship with the rapid urbanization of a rural population. Today a large proportion of African Initiated Churches (Chidester et al. 1997), and the Zionists in particular, are found in peri-urban areas.[7] Their members face great difficulties accessing education, health, safe water, electricity, transport, sanitation, and communications. They experience subemployment or unemployment, surviving mainly by means of the informal economy. They endure high rates of criminality and a general sense of social and physical insecurity. Excluded from society and access to its privileges, they are the peripheral and marginalized *par excellence*. The poverty, illiteracy, and fragmentation of many peri-urban evangelical congregations mean that many are not formally recognized by the state, often lacking as they do knowledge of the necessary statutes and the procedures for formal registration.[8]

The churches that do manage to register are listed in files in the Ministry of Justice. My research team searched these files between October 1999 and May 2000, singling out churches that could be characterized as evangelical. We located at least ninety-seven distinct evangelical churches, of which fifty-one were Zionist, and seven different evangelical associations. They were spread throughout Maputo, but with a heavy concentration in peri-urban and "marginalized" urban areas.[9] Most of them achieved official recognition during the second half of the 1990s, during the period of wider political and religious tolerance (Agadjanian 1999).

Such data, of course, give only one side of the picture: Those evangelical churches with a leadership able to claim the level of skills necessary for registration, a relatively stable financial base, and a certain number of believers. There are many Zionist churches with illiterate leaders and a fluctuating membership that escape the notice of state bureaucrats. We focused on these less visible churches during our fieldwork.

As for evangelical associations, apart from the long established Christian Council of Mozambique, founded in 1948, and the Aliança das Igrejas Cristãs Independentes de Moçambique, which includes fifty-eight churches, founded in 1957, most of the associations emerged during the 1980s and 1990s. Among them are

- *Associação Evangélica de Moçambique*, or AEM (Evangelical Association of Mozambique) affiliated with the Africa Evangelical Association;
- *Conselho das Igrejas Pentecostais de Moçambique* (Council of Pentecostal Churches of Mozambique), in formation;
- *União Bíblica de Moçambique* (Mozambican Bible Association) founded in 1986;
- *Conselho dos Patriarcas Pentecostais de Moçambique*, or COPAPEMO (Council of the Pentecostal Patriarchs of Mozambique);
- Association of Churches of Luis Cabral suburb, a group found in many urban districts and also in some suburbs. They also have associations of churches, under the supervision of the local administration.

The statutes and membership of most associations clearly show several things. They show the high visibility of the evangelicals who emerged from the historical mission churches and who play the most important role in well-established institutions such as the CCM. They reveal the importance of evangelical churches with international links in the formation of associations such as the Evangelical Association of Mozambique. They show the lesser involvement of pentecostal churches, and in general terms the new "African Initiated Churches" (AICs) in these bodies, though some now have the status of observers in the CCM. Finally, the marginalization of the AICs (including Zionist churches) is deepened by a new wave of exclusively pentecostal associations (Freston 2001). By the means of these various associations, evangelicals try to occupy public space, voice their interests, and achieve legitimacy; however, their fragmentation often makes the creation of effective associations difficult.

In the two case studies that follow, I focus on the contrasting democratic experience of two kinds of evangelicals: the highly visible inheritors of the historical mission churches, on the one hand, and the marginalized and fragmented evangelicals of the peri-urban areas, on the other. The first type I shall illustrate by a study of the United Methodist Church in Mozambique (UMCM). The second, I shall illustrate by a study of the Zionists in Maputo City. In the first case, there was much openness and collaboration by Methodist and other Protestant associations, which facilitated research. The fragmented Zionists are more difficult to study, but my research group had already carried out a study of pentecostal churches in Maputo and had identified the pattern of Zionist networks.

My decision to use a wide definition of evangelicalism worked in my favour, allowing the research team to interview many very different people and to explore many different meanings of democracy. Our study involves a world of contrasts. The large majority of the Zionist members are illiterate or poorly educated and their communication is largely oral. The UMCM largely uses written texts in both Portuguese and the written vernaculars, which the Protestant churches have done so much to create (Cruz e Silva 2001a, 2001b; Harries 2001). New churches, like the UCKG, make use of the electronic media, particularly television.

In a country marked by religious pluralism, the study of churches so different in origin and social composition enables us to understand evangelical action in diverse contexts: among the most marginalized and excluded; among the middle class; and, in some cases, among the upper classes and national elites. However, there is enough in common in the evangelical Christianity of these diverse groups to allow us to claim that evangelicals have contributed to the emergence of a democratic culture in many different ways: through meetings, discussions, and education; through focus on the Old Testament with its emphasis on liberation from oppression and on the social involvement of believers and their institutions; by means of the socially integrative practices of the churches; through the evangelical emphasis on citizenship, and on respect for law and authorities, while attempting to maintain an institutional distance and a readiness to challenge corruption and violations of human rights; and finally, by means of their general moralizing function in society. The choice of the two major case studies also allows us to contrast a church originating from a missionary movement with its long history and its traditions of indirect anticolonial struggle, with the more recent and less clearly political Zionist churches.

The United Methodist Church in Mozambique (UMCM)

The work of the American Methodist missionaries in Mozambique began in 1880, when they reached the areas of Inhambane and Gaza. During the 1880s, they reached Manica and Sofala. By 1910, the Methodist Episcopal Mission had established itself all over Inhambane province and exercised a strong influence in the area. Although it tended to be particularly associated with the use and development of the Tswa language, it also had influence in what are today the Gaza and Maputo provinces (Cruz e Silva 2001a, 2001b).

The United Methodist Church was born in 1968 by means of a merger between the former Methodist Episcopal Church and the Methodist Church (Helgesson 1994). Historians have shown that during Portuguese colonialism, the UMCM contributed greatly to the political awareness of its believers. It also assumed a political and social role in society, undertaking underground work to give indirect support to young people who later joined the armed struggle for liberation (Helgesson 1994; Cruz e Silva 2001a, 2001b) and to other nationalists in opposition to the colonial state. The original mission structures of the church were modified by a process of "Africanization," which began in the 1920s and was consolidated during the 1960s (Helgesson 1994). The UMCM was securely based in the rural areas; however, later on it came to link its rural constituencies with an urban membership, drawn from the lower and the middle classes, and including a certain proportion of the national elite, particularly in the Inhambane and Maputo areas. This continues to be the case today.

The church was a member of the CCM from its earliest days. After independence, the UMCM worked under the umbrella of the Council towards national reconstruction, seeking to define strategies of social intervention and to work out a relationship with the FRELIMO government. Like the other Protestant member churches of the CCM, it has played an active role in politics, particularly in recent years.

Here I seek to analyze this political participation. In particular, I focus on the role of the UMCM in the peace process, in post-conflict reconciliation, and the construction of democracy. I also ask whether the fact that the president of the National Elections Commission was a UMCM pastor has influenced the electoral behaviour of Protestants as a whole and of United Methodists in particular.

Apart from a review of the literature and a search of the press, I carried out semistructured interviews with members of both MNR/RENAMO and FRELIMO; with church leaders; with leaders of CCM; with the pastors of two of the UMCM parishes in Maputo city and surroundings (Matola—Bairro Liberdade); with Methodist believers; and with Pastor Jamisse Taimo, the president of the last two National Elections Commissions.

Toward a Culture of Peace

The formal position of the United Methodist Church of Mozambique during its missionary days was that it was concerned with the kingdom of God rather than the kingdom of the world. Nevertheless, during colonialism, the UMCM came to assume the position of an informal opposition to the Portuguese system. Yet after the start of the war for national liberation (1964–1974), the Church questioned the legitimacy of making war in order to obtain peace and to liberate men and women from oppression. The war caused many divisions within the churches, and differences among Protestant missionaries in Mozambique paralleled the well-known divergences within the Catholic Church (Cruz e Silva 2001a, 2001b).

After independence, even though they were operating in a closed, and in some ways hostile, environment, many of the ex-mission churches found themselves, as national institutions, in a more favourable position to participate openly in shaping the destiny of the country by functioning as pressure groups in the struggle for social justice.

It is clear, however, that the old debate about whether the church should take part in politics is still very much alive. When questioned on the matter, some of our Methodist interviewees reacted almost instinctively at first, stressing their dislike of talking about politics, even when their later comments gave a different picture. Others adopted a more or less open attitude. For example, Mr. Nhancale, who is fifty-six years old, made a point of emphasizing that:

> The ultimate aim of the Church is to preach the word of God and it
> is not the church's mission to participate in politics. But as life
> evolves and times change the Church is also involved in contribut-
> ing to the success of democracy so that people may live in peace—
> even if this is not the mission of the church.

Many believers mentioned to us the still difficult matter of separating the individual's personality as a believer from their personality as a citizen. T. Simbine gave the following testimony:

> To say that the Church should not involve itself in politics is a
> great error. This was the case in the post independence period. It is

difficult for a believer to see evil and not react. But the reality shows us the opposite. When a Church aids the state itself, it ends up involving itself in politics. The Church incorporates citizens and has to be there when necessary. We have witnessed the moral disintegration of society. We have fallen and are we not to recover? Young people have no direction and few respect the advice they receive. The mission of the Church is to educate the people and to avoid evil, and it would not be a Church if it did not speak out!

As the secretary-general of the CCM, the Reverend Amosse told us, when dealing with Church participation in politics, we should not forget "that the theology of oppression belongs to the older generations,"[10] and that the Church has to involve itself in the society of which it is a part. Indeed, this view turned out to be the opinion of the majority of our Methodist informants, many of whom insisted that preaching the word of God and the Holy Scriptures is the basis for teaching the democratic principles that should guide the Church's activities.

Some of our informants referred to the democratic culture that had long characterized the Methodist Church, including the debates and discussions in assemblies, as well as the education offered to the young. From this perspective, the Church's own principles and practices could be taken as a starting point for the development of a culture of peace, dialogue, and respect for difference. However, other informants, particularly those belonging to the younger generation, questioned the difference between the official position of the Church and the actual practices of the leadership, where centralized authoritarianism rather than democratic practice often predominates. From their perspective, the creation of a general democratic culture needs to feed back into and democratize the Church.

At any rate, political and economic change in the 1980s and 1990s created effective space for church action. The "center" needed local, nonstate "partners" to help carry through development activities and to channel international aid. There was an explosion of national social organizations in the 1990s (Sogge 1997). Many of these were religious. They participated in the quantitative and qualitative growth of civil society.

The Church now has to confront the challenges that such a situation offers, and has to work out how to respond to the legacy of violence and the effects of neo-liberal policies on the poor. The Church is called upon to play a vital role in national reconciliation, and one of the most notable contributions of the evangelical churches in Mozambique in the last twenty years has been the development of a peace culture—a fundamental step towards greater dialogue. The United Methodist Church has been much involved in this (as we shall see, so also have the Zionists, though in very different ways).

From prayer, vigils, and ecumenical meetings to their more visible role in the process of peace and reconciliation under the umbrella of the CCM (whose role in the establishment of dialogue between FRELIMO and MNR/RENAMO was very important), the United Methodists have struggled in various ways to help to establish a peace culture. Some of our Methodist informants told us that in time of war the Church cannot be neutral; it has to promote reconciliation. Thus, R. Whate told us:

> During the war, more than 90 percent of the parishes organized prayers for peace. This was the first weapon the Church used. Through the CCM our bishop participated in the peace process, and God heard us—not only Methodists and other Protestants, but even Catholics.

As a member of the CCM, the United Methodist Church took part in the first meetings with the Mozambique government, meetings that initiated the dialogue between FRELIMO and MNR/RENAMO. Although the final phase of the search for peace through dialogue lay in the hands of the Catholic Church, the members of the CCM played a crucial role in the initial stages of the negotiation, managing to bring the belligerents face to face.

The postwar process required greater effort on the part of the Church because it was now cast in the role of conciliator, and, to a certain extent, guarantor of the maintenance of stability in the country. Ten years later, the UMCM and other members of the CCM continue in this role—maintaining regular meetings with FRELIMO and MNR/RENAMO, promoting Methodist and ecumenical discussion, organizing prayers and vigils for peace in Mozambique at the national and regional level, all the while not neglecting its own role as a pressure group. Its leaders and members participate in movements for peace and democracy that have taken root in the country as well as in campaigns against human rights abuses and discrimination.

A rapid survey of daily and weekly newspapers over the last ten years reveals the active participation of the UMCM in the peace process. This participation emerges even more clearly during the period of high political tension that followed the second democratic general elections in 1999. The UMCM and other churches have openly denounced evident electoral irregularities and maintained dialogue between the contending political parties. During this period, the UMCM organized numerous meetings whose main objective was the maintenance of peace and the promotion of reconciliation. The Church is even setting up its own peace institute[11]—all a clear sign of Methodist activity in the political arena and of the impact that the development of democracy has had among evangelicals, as well as of the impact evangelicals are having on democracy.

The Methodist Vote

The first multiparty elections in the country had a special symbolic and sub-stantive importance, representing a moment of decisive change toward the construction of a democratic society. The first National Election Commission was headed by Brazão Mazula, a former Catholic priest, long involved in the educational arena as a high-level administrator in the Ministry of Education. The emphasis given at the national and international level to the elections and to the role of the Catholic Church in the preliminary phases of the peace process tended to obscure the fact that Mazula was an ex-priest. There was active but discreet participation by the evangelical churches. However, little has been published about the role of the churches in the elections and no analysis has been made of the religious vote (Balói 1995). There has been no treat-ment of Mazula as a Catholic, though the prestige he acquired as a result of the successful elections earned him an appointment as Rector of Maputo's Eduardo Mondlane University, the country's oldest and largest institution of higher education.

The parties largely accepted the results of the first general election. This outcome was very different from that of the second elections, held in 1999, in which MNR/RENAMO was convinced that it had been cheated of vic-tory. Eighteen months later, the results were still being contested by MNR/RENAMO, despite being upheld in the High Court. Since the elections, there have been deep political tensions between the political parties and much po-litical violence. The Presidency of the 1999 National Election Commission, therefore, was a much more contentious office than it was during the first multiparty elections.

The president in 1999 was Jamisse Taimo, a UMCM pastor[12] and Rector of the Higher Institute of International Relations in Maputo. (Despite the controversy over the elections, Taimo was reelected as president of the National Election Commission in 2000.) In his first period as president, Taimo was active and prominent as a Methodist Christian; the leader of his church, Bishop Machado, was also very visible. To what extent did Taimo use a Christian platform to reinforce his position on the Commission? Was there pressure from the churches in general, and from the UMCM in particular, for him to accept the position of president? Did his role have any effect on the Protestant vote?

Jamisse Taimo had been a teacher in the combined theological college at Rikatla and pastor-in-charge of a new UMCM parish in Liberdade suburb, Matola, itself formerly a suburb, though now a neighbouring city, of Maputo. He became a noted figure in the UMCM when he completed his Masters degree in Brazil. His links with the younger generation and his method of working by listening closely to people of different age groups and experiences gained him the support and respect of church members. He had been a member of one of the first peace organizations in Mozambique.

During the preelectoral period, when Taimo was president of the Election Commission (for the 1999 elections), he was very active in the United Methodist community, thus giving the UMCM increased visibility. For example, his visit to the parish of Malanga—the largest UMCM parish and the headquarters of the Church—though ostensibly for a simple religious service, was covered by the country's major TV channel, TVM, in great detail, and the image transmitted was one of civic propaganda in the midst of a crowded religious ceremony. Bishop Machado, the head of the UMCM, appeared on television to urge people to vote in the elections. The UMCM thus appeared fully committed to the electoral process. Our Methodist informants frequently referred to the difficult task Taimo had in separating his personality as a believer from that of president of the Commission when he visited parishes or took part in services. They pointed out that his speeches there always referred to the elections and to the necessity of citizens fulfilling their duty by voting.

We found no evidence of party propaganda on Taimo's part during the campaign, but we can affirm that he employed his religious platform and connections to reinforce his position in the Election Commission, making the fullest possible use of church networks to guarantee the success of the elections through his advocacy of the importance of voting. As he personally informed me,[13] the Commission planned that religious leaders should appear in the media to speak on the importance of voter registration. Taimo himself used his contacts with the various religious denominations to ensure that they urged upon their members the importance of the elections, and, in particular, the importance that they take place according to the original timetable, despite the objections of the opposition. The municipal elections of 1998 had been marked by a very low turnout (Serra 1999). Taimo was determined that this be avoided in 1999.

There is no doubt that Taimo's influence reinforced the Methodists' emphasis on the necessity of voting. In any case, the UMCM makes constant appeals to its believers to exercise their rights as citizens. The Church attributes to itself a special role in society, as a moral and civic educator, emphasizing the value of the individual.[14] Although the right to choose political leadership through an electoral process is part of the recent history of the country, the Church sees it as a fulfillment of the fundamental rights of citizenship, which it has consistently emphasized in the past.

As we have seen, the majority of Methodist informants believe that their church has a role to play in the political arena. Many of these informants approved of the choice of Jamisse Taimo as president of the electoral commission. Some hold that he earned the post through his personal qualities rather than because of his position as pastor. As a fifty-three-year-old woman, Z. Quepiço, put it:

The nomination of Pastor Jamisse Taimo to the presidency of the CNE was a very important event for the Methodist Church, despite his not being nominated because he was a pastor. The Church, particularly in Liberdade parish, felt vindicated because it had always encouraged the pastor to expound his ideas and opinions on political questions, and with this nomination, we felt it was another opportunity to show that the Church is responsible for the establishment of [a] moral equilibrium in society.

E. Matsinhe, a forty-nine-year-old woman, was also happy with the nomination because it helped the Church to participate in the construction of democracy. Among the youth of the UMCM, Taimo also seemed the best choice because of his personal qualities.

Others put less emphasis on Taimo's personality and believed that he had been chosen because of his Church office. Twenty-six-year-old N. Zunguza explained:

Pastor Jamisse Taimo as President of the CNE shows the Church contributing to the success of democracy. The State chose a religious figure for such an important task because having a politician in that position would raise lots of doubts.

Yet more convincing than all these testimonies as a confirmation of the pride with which members of the UMCM greeted the nomination of one of its "offspring" to this important task was the religious ceremony of Thanksgiving held to mark the appointment. During the ceremony, prayers were offered that Taimo would show much courage and determination. He was encouraged with the words "success in your duties," "impartiality," and "dignity."

Before Taimo accepted the position, he approached Bishop Machado of the UMCM, Archbishop dos Santos of the Catholic Church, and Bishop Mandlate of the CCM; all gave their encouragement and support.[15] He explained to us how Bishop Machado reacted to the invitation: "You cannot refuse because it is important that it be seen that it is the Church that is being invited to direct the CNE. We as a Church will support you and stay close to you whatever may happen. The Church is your home."

We did not carry out research designed to show how evangelicals voted individually. However, our interviews revealed three types of response among Methodists to Taimo's nomination: first, pride and pleasure on the part of most Methodists and Protestants generally; second, general acceptance by the wider Christian community; and third, acceptance with some concealed reservations by some Protestants, anxious about the involvement of the church in a controversial process. We have not tried to discover for which candidate Protestants voted, but we believe the evidence suggests that Taimo's influence helped to ensure widespread participation in the electoral process.

The Zionists in Maputo City

The extent to which the Methodist Church was ready to be publicly associated with the formal institutions of multiparty democracy in Mozambique is perhaps surprising. Nevertheless, its whole history prepares us for its contemporary political role. The case is very different with the Zionists, whose role in Mozambique has never been studied in detail but who are portrayed as apolitical in almost all the studies made of them in southern Africa.[16] Since Zionism in Mozambique originated in South Africa, Zimbabwe, or Malawi, its character there might be expected to be the same. But whatever may be the case elsewhere, in Mozambique Zionism grew out of the crises of war, refugee flight, the movement of peasants to the towns and their subsequent impoverishment and marginalization. In Mozambique, Zionism is clearly part of the politics of the poor.

This case study is based on information contained in the Ministry of Justice archives; on a literature review for Mozambique (Honwana 1996; Roesch 1994; Balói 1995; Helgesson 1994; Hastings 1991; Figueira 1972; Freitas 1956–1957; Agadjanian 1999, among others); on a literature review for the region as a whole (Comaroff 1985; Gifford 1993, 1995, 1998; Maxwell 1998; Venter 1999; Sundkler 1961a, 1961b, 1976); and, above all, on field work undertaken in the peri-urban Luis Cabral suburb of Maputo.

The Luis Cabral suburb was originally called "Chinhambanine" because most of its inhabitants originated or descended from Inhambane Province. It was given its current name after independence when President Samora Machel visited the suburb with the former president of Guinea-Bissau, Luis Cabral, but it was founded during the colonial period because of movement from the countryside into the town. Its culture derives from its predominantly Chopi population, though there are other immigrants from Inhambane, such as the (bi)Tonga and (ma)Tswa. During the violence of the 1980s and 1990s, the suburb grew and received immigrants not only from Inhambane, but also from other rural areas, particularly Shanganes from Gaza Province and Rhonga from the general Maputo area.[17]

Situated within the Maputo urban administrative district No. 5, Luis Cabral borders on other peripheral areas of the city, and makes a bridge between the town and the green belt, a valley where most of the vegetables consumed by the city are produced in small and medium-sized farms. Its total population is about thirty-four thousand inhabitants.[18] Many inhabitants work in towns or in factories in greater Maputo; a considerable number, however, work on the vegetable gardens. However, the main characteristic of the neighborhood is the number of the population practicing alternative survival strategies. On every corner one can see men and women of all ages selling almost everything. Informal trade and permanent subemployment are the main way to survive. Safe water and electricity are only available to families who can afford to pay utility bills. Schools are unavailable to most children—there are only three primary schools—and the majority of the population cannot afford access to transport, communications, and healthcare.

The Zionists at Luis Cabral

In 1999, I undertook a pilot study, followed by fieldwork in Luis Cabral sub-urb, which focused on the establishment of religious and social networks. The results allowed us to make a preliminary mapping of the religious field in the area. Initially, we noted the existence of at least fifty different pentecostal churches, but during January and February 2000, carrying out fieldwork for the present study, we realized that there are in fact many more than the fifty originally estimated. We became aware of how difficult it is to estimate the number of churches in the area. Most of them are based in the private homes of their pastors or bishops, are not registered, and are permanently mobile.

A Sunday visit to the suburb gives an excellent appreciation of the pro-liferation of pentecostal churches in Luis Cabral. There are innumerable meet-ings held simultaneously in homes or in small church buildings, filling the air with hymns. The streets are full of people dressed in the colorful uniforms typical of many of these churches. Such a picture could be repeated in many of the outer suburbs.

Although my focus was on Zionist churches, it was difficult to distinguish them from other churches, particularly pentecostals.[19] As a result, we also interviewed people from Ethiopian and Apostolic churches, as well as various types of pentecostals. Thus, the churches approached by our research team were:[20] Igreja Santa Cristã de Moçambique; Igreja Zione Apostólica; Igreja Evangélica de Deus Pentecostal de Moçambique; Igreja Sião Apostólica S. Marcos de Moçambique; Igreja Evangélica da Santíssima Trindade; Igreja Zione Evangélica Chilembene Malhazine de Moçambique; Igreja Sião União Apostólica de Moçambique; Igreja Filadélfia Apostólica de Moçambique; Igreja Betania Sagrada de Moçambique; Igreja Zione Jerusalém de Moçambique; Igreja Herman Genesareth Apostólica Galileia de Moçambique; Holy Speed Zion de Moçambique; Igreja S. Marcos de Moçambique; Igreja Luz de Mo-çambique.

Since some churches in Luis Cabral suburb extend into other neighbor-hoods, or are simply branches of churches settled in other areas of the city, we had to conduct some of our research in other areas. The churches that we studied in Luis Cabral were usually small, with some fifty to sixty members each. Most of them were based at the house of the bishop, the pastor, or the prophet, and constructed of local and precarious materials.

Healing and Purification: Key Points for Social Reintegration

Zionists work within a Christian framework where the Holy Spirit is believed to intervene when various rituals are performed, particularly rites of healing and purification. The Zionist movement in Mozambique is made up of a variety of churches, with differences in doctrine, liturgy, and rituals (Agadjanian 1999). Apart from these differences, however, most churches have in common some dietary taboos (against alcohol, some kinds of freshwater fish, pork, duck, and rabbit) and behavioral restrictions, particularly directed to women (after childbirth and during menstruation). The use of drums and prescribed uniforms (Comaroff 1985, 167, 187), where colours have different meanings, according to each prophet's dreams, are also characteristic. Depending on the type of Zionism, churches appeal to or reject spirit possession and the interpretation of dreams in healing rituals.

Hierarchy is very similar in Zionist churches. Most have a bishop, pastors, evangelists, advisers and other officials, and usually associations of women and youth. As was described by Agadjanian (1999), the relationship between the bishop and other members of the hierarchy is a symbolic one, allowing them greater autonomy. However, the role of a charismatic prophet, around whom believers gather, is a central feature of Zionist churches, especially when it comes to healing and purification. Such rituals are pivotal to understanding adherence to Zionist movements, particularly in periods of social crisis such as the 1980s and 1990s in Mozambique.

Isabel J., fifty years old, born in Inhambane, and originally a Catholic, joined the Igreja Jerusalém in 1974, while attempting to solve her problem of infertility. Laura F. Macave, also fifty years old, was also originally a Catholic and joined a Zionist church because it resolved her daughter's health problems. G. B. Leão, fifty-two years old, again originally a Catholic, joined the Igreja Sião Apostólica Cristã de Moçambique when his son was healed in a mere two weeks and without cost after all efforts in the hospital failed. He believes that the Holy Spirit brings physical healing through the ministry of the Zionist churches.

Healing and purification rituals take many forms, from the simple use of prayers, the Bible, and invocations of the Holy Spirit, to the use of leaves, roots, water, salt, candles, ashes, amongst many other examples. In other cases, there are animal sacrifices and sometimes invocation of the ancestral spirits. Colours play a part in the rituals, as they figure in the symbols of the church, in dress or simply in the ropes used to heal. Water is used to baptize, to heal and clean the socially dirty and polluted. G. B. Leão told us about healing rituals: "Our work is based on the Holy Spirit. The Holy Spirit indicates the correct root or leaf and also the way to boil and drink it, to heal a particular person."

Celeste T. G., age fifty-eight, born at Inhambane and a believer in the Igreja Santa Cristã de Moçambique, told us that Zionists are playing an important social role by healing poor people who lack the money to go to the hospital.

Reviewing the statutes of some registered Zionist churches, one observes that most are not hostile to "Western medicine," and hospital treatments are allowed and even advised. Contrary to the opinion expressed by Agadjanian (1999: 417), our testimonies show that Zionist healing is not an alternative to Western medicine for most people, but the only means of healing certain diseases that hospitals are unable to cure, and in many cases the only form of healing they can afford. In such a situation, Western medicine becomes the alternative solution (Meneses 2004). Zionist healing, however, does serve as an alternative to traditional doctors (Agadjanian 1999, 417).

Rituals of purification, usually related to traumatic disorders, are very characteristic of Zionism. Social pollution may arise "from being in contact with dead people and bloodshed." People exposed to such situations "are believed to be potential contaminators of the social body" (Honwana 1996: 355–356). Our informants described to us the necessity of cleansing, giving many examples, such as after childbirth, after a period of menstruation, or contact with death, even if only a visit to a cemetery. Purification rituals to reintegrate people into society are mentioned quite often, particularly in relation to migrant workers coming back home and individuals who have been in war or in other contexts and situations related to violence. However, very few people admitted that they had had personal experience of rituals relating to war and death. Our interpretation of their refusal to discuss such topics is that they prefer to forget this phase of their lives as a form of self-protection.

This was the case, for example, with one informant, Catarina E., a fifty-eight-year-old widow born in Manjacaze district, Gaza. Catarina was formerly a pastor in a Zionist church, the Igreja Zione Apostólica. But when her husband died she had so many problems in the church that she gave it up and joined the Universal Church of the Kingdom of God. She told us:

> I feel very weak in speaking about the past. I prefer to speak
> about real things. The war is over, but my nephew was killed and
> quartered into slices, and his wife was obliged to eat his meat cooked
> with maize. . . . So I do not want to speak about things that to me are
> over!

However, a Zionist healer, Celeste T. G., told us that she had performed many rituals of purification and cleansing. People who have been kidnapped and raped have approached her for healing, and recently she performed cleansing rituals for a man who had been a soldier. This kind of ceremony is also part of the creation of a culture of peace; such rituals restore individuals' identities and facilitate their reintegration into society (Honwana 1996).

Among the objectives stated by the Zion churches registered at the Ministry of Justice is the expulsion of Satan. Satan is held to cause disease among people, and to drive him out there is a need for special rituals and prayers.

Our observations showed that most believers in Zionism belong to the poorest levels of society. The social networks built up around Zionist religious identity offer moral even more than material support, particularly in situations of disease and death. They assist in resolving family and community conflict. The more stable churches collect a tithe, sometimes only annually (an illustration of the economic situation of most Zionists), to help believers in times of crisis.

Comparing the results of our research in Luis Cabral with the records held at the Ministry of Justice, we concluded that, although registered churches have to be headed by literate people with at least a minimum of education, most Zionist churches are composed of and headed by illiterate people. They are organized not according to bureaucratic rules but around a charismatic leader, usually a prophet and senior kinsman. In Luis Cabral, the churches reflect kin and ethnic identities, and allowed small clusters of people to express their own culture and to celebrate their own capacities for religious inspiration and leadership.

Zionists and Gender Relations

The concentration of women within the Zionist churches is typical of many Christian churches, which tend to be movements of women led by men. When questioned about the reasons for the high membership of women, the majority of those interviewed argued that women's traditional role within the family, as wife, mother and educator, naturally leads to devout attendance at worship and at other ceremonies. Women attend Zionist churches because they have a primary need to ensure the health of their children. According to our informants, women express the greatest need for healing and purification.

The Zionist churches are not very different from other evangelical churches in placing a strong emphasis on the role of the family, with particular insistence on monogamous marriage and the education of children. In a society where the ties of belonging, and, more generally, the whole social fabric, have been eroded by successive crises, including war and dislocation (Andrade, Loforte, and Osório 1998), the remoralization of society and the appeal to Christian moral values can itself be interpreted as a form of social reconstruction. In this process, the Church plays an integrative function, contributing to the reestablishment of social cohesion (Andrade, Loforte, and Osório 1998).

A Zionist informant, Isabel J., told us that most believers in her church are women but that the power belongs to men. Other female informants, like

Ermelinda T. and Alice S., both members of the Igreja Sião Apostólica de Moçambique, agreed with her.

The fact that authority in Zionism is in male hands usually means that women have access to leadership only when their husbands occupy positions in the hierarchy of the church, as a sort of delegated power. This is the case with wives of bishops or pastors, who, as such, are entitled to play a leadership position in the church. According to our informants, a single woman is not allowed to assume a leadership position and can only occupy the position of adviser, church organizer, or youth worker. The main role of a woman in the church is related to her capacity as mother, educator of children, or exemplar of a good Christian wife. The churches thus in many ways reproduce the dominant models of patriarchal society.

There are certainly women playing leadership roles in Zionist churches, even as pastors and prophets and heads of associations. Women are not absent from public spaces. An attentive reading of gender relations within the churches would lead us to conclude, however, that this public space is, in reality, an extension of domestic space and is almost always separated from the space of males.

Zionists and Politics

We have seen that the Methodist Church has been committed to democracy, citizenship, and the electoral process. Although Zionists have not played public roles on electoral commissions or in convening meetings with parties, their position is essentially the same. Isabel D. J., a Zionist believer in Luis Cabral, told us:

> Every day, at the end of worship, we pray for the country, for the political leaders, people with diseases and people in prison. We begin with prayers directed to the hospital and we pray to God in order to give strength to the nurses that they should take good care of people suffering from diseases. We pray also for peace and peace keeping.

Other informants confirmed her testimony. Laura M. told us that during the first and second general elections, and also during the municipal elections, her church organized civic education classes. All members were taught their rights as citizens, how to vote, though they were not told to vote for one or other party. Most of our informants gave us similar testimony, stressing that they were taught to act as individual citizens rather than as a bloc of church members.

A glance at the results of the last presidential elections in 1999 shows that FRELIMO and its candidate, Joaquim Chissano, had a good margin of advantage in the southern provinces, and in Maputo in particular. Despite its earlier antireligious stance and its disapproval of "obscurantist practices," FRELIMO now tolerates pentecostalism and is supported by most Zionists. In Samora Machel's day, one would not have witnessed the numerous public rituals carried out today by Zionists and Apostolics on the beaches of Maputo nor such high levels of pentecostal activity in the suburbs. But the Zionist churches make useful contributions to the new democratic pluralism of Mozambique. They teach respect for the nation's laws and the obligation to exercise the duties of a citizen.

We concur with Otto Roesch's conclusion that the recent waves of evangelical Christian movements in Mozambique, and the Zionists in particular, though diffuse in nature and strongly orientated towards local issues, are "a rather heterogeneous political force, and are not likely ever to form a significant national, or even regional, voting bloc. . . . At the community and local level, however, they may prove to be a political and social force to be reckoned with" (Roesch 1994, 14).

Conclusion

The history of Mozambique, as of most other African countries, offers plenty of evidence of the way religion is always present in the life of the people, either to benefit their interests or to be used against them. During the wars of the 1980s and 1990s, cults of counterviolence emerged (Vines 1991; Wilson 1992a, 1992b; Pereira 1999). The war became also a "war of spirits" (Wilson 1992a) and a contest of beliefs. Refugees developed their own new churches, often Zionist, in the camps. After the war ended, rituals of healing and cleansing (Honwana 1996) contributed powerfully to political reconstruction and thus to efforts to build a democratic society (Ranger, quoted by Shah, 2000). "Religion has allowed people to experiment in different ways of being human," writes Chidester (1992, xi).[21]

Many of these experiments have been evangelical. The history of evangelicalism in Mozambique has been marked by an ideological tradition of separation between church and state. This ideology is still expressed today. Our research in the Ministry of Justice files reveals that many registered evangelical churches declare as a principle the separation between religion and politics. Yet throughout the decades in which this ideology has been expressed, evangelical Christianity has in fact assumed one political position after another.

In the colonial period, evangelical Christians in effect took a political position by refusing to take one. Unlike Catholics, they made a clear distinction between their churches and the colonial state. This distinction ensured that, while they were not directly involved in politics, they were free to act as pressure groups and sometimes as a *de facto* opposition to colonialism. In the immediate postcolonial period, with the new state taking strongly authoritarian and antireligious positions, the evangelical churches resumed their role as critical pressure groups, seeking to moralize the country and "generally acquiring a voice in the public forum" (Martin 1999, 39), though (with some exceptions) in a fragmented way. The war between FRELIMO and MNR/RENAMO gave them a more positive role—a leading part in the search for peace, and thereafter in the peacekeeping process and the construction of democracy.

In the process, churches with international links made the most visible political interventions (Ranger 1995). Members of smaller churches, and particularly the pentecostals, expressed their politics in a less visible way by playing their role as citizens during the electoral process, participating in civic education, and exercising their voting rights. With the presidential, Assembly and local elections in 1994, 1998, and 1999, Mozambique experimented with a multi-party democratic system. Our case studies of the Methodist church and of the Zionists have shown that the civic culture of elections is a process in which evangelicals can be involved not only as citizens but also as believers.

On the other side, the history of Mozambique provides many examples of religion being used—along with race and ethnicity—to justify division and exclusion, as a means of demarcating *oneself* from the *other*. During colonialism, religion and religious identities were utilized to divide and to establish difference, and to justify inclusion and exclusion. More recently, the utilization of religion has been illustrated in the history of the post-independence war. The appeal to religion has been at the heart of attempts to "retraditionalize" the country. Use has been made of both religion and ethnicity to legitimize political power.

For example, we analyzed the reports published by the daily newspaper, *Noticias*, and the weekly newspapers, *Savana* and *Domingo*, published in Maputo between October and December 1999, covering the period of preparation for the elections, and the elections themselves. We focused on MNR/RENAMO and FRELIMO speeches; statements from the National Electoral Commission; statements by the churches; and comment by journalists. The analysis shows that during the electoral process FRELIMO often made appeals to the realm of the traditional, either using religious and kinship rituals to appeal to the spirits of ancestors, or else approaching chiefs. At the beginning of their campaign, in each region of the country they held a religious ceremony, which reflects both a clear illustration of their need to legitimate their authority and power and an example of the process of "retraditionalization." Traditional religion was used to reanchor the political regime in the history of the country (Cruz e Silva 2000a, 2000b). Discussing the elections of 1994, Balói (1995, 501–502) maintains that there was no religious vote. However, he points out that the churches played an active role in the preparation of the elections and during the elections themselves. He emphasizes that apart from the Jehovah's Witnesses, there was no clear example of abstentions specifically related to religion (Balói 1995, 516). A similar situation prevailed in the elections of 1999. There are no statistical or contextual analyses of religious voting patterns. However, the news transmitted by television and the national newspapers, and the data collected during our fieldwork, offers abundant evidence of the intense involvement of evangelicals in the electoral process.

A glance at the daily and weekly national papers published in Maputo, like *Noticias, Savana, Domingo*, after the announcement of the 1999 presidential election results,[22] shows that various evangelical Associations, such as the CCM (*Savana*, January 14, 2000) and the AEM (*Noticias*, January 12, 2000), issued calls for evangelicals to pray for newly elected MPs and to accept the results of the elections and also made appeals to other parties to accept these results.

Based on such evidence, some authors hold that the evangelical churches, with their style of organization, education, and training, naturally stimulate the exercise of democratic values. However, we found that there was often some distance between discourse and practice, and thus a distance between leaders and members. The hierarchical forms of many churches can function as a means of domination, leading to the emergence of authoritarian leadership.

In Mozambique, the churches as such do not enjoy representation in parliament, and their only form of political participation can be through political parties. The model of representative democracy adopted in the country excludes the majority of the citizens from decision-making. As the Reverend Amosse told us, "Politics is not free in the country. People represent their parties. It is difficult for the churches to enter this process."[23]

In view of this limitation, the evangelical churches can intervene in political life only by continuing to act as pressure groups, through their management of social alternatives, and their stress on the exercise of citizens' rights. At the same time, they play an integrative role that enables them to contribute to social cohesion through healing and purification rituals, the re-establishment of families, the moralization of society, and efforts in favour of reconciliation and the permanence of a culture of peace. Even though evangelicals do not consistently practice their own values in their internal governance, the great support they give to the individual and the work they do in defense of reconciliation and human rights are forms of political participation conducted on, as well as conducive to, basic democratic principles.

NOTES

1. I would like to thank the team of assistant researchers, who collaborated in collecting information on the two case studies, particularly Hilário Diuty, Zefanias Matsimbe, Sonia Massangaia, Mário Rui Tsaquice Antonio Langa, Padil Salimo, and Adriano Biza. I am also grateful to: the direction of the United Methodist Church in Mozambique (UMCM) and the leaders of UMCM parishes at Malanga and Bairro da Liberdade; Dr. Jamisse Taimo and Dr. A Zunguze from UMCM; the Reverend Amosse from the CCM; leaders of the local administration, churches, and churches

commissions from Luis Cabral Suburb, and all interviewees for all their support and collaboration.

2. According to Sundkler (1961a, 54–55), "The reason for the use of this term is simply that the leaders and followers of these churches refer to themselves as '*ama-Ziyoni*,' Zionists. Historically they have roots in Zion City, Illinois, United States. Ideologically they claim to emanate from the Mount Zion in Jerusalem (. . .). There are numerous denominational, local, and individual variations of Zionist groups (. . . .), and they have in common, healing, speaking in tongues, purification rites, and taboos as the main expressions of their faith" (Sundkler 1961a, 55).

3. Although aware of limitations in using the concept "Africanisation," in our analysis we adopted its use as meaning the introduction of elements of African culture in Christian rituals. Sometimes however, as in this case, the concept is more related to: (1) African leadership, involving both the training of African Pastors, personnel, and the religious leadership, on the one hand, and the movement toward church autonomy, on the other, and (2) the formation of an educated elite.

4. This point was also made by Job Chambal, director of the Religious Affairs National Department in an interview with T. Cruz e Silva in Maputo, 2000.

5. Jamisse Taimo, interviewed by T. Cruz e Silva, 2000.

6. Venter uses "African Indigenous Churches" (AICs); in the literature it is common to find various other names such as "African Initiated Churches" or "African Independent Churches" (Venter 1999, 106).

7. The term Zionist has been variously used. Some studies combine Zionist and Apostolic churches into one category; others distinguish between them. Some African Initiated Churches reject the label "Zionist" (Chidester et al. 1997; Venter 1999). I will use the term "Zionist" to refer only to the churches that call themselves by the name.

8. For recognition as the leader of a registered church, the Ministry of Justice (Department of Religious Affairs) requires a basic level of education and biblical training.

9. Such as Bagomoyo; Boquisso; Luis Cabral; Machava; Magoanine; Aeroporto; and so forth.

10. The Reverend Amosse, interviewed by T. Cruz e Silva, Maputo, 2001.

11. Centro de Estudo e Transformação de Conflitos (Center of Conflict Transformation Studies).

12. A similar situation, where a church person assumed a position in the Electoral Commission, happened in South Africa, when Miss Brisalia Bam, formerly General Secretary of South African Council of Churches, became the chairperson of Independent Electoral Commission in South Africa (Moss Ntlha's personal information, 2001).

13. Jamisse Taimo interviewed by T. Cruz e Silva, Maputo, 2000.

14. Amosse, interviewed by T. Cruz e Silva, 2001.

15. Jamisse Taimo, interviewed by T. Cruz e Silva, 2000.

16. Confirming this idea, while discussing "African Traditional Religion" in South Africa, Chidester wrote: "Zionist Christians have gained a reputation for being apolitical" (1997, 329).

17. The history of Luis Cabral suburb was collected by Zefanias Matsimbe and Padil Salimo, during July 1999, as part of a study of social networks in Maputo's peri-urban areas undertaken by the Centre of African Studies at Eduardo Mondlane University, with the participation of students from the University Social Sciences Unit.

18. Interview with Albert Safu, administrator of Luis Cabral suburb, 1999.

19. Agadjanian calls a wide variety of churches Zionist, using the presence of divine healing and the appeal to the Holy Spirit as defining characteristics. We describe churches as Zionist where they themselves employ the classification.

20. Not all our informants were prepared to inform us about the full or correct names of their churches. Thus, it is possible that some of these names are not correctly written. Some are also incorrect translations from English to Portuguese.

21. He adds: "Not only humanizing, however, religion has also been implicated in forces of dehumanization . . . entangled with economic, social and political relations of power that have prevailed some but have excluded many from a fully human empowerment."

22. It is important to underline that the results of the elections and the victory of FRELIMO and its presidential candidate, Joaquim Chissano, were contested by RENAMO, so that the final results were only published in January 2000.

23. The Reverend Amosse from CCM, interviewed by T. Cruz e Silva, Maputo, 2001.

6

From Apartheid to the New Dispensation: Evangelicals and the Democratization of South Africa

Anthony Balcomb

A seismic political shift has occurred in South Africa since the democratic elections of April 1994. One analyst describes the new South African constitution as "one of the most luxuriously democratic instruments in the world" (Southall 1999, 19).

> A democratic constitution, democratic institutions and substantially democratic practice have replaced the racial dictatorship of apartheid. South Africa's system of parliamentary government, if it works correctly, entrenches an advanced array of political, social and economic rights, is controlled by an extensive separation of powers (between legislature, executive and judiciary and between different levels of government), and is buttressed by an array of democracy-supporting institutions such as a Human Rights Commission, a Gender Commission, an Ombudsperson, and an Auditor-General's office. (Southall 1999, 18)[1]

The role that Christianity has played in the democratization of South Africa has been significant. The Freedom Charter of 1954, the precursor of the present constitution, was compiled primarily by people who "had gone through mission schools and colleges, and it was this strong Bible knowledge that informed them how to phrase, articulate and put into shape the sentiments of many people who were wanting a summary of the vision of the oppressed for a free and democratic South Africa" (Xundu 1988, 14).

Christianity features on almost every page of the four-volume record of African politics in South African history edited by Karis and Carter (1972–1977). Records of speeches made at the early establishment of the South African Native National Conference, the forerunner of the African National Congress (ANC), read like the charismatic sermons of evangelical preachers. "Truly the harvest is great," said the Reverend John Dube, the first president of the ANC, in 1892, "but the reapers are few. Millions of those for whom Christ died, are sitting in the darkness of sin and superstition, and almost crushed under the iron heel of heathen oppression" (Johns 1972, 68).[2] Decades later, at the dawn of the new dispensation, Christianity's impact was as pervasive as ever. David Chidester, a leading South African historian, in his annotated bibliography of Christianity in South Africa, notes that virtually all the major political parties, including the "secular" ANC, laid claim to the message and authority of the gospel in their election campaigns in 1994.[3]

These factors demonstrate the profound importance and influence of the Christian message on the South African political scene, from the earliest rumblings of democracy in the nineteenth century to its culmination on April 27, 1994. That many of the early movers and shakers for genuine political democracy in South Africa were evangelical, at least in their general theological orientation, is quite clear. That they closely associated Christian redemption with political freedom is equally clear. Moreover, the fact that contemporary political parties believe it necessary to appeal to the gospel message, in some form or another, in order to win the votes of the people is profoundly indicative of the pervasive and ongoing influence of the *evangel* on South African society.[5]

Obviously, however, this is not the whole story. The role of evangelicals in the democratization of South Africa has been ambivalent. Particularly salient today is that many evangelicals actively *oppose* some features of the present liberal-democratic constitution and bill of rights. Indeed, some of its most "progressive" features helped bring some (especially white conservative) evangelicals out of their political closets, onto the streets, and into politics with a new and combative zeal. Many evangelicals condemn the constitution's emphasis on individual rights and civil liberties when it comes to freedom of speech and choice, especially with reference to its pro-choice position on abortion, the forbidding of discrimination based on gender or sexual orientation, and pornography. One member of parliament from the African Christian Democratic Party (ACDP) asserts that his party exists and is growing precisely because it has mounted a "resistance" struggle against political liberalization (Advocate Mighty Madasa, member of parliament for the ACDP, at a workshop arranged by The Evangelical Alliance of South Africa in Johannesburg, August 30–31, 2000).

The ambivalence is even deeper because South African democracy and democratization cannot be understood except in relation to the *ancien régime* of apartheid, which for decades set the terms of political participation for all South Africans, evangelical and nonevangelical alike, and which also enjoyed substantial evangelical legitimation.

Insofar as apartheid was based on categories of race, it inevitably fostered differences in political approach between blacks and whites. Race was the dominating reality of South African society at every level. It affected even the available modalities of resistance to or support of the system. It was hardly possible, for example, for the disenfranchised black majority in South Africa to legitimately fight against racial prejudice on a political level because their participation would by definition be dictated by apartheid policy: they could vote and "have democracy," but only as long as it was in their own "home-lands" and not in the central government. For many, this was tantamount to supporting their own disenfranchisement. For such people, only two options seemed readily available: illegitimate means of opposition, such as nonviolent noncooperation with the authorities, as in the Defiance Campaign of the fifties; or, outright and violent overthrow of the regime, as in the armed struggle of the sixties, seventies, and eighties. However, the price of either kind of action was often so brutal that other means of tacit resistance needed to be found. The *modus operandi* of most blacks, therefore, was to develop forms of resistance in the interstices between activism and acquiescence. This not overtly political, but profoundly effective, form of resistance, which often took Christian and specifically evangelical forms, played a significant role in the struggle for de-mocracy and, therefore, demands attention in this study.

If one set of rules for participation in the struggle for democracy obtained for the disenfranchised black population, a completely different set of rules applied to the enfranchised white population. Enfranchised whites frequen-tly perfected not the arts of resistance but the arts of avoidance, not the "weapons of the weak" but the defenses of the strong. Reasons needed to be found either to legitimate the status quo that favored them or avoid, delay, and compromise its demise as much as possible. Insofar as (white) evangel-ical Christianity was concerned, a whole range of theological rationalizations emerged to do precisely this. This reality cannot be ignored in any honest study of evangelicals and democracy in South Africa, though neither can the fact that some whites, albeit a minority, joined in the active struggle against apartheid.

The 1994 democratic elections effected a complete transformation of po-litical conditions. The forces of liberation became the forces of the status quo. Those who were in power found themselves in opposition to power. Those who were previously silent became vocal, and those who were previously vocal became silent. Protagonists of socialism became protagonists of capitalism; supporters of the status quo became supporters of the opposition, and so on. The racial categories and divides generally still exist, though the political roles have generally been reversed. Majority rule means that at the political, if not the economic, level, power lies in the hands of blacks.

With this shifting of the ground came a shift in the priorities and values that drive South African politics. All except the far right have condemned apartheid. However, although most condemn it, not all have confessed their collusion with it. In addition, of those who have confessed their collusion with it, not all have demonstrated a change in their fundamental attitude, theology, or practice. The shifting of the ground also means that the elements and people that made democracy happen are not necessarily the elements and people that will make it work. Those who opposed it *then* may be the ones who will sustain it *now*, and vice-versa.

The Present Study: Purpose and Structure

The purpose of this study is to ask what role evangelicals have played and continue to play in the democratization of South Africa before and after the demise of apartheid. Because of the immense ambivalence, variation, and complexity of evangelicalism's relationship to democratization, I address this question by offering a typology of five different evangelical responses to the political situation in South Africa, before and after April 27, 1994. Each response is illustrated by a case study of an evangelical leader and a church or movement associated with that leader. Within each case study, I develop a qualitative assessment of each type of evangelical contribution to South African democracy based on four criteria: (1) its relationship with the apartheid system prior to April 1994 and the extent to which it supported and/or resisted it; (2) its position—whether engaged or disengaged, whether critical or supportive—with respect to the new democracy; (3) its role in creating conditions conducive to the new democracy; and (4) the relative strength of its influence in South African society as a whole. Before proceeding, however, I must add the usual caveat: my categorization of these cases into distinct types should not imply that these are hard and fast or that a "bright line" separates one type from the next.

Based on my observation and analysis, evangelical responses to the political situation in South Africa before and after the end of apartheid in April 1994 fall broadly into the following five categories:

First, there are those who supported apartheid because of the biblical injunction to submit to the authority of the day, opposed, or supported attempts to oppose, any resistance to apartheid, and also now oppose various changes that have taken place in the new dispensation. These may be called the *conservatives.*

Second, there are those who were apolitical and therefore indifferent to apartheid and to resistance to it but who subsequently quite consciously changed both their theology and their political beliefs when the forces against apartheid acquired greater influence in the late eighties. These may be called the *pragmatists*.

Third, there are those who opposed apartheid but believed their major contribution was to work toward reconciliation and gradual change. These may be called the *protagonists of the "Third Way,"* because they opposed both apartheid and violent efforts to overthrow it.

Fourth, there are those who suffered under apartheid and were against it but who remained aloof from the political attempts to destroy it. Theirs was a theology that transcended political categories and asserted the alternative values of the kingdom of God. Their aloofness from politics in the old order usually translates into skepticism of politics in the new order. These may be called the *protagonists of the "alternative" community.*

Fifth, there are those who were against apartheid and who found it necessary to join the political struggle to overthrow it. They did so by open affiliation with the democratic forces committed to its downfall. In the new order, they continue to believe in the necessity of political engagement, but from the center and not from the margins of power. These may be called the *liberationists.*

I have chosen five leading figures and associated movements that illustrate these positions. Representing the conservatives is Bishop Frank Retief and the Church of England in South Africa (CESA); representing the pragmatists is Ray McCauley and Rhema Church; representing the Third Way is Michael Cassidy and African Enterprise; representing the alternative community is Nicholas Bhengu and the Back to God Movement; and representing the liberationists is Frank Chikane of the Apostolic Faith Mission (AFM) and the ANC. Besides the fact that these individuals powerfully illustrate the positions characterized above, they have been chosen because (1) they are, or have been, leading figures whose interventions have influenced or are influencing the South African political scene; (2) they are all evangelical but represent different modes of intervention in the political arena; and (3) they are broadly representative of wider and important groupings within South African evangelicalism.

The problem of defining evangelicals as a distinct group is difficult and is dealt with elsewhere in this volume.[6] For the purposes of this chapter, evangelicalism designates that brand of Christianity that emerged from the Pietist stream of the Reformed tradition and whose emphasis is on the universal need for salvation through personal encounter with the risen Christ.[7] Evangelicalism has a strong biblicist component because evangelicals, as I understand them, believe that personal salvation and Christian discipleship depend on close (though not necessarily literal) adherence to the teachings of the Bible. It thus includes pentecostal/charismatic, as well as other evangelical movements. This definition also includes many in the "mainline" or ecumenical churches traditionally associated with the South African Council of Churches (SACC).[8]

Each of these streams or branches of evangelicalism is represented by one of my case studies: Michael Cassidy and African Enterprise represent "mainline" evangelicals; Nicholas Bhengu and the Back to God Crusade represent pentecostal evangelicals; Ray McCauley and Rhema represent charismatic evangelicals; and Frank Retief and the Church of England in South Africa represent nonpentecostal evangelicals.[9] The numerical strength of each of these groups, relative to the wider demographics of the church and nation, is discussed at the end of each case study and in the conclusion.

Conspicuous by their absence from this study (but present in other studies in this volume) are the African Initiated Churches (AICs). These churches bulk large on the South African religious field: they are estimated to number 10,668,515, or 32 percent of South Africa's population (Hendriks and Erasmus 2001, 42). They therefore constitute by far the country's largest church grouping. Elsewhere, I have argued for their inclusion within the ambit of evangelicalism (Balcomb 2001, 7). However, I have largely excluded them from this analysis, mainly because I believe they demand a separate study on account of their sheer size and impact. At the same time, I say I have only "largely" excluded them because the subject of one of my case studies, the enormous and influential Back to God movement founded by Nicholas Bhengu, possesses some of the characteristic features of the AIC family of churches, even though it is not generally considered an African Initiated Church.

Case Study 1: Bishop Frank Retief and St. James Church, Kenilworth

The Church of England in South Africa (CESA) is the most theologically conservative evangelical denomination in South Africa. This is ironic because its origins are associated with one of the most radical churchman that ever lived in South Africa, John William Colenso. Bishop Colenso was a mathematician and churchman known for his liberal views of the Bible and radical views of politics. He was a champion of the Zulu cause when the British were at war with the Zulu people. Because of his unconventional theological views, he was tried for heresy and excommunicated from the Anglican Church. CESA was established by his supporters.[10]

Yet Bishop Frank Retief, the present leader of CESA, and its biggest congregation, St. James Church Kenilworth, could not be more theologically and politically distant from Colenso. Retief describes the early beginnings of CESA as a "struggle for survival." Through this struggle, the denomination ultimately emerged as a locus of conservative theological and political convictions. As Retief states, it emerged "as a small group of people . . . committed to the evangelical, Reformed, and Protestant convictions of its forbears" (Retief

1997, 1). As a denomination, CESA has profound significance for at least three reasons: (1) it consciously adopts a theological position opposed to that of its more liberal counterpart, the Church of the Province of South Africa (CPSA) or the "Anglican" church; (2) it has its own history of struggle centered on issues of theology and political practice; and (3) during the seventies and eighties, it became a haven for conservative whites fleeing the liberal positions of Desmond Tutu and others in the CPSA and SACC.

St. James Church Kenilworth is not only the largest congregation of CESA but is especially significant for understanding conservative evangelicalism's relationship to South African politics. One of the chief advisors of the conservative ACDP is a member of St. James. An influential psychologist and ordained minister of the church, Dr. Angelo Grazzioli, leads the church's Social, Ethics, and Morals Committee, which acts as a "watchdog" with respect to the liberalization of South African society and makes frequent interventions in this area through the media. He was also elected chairman of a similar committee established by The Evangelical Alliance of South Africa (TEASA). Grazzioli's criticisms of the constitution concerning gay rights, pornography, and abortion are articulate and intense. In addition, St. James is connected with United Christian Action, an umbrella for fourteen organizations, including Frontline Fellowship and the Gospel Defence League, widely believed to constitute the extreme right wing of the South African church. These organizations were in the forefront of the attack against the South African Council of Churches at the height of its resistance to apartheid under Desmond Tutu's leadership because of what it considered its liberal theology and communist associations. They continue to be vociferous in their attacks on the present regime, which they consider excessively tolerant of crime, corruption, and sexual immorality.

However, the most spectacular reason for the sociopolitical significance of St. James was an event that attracted national and international attention on July 25, 1993. The armed wing of the Pan Africanist Congress staged an attack on the church during one of its Sunday evening services. Two gunmen with machine guns and a hand grenade sprayed the congregation with gunfire and blasted the people-filled pews. The attack lasted only thirty seconds but left scores dead and wounded. In a book published only a year after the attack, *Tragedy to Triumph: A Christian Response to Trials and Sufferings,* Retief describes the impact of this event, known as the St. James' Massacre:

> The attack on our church did not last more than thirty seconds, but it
> was thirty seconds that shook the nation, brought worldwide con-
> demnation of political violence and changed the lives of literally
> thousands of people forever. It made us face the deep questions of
> life. It forced us to confront the mysteries of our existence in this

world, the fearsome reality of evil and the massive display of good will
and sympathy. It forced us to reflect on our view of God and his
relationship to good and evil, and it forced us to look the world in the
face and answer for the things we believe. (Retief 1994, 25)

This description is profoundly significant both in what it says and in what it
does not say. Although it reflects on the significance of the attack from a
theological and existential point of view, no attempt is made, either in this
short passage or in any of the book's 230 pages, to reflect on its significance
from a political or sociological point of view. No connection is drawn between
the attack, on one hand, and the church's conservatism and implicit support of
the apartheid regime, on the other. There is no mention of a political agenda
besides a blanket condemnation of political violence, and there is no re-
appraisal of the church's theology—political or otherwise—in light of the attack. Indeed, the book shows a remarkable ability to reflect on the meaning of
Christian forgiveness and the suffering of individual Christians without undertaking political or social reflections of any kind.

Besides this book, there is very little published material available to illustrate CESA's theology and its political implications. However, Retief has
preached significant sermons on South Africa's new democracy. These sermons are succinct, clear, and masterfully delivered. Through them, he appeals
to his listeners to develop "a Christian perspective on the South African reality."

In a sermon entitled, "South Africa and my Future," delivered on January
5, 1997, Retief deals primarily with the issue of white flight from South Africa.
Should we leave South Africa? What are the reasons for staying or leaving?
What does the Bible have to say? In this sermon, he addresses the deep fears of
his white congregation. Through critical commentary on secularism, human
rights, and religious pluralism, the sermon outlines a political theology that
has profound implications for democratic theory and practice. Retief puts forward a series of dualisms that, *mutatis mutandis*, yield conservative and sharply
critical positions vis-à-vis the values of South Africa's new democracy: democracy versus righteousness (democracy has its limits because of human
depravity); secular government versus "godly" government (secularism is tantamount to "turning your back on God" and is therefore the root of all evil in
society); human rights versus human punishment (retribution is more important for criminals than forgiveness); Christianity versus other religions
(tolerance has its limits); spiritual values versus material values (the poor need
the gospel before they need material goods); right versus wrong (there is little
place for debate and ecumenism in the kingdom of God).[11]

When Retief was asked to appear before the Truth and Reconciliation
Commission (TRC), his submission demonstrated that he is well aware of
the wider Anglican Communion's opinion that CESA is, in his words, "a
recalcitrant, schismatic group of unreasonable right-wing evangelicals" (Retief

1997, 1). Moreover, he says, "We have no one to blame for these views but ourselves." He also admits that on issues of injustice his church had been "insensitive" and that its identification with the apartheid regime had been based on its belief in the biblical teaching of support for political authorities. "Our failure to be involved in the political struggles of our land," he says, "was a major error in both understanding and judgment" (Retief 1997, 1). Retief makes it clear, however, that CESA will "continue to clearly teach and preach the Word of God" and that it will not shirk its responsibilities in the socio-political sphere in the future, naming specifically the "ethical challenges of the day in relation to crime and corruption, abortion, pornography, gambling and the proposed decriminalization of prostitution." With respect to CESA's position concerning other faiths, Retief insists, "We have distinctive convictions that are non-negotiable" (Retief 1997, 1).

How, then, should one assess CESA's contribution to democratization in South Africa in terms of the criteria of assessment set out above? By its own admission, reflected in Retief's submission to the TRC on behalf of his denomination, the church was compliant with the apartheid system. With the benefit of hindsight, he admits that this was a "major error in both understanding and judgment." This admission exhibits a sense of remorse and suggests that the church will in the future be more engaged in political issues. However, notwithstanding CESA's apparent recognition of its past mistakes vis-à-vis apartheid, it is already clear that its political activism is confined to a relatively narrow range of moral issues. At the same time, the practical upshot of this political activism is fierce "resistance" to the new dispensation. Its support for apartheid was biblically derived from the Pauline injunction that all should support the government of the day as ordained by God. Although there may seem little in CESA's public stands to suggest that it offers the same "biblical" support for the new government, Retief's preaching calls on his congregants to adopt an approach to citizenship in the new South Africa that combines both compliance and resistance.

In spite of CESA's failure to oppose apartheid in the past, Retief's sermons on the present situation in South Africa constitute one of the few sustained evangelical attempts to reflect on Christian social responsibility in light of the Bible. In these sermons, Retief regularly endeavors to give members of his congregation reasons to engage in the political processes affecting the future of their country, though, again, primarily in order to resist the new "establishment" on the issues of abortion, pornography, religious pluralism, and the death penalty. At the same time, Retief's belief in the sovereignty of God and authority of the Bible leads him specifically to impress on the white members of his congregation that God ordains the present regime. This no longer means that Christians should uncritically endorse it. Interestingly, however, he preaches that it does mean that whites should not leave South Africa but stay and seek to make a difference in society.

In trying to determine CESA's overall impact on evangelicals in South Africa, it is necessary to remember that it is highly visible and fast-growing, in spite of its relatively small base. Numerically, the denomination is not as large as the CPSA (the Anglican Church in South Africa). However, indications are that it is growing faster than the CPSA. Five full-time white male ministers and ten support staff, of whom two would previously have been classified as colored, serve St. James Church Kenilworth. Membership at St. James is 1,700, with average Sunday-morning attendance being 1,800 and average Sunday evening attendance being 1,000. Midweek Bible studies attract about six hundred people. Membership is roughly 70 percent white and 30 percent black. The high income of the church (probably around three million rand a year, or about $300,000) makes it the richest church in the denomination. For the purposes of this research, a visit was also paid to a black counterpart of this church, which was discovered to be hopelessly underresourced and struggling to survive numerically and financially.

CESA is an overwhelmingly white denomination in a country where the power of whites remains disproportionate. Although Retief's passionate articulation of a conservative position on many issues is attractive to traditionalists who are white and nonwhite alike, in many ways the church's function is to both represent and speak to the concerns, hopes, fears, and values of much of the white minority. Of course, though whites are in the minority in South Africa, they still largely control its wealth and possess the lion's share of the skills essential to its functioning. The influence of a denomination such as CESA therefore goes far beyond its numerical size.

Case Study 2: Ray McCauley and Rhema Ministries

Ray McCauley started Rhema Ministries in 1979. McCauley is a "born-again" body builder who placed third in the Mr. Universe championships in London in 1974. He studied at Rhema Bible Training Center in Tulsa, Oklahoma, and started a church in his home in 1979. The so-called faith message of the American preacher Kenneth Hagen was the initial inspiration for McCauley's new church. This message included the "prosperity gospel," which emphasizes biblical texts that promise material power and success. Appealing to young, white, and upwardly mobile city-dwellers, the church grew rapidly, and in 1981, McCauley bought a warehouse and converted it into a two-thousand-seat auditorium. In 2001, the church is housed in a seventy-five-million-rand (around 7.5 million U.S. dollars) complex and enjoys a membership of twenty-three thousand and a full-time staff of seven hundred.

It is difficult to enumerate all of Rhema's activities. Its social outreach program consists primarily of a ministry called the "Hands of Compassion," which runs soup kitchens and has an outreach to AIDS victims, alcoholics, and drug addicts, among others. It has a specialized street-children ministry called "Paradise for Children," which provides children with a permanent home, schooling, and sports facilities. There is a Rhema Care Centre in Alexandra Township, one of the poorest black townships in the country.

McCauley has made intentional and high profile interventions in the so-ciopolitical arena. According to his friend and assistant, Ron Steele, an ex-journalist who has written his biography and coauthored several books with McCauley, a turning point in his life was the Rustenburg Conference in 1990. At this conference, "an overwhelming majority of church leaders from across a very wide denominational spectrum unequivocally rejected apartheid as a sin, confessed their guilt in relation to it, and pledged themselves to the struggle for justice and equity in the land" (de Gruchy 1991, 21). Significantly, McCauley sat on the steering committee that organized the conference and was one of the church leaders in attendance who publicly apologized for his "apolitical," pietistic stance vis-à-vis the political situation in South Africa. After this, Rhema adopted observer status in the SACC, and Ray McCauley became involved in numerous public as well as behind-the-scenes political interventions. With Dr. Johan Heyns of the Dutch Reformed Church and the Reverend Frank Chikane of the SACC, himself a pentecostal belonging to the AFM,[12] he served on the steering committee for the formation of the National Peace Accord in April 1991, an advocacy initiative that "managed to get the major political parties to pledge themselves to seeking peace through negotiation" (Steele and McCauley 1996, 37).[13] McCauley's behind-the-scenes activities included meetings with Brigadier Oupa Gqoza—the "puppet" leader of the "independent" homeland of the Ciskei—and with Chief Buthelezi, leader of the Inkatha Freedom Party. These meetings were designed to persuade black leaders whom many blacks considered "sellouts" to the apartheid regime, and who were reluctant to relinquish power, to enter into negotiations with the ANC.

Since the advent of the new regime, McCauley has been instrumental in launching the Stop Crime Campaign and has been involved in arranging the Morals Summit of 1998, the Civil Society Initiative, and the Cape Peace Initiative, which attempted to bring gang leaders together to stop gang violence. He also became the "unofficial" chaplain for the South African cricket team and the South African Olympic squad that went to Sydney in 2000.

Rhema's position on political issues such as abortion, pornography, freedom of expression, gay rights, interfaith dialogue, Christian political involvement, and social transformation are spelled out in a small 1996 book, *Power and Passion: Fulfilling God's Destiny for the Nation*, jointly written by McCauley and Steele. On some of these issues, Rhema's views are remarkably "liberal," and on most issues, they appear to take a conscious stand against what they call the "fundamentalist" position. The following quotation from

202 EVANGELICAL CHRISTIANITY AND DEMOCRACY IN AFRICA

Steele's book provides an apt summary. It also gives a good impression of the straightforward, "down-to-earth" style, characteristic of McCauley generally, in which the book is written:[14]

> Christian fundamentalists have two distinctive characteristics: they are usually intolerant of other people's views and they want to impose their truth on other people. On the surface, this misplaced zeal may be forgiven. At the heart, though, is a dangerous defect in the make-up of this type of Christian. It is precisely this intolerant, imposing attitude which has stereotyped much of the Pentecostal and evangelical movement and offended many good people who otherwise may have responded to the gospel.
>
> Despite New Age, pro-choice, gay rights, pornography and the many other activist organizations that challenge standards, Christians may have failed to recognize their role in allowing people to oppose accepted Christian views. That may sound surprising, but martyrs of the church have spilt their blood over the centuries for the jewel called "freedom of religion." The church has always placed the highest premium on free speech because it recognized the need to proclaim the gospel message. (Steele and McCauley 1996, 73)

McCauley and Steele signal their strong support for most of the new government's steps in promoting its brand of democracy and strongly criticize conservative evangelicalism, or "fundamentalism," for what they consider its illiberal resistance to the spirit of the new dispensation. They are eager to demonstrate their own decisive break with the apartheid past and that—precisely as evangelicals—they embrace the New South Africa.

Although many evangelicals are favorably disposed to South Africa's new and strongly conservative Christian political party, the African Christian Democratic Party (ACDP), McCauley and Steele are vociferous in their criticism:

> The ACDP is suffering from the same perplexing problem that plagues Christians when they enter into the political domain—and even more so when they bear the title "Christian" and are driven by fundamentalist zeal. The ACDP has the basic problem of not knowing whether it wants to be a church or a political power. In the process, it crosses over into the territory of the church and tries to be the church. The result is that it fails to maintain its political integrity and does not carry the weight of the church behind it when it makes so-called spiritual judgments in parliament. It unfortunately plays directly into the hands of those who advocate a purely secular government for South Africa because they claim the ACDP is propagating a religious message. (Steele and McCauley 1996, 65)

It probably must be conceded that McCauley and Steele have adopted a strongly antifundamentalist political position—and communicated it so publicly and vigorously—partly in order to be acceptable to the new regime. Indeed, ANC MPs are among Rhema's members, and its church complex was used for the funeral of a leading ANC stalwart and erstwhile minister of foreign affairs, Alfred Nzo.

As in the case of Retief, McCauley admits to past mistakes due to the apoliticism of his prior understanding of the gospel. He particularly regrets having excluded from his ministry a clear condemnation of the injustices of apartheid. He insists that he has subsequently undergone a change of heart and is now attempting to address issues of political and social injustice. Rhema's recent social and political interventions, whose primary aim has been the economic and social uplift of the poor, indicate a genuine change in McCauley's outlook and priorities.

Although McCauley's specifically political interventions have been relatively ineffective, the political position he has elaborated represents an articulate evangelical alternative to that of CESA, the ACDP, and other conservative evangelical groups. Though not uncritical of the new government, Rhema's leaders obviously intend to align their evangelical following with South Africa's progressive direction under the ANC. If nothing else, the tone and content of their political views indicate the diversity of evangelical political positions and the vitality of evangelical debate concerning the politics of the new dispensation.

With respect to Rhema's impact on South African democracy and democratization, it is clear that the church strongly encourages its membership to become positively engaged in the transformation of society. And it provides various opportunities to do so. However, the extent to which this approach nurtures democracy in the New South Africa is open to question. Once again, the question of race is crucial. Although the public relations material produced by Rhema boasts that the congregation is "fully multiracial," our investigations have shown that most of the blacks that attend the Rhema meetings are bussed in from black areas. Blacks do not necessarily "feel at home" in Rhema, and the extent to which Rhema's black and white communities are integrated is limited. There is a separate service for vernacular speakers that is supported only by blacks and is more African in its worship. There is a black church based on the Rhema model and populated by its exact social counterparts, the only difference being skin color, in the black township of Soweto. This is run by Musa Sono, who was trained in the Rhema Bible School. In one sense, Rhema might be considered politically empowering in that it unquestionably helps to build up what Robert Putnam called "bonding" social capital among blacks and also provides them institutional settings for the acquisition of leadership and organizational skills that may be transferred to civic life. However, it largely fails to build up the "bridging" social capital that is needed to enhance sociopolitical cooperation and harmony—essential to the effectiveness of democracy—across South Africa's ongoing racial divide (Putnam 2000).

The impact of Rhema should be viewed in light of the fact that it represents the charismatic Christian tradition, which has a strong presence in South African society. It is part of the International Fellowship of Christian Churches, a loose association of like-minded charismatic churches that includes large churches such as the Hatfield Christian Church in Pretoria and the Durban Christian Centre. Similar movements include the Vineyard movement and the New Covenant fellowship of churches. These movements are strongly oriented to mission and evangelism and maintain strong international connections. I have focused on Rhema because it is probably the most politically aware and engaged. A conservative estimate would put the membership of these churches at around 250,000.[15] They are largely white and middle-class in composition and have had little impact on the black community, but they have black counterparts (i.e., large charismatic churches composed of upwardly mobile urban blacks). However, these churches are not as large as their black counterparts in other parts of Africa and are far fewer in number than their white South African counterparts. In addition, they lack an umbrella association or organization. The fact that the charismatic movement is generally a middle-class phenomenon, combined with the fact that the South African middle class is predominantly white, may explain why relatively few blacks are part of churches such as Rhema.

Case Study 3: Michael Cassidy and African Enterprise

Michael Cassidy started African Enterprise (AE) in 1964. The vision of AE is to evangelize the cities of Africa. The ministry of Billy Graham has strongly influenced Cassidy in terms of evangelistic method. Like Graham, Cassidy undertakes citywide missions in the main urban centers, holding large rallies where people are called to personal conversion. Frequently, Cassidy's approach has included a method that might be called "stratified evangelism," which targets different sectors in the urban centers, including businesses and schools, prior to the rallies. These citywide missions are usually interdenominational and serve to unify the church in local cities. Over the years, AE has developed considerable credibility among the churches throughout South Africa because of its ability to mount such missions and unite the church.

AE also mounts major congresses of church leaders on particular topics. Three have been particularly significant: the Durban Congress on Mission and Evangelism (1973), the South African Christian Leadership Assembly (1979), and the National Initiative for Reconciliation (1985). Two other foci in Cassidy's ministry are important: his keen interest in influencing leaders, both political and ecclesiastical, and his untiring efforts to bring leaders together. His efforts to reconcile warring political parties in the province of Kwazulu Natal during the 1980s were significant. In the National Initiative for Reconciliation, convened at the height of that period's political unrest, AE under Cassidy's leadership proved itself the one Christian group with the credibility to organize a meeting of racially, politically, and denominationally diverse church leaders, even though the conference and subsequent follow-up meetings served mainly to highlight the vast differences between blacks and whites on the issue of reconciliation. Whereas blacks consistently understood it as requiring equality, starting with the universal franchise and proceeding to equal opportunity in every field, whites consistently interpreted it as requiring a vague "unity in Christ" that did not translate into sociopolitical reality. Few in the National Initiative for Reconciliation were bold enough to unpack these differences and analyze their roots.[16]

Cassidy has endeavored to build into his evangelistic thrust a concern for sociopolitical issues. He models his position on that of the Lausanne Covenant, a statement issued at a major international congress of evangelicals in 1974. The Lausanne Covenant draws a distinction between evangelism and "social action" but acknowledges the need for both. For Cassidy and Lausanne, the gospel is closely associated with the imperative to denounce evil and injustice. Consequently, Cassidy believes that evangelicals must consciously explore the implications of the gospel for society and politics.

Theologically, Cassidy has been shaped by that particular brand of Anglo-American evangelicalism exemplified by such "thinking" evangelicals as Michael Green and John Stott and such seminaries as Fuller Theological Seminary, where Cassidy did his theological training. By "thinking" evangelicalism, I mean that brand of evangelicalism that believes that the truth of the gospel can be defended intellectually, and that its relevance can be intelligibly validated in all spheres of life because it constitutes the very foundation on which the universe is established.

Cassidy outlines his political views in two major works: *The Passing Summer* (1989) and *The Politics of Love* (1991). The latter is an updated and abbreviated version of the former. These books have enjoyed wide circulation, which is indicative of Cassidy's wide-ranging influence within English-speaking churches. The main concern of these books, written during the apartheid era, is to emphasize the need for change in South Africa and to inaugurate a just and peaceful sociopolitical dispensation. In effect, they take the reader on a tour of South Africa's diverse groups and seek to encourage his largely white conservative audience to understand the hopes, fears, and aspirations of each group. Cassidy hopes that this will induce whites to adopt a posture of progressive and gradual change. Following these publications, he has articulated his positions on matters that have arisen in the new dispensation, such as homosexuality and abortion, in a series of pamphlets and occasional papers called *Theologically Speaking*. These pieces recall evangelistic sermons in which the preacher attempts to convince his audience of the truth of what he says by quoting the widest possible array of authorities. Cassidy derives his views concerning political and social ethics from the age-old approach developed by Thomas Aquinas, that of natural theology and natural law. In Cassidy's terminology, this approach consists above all in reverence for "the way":

> "The way" is the way to do everything—the way to think, to feel, to act, and to be in every conceivable circumstance and in every relationship. The way is written into the nature of everybody and everything. This makes the moral universe all of a piece, with its laws inherent in reality itself. This means that the way we are made to work is also the way God wants us to work. Creation thus works His way or else works its own ruin. And the history of humanity is nothing but a long confirmation of this truth. (Cassidy 1989, 221)

Cassidy used natural theology to expose the unacceptability of apartheid, by arguing that apartheid law is against the law of God, and he uses natural theology to argue against abortion and homosexuality in the new dispensation. An antipathy for nationalism, which is evident from the very earliest days of his evangelistic ministry, informs his political theology. He feared that the clash of two nationalisms, Afrikaner nationalism and African nationalism, would eventuate in a terrible bloodbath and destroy South Africa. The way to avoid this outcome was to develop a "third way." The third way was the transcendent middle way of love and reconciliation. Politically, it translated into an emphasis on gradual change based on negotiated settlement and compromise.

As with Retief and McCauley, Cassidy is a skilled preacher and leader. His style is to lead publicly and assertively, with maximum visibility and drama. AE stages each of its events against the apocalyptic background of the imminent destruction of the nation. Each of its events has a "watershed" significance that is "pivotal" in the "destiny" of the nation, with each one taking place at "one minute to midnight." When a radical black youth embraces a white in an AE meeting where the Spirit is "tearing down the barriers," a "seismic shock" is sent through the township. "Massively powerful" calls are made to leaders amidst "volcanic political pressures and desperate emotions" to "bring them back from the brink," and so on.[17]

Despite the obvious extravagance of these assertions, the achievements of Cassidy and AE in facilitating dialogue between South Africa's racial, political, and religious groups have clearly been significant. During the apartheid era, Cassidy and AE worked constantly behind the scenes, especially during the violence in Kwazulu Natal. Before the elections there, they fought tirelessly to get the various parties to the negotiating table.

For many living under apartheid, however, justice outweighed reconciliation, and many criticized the ministry of AE for not addressing justice issues strongly enough. The 1973 conference in Durban, for example, said little about the need for a new day in South Africa. This conference took place thirteen years after the Sharpeville Massacre[18] and three years before the Soweto Uprising,[19] both of which were crucial and pivotal events indeed in the destiny of South Africa. The only statement at this conference unambiguously condemning apartheid and calling for immediate political change was made by Beyers Naude, founder of the Christian Institute of South Africa, a group ultimately banned by the government, as was Naude himself. The other significant paper, which was to be given by Bishop Manas Buthelezi of the Lutheran Church, could not be read because Buthelezi had already been given orders by the government that he could not gather in a group of more than three people.

Still, Cassidy's influence on the more conservative white sectors of society should not be underestimated. Whereas the SACC was a powerful voice for South Africa's oppressed, AE and Cassidy were significant influences in society's broad middle sector, particularly because the church was, and still is, a well-respected institution and important agent of change in this sector. Once again, however, AE had little impact or influence in the black sector. Although AE is respected by whites of many socioeconomic and political backgrounds, it has consistently struggled to gain the same level of credibility among blacks, and it has been unable to find a black leader to replace Cassidy.

In summarizing the role of AE and Cassidy in the democratic transformation of South African society, one can draw the following conclusions: First, unlike in the previous cases, Cassidy has consistently opposed apartheid, even from the earliest days of his ministry. He was overjoyed at the demise of apartheid and the arrival of a new dispensation. Second, with the advent of the new regime, AE has focused mainly on evangelism and social programs, and it increasingly conducts its missions in other African countries. In other words, since April 1994 Cassidy has had a significantly reduced profile in the South African social and political arena. As with most other evangelicals, however, he offers vigorous social and theological commentary on the front-burner evangelical issues—interfaith dialogue, abortion, and homosexuality—and his position on these is broadly characteristic of conservative evangelicalism. Third, with regard to contributions to the present democracy, AE runs leadership and development programs aimed at empowering the previously disadvantaged. Furthermore, the broader church, including the SACC, has formally asked Cassidy and AE to mount a conference that will unite the church in South Africa's new era to address issues of common concern. These include justice and reconciliation, HIV/AIDS, poverty and job creation, and Christian morality. The overall aim will be to inspire the church to adopt a common understanding of Christian faithfulness in South Africa today, as well as a common program of action flowing from this understanding. The fact that such a broad spectrum of the church has chosen AE for this task indicates the credibility the organization generally continues to enjoy in contemporary South Africa.[20]

The overall impact of Cassidy and his AE team during the apartheid era should be measured in terms of the particular constituency he represented: the English-speaking, white, middle class that held many of the levers of power in the economic arena. He was a progressive evangelical whose main calling was evangelism but who found himself unable to escape politics early in his ministry. On one level, he used his considerable leadership skills to move this constituency to work toward a more democratic South Africa. On another level, he attempted to bring together in dialogue different sides of the political divide. Cassidy never went as far as some church leaders, for example Beyers Naude of the Dutch Reformed Church and Desmond Tutu of the Anglican Church, in the denunciation of apartheid. However, on the injustice of the old regime, he probably pushed his constituency as hard and as far as he could without losing it entirely.

Case Study 4: Nicholas Bhengu and the Back to God Crusade

It is difficult to describe the impact of Nicholas Bhengu on the South African scene. A former member of the Communist Party, he converted to Christianity in 1929 and started the "Back to God Crusade" in 1950. He converted thousands of men and women to a form of evangelical faith, and lorry-loads of stolen goods and weapons were carted away from his tent meetings.

Although Bhengu eschewed direct political involvement, he directed his preaching and ministry to specific areas of social concern that he considered crucial: the strengthening of the self-confidence and dignity of blacks in relation to whites, addressing the needs of both traditional and modern Africans, and combating crime.

Self-Confidence and Dignity

Watt describes the theology of Nicholas Bhengu as a form of black theology that "developed around the dignity of . . . black leaders" (Watt 1992, 54). In a speech given to the Ciskeian legislature on May 5, 1984, Bhengu spoke from 2 Chronicles 7:14 and established the "biblical," "historical," and "legendary" significance of Africa. He noted that Abraham sojourned in Africa, the Ethiopian eunuch was an African, Augustine was an African, Christianity was in Ethiopian Africa before it was in Europe, and that present Africans "came from the North." "I am not trying to persuade you to accept or adopt a Western God," he said, "but the God of our Ancestors, the God of the Bible" (Diko, unpublished, 37).

Linking Tradition and Modernity

A remarkable feature of Bhengu's ministry was that it reached both the modern or "school" people and the traditional or "red" people.[21] These categories applied especially to the Xhosa people at the time, and Dubb argues that Xhosas "unhesitatingly classify themselves into one or other category":

> Reds are traditionalists: they value the preservation of and adherence to the tribal way of life, and are opposed to Christianity, schooling and European culture generally. They regard School people—who are, ideally, Christian and educated and value "European ways and things"—as traitors to Xhosa survival. School people return this contempt and scorn the conservatism of the Reds. (Dubb 1976, 29)

Dubb's research on the Bhengu revivals of the 1950s demonstrates that, although profound social, cultural, and economic differences separated these two groups of people, many in both groups committed themselves to the Christian faith under Bhengu's ministry. The "red people" came to Bhengu's meetings mainly for healing and the "school people" generally out of curiosity. He managed to convince red people that their traditional religious goals could not be attained by traditional religious systems but only through Christianity. Dubb notes that most of the school people in the East London district went to hear Bhengu at least once. They were persuaded, according to Dubb, because Bhengu's message was able to meet their deep-seated spiritual and social needs in a way that mission Christianity had not, because it reconnected them with their traditional African roots.

Combating Crime

> One of the strongest Christian influences in Africa is a 50-year-old Zulu ... who has a knack of persuading criminals to turn in their weapons—and often themselves. The Rev. Nicholas Bhengu stands on a packing case platform and says. ... "Crime does not pay, surrender your arms and yourselves to God." He continues and a pile begins to grow at his feet—knives, blackjacks, brass knuckles and quantities of stolen goods. At one meeting police carted away three vanloads, and it is not unusual for Bhengu to walk down to the police station hand in hand with someone on the wanted list. ... In some areas, [the crime rate] has dropped by a third. (*Time*, November 23, 1959)

Thus read a *Time* magazine article on Bhengu from the 1950s. Other newspapers reported on the impact that Bhengu had on crime in various parts of the country. A 1958 issue of *The Star* newspaper said, "So phenomenal is his power ... that tributes have been paid to him by [then prime minister] Dr. Verwoerd and by police chiefs throughout the country."

The impact that Bhengu had on South African society through these aspects of his ministry was obviously considerable. At the same time, Bhengu clearly became disillusioned with the possibility of a political solution to the problems of South Africa. When he converted to Christ, he became convinced that the gospel was the answer. He believed that a "new nation" would emerge "born from above with the likeness of God."[22]

Yet Bhengu was clearly no Pietist who believed only in an "internal" and "personal" gospel. He was acutely aware of the injustices of the day and convinced that the gospel would have a direct and profound influence in changing them:

> Our liberty may be whittled away, our facilities curtailed, our freedom of movement controlled, our food rationed, our speech stopped, our rights to sell our products in the open market denied, our residential areas portioned ethnically and land tenure threatened by insecurity, but the right to reach our hand to God in the Unseen World remains mysteriously guarded by God Himself against infiltrations, infringements, entrenchments and encroachments. Let us look to God, my people! (Diko, unpublished, 63)

After his early involvement in Marxism before his conversion, Bhengu eschewed politics. He hints at the reasons for this in one of his addresses at the 1973 Congress on Mission and Evangelism in Durban:

> Political awareness plus race consciousness had made it impossible for a White preacher to reach African people a few years ago. Later it became difficult for even an African preacher to do this unless he identified himself with the struggles and feelings of the people. *Those who did not endanger their lives for others eventually succumbed and lost their spiritual impact.* (Bhengu 1974, 157; emphasis mine)

Bhengu believed in a stark choice between political struggle and spiritual impact. But it was not an easy choice: those, like him, who chose the path of spiritual impact "endangered their lives." The language he uses indicates the enormous pressures on Bhengu to become involved in political activism. At the same time that Bhengu was conducting his evangelistic crusades in the townships of the Eastern Cape, one of the most activist regions of South Africa, the Defiance Campaign was in full swing. Anyone not actively engaged in the struggle against apartheid was branded a "sellout." None other than Manilal Gandhi, the son of Mahatma Gandhi and president of the Natal Indian Congress, leveled this accusation at Bhengu. Many educated blacks and politically active clergymen also accused him of being a traitor to the cause of liberation.

If Bhengu was disillusioned with political struggle, it was because he believed that it could not deliver true liberation. Dubb argues that he made no attempt to whitewash the conditions in which his people lived under apartheid, but he believed that it was futile to combat them at a political level. Bhengu refused to compete for political equality, because if blacks merely craved whatever whites had, they were in effect inviting whites to define the content of their aspirations. He sincerely believed that blacks should develop their own abilities, talents, and goals and did not need whites to help them to do so. According to Dubb, Bhengu also argued that entering the political fray merely meant giving whites, who monopolized political power, yet another opportunity to display their superiority to blacks. This Bhengu was unwilling to do. For these reasons, Bhengu disapproved of his people joining political parties (Dubb 1974, 120).

There seem to be two parallel strands to Bhengu's argument. On the one hand, there is his argument against overt political activism, and on the other, there is the alternative path of spiritual struggle and liberation. Clearly, Bhengu was not blind to apartheid's injustices and the need for freedom. Indeed, in the spirit of liberation theology, he likened the situation of the South African black to that of Israel in Egypt. However, it is also clear that he did not believe, at least in the years of his active ministry, that one could combat them on a political level. This was partly for the reasons just outlined: Efforts to oppose them would only further undermine black dignity and self-determination. But it was also because of the sheer might of the apartheid system and the comparative powerlessness of its victims. Due to this imbalance of power, agitation simply yielded further repression. And the second state of oppression would be worse than the first.

With respect to the alternative to political activism, Bhengu offers remarkable insights. First, he suggests not only that he is politically unequal with the white man but also that he does not *want* or *need* political equality with the white man. A Marxist might observe in Bhengu an attempt to escape his condition of material alienation by reification—that is, by projection of his desire for the material onto the spiritual—which begins in an irrational refusal to accept that there is only one (material) reality. Bhengu, however, seems to have been genuinely unimpressed with what he saw of the white man's material reality. If it was real, it was not necessarily desirable. Bhengu believed that true reality and true liberation were to be found elsewhere.

A second feature of Bhengu's alternative is his insistence that blacks do not want to be "with" the whites but to be able to improve their situation in life as they see fit and on their own. In other words, he wants the space to make himself independent of the white man's control and values. Bhengu had constantly, and politely, demonstrated his own independence of white control—with respect to both white money and white values. Why should he "lower himself" to fight for an "independence" or "freedom" already predefined by the white man?

A third feature is that emancipation depends on blacks themselves and not whites. This, of course, was the basic tenet of Steven Biko's "Black Consciousness" ideology. However, Bhengu believed that entering a political struggle against the white man was by definition recognizing that the white man had the power to "free" the black man. He was unwilling to give the white man that power or recognition.

Finally, there is the "social and moral" aspect of Bhengu's teaching. Bhengu's understanding of what constitutes sound social and moral teaching has already been outlined. It includes dignity, self-sufficiency and self-determination, respect, honesty, equality between traditional and modern Africans, trust in God, and upholding the law.

Although Bhengu did not enter the struggle against apartheid on a political level, it is clear that his ministry had profound effects on apartheid. That he bequeathed a moral and social legacy affecting the future of democracy—indeed, one that helped prepare the way for democracy—is clear. Individuals converted to evangelical Christianity through the Back to God movement populate every sector of black society: teachers, lawyers, traders, clerks, businessmen, gardeners, and even politicians. Bhengu's teaching emphasizes the preeminent existence of a transcendent reality that relativizes the material realm, centralizes spiritual values, exalts the dignity of the individual, and compels political reflection to imagine radical alternatives.

A Marxian critique of such a legacy (one thinks of E. P. Thompson's *The Making of the English Working Class*) would perhaps give it short shrift, but the facts concerning Bhengu's movement speak for themselves. It is a completely self-supporting, self-governing, and self-propagating initiative; and it continues to grow. The Back to God crusades are funded entirely by the women in the movement who, in the year 2000, raised four million rand (approximately $400,000) through the selling of handicrafts.[23] Some nine hundred churches have been established, the biggest being about five thousand and the smallest two hundred in number, with probably over a million adherents nationwide.[24] This makes Bhengu's Back to God Crusade numerically by far the largest evangelical movement examined in this essay. With its adherents distributed throughout society, including the ranks of government, it is profoundly significant for understanding evangelicalism's contribution to democracy and democratization in South Africa.

Case Study 5: Frank Chikane

If Bhengu refused to engage in political activism, Frank Chikane felt he had little choice. Two forces profoundly shaped Chikane's life: the Christian message and the struggle for liberation in South Africa. Born into a pentecostal family on January 3, 1951, he has been a staunch member of the Apostolic Faith Mission (AFM) ever since, serving in this church in various capacities, including that of secretary of the congregation (at age eighteen), evangelist, pastor, and later vice president. A brilliant student and gifted leader, he studied mathematics and physics at university where he became a member of the Students Christian Movement (SCM) in the early 1970s. The SCM was a strongly Pietist movement that refused to become politically involved. At one stage, the students banned it from campus because it was believed to have "sold out" to the government. However, under the leadership of Chikane and Ramaphosa (another prominent black South African and erstwhile leader of the National Union of Mineworkers, who played a crucial role in the demise of apartheid and the transition to a new regime), the SCM became a more politically conscious institution. Chikane began to demonstrate that he was prepared to abandon neither his faith nor his political consciousness. This struggle, to keep what he has called the "vertical" and the "horizontal" together, has become a hallmark of his career as a Christian political activist.[25]

Chikane met great resistance from both ends of the religious/political spectrum: on one hand, from his politically conscious peers, who identified him with the oppressor because of his faith; and on the other, from his fellow Christians because they identified him with political radicalism. Both Christians and political activists continually pressured him to choose either Christ or the struggle (an experience shared by many evangelicals who joined the struggle against apartheid during the 1970s and 1980s). However, the more he was pressured to reject his faith, the more intense it became, and the more he was pressured to reject politics, the greater his activism became. As General Secretary of the Institute for Contextual Theology (ICT) and then later the SACC—both ecumenical institutions that do not normally associate with evangelicals, as evangelicals do not normally associate with them—he insisted that worship and Bible study take place alongside political and social activism and refused to separate them.

However, Chikane began to undergo a profound internal theological struggle as he became increasingly aware of what he believed were the evangelical tradition's inadequacies in equipping him for political struggle. His time in the ICT enabled Chikane to develop his theological understanding with respect to politics. Chikane lists the theological influences on him at that time: Black Theology, Liberation Theology, African Theology, and some Asian theologies. He describes the result:

> After long periods of reflection and sharing we reached a consensus: that the traditional, and dominant, position that looked at reality and understood our faith from the point of view of the powerful dominant forces in society and their ideology-theology was not compatible with the demands of the gospel. Surveying the history of the church since Constantine, we agreed that the church had taken sides, in the main, with the dominant classes of society which were responsible in the main for the pain, suffering, misery and even death of many, especially the weak, poor and powerless.... It is for this reason that ... the church failed to see the injustices perpetrated by

the powerful and rich against the powerless and poor.... [W]e were conscious that we were called to minister to all in the world, both oppressors and oppressed, white and black.... Taking sides with the victims of society in our situation means taking sides with the ideals of the Kingdom of God proclaimed by Jesus. This is a kingdom of justice, righteousness and peace where goodness will always prevail. (Chikane 1988, 90)

During Chikane's tenure of leadership in the ICT and SACC, their profile and influence as instruments of change became extremely significant. Chikane led them through one of the most crucial periods in the history of the struggle against apartheid, just before its demise. He won wide-ranging respect in both the political and ecclesiastical spheres, as well as the admiration of the townships' youth, who can be described as the anti-apartheid movement's "storm troopers." He also enjoyed extensive contacts with key overseas governmental and nongovernmental organizations whose influence and help he was able to bring to bear with great effectiveness within the borders of South Africa. During the late 1980s and early 1990s, he was able to mediate between the South African government and the ANC, right up to F. W. De Klerk's announcement of the release of Mandela. It is difficult to overstate Chikane's influence during this period.

However, the dramatic changes in South African politics due to the 1994 elections left Chikane in a quandary. Initially, he did not know where his future lay. For a brief period, he took up a lectureship at the University of Cape Town. Shortly thereafter, then President Mandela approached him and challenged him with the observation that he was one of those Christians who said a lot about what government should do but would not actually join a government to help it to do it. Chikane responded by accepting an invitation to be the administrative director in the president's office, a post he held through 2007.

From being an activist who criticizes government from the outside, Chikane is now a functionary on the inside who helps the new government to both govern and defend itself from the activist critics of today. This radical change in his political position puts his previous comments concerning the prophetic role of the church in an interesting light. His claim had been that the church should side with the "powerless and poor" against the "powerful and rich," though it was in the habit of doing the opposite. What are the implications of this claim now that political power has shifted so radically in favor of the ANC? Of course, the ANC still claims to be the voice of the poor. The fact that it has not lost its mass support in the transition from powerlessness to power—with its concomitant shift from a socialist to a capitalist posture, for example—suggests that this claim is not without some legitimacy. However, parties to the left of the ANC have now emerged that claim to be the real voice of the poor and challenge the government in ways that recall Chikane's earlier prophetic activism. Although they clearly do not enjoy the popularity of the ANC, the ANC can no longer take for granted that it is the voice of the underdog: after all, it cannot govern effectively without its main allies—the Congress of South African Trade Unions (COSATU) and the South African Communist Party (SACP)—and tensions within this alliance are already discernible.

Chikane's present position, in fact, differs little from that of many of South Africa's erstwhile liberation theologians. They joined the struggle against apartheid when they were powerless and now, with apartheid's demise, have become powerful. And, clearly, they have also ceased to be poor. However, having left the ranks of the poor and powerless, it is fair to ask whether erstwhile liberation theologians such as Chikane still speak with the same clarity and vigor on their behalf. It is also fair to ask whether liberation theology provides a usable political framework or public language for the government and citizens of the new dispensation, given that contemporary South African society is more complex than a Manichean dichotomy of "oppressor" and "oppressed." A theology of liberation, even in Chikane's evangelical form, draws its power from the moral high ground that a lack of political and economic power provides. Once this disparity is eliminated or reduced, and there is no longer a readily identifiable oppressor, liberation theology can no longer sustain a conceptual footing. In addition, the reality in South Africa is more complex than liberation theology allows in that, although formal political disparities have been eliminated, severe economic disparities remain. The erstwhile liberation theologians no longer suffer by these disparities (since many of them are now government functionaries enjoying generous salaries), and liberation theology itself can hardly recognize them unless an obvious "oppressor" has inflicted them on the "oppressed." But these disparities cry out for a just political response nonetheless.

The vacuum created by the absence of a distinctive Christian voice on the side of the economically downtrodden has been filled by Christian voices of resistance finding their *raison d'être* not in economic disparity but in the "liberal" atmosphere created by the new regime's reaction against the authoritarianism of the apartheid era. The call for human rights has had its inevitable consequence in the outbreak of a "culture war" of left versus right with respect to abortion, pornography, gay rights, and the death penalty. In this sense, South Africa may be welcomed into the liberal West in a way that no other African country can yet be welcomed, as such questions are generally nonissues in these countries. This cultural and moral debate has somewhat eclipsed the economic debate and given the evangelical right (in the form of Frank Retief and the ACDP, for example) the space to gain power. "Progressive" evangelicals such as Chikane now find themselves at loggerheads with "conservative" evangelicals on what the latter consider the "front-burner" moral issues. In other words, one of the main faultlines of contemporary South African politics runs *through* the evangelical community.

So-called progressive evangelicals are drawn from a group that used to be known as Concerned Evangelicals. The evangelicals in this movement were supporters of the democratic struggle in the 1980s and are now largely adherents of the ANC. The Concerned Evangelicals were individuals from across the evangelical segments of the various churches who signed a document published in 1985 known as Evangelical Witness in South Africa. This document, which followed the Kairos Document, was a critique of the right-wing stand taken by most evangelicals under apartheid. It attacked the conservative tendencies of evangelical theology and practice that tilted the evangelical community toward legitimating apartheid. It was formed in conscious opposition to the more conservative Evangelical Fellowship of South Africa (EFSA), which linked with other evangelical groups throughout the world. Chikane was a signatory of the document. (After 1994 these two groups merged to form TEASA, which attempts to unify evangelicals on mainly sociopolitical issues.)

Both Chikane and the General Secretary of TEASA, Moss Ntlha, have expressed themselves on the matter of the ACDP.[26] Their critique is significant partly because it demonstrates the deep diversity of evangelical positions with respect to political engagement. It centers around two sets of criticisms concerning the party: one relating to representation, the other relating to salvation. Both Chikane and Ntlha are disturbed by the fact that the evangelicalism they share with the ACDP associates them and many other evangelicals with the values and practices of the party, which they find distasteful. Although they acknowledge the ACDP's right to exist in a democracy, they are clearly embarrassed by its lack of political acumen and expertise, the identification of its political agenda with the values of the gospel, and its narrow concern with what Ntlha calls "the sins of sex—abortion, pornography, and homosexuality." In his unpublished paper titled "The ACDP God-Talk," Ntlha goes so far as to say that the ACDP is "doing the Christian label a giant political disservice in creating the impression that Christian political practice must remain in a grid of narrow fundamentalist concerns." He writes:

> The tragedy of the ACDP is that it has not demonstrated an adequate grasp of the challenges we face as a nation rebuilding from the ashes of apartheid. It is yet to come to grips with the fact that South Africa is, correctly, suspicious of a Christianity that is aloof, fundamentalist, soul-less, uncaring and devoid of compassion. This brand of Christianity is all too familiar to many as having helped to undergird apartheid. The history of the ACDP, its genesis and practice from inception, also points to such a Christianity.

In spite of these criticisms from politically engaged evangelicals who sympathize with the ANC, the ACDP clearly enjoys substantial support from many evangelicals who view it as a party that accurately expresses their views concerning the very "sins of sex" that Ntlha mentions. The leader of the party,

Kenneth Moeshoe, is the minister of a charismatic church who combines his activities as a pastor and a member of parliament.

Frank Chikane has evidently played a significant role in South Africa's democratic development. His powerful leadership skills, charisma, acute intelligence, and deep spiritual commitment have brought him into key positions throughout his career—youth leader, student activist, pastor, general secretary of the ICT when this organization was the main catalyst of liberation theology, general secretary of the SACC when this organization led the church's activism against apartheid, and now administrative director in the president's office. This pedigree makes Chikane the most high-profile and best-known evangelical in South African politics. As such, how anomalous or representative is he with respect to other evangelicals in South Africa? Is he one-of-a-kind, an outlier? Or, does he represent a large swath of South African evangelicalism?

The AFM, Chikane's home church, is one of the largest pentecostal denominations and, with the Assemblies of God and the Full Gospel Church, forms part of the classical pentecostal tradition in South Africa. These churches differ from the newer charismatic churches that were, in many cases, breakaways from the historic pentecostal churches. These denominations— with the exception of the Assemblies of God, whose organization was strongly influenced by Nicholas Bhengu—are under strong white control. Conservative whites in the AFM persecuted Chikane himself. Overall, the historic pentecostal churches all fall into the political position of the first case in this study, and Chikane therefore can in no way be taken to represent their politics. Chikane's political position within evangelicalism reflects the position of the Concerned Evangelicals, which, as mentioned above, constituted a small but influential group within the evangelical family in South Africa.

Conclusion

I have attempted in this chapter to distinguish between five responses to the political situation in South Africa made by evangelicals before and after the end of apartheid in April 1994. I have characterized the adherents of these positions as the conservatives, the pragmatists, the protagonists of the Third Way, the protagonists of the "alternative" community, and the liberationists. I then attempted to demonstrate their influence in the transformation of South African society toward democracy by undertaking a series of typological case studies of prominent representatives of these positions. In the process, I have attempted to unpack some of the theological and political thinking that underlies and explains each position. What conclusions can one make concerning the evangelical contribution to the democratic transformation of South African society?

The first conclusion to emerge is that, despite theological similarities, the nature and content of evangelical political interventions differ considerably.

They vary from active opposition to change and preservation of the status quo, to apparent neutrality and indifference, to active participation in the democratic processes of change, including the formation of an evangelical political party, the ACDP. The differing attitudes among evangelicals toward the ACDP indicate their differences in approach and their varied views of the appropriate aims and methods of political engagement. The fact that evangelicals vary considerably in their political attitudes and interventions suggests that in this respect they are no different from other sectors of society and that their political contribution depends on factors other than faith, such as race, class, and culture. At the same time, most evangelicals respond more or less predictably on certain moral issues, such as abortion and homosexuality, no matter what their race, class, or culture, varying from zero tolerance on these issues to qualified intolerance. Yet it is not appropriate to conclude that because evangelicals are "intolerant" with respect to these issues and others are "tolerant," evangelicals are antidemocratic or at least unable to contribute to democratization. On the contrary, their vigorous exercise of their constitutionally protected right to express themselves on these issues demonstrates that, rather than being alienated from the New South Africa, they regard themselves as citizens who have a stake in its well-being. And they are contributing to a healthy climate of debate essential to any democracy.

It has been argued in this chapter that South Africa is a unique democracy in at least two respects: it has emerged from a system of institutionalized racism, and it now has one of the most liberal constitutions in the world, certainly the most liberal in Africa. Any assessment of the evangelical role in South African democracy must examine evangelical attitudes toward these unique features of South African politics. With respect to resistance to apartheid, it has been shown that not many whites participated in this struggle, as this would inevitably have involved eroding their own positions of privilege. There were, of course, notable exceptions. However, avenues of black resistance were limited. Evangelical blacks creatively pursued whatever options were available, two of which were characterized in this study as the "alternative" and "liberationist" routes. With regard to the new constitution, I have argued that it is precisely its liberalism that has stirred many evangelicals to participate in the new democracy. Some evangelicals have entered the debates on the liberalism of the constitution because they saw an opportunity to engage in an important debate concerning the nature, extent, and appropriateness of individual rights and civil liberties, while others have done so with a view to resisting what they consider the moral degeneration of society.

Taken together, then, how have the opinions, beliefs, interventions, and attitudes of the evangelicals discussed above contributed to the democratization of South African society? The relative influence of the evangelical leaders and movements discussed, or their ability to effect change in accordance with their beliefs, depends on two factors: their strategic placement within the South African society and politics and their numerical size. Frank Chikane and the Concerned Evangelicals were small in number but highly strategically situated, first within the church, then in anti-apartheid organizations, and finally in government. The influence of these "progressive evangelicals" has therefore been disproportionate to their numbers. Similarly, Michael Cassidy and AE were not numerically large but found their constituency in the influential and moneyed white middle class and were therefore also strategically placed to make a significant political difference. Retief and CESA were small in number but showed considerable growth as conservative whites left the Anglican Church and flocked to them when the Anglican hierarchy publicly joined the struggle against apartheid. They became an ideological haven for whites trying to escape or resist the processes of change. What McCauley and Rhema lacked in terms of overall spread of numbers throughout the nation they made up for in terms of concentrated, high-profile, and media-savvy interventions.

Of all the groups discussed, the most substantial numerically is Bhengu's Back to God Crusade. Estimates put this movement at about a million adherents. Furthermore, membership is spread across the economic and political spectrum. It seems beyond doubt that the movement's message of dignity and its self-supporting character help equip its adherents to be more confident and effective participants in South African politics and society.

The relative numerical strength of these groupings raises the question of their numerical strength with respect to the church and nation as a whole. A 1996 census placed the overall population of South Africa at 40,583,574, with the racial breakdown being 5,346,000 (10.9 percent) white and 35,237,574 (76.7 percent) black, and the balance consisting of people of mixed race, Asian and other ethnicities (Hendriks and Erasmus 2001, 42). Given that whites constitute such a small proportion of the population, one may well ask why this study has focused so heavily on the white sector. Besides the argument concerning strategic placement and influence made above—which would have been particularly important during the apartheid years when blacks did not have the vote—the answer lies in the nature and definition of the term "evangelical." The definition used in this study has placed the target group in a particular historical tradition traceable back to the Pietist and pentecostal streams of Europe and America. These have become independent of the mainline churches whose numbers are far greater (14,567,569—9,956,189 of whom are black) than, for example, the pentecostal churches (2,683,314—1,732,798 of which are black).

The other nonpentecostal evangelical branch of the church consists of Baptists, Brethren, Church of the Nazarene, and CESA. These all have small, white-dominated black sectors[27] and the discussion of CESA more or less covers their role politically. Nonpentecostal evangelical black denominations include the African Gospel Church and the Mahon Mission Church, which are comparatively small.

The figures cited bear out the importance of Bhengu's Back to God movement. The fact that his group was constantly confused with the AICs—with which his movement has important similarities—reinforces the important observation that the Back to God Crusade was perceived as being truly African. On the other hand, Bhengu insisted that he identified with the revivalist traditions of European and American evangelicalism as well as with the "God of our (African) ancestors." Bhengu thus manages in a remarkable way to assert a Christian identity that brings together both Western and African traditions. The numerical superiority of his movement makes it by far the largest black pentecostal church in South Africa, if movements such as the Zionist Christian Church (which is a part of the AICs) are not included in this category.

In conclusion, the role that evangelicals have played in South Africa's democratization has been varied, complex, and ambivalent, and yet significant nonetheless. Although the relationship of evangelicals to apartheid varied significantly, from support to protest to resistance, the advent of the new dispensation in 1994 was accompanied by a sharp increase in their participation in active politics. The new era has demonstrated how quickly the past, with its tortured theological and ideological justifications and awkward silences, can be forgotten and the new can be embraced with enthusiasm and the possibility of fresh opportunities. There is not only a new sense of freedom but also a sense that ordinary men and women can determine the way South African society evolves. With this freedom and freshness have come excesses. Perhaps there is a democratic parallel to the tendency of the *nouveau riche* to overindulge. These excesses have, in many ways, begun to threaten the new democracy in its infancy, in spite of all the instruments that have been put in place to prevent its corruption and dilution.

No political or legal instrument in the world can reach into human hearts and inculcate all the habits and dispositions on which a healthy democracy depends. South Africans are learning that, without these habits and dispositions, a culture of human rights can easily become a culture of entitlement, that power can lead to corruption, and that freedom is apt to abandon duty and social responsibility. In many ways, the story of the democratic revolution in South Africa, hailed by many as a miracle, is the story of democratic revolutions that have occurred throughout history. Evangelicals, with their distinctive emphasis on matters of the heart, are well placed to make a difference.

NOTES

1. Analysts are also quick to point out, however, that there are worrying signs that threaten the new democracy. Among these are the following: (1) The continued existence of substantial economic disparities between the rich and poor. Even though the new regime has brought about the rapid expansion of a black middle class, the poor have effectively remained poor or become poorer. (2) "A desire for total control over

society, including the organs of civil society." (3) "Increasing intolerance of opposition, coupled with increasing tolerance of errant party apparatchiks" (1999, 29). (4) The dominance of the ANC on the political landscape, highlighted by the 1999 elections, which brought the party to a hair's breadth of enjoying, entirely on its own, the two-thirds majority in the House of Assembly required to change the constitution.

2. These records not only reflect the influence of Christianity at the level of the rhetorical. They also demonstrate that Christianity profoundly shaped the core identity of its converts. This is illustrated in a fascinating exchange between a certain Chief Stephen Mini, then chairman of the Natal Native Congress, and the chairman of a meeting of the Select Committee on Native Affairs, taking place on June 15 and 18, 1917. In paragraph 4398 of the records of this report, the question is put to Mini: "What tribe do you belong to?" He replied, "The Christian people at Edendale" (Document 28, in Johns 1972, 94).

3. The African National Congress issued a full-page advertisement, supported by the signatures of Christian clergy, "proclaiming the gospel as the only framework for establishing full political inclusion and guaranteeing social justice in South Africa." It also pointed out that five other parties in the election used Christian slogans or rhetoric. While the ANC appealed to Christian justice, the Nationalist Party (the former party of apartheid) appealed for Christian mercy: "The NP apologised. As a Christian I accept that. The NP is now the party for me." The right-wing Freedom Front promised to defend Christian principles against Communism, the African Christian Democratic Party declared that it was "time to do it God's way," and the Inkatha Freedom Party, the party of Chief Buthelezi, after a classic display of political posturing, delaying tactics, and threats of violence, finally came into the campaign promising apocalyptic redemption when its name appeared last on the ballot, biblically asserting that "the last shall be first" (Chidester, 1).

4. For the definition of "evangelicalism" I use in this study, see below.

5. In a recent survey (2000) carried out by the Human Sciences Research Council, it was found that of all the institutions of South African society, the church remains, in the minds of most people, the most trustworthy.

6. See Terence O. Ranger's introduction to this collection.

7. This definition is consistent with the broad definition outlined by Terence Ranger in his introduction and with the definitions used by other authors of chapters in this volume.

8. On the perils of drawing a sharp distinction between evangelical and "mainline" churches, especially when it comes to the Third World, see the introductory chapter in Freston (2001).

9. For one discussion of some of the differences between charismatic and pentecostal Christianity, see Coleman (2000, 20–24).

10. The link between Colenso and CESA has never been a doctrinal one. It was structural in the sense that the Anglican Church in South Africa was originally the Church of England. Bishop Grey's attempt to assert a degree of autonomy for the Church of England in South Africa by establishing the Church of the Province of South Africa (CPSA) was resisted by Colenso, as well as by a cleric by the name of Long, who insisted on the association of the Church with the British Crown. Long was personally an evangelical, though in general South African Anglicanism at the time could be

characterized that way. Colenso was partially vindicated: His diocese officially re-mained a part of the Church of England, though under Grey's oversight. However, Grey subsequently excommunicated Colenso on doctrinal issues: theologically, Colenso had adopted a "modernist" scepticism concerning the historicity of the Bible, especially the Old Testament. But Bishop Grey also found Colenso's friendship with the Zulu people and support for their cause in the Zulu war unacceptable. When Colenso died, his diocese came under the CPSA. In the meantime, another Church of England diocese in the Cape had linked up with the Anglican Church in Sydney, Australia, and became the Church of England in South Africa (CESA).

11. Grazzioli gives a classic rendition of this: "CESA's desire to be present and vocal when the evangelical position is corrupted by other agendas is shared by many equally concerned with upholding the gospel and truth. The dangers of a social/political gospel and ecumenism are fully understood by the majority of members and TEASA's [The Evangelical Alliance of South Africa's] position continues to keep groups such as SACC, CPSA, and Methodists from membership" (1996 report of the Morals and Ethics Committee, 19).

12. On Chikane, see case study 5.

13. Heyns paid the ultimate price for his involvement in these activities by being assassinated by right-wing forces on November 5, 1994, seven months after the in-auguration of a democratic dispensation in South Africa.

14. Steele and McCauley work so closely together that one may be forgiven for putting into one's mouth the words of the other and vice versa. The book quoted here was clearly written by Steele, as was McCauley's biography and probably most of the writings put out by Rhema. But it no doubt sums up not only McCauley's own position on these matters but also his style.

15. This figure is speculative.

16. A notable exception to this was Klaus Nurnberger, who made it clear from the beginning of his involvement in the NIR that reconciliation would ultimately mean the necessity of surrender of political hegemony by the white minority.

17. Reported by African Enterprise in *The Star*, April 12, 1994.

18. The Sharpeville Massacre took place when people peacefully marched on the Sharpeville Police Station in Soweto, objecting to the Pass Laws that forbade blacks access to white areas after certain hours. Sixty-nine people were killed, most of them shot in the back as they were fleeing.

19. The Soweto Uprising took place when schoolchildren objected to being taught in the medium of Afrikaans, the language they deemed to be that of the oppressor. As in the case of Sharpeville, it was brutally repressed. Following the uprising, many left the country to join the armed struggle.

20. This conference took place on July 7–12, 2003, in Pretoria and was attended by up to 4,800 people. It was jointly organized by the South African Council of Churches, The Evangelical Alliance of South Africa, and African Enterprise. It had representatives from sixty church groupings and addressed the issues of HIV/AIDS, crime, poverty and unemployment, the family, violence, racism, and sexism. The four days that it lasted were organized respectively under the themes of repentance, hope, unity, and commitment to action.

21. The term is derived from the traditional Xhosa practice of covering the skin with red mud.

22. "Do you call this Utopia? Wait and see. Remember what Luther's message did for Europe. Look at John Wesley's message in England. We have a message for the continent of Africa. Pray for us, help us now. We are desperate, we mean business and have the confidence that God is going to move and change the continent of Africa. God save Africa or we die, is our plea. We are not preaching for the sake of preaching. We are not motivated by the selfish desire to have a following and finances but we are burdened for Africa. We have suffered, and things cannot go on like they are forever. Where is our God? Let us face Him and claim our birthright through Christ Jesus and see if He is going to fail Africa at this hour of need." Bhengu, in the *Back to God* magazine, 1958, quoted by Diko, unpublished, p. 64.

23. Interview with the Reverend Victor Nkomonde of the Back to God movement, March 23, 2001.

24. This figure was suggested in an interview with the Reverend Victor Nkomonde of the Back to God movement, March 23, 2001, but is not confirmed.

25. But the road has obviously not been an easy one. In Pauline style, he describes what he has experienced: "Six times I have been detained, at times for long periods without charge, and in three of these detentions badly tortured. Once I have been charged with high treason and acquitted, my house was petrol-bombed, and I have appeared on a hit list of a death squad" (Chikane 1988, 90).

26. They articulate their views concerning the ACDP in two short unpublished documents written in 2000: "Jesus Crucified in Parliament" and "The ACDP God-Talk," written by Chikane and Ntlha respectively.

27. Toward the end of the apartheid era, the Baptists had the equivalent of the Concerned Evangelicals, which was called the Fellowship of Concerned Baptists. It was essentially a group of dissenting blacks and people of mixed race, along with a handful of whites.

7

Evangelical Christianity and Democracy in Africa: A Response

Paul Gifford

The contributors to this volume on evangelical Christianity and democracy in Africa are to be congratulated. All of their studies are most illuminating; I wish I had known much of this before. I would also like to thank the organizers and funders for making such a significant project possible.

In reflecting on this volume and the issues it raises, I wish to make seven comments. None is a point of major disagreement. All are more akin to observations made from a complementary perspective or conclusions resulting from a slightly different weighting of evidence.

The first point concerns labels and particularly the crucial labels "evangelical" and "pentecostal." My recent experience in Ghana has led me to see the enormous range of churches involved in this kind of study. It is no longer clear that we can talk of "pentecostal" as a simple category, and the complexity increases when we talk about their public effects. I have problems even with the word "evangelical." In the studies in this as well as the other volumes, which are based on David Bebbington's widely used definition, "evangelicalism" is given four qualities: biblicism, crucicentrism, conversionism, and activism. But many of these churches would not be marked by that crucicentric quality at all; many have little reference to suffering, little to sin. The same is true for the stress on conversion, and maybe we distort the picture by presuming that membership implies a sharp change of life.

It may be that the word "evangelical" is another of those words not immediately applicable outside the West. I suppose I would opt for a less theological and perhaps more organizational definition: The churches we are dealing with are not the Roman Catholics, not the mainline Protestants (who tend to congregate in national Christian Councils and who paradoxically may well be theologically evangelical themselves), not the classical AICs, but the rest.

The second point relates to "democracy" and politics. I think the last ten years has seen a growing consensus about the great systemic ill of Africa, which is not necessarily that of Asia or Latin America. This neo-patrimonialism is marked by clientelism, access to state resources, centralisation of power, and hybridity of regimes (see van de Walle 2001, 118–129). To illustrate briefly what this means, take Angola. In mid-2002 it looked as though the war had stopped. Why? According to the *Economist*, "the peace has been negotiated, and is being implemented, by soldiers, not politicians: several of the latter pocketed huge 'commissions' on arms to blast the rebels, and so had an interest in postponing peace" ("The War Is Over, the Rebels Come Home," May 23, 2002). Unlike prior ceasefire agreements, in which rebel soldiers did not report for disarmament, in 2002 in just five weeks, around 80 percent of rebel troops—more than forty thousand men plus their families—have converged on refugee camps. However, continued clientelism threatened the disarmament and reintegration process. The *Economist* continued:

> Sixty inmates have already starved to death. If conditions do not improve, UNITA's leaders say their men will be forced to desert the camps and revert to armed banditry to survive. Foreign donors are ready to send help, as the Angolan army has repeatedly requested. But the donors cannot intervene without permission from the Angolan government, and this permission has been denied. Why? In the absence of war, senior political figures are now trying to cash in on the peace. The same men who used to grow fat on weapons contracts have now taken charge of ordering tents, medical kits and rations for demobilised rebels. If the UN took over, this avenue for profiteering would be closed. (May 23, 2002)

This political culture is the problem—the problem with a capital "P."

I was trying to think of an illustration: a man might be ill with TB but have eczema, a migraine, and a stomach ulcer as well. All are important, and for certain purposes it will be justified to treat the ulcer, say, or the eczema. But nevertheless I think it is still arguable that that man's big sickness is his TB; that's his sickness with a capital "S." When talking about the evangelical churches' role in African politics, it might help to keep in mind that some evangelical contributions bear on this major problem, others on lesser problems. It may even be that in treating the major one they inflame some minor ones, or *vice versa*. But the diagnosis is in: Africa's major problem is the neo-patrimonial culture of the political elite.

Third, this raises the question of how leading evangelical church figures relate to that elite behaviour. It is not immediately evident that they necessarily challenge it. I observe in Ghana, for example, an enormous increase in the status of leaders. What may have begun as egalitarian spiritual brotherhoods may be very different now. Just watch the evolution of titles: from pastor, to general overseer, to bishop, even archbishop or even megabishop; from prophet to megaprophet. It is conceivable that in some cases, these leaders, far from challenging the characteristic way political elites exploit and oppress, replicate it. It is interesting that Karl Maier's book *This House Has Fallen*, which was reviewed extremely positively in Britain, with everyone remarking on his sympathy with Nigerians, loses that sympathy in only one case—that of the new church leaders David Oyedepo and the prophet T.B. Joshua, the first (in his view) trading on the greed of his followers, the second on their gullibility (Maier 2000, 252). If Maier's view is correct, these leaders are replicating, not challenging, the attitudes of Africa's political elites.

Fourth, there may be a danger of placing too much stress on the change of character of those individuals joining such churches—as I mentioned above in my criticism of the use of "conversion" as one of evangelicalism's distinguishing marks. Sometimes it is almost presumed that a total transformation is inevitable. However, all sorts of other things may be going on. This was brought home most forcibly in June 2002 with the death of Hansie Cronje, the South African cricket captain. He made much of being a committed Christian from Ray McCauley's evangelical Rhema church (which is discussed in detail in Anthony Balcomb's contribution to this volume), and he was probably South Africa's best-known born-again Christian. Not only was Cronje discovered to have been taking hundreds of thousands of dollars from match-fixers, but he had actually tried to embroil the two newest and only two nonwhite players in the team in his corruption. Having done so, he cheated them out of half the fee they were owed. In short, he cheated everyone, all the time wearing a bracelet engraved with the letters "WWJD"—"What would Jesus do?" I am not necessarily questioning the importance of conversion in Africa's new churches, just the assumption that it must always and everywhere be a defining and transformative characteristic.

Fifth, there is another factor to be considered: the economic. Africa is marked by enormous poverty; that is what underlies the behavior of the elite. If they have used the state to enrich themselves, the way they now use the aid business looks somewhat similar. After the state, aid is now the second biggest employer in Africa. I think one might speculate that Christianity may well be the third. Christianity is not just a religion; it is also a business. Please note that I am not reducing Christianity to a business. I am merely pointing out that if you omit the economic angle, you may be omitting something important.

For example, Reinhard Bonnke has revealed that his 2000 Ibadan crusade and Fire Conference cost £1.3 million (Bonnke's *Revival Report*, April 2000). Even if only half of that reached Ibadan, can you think of any other enterprise investing £600,000 in the economy of Ibadan? For Bonnke's Sudan Crusade in April 2000, it cost £117,500 to fly in the equipment, and he hired a fleet of three hundred buses for transport for the crusade, at a cost of £50,000. Again, who else is investing £50,000 in the Khartoum transport business? His Ethiopian Crusade about the same time cost £805,000 just for the literature distributed (*Revival Report*, May 2000). Bonnke calculated that an upcoming crusade in Khartoum would cost £310,000 (*Revival Report*, February 2001). Christian publishing offers another example. In Ghana, publishing has been very hard hit, especially since the collapse of Ghana's currency, the cedi, in 1998. The only people that seem to publish books are church pastors. Part of the dynamic here is the book launch, effectively an auction at which followers outbid one another for the first copies. At a recent book launch, Duncan Williams, one of Accra's most prominent church leaders, received ten million cedis ($1,500 U.S.) for each of the first three copies; the next three went for five million; after that launch and the auctioning at both church services the next day, six hundred books (out of a print run of two thousand) had been sold with a turnover of one hundred million cedis ($15,000 U.S.; *Daily Graphic* [Accra], April 8, 2002). And this in a country where the average annual income may still be under $400 (U.S.).

In short, the material aspect of Africa's new Christianity cannot be ignored. It is against this background that I understand the Gospel of Prosperity to be so functional, especially with its "law of sowing and reaping." I simply note how little is made of the Gospel of Prosperity in these studies, whereas I tend to give it more prominence.

Sixth, it is possible that the "powers that be" may directly use evangelical Christianity for political purposes. Naturally, the scope for this varies enormously from country to country. But as an example of what I mean, consider Liberia. Until his recent exile, Charles Taylor was one of Africa's most destructive warlords. He destroyed and brutalized two countries, Liberia and Sierra Leone, yet made an estimated $70 million (U.S.) annually from selling off the assets of Liberia alone. In early 2002, he staged a national three-day prayer crusade, the largest gathering in the history of his administration; more than sixty-five thousand people attended. This was well covered in the international media. *West Africa* (London) reported it at face value:

Then came Taylor's prayers, accompanied by serious weeping. "O Father, we cry before you. Father we mourn before you.... O Father men have sinned against you. Have mercy on us," he said. As his voice echoed, some people nearby said, "This man is gifted. He knows how to pray. Look, see, he knows the Bible well." [Taylor continued,] "I am not your President. Jesus is [the crowd went wild].... Let not our enemies triumph before us. Let not them ask, where is their God? Let them never laugh to say, "Ha ha ha, and where is their God?" Liberia is calling upon you. You are my strength. You are my everything," Taylor said in tears. (*West Africa* [London], March 4–10, 2002)

West Africa continued:

Historically, Liberia was built on proclaimed Christian principles... this made the early settlers name Monrovia Christopolis, meaning "City of Christ." Indeed, the City of Christ is gaining its status in the difficult days under Taylor.

By contrast, *Africa Confidential* (London) and the *Economist* saw this—correctly, in my view—as a blatant attempt to manipulate Christianity for political ends. An *Africa Confidential* article stated: "Taylor reaches out to the Christian right in the USA, calling for support against Muslim rebels backed by neighbouring Muslim states. There are suggestions that Liberia should formally declare itself a Christian state which...might appeal to some U.S. politicians" (February 22, 2002). The *Economist* wrote that Taylor "accuses the rebels of being part of a shady Muslim conspiracy, which has launched a jihad against Liberia's majority Christians and threatened to burn their churches," while in the meantime possibly sponsoring an attack by the same rebels "in order to manipulate international opinion into lifting the UN sanctions that were imposed on Liberia for backing the rebels in Sierra Leone's civil war" ("Liberia's Curious State of Emergency," February 28, 2002). I think that at least Moi, Chiluba, Gbagbo, Obasanjo and Kerekou have all at times used Christianity in similar ways in order to further political aims.

Seventh, there has been little reference to the enchanted worldview that may underlie much evangelical and pentecostal Christianity in Africa. In Ghana, this phenomenon is called the "primal religious imagination," which has given rise to the deliverance explosion in the last five or six years. To link this up with a previous point, I would suggest that, far from being democratic, these churches are characterised by leaders with special powers to cast out evil spirits and hence a unique and unimpeachable ecclesial authority. This is all very difficult to handle, especially in its political effects. The attempt to view this new Christianity as rooted in traditional forms of religion is sometimes dismissed out of hand. Philip Jenkins, the author of *The Next Christendom: The Coming of Global Christianity* (2002), is reported as dismissing this as nothing more than a "racist, they've-just-come-down-from-the-trees" kind of argument (Toby Lester, "Oh Gods!" *The Atlantic Monthly*, February 2002). Yet Birgit Meyer has effectively demonstrated that for the Ghanaian Christians she was studying, a linking of witchcraft with Satan made witchcraft an essential category of their Christianity. And she is not a racist. In talking about the role of sorcery in African politics, she has written something that deserves quoting in full:

> How can one write about politics and sorcery in Africa without evoking an image of the continent as hopelessly backward, fundamentally different and exotic? This question kept haunting me during my struggle to write this essay and I am still not sure what my answer is. But for me *not* writing about this relationship at all was out of the question. (Meyer 1998, 32)

Like Birgit Meyer, I do not know how to treat this subject adequately. But I strongly agree that to omit discussion of this very difficult dimension would be to omit a key part of the dynamic. I had hoped that local scholars coordinated by Terence Ranger—who some years ago gave the Wiles Lectures at Queens University on witchcraft and must know as much about this subject as anyone— might deal with this issue sensitively and instructively.

Again, however, let me express my gratitude for these studies and all they contribute to our understanding of evangelical Christianity and democracy in Africa. To their authors and their editor, we are very much indebted.

Afterword

Terence O. Ranger

When the chapters in this book were written, they were all very up to the moment. Of course events and understandings have developed since then, and it seems necessary to summarize some of these developments here. In this afterword I comment on more recent developments in four of the cases presented in this book: northern Nigeria, Zambia, Kenya, and Zimbabwe.

Islam in Northern Nigeria

So far as the confrontation between Christians and Muslims in northern Nigeria is concerned, it is not so much that there have been dramatic new developments since Cyril Imo wrote his chapter. But there have been important fresh analyses. Imo is mainly concerned with tracing developments within evangelical Christian thought that result from its confrontation with radical Islam—a confrontation that has wide implications for Christian thinking about politics, democracy, and the state. Lamin Sanneh (2003) has now explored the debate *within* northern Nigerian Islam rather than the confrontations between Muslims and Christians. His analysis does not so much as mention evangelical Christianity, but it raises fascinating contrasts and comparisons between what might be called "evangelical Muslim" and "evangelical Christian" responses to democracy.

Sanneh argues that some of the radical Muslims who have promulgated Sharia law in northern Nigerian states make a crucial distinction between "the Islamization of the state," which they oppose, and "the Islamization of society," which they favor. Sanneh thinks that

> the distinction offers a potentially productive way of re-framing the debate on the proper relationship between religion and statehood in Muslim thought in general, and among Nigerian Muslim leaders in particular. Its great intellectual merit is the shifting of the focus from the role of the state exclusively, to the role of civil society in dealing with issues of tolerance, diversity and pluralism. The distinction does not deny the challenge of secularism, but instead mitigates it by restructuring it as a matter of the civil order.... The Islamization of society in Nigeria would not politicise religion, or oppose democracy, in the way that the Islamization of the state would. Furthermore, the Islamization of society, involving a code of strict personal standards of religious observance ... could proceed with the dual affirmation of a laic state, on the one hand, and, on the other hand, of the role of Muslims in promoting Islam without denying a similar role for members of other religions. In other words, the effects of civil agency could neutralize at the same time combative secularism and religious fundamentalism. (Sanneh 2003, 237)

Other Muslim radicals argue for the Islamization of the state, holding that "a Muslim delinquent at his or her prayer and devotion brings harm only to himself or herself, whereas a politically negligent Muslim implicates the larger Muslim community, both present and future." One side argues that "religion is too important to abandon it in private hands as personal choice"; the other side argues that "religion is too important to entrust to the state, whether civil or military." Sanneh himself comments that "religious or secular anointing of the state does not solve the problem of the state; they merely exacerbate it" (Sanneh 2003, 238). He sums up the debate among northern Nigerian Muslims:

> One side feels that the Islamization of the state, with religion and government united in a single source, will make government a source of grace and assure immunity for God's truth, while the other side feels that such a step will result in double jeopardy for political stability and religious integrity. (Sanneh 2003, 241)

As other chapters in this book show, the choice between moralizing the state and moralizing society is one that evangelical Christians have been making and debating. Meanwhile, since these chapters were written, the question of Muslim ideas about democracy and society has assumed importance not only in Nigeria but in some of the other cases presented in this book as well. I shall seek to bring this out in my comments on Kenya and Zimbabwe.

Political Change in Zambia

Two of the remaining five chapters in this book need no additional closing comment. Tony Balcomb has updated the South African chapter. Teresa Cruz e Silva feels that in its essentials the Mozambican situation remains the same as it was when she wrote. But in Zambia and Kenya there have been crucial elections since those chapters were written, and the political and moral crises in Zimbabwe have reached depths that would have been impossible to foresee even a short time ago.

I am not, of course, going to attempt a narrative of events in these three countries in this short afterword. I shall maintain, however, that although their authors could not have foreseen in detail what has developed in Zambia, Kenya, and Zimbabwe, their chapters establish the basis for understanding these changes. The chapters set out trajectories for the interaction of evangelical Christianity and democratic politics that have persisted in the subsequent period. Zambia is perhaps the best, if most paradoxical, example.

Anticipating the forthcoming Zambian triple election—presidential, parliamentary and local—in December 2001, Isabel Phiri's chapter predicted that Christian women would make a significant impact. She also believed that the evangelical leader, Nevers Mumba, would play an important role. These developments would be the result of evangelical ideology and organization in Zambia, and a part of the fallout from then President Frederick Chiluba's concept of Zambia as a Christian nation. Evangelical morality could no longer be far from the core of Zambian politics.

The results of the December 2001 elections seemed at first sight totally to confound these expectations. As Dr. Mutumba Mainga Bull's 2002 analysis of "Gender Dimensions of Multiparty Politics" in Zambia shows, the women's movement throughout the country

> embarked on its Programme M2000 to promote the political aspirations of women within political parties and in decision-making positions at all levels. Earlier this year, 2001, a Zambia Women's Manifesto was produced by Women in Politics and the Women's Movement was adopted by almost all the major political parties in the country to help women, especially those seeking elective office in the 2001 elections. (Bull 2002, 2–4)

The Women's Movement organized campaign teams and distributed resources to all women candidates. Virtually every political party gave preference to qualified women in candidate selection. Some 180 women stood as candidates, divided among twelve parties—"the largest number of female candidates in the country's history" (Bull 2002). Two women stood as presidential candidates, Gwendoline Konie, founder and president of the Social Democratic Party, and

Dr. Inonge Mbikusita Lewanika, leader of the Agenda for Zambia party. Yet as Dr. Bull remarks, "the two female Presidential hopefuls scored the lowest number of votes, while only 16 candidates out of nearly 190 female parliamentary candidates have won" (Bull 2002, 5). "I am shocked," said Dr Lewanika, "I did not know that there is still so much bias against women in this country."[1]

As for the presidential candidacy of Nevers Mumba, despite hearing God "telling him to save Zambia through the ballot box . . . to cleanse the country of corruption," he "was one of the more spectacular flops, when he polled only 2% of the vote" (Dale 2003a). Evidently, the evangelical campaign to moralize and equalize Zambia was not yet politically attractive, at least not at the ballot box.

And yet in a quite extraordinary way the moralizing and the feminizing agendas emerged as central to Zambia's politics after all. Zambia's unpredictable president, Levy Mwanawasa, has drawn upon both in his struggle with the entrenched corruption of Frederick Chiluba, his predecessor as leader of the Movement for Multiparty Democracy (MMD) and as national president. Having indicted Chiluba for abuse of office, Mwanawasa threatened to sack corrupt cabinet ministers. In May 2003 he did indeed sack his vice president, Enoch Kavindele, together with the finance and information ministers. Sensationally, Nevers Mumba, disbanding his own party to join the ruling movement, was appointed the new vice president:

> Never in the history of Zambian politics has someone's rise to power been as meteoric as that of Nevers Mumba [exclaimed the BBC correspondent in Lusaka]. Almost overnight, Mr. Mumba has moved from being an unimpressive opposition leader to holding the country's second most prestigious job. (Dale 2003a)

It is abundantly clear that Mumba was appointed not because of any party political strength but because of his reputation as a fiery and charismatic evangelist. His job is to exemplify incorruptible morality in the Zambian state. The flavor is given by a statement on the website of his Victory Ministries International:

> His statesmanship has remained on the cutting edge of the quest for a better nation spiritually, politically, economically, and socially. . . . His clearest purpose is to champion and bring a full spiritual, economic, and social emancipation for his generation . . . and to bring the restoration of dignity lost through the oppressive history by highlighting God's values. He believes the Scripture that says, "When the righteous rule, people rejoice."[2]

This message evidently had little electoral appeal. Equally evidently, it offers a crucial resource to President Mwanawasa in the rough and tumble of

Zambian politics. As he beat off a recent impeachment attempt, it was an enormous asset to have the "righteous" Mumba on hand to oversee the voting.

The tantalizing update to this episode, however, is that in October 2004, after Nevers Mumba publicly accused Zambian opposition parties of receiving funding from the Democratic Republic of the Congo without discussing these allegations with Mwanawasa beforehand, the President sacked him. Mumba indicated soon afterwards that he will contest the MMD candidacy for the presidency in 2006, and an impressive website already details his "Vision and Plan for a New Zambia."[3] Thanks partly to Mumba's candidacy, evangelical Christianity again played a visible role in the run-up to the 2006 presidential election.

Mwanawasa offered other surprises, however. In May 2003 he threw down the gauntlet to the women of Zambia, announcing that when his time in office is up, he wants a woman to take over: "He boasts that his 'new deal' government has made significant strides in narrowing the gap between men and women in politics. Every female ruling party MP holds some sort of ministerial portfolio. There is even a woman from the opposition in cabinet" (Dale 2003b).[4]

So, despite all appearances at the time of the 2001 election, Isabel Phiri's agenda is alive and well.

Political Change in Kenya

In Kenya, too, a presidential election took place soon after John Karanja's chapter came to an end. At the end of December 2002 the candidate of KANU, which had been in power for nearly forty years, accepted defeat by Mwai Kibaki, candidate of the National Rainbow Coalition. The Kenya Domestic Observation Programme, K-DOP (2003), rejoiced:

> Never before were there crowds seen in Kenya as those witnessed at Uhuru Park. The Park became a symbol of its name, UHURU which means FREEDOM; freedom for Kenyans from suppressive and oppressive politics; freedom to usher in a new dawn of hope for the country, a hope of a better life; and most of all, freedom to decide their own destiny and to achieve self-actualization and self-determination. The 2002 elections illustrated that power indeed belonged to Kenyans.

Newly elected President Mwai Kibaki hailed "Kenya's long awaited second liberation" (Kenya Domestic Opposition Programme 2003, 9).

John Karanja describes in his chapter how evangelicals of the historic churches, together with Catholics, Muslims, and Hindus formed an alliance in order to participate in the constitution-making process. This alliance was extended during the presidential elections, which were held under the old constitution. As their June 2003 report describes:

> The religious organizations that had formed the *Ufungamano* [constitutional] Initiative realized that they could work together and, as a united front, formed the Kenya Domestic Observation Programme (K-DOP). These organisations were the Catholic Justice and Peace Commission (CPJC), National Council of the Churches in Kenya (NCCK), Supreme Council of Kenyan Muslims (SUPKEM) and the Hindu Council of Kenya (HCK).

In June 2002 these partners appointed regional coordinators, constituency observers and organizers, and a secretariat. Before Election Day, K-DOP recruited and trained an additional 18,366 poll watchers. Significantly, the churches ran civic education programs. In his report a year later, the chairman of K-DOP's Strategic Board, Archbishop John Njenga, rejoiced in the success of the operation:

> All the faiths, Christians, Muslims, and Hindus worked extremely well, in this memorable and historic joint venture.... The peaceful elections and the smooth transfer of power were a fitting tribute to the intrinsic peaceful nature and maturity of Kenyans. The solid resolve by the people of Kenya for peaceful change had materialized. The people had elected a government of their choice. (Kenya Domestic Opposition Programme 2003, 7)[5]

As a fulfillment of the trajectory documented by Karanja in his chapter, all this sounds almost too good to be true. And in a way it has turned out to be so. In the months since the presidential election in December 2002, fascinating new patterns of evangelical participation have emerged in Kenya.

Evangelicals of the historic church tradition had played a leading role both in the debates on the constitution and in the monitoring of the 2002 election. Of the newer evangelical churches only the Assemblies of God were members of the National Council of Churches in Kenya. Other evangelical, pentecostal, and charismatic churches had opposed political participation and had even gone so far as to take legal action to prevent the historic churches from participating in the constitutional review. They did not join in election monitoring and there is little available evidence concerning their role in the election itself.[6]

After the election and with the publication of the draft constitution, however, everything changed. The draft provided that Islamic *Kadhi* courts, which had existed on the costal strip since the nineteenth century, should be established in every part of Kenya. There was an instant outcry from Kenyan Christians in which the new evangelicals, pentecostals, and charismatics have been the most vociferous. Having tried to prevent the historical churches from participating in the constitutional process, the new evangelicals blamed them

for having allowed the *Kadhi* recommendations. For their part, Muslims demonstrated in the streets of Nairobi; withdrew from the united *Unfungamano*
initiative; and said they will not negotiate on the question of the *Kadhi* courts.
The sharp contrast between Cyril Imo's and John Karanja's papers so far as
Islam is concerned looks somewhat less sharp now (Nguru 2002).[7]

This issue has transformed the new evangelical attitude to politics. In
order to oppose the *Kadhi* recommendations, the pentecostals have taken the
initiative in forming a new body, "The Kenya Church," which includes Roman
Catholics also, and runs parallel to the National Council of Churches. Charismatics pray in the streets, send out prayer teams, and issue monthly action
bulletins against the constitutional draft; charismatic representatives were also
among the six hundred delegates who had to make the final constitutional
recommendations. There was no attempt, however, to replicate a Zambian
"Christian nation." Instead, "The Kenya Church" argued that there should be
no religious law courts in a secular state.[8] In a national referendum in November 2005, pentecostals and other evangelicals helped mobilize 58 percent
of voters to defeat the draft constitution.

Political Change in Zimbabwe

In Zimbabwe also there were presidential elections in 2002, but with very
different results from those in Zambia and Kenya. In violent, embittered, and
contested polls, victory was declared for the incumbent, Robert Mugabe, who
has ruled Zimbabwe since independence in 1980. The incoming President did
not, like Kenya's Kibaki, hail a second democratizing liberation in which NGOs
and especially the churches would play a full part. Mugabe's very different
slogan was one of permanent revolution and constant mobilization against
global imperialism with its false slogans of human rights and civil society
(Ranger 2002, 2004). The Zimbabwean churches were not able to launch
widespread campaigns of civic education, to monitor polling stations, or to
issue a detailed report like their Kenyan counterparts. Indeed, since the election, the churches have been regularly rebuked by the government for playing
the game of Zimbabwe's Western enemies by talking about "international
human rights" and "regime change" (*Herald*, "Non-State Actors Doomed,"
November 14, 2003).[9]

Nevertheless, the Zimbabwean churches—and especially Zimbabwean
evangelicals—have come to play a much more open and systematic role in
democratic politics than was the case when Isabel Mukonyora completed her
chapter. The trajectory she establishes there, however, has carried Zimbabwean evangelicals irresistibly forward. This is largely the result of what they see
as the increasing immorality of the state. Thus, leaders of the Evangelical Fellowship of Zimbabwe, especially its chairman Bishop Trevor E. C. Manhanga,

and his deputy, Pastor Charles Chiriseri, have played a leading role in public protest in the years since the 2002 elections. Manhanga is one of three bishops, together with an Anglican and a Catholic, who have been mediating between President Mugabe and Morgan Tsvangarai of the MDC. Chiriseri is chair of the National Peace Building Committee of the National Crisis Coalition. In this capacity, he has brought together representatives of the churches and of NGOs in a series of important conferences that have issued increasingly radical political and theological statements.

A National Peace Convention was held in Bulawayo, Zimbabwe, in December 2002 "to develop an action oriented, non-partisan response to Zimbabwe's growing crisis and spiralling [sic] violence." It was attended by 8 bishops "from a variety of denominations such as Catholic, Anglican, Brethren in Christ, and Evangelical churches," including Manhanga; and by over seventy pastors and delegates from fifty civil society organizations, including women's, youth, and labor organizations. Chiriseri opened the meeting by urging everyone "to shun stone age politics that base human relationships on who has a bigger stick to beat with or a larger stone to throw." The delegates unanimously called for a restitution of democratic institutions and civil rights as well as for the cessation of the politics of chaos. Patson Netha of the Association of Evangelicals in Africa said that the convention was not an event but a process. "The church is coming together to stand and say 'we have a role to play in Zimbabwe—a prophetic, priestly, pastoral role as the conscience of the nation.' "[10]

In February 2003, Manhanga was illegally detained for over five hours at Borrowdale Police station when he went to submit a petition there. He reminded his audience of this in July 2003, when he addressed a Stakeholders Conference on Dialogue and Transition in Harare. He opened with a joke, reminding the gathering that "the last time I accepted an invitation from [the National] Crisis [Coalition] I was arrested even though I did not speak!" A jailbird chairman of the Evangelical Fellowship was unusual enough. Perhaps even more unusual was the range of Manhanga's speech, which covered issues of political will, economic reality, human rights, land reform, and legal constitutional concerns. He defined the key problem as the "failure of the people of Zimbabwe to hold accountable those they have elected to lead them.... We need to disabuse ourselves of the idea that democracy is simply the holding of elections.... People of Zimbabwe need to take ownership of the processes that determine their fate and well being." Citizens must test leaders by criteria of integrity, morality, and accountability. There must be immediate repeal of oppressive legislation; an immediate end to political violence; reparation and healing for victims; and healing for perpetrators. "I have made myself clear on my stance as a servant of God," Manhanga concluded, noting that "there will be no transition or dialogue without leverage of some kind. Others present might seek to exert mass pressure or popular campaigns, but as a clergyman my perception of leverage is mediation" (Manhanga 2003).

In September 2003, 109 clergy from fifty-nine denominations met in Kadoma, Zimbabwe, inspired by the ideal of good government portrayed in Romans 13:1–17, which, they said, is regrettably abused by oppressive regimes to legitimate their rule.

> We maintain that a good government comes from God and is charged with the tasks of protecting the common good of the nation, ensuring justice for all . . . as well as being a custodian of the nation's social and moral values. Such a government is worthy of the obedience and loyalty of its citizens as demanded in Romans 13. Any government that negates these fundamental principles, to which we are committed, forfeits its God-given mandate to rule. It therefore cannot demand submission and obedience of its citizens. It is like the "beast" in Revelation 13, which usurps power. (Kadoma Conference 2003)

Romans 13 was "an indictment of the government, people, and the Church of this country in the current situation." The gathering proceeded to identify the beast-like nature of the Zimbabwean state: "irresponsible, violent, partisan . . . rampantly corrupt; perpetuating physical, psychological and emotional violence upon students in institutions of higher learning; inflicting violence on women; and corrupting the minds of youth." The fifty-nine denominations committed themselves to a "prophetic voice to transform fear into faith" and "to a campaign that will lead to the realisation" of a good society (Kadoma Conference 2003).

Clearly the political declarations of the Zimbabwean Church—and of evangelicals in particular—have become more and more radical. Late in 2003, Bishop Trevor Manhanga joined with the Catholic Archbishop of Bulawayo, Pius Ncube, the Anglican Bishop of Mutare, Sebastien Bakare, and two South African prelates, to form the Solidarity Peace Trust. Its first publication was a damning document concerning government-sponsored militia training camps for youth. The bishops noted: "It takes great wickedness for those in power to be prepared to sacrifice a whole generation, the youth of the nation, in order to maintain their hold on power. But that is precisely the wickedness revealed in this report." Zimbabwean youth were being taught "blatantly anti-democratic, racist and zenophobic [sic] attitudes" and used to commit "torture, rape, murder and arson" (Solidarity Peace Trust 2003).

It is not surprising that the Zimbabwean regime, accustomed for so long to the acquiescence of evangelicals, should have responded to their new boldness with paranoiac anger. On March 28, 2003, the state-owned Bulawayo *Chronicle* fulminated that:

> [a] coalition of church organisations, businessmen, and civic groups . . . has been engaged in a plot to undermine the democratically

elected Government of Zimbabwe. Church leaders have been
preaching anti-Mugabe and anti-government vitriol and were allegedly heavily involved in organising mass actions aimed at inciting
an uprising against the Government... Groups that have been
named in this sinister plot include the Habakkuk Trust, Zimbabwe National Pastors Conference, the Evangelical Fellowship of
Zimbabwe.... Their financiers include shadowy satanic sects from
the United States and some gay and lesbian groups... Archbishop
Ncube has reportedly broken the Catholic Church's pagan doctrines to go into an unholy alliance with Pentecostal churches in
the city... scores of the United States CIA and British intelligence
services' agents have been infiltrated into the country disguised
as pastors.

The best evangelical ammunition the *Chronicle* could muster against this
alleged ecclesiastical conspiracy was the Reverend Obediah Msindo of the little-
known Destiny of Africa Network, who invoked Romans 13: "We are questioning the unholy alliance between Archbishop Ncube and people like Pastor
Goodwill Shana from the pentecostal churches. On theological grounds, they
don't agree but they have been brought together solely by a desire to gain
political power and profit from donor funds." Quoting from the Bible, the
Reverend Msindo said, "In Romans 13 the Chief Apostle Paul wrote; 'Let every
soul be subject to the governing authorities; for there is no authority except
from God.' " Further testifying to the vigor of its newfound voice, the Evangelical Fellowship took out a full-page advertisement in the *Chronicle* in order
to refute the newspaper's charges.

As we have seen, Romans 13 does not silence Zimbabwean evangelicals
any longer.[11] However, the extraordinary unanimity of the fifty-nine denominations on equality and democracy within a secular state does open the door to
some unexpected demands, which in a very small way have echoes of what has
happened in Kenya. Muslims in Zimbabwe number less than 1 percent of the
population, yet in August 2002 the Islamic Convent of the Strict Observance
threatened to take the issue of religious education in Zimbabwe's state schools
to the Supreme Court. The focus of such education on Christianity, they said,
was in breach of Section 19 of Zimbabwe's constitution, which provides for
freedom of conscience. This threat produced some less nuanced and edifying
Christian statements about democracy. "Moslems had to be grateful that they
could practice their religion in this country," said one commentator, "while
Christians could not do the same in countries dominated by Islam." Another
insisted that "those Moslems need to appreciate that it's always about the
majority" (*Sunday Mirror* [Harare], "Ultimatum by Muslim Community Stirs
Hornet's Nest," August 17, 2003).[12]

Conclusion

These brief remarks on recent developments in the countries represented in this book once again reveal the importance and vitality of its subject. The question of the interaction of evangelical Christianity and democracy has grown more and more important. Different national situations have produced different forms of collaboration and opposition. The varying demands of Muslims have produced sharp responses. A broad Christian consensus on governance has been reached, more biblically based than traditional Roman Catholic responses and less literalist than traditional evangelical ones. Many issues remain to be worked out, particularly the questions of where religious schools and religious law courts fit in to a secular state and a plural civil society. By the time this book is published there will no doubt have been further fascinating developments. I hope that it will nonetheless give readers both a powerful motive for observing the situation of African evangelicals and a reliable basis for understanding it.

NOTES

1. Interview between Mutumba Mainga Bull and Inonge Mbikusita-Lewanika, December 26, 2001.

2. Victory Ministries International, "Zambia Shall Be Saved," June 2002: http://www.zambiashallbesaved.org/Profile.html. Last accessed June 30, 2005.

3. See http://www.neversforpresident.com/ and http://www.neversforpresident.com/plan.cfm. Last accessed June 30, 2005.

4. Invited to comment by the BBC, many Zambians reflected that it would be good to have a woman president, provided it was not Mwanawasa's wife.

5. Chapter 14 of the K-DOP report, "Gender and Politics: Suffer the Women of Kenya," discusses the still not very impressive performance of women candidates in the 2002 election.

6. K-DOP's *When Kenyans Spoke* contains no comment on the charismatic and pentecostal churches. On page 167, however, it does discuss the support given to KANU by the "traditionalist" Mungiki sect.

7. Nguru says that Muslims claim 30 percent of the Kenyan population; there is an Islamic university, schools and hospitals; and Islam is growing rapidly. Kenyan Muslims argue that *Kadhi* courts deal only with questions of marriage, divorce, and inheritance and do not administer Sharia law in its totality.

8. Interview with Sara Muhoya, November 5, 2003. Ms. Muhoya was the main compiler of the K-DOP report on the 2002 presidential election and is currently writing a doctoral dissertation on the churches and democracy in contemporary Kenya.

9. The Zimbabwe Minister of Information, Jonathan Moyo, in a lecture at Midlands State University, said that "non-governmental organisations, churches, and businesspeople" were talking of regime change. "They will never succeed. Their future

is ill-fated. Non-State actors across the country were playing a negative and counter-productive role. There was a total onslaught on the state with the non-State actors undermining the Government. . . . The first people who started selling out are the intellectuals. They made the simplistic definition of State as Government and rest as civil society. Everyone left the State and created civil society. They need to come back home and home is the State."

10. Statement on the National Peace Convention, December 14, 2002.

11. This afterword has concentrated on the new evangelical and pentecostal churches. Isabel Mukonyora's chapter, of course, says a great deal about the Masowe Apostles. Their responses over the last two years have been complex, inevitably so for a movement with many subdivisions. Some Apostles have drawn upon their founding myth of expulsion from the promised land in order to offer support to Mugabe's land seizures. Mugabe, in turn, has done his best to exploit these groups, gathering them together for ceremonies at Heroes Acre. Their leader, Nzira, has fallen afoul of the law, however, and been imprisoned for abduction and rape. Other Apostles have drawn upon their tradition of self-help to dominate the parallel exchange market so that in Bulawayo Apostolic women in their white robes are being brutally attacked by police. The great bulk of mainstream Apostles, meanwhile, are still working out on the ground the increasingly desperate social and economic problems of Zimbabwe. Isabel Mukonyora deals fully with this variety of responses in her book *Wandering a Gendered Wilderness: Suffering and Healing in an African Initiated Church* (2007).

12. The issue drew fascinating comments from other religious traditions in Zimbabwe. The leader of Zimbabwe's Rastafarians, Trevor Hall, backed the Muslim demand: "Christianity was imposed on Africa through colonisation [and] there was still a lot of discrimination in schools against people of minority religious persuasions." Professor Gordon Chavunduka, president of the Zimbabwe National Traditional Healers Association (ZINATHA), demanded that the Muslim demand be dismissed "with the contempt it deserves. We consider that as very arrogant. The majority of Zimbabweans belonged to the African traditional religion and by converting to Christianity, they did not resign from their traditions but still participated in African religion." But he added that ZINATHA has "been lobbying [the] government and the Ministry of Education, Sports and Culture, to give African culture and religion room in the school curriculum."

References

Abuom, Agnes. 1994. *Mission Outpost 1943–1969*. Nairobi: NCCK.

Agadjanian, Victor. 1999. "As Igrejas Ziones no espaço sócio-cultural de Moçambique urbano (1980–1990)." *Lusotopie*, 415–423.

Ahanotu, Austin M. 1992. "Muslims and Christians in Nigeria: A Contemporary Political Discourse." In *Religion, State, and Society in Contemporary Africa: Nigeria, Sudan, South Africa, Zaire, and Mozambique*, ed. Austin Metumara Ahanotu. New York: Peter Lang.

Ake, Claude. 1991. "Rethinking African Democracy." *Journal of Democracy* 2 (1): 32–44.

———. 1992. "Keynote Address to Conference on Democratic Transition in Africa." Organized by CREDU, at the Institute of African Studies, University of Ibadan.

———. 1996. "Rethinking African Democracy." In Diamond and Plattner 1996, 63–75.

Akinkoutu, Ayodele. 2000. "A Dangerous Agenda." *Tell: Nigeria's Independent Weekly* (Ikeja, Nigeria), March 10, pp. 12–20.

Akinola, Wule, and Nathaniel Ikyur. 2000. "North Regroups for Sharia." *Sunday Vanguard* (Apapa, Nigeria) March 5, p. 1.

Akpena, Mamman. 2000. "Gov. Flays Sharia Advocates: Angry at Sultan's Letter." *The Nigerian Standard* (Jos, Nigeria), April 18, p. 1.

Akwetey, Emmanuel Obliteifio. 1994. *Trade Unions and Democratisation: A Comparative Study of Zambia and Ghana*. Stockholm: University of Stockholm.

Ali, Mohammed. 2000. "Sharia and Hypocrisy." *Vanguard* (Apapa, Nigeria), March 31, p. 11.

Anderson, Allan. 2000. *Zion and Pentecost: The Spirituality and Experience of Pentecostal and Zionist/Apostolic Churches in South Africa*. Pretoria: The University of South Africa Press.

Anderson, J. N. D. 1959. "Conflict of Laws in Northern Nigeria: A New Start." *International and Comparative Law Quarterly* 8 (July): 442–456.

———. 1976. *Law Reform in the Muslim World*. London: The Athlone Press.

Andrade, Ximena, Ana Loforte, and Conceição Osório. 1998. *Famílias em Contexto de Mudanças em Moçambique*. Maputo, Mozambique: WLSA Mozambique e Centro de Estudos Africanos.

Araújo, M. 1990. "Migrações Internas e o Processo de Urbanização." In *Dinâmica Demográfica e Processos económicos e Sociais*, Ministério do Plano e Finanças, 72–89. Maputo, Mozambique: Direcção Nacional de Estatística.

Arrand, Ken. n. d. *Zimbabwe for Biblical Government (ZBC). Basic Party Principles: What We Value*. Harare: Westgate.

Aso, Director. 1999. "Sharia Time Bomb: The New Plot against Obasanjo." *Tell: Nigeria's Independent Weekly* (Ikeja, Nigeria), November 15, pp. 12–18.

Balcomb, Anthony. 1993. *Third Way Theology: Reconciliation, Revolution, and Reform in the South African Church during the 1980s*. Pietermaritzburg, South Africa: Cluster Publications.

———. 2001. "Evangelicals and Democracy in South Africa: Another Look, Another Method." *Journal of Theology for Southern Africa* 109 (March).

Balói, O. 1995. "O Posicionamento das Igrejas face ao processo eleitoral de 1994." In *Moçambique: eleições, democracia e desenvolvimento*, ed. B. Mazula. Maputo, Mozambique: Edição do autor.

Banana, Canaan. 1991. "The Church and State." *Southern African Political and Economic Monthly* (SAPEM), 4: 11.

———. 1996. *Politics of Repression and Resistance: Face to Face with Combat Theology*. Gweru, Zimbabwe: Mambo Press.

Barnes, Terri, and Everjoyce Win. 1992. *To Live a Better Life: An Oral History of Women in the City of Harare, 1930–1970*. Harare, Zimbabwe: Baobab Books.

Barrett, David B. 1968. *Schism and Renewal in Africa: An Analysis of Six Thousand Contemporary Religious Movements*. Nairobi: Oxford University Press.

Barrett, David B., and Todd M. Johnson. 1998. "Annual Statistical Table on Global Mission: 1998." *International Bulletin of Missionary Research* (January): 26–27.

Barrett, David B., George T. Kurian, and Todd M. Johnson, eds. 2001. *World Christian Encyclopedia: A Comparative Survey of Churches and Religions in the Modern World*. 2nd ed. New York: Oxford University Press.

Bashir, Ibrahim L. 1999. "Cultural Resources for Sustainable Democracy in Africa." *Development Studies Review* 4: 10–20. Centre for Development Studies, University of Jos, Nigeria.

Baur, John. 1994. *2000 Years of Christianity in Africa: An African History, 62–1992*. Nairobi: Paulinas.

Bayart, Jean-François. 1993. *The State in Africa: The Politics of the Belly*. London and New York: Longman.

Bebbington, David W. 1989. *Evangelicalism in Modern Britain: A History from the 1730s to the 1980s*. London: Unwin Hyman.

Becker, David G., Jeff Frieden, Sayre P. Schartz, and Richard L. Sklar. 1987. *Postimperialism: International Capitalism and Development in the Late Twentieth Century*. Boulder, Colo., and London: Lynne Rienner.

Beetham, David. 1995. "Problems of Democratic Consolidation." In Gifford 1995, 61–73.

Bennett, George. 1963. *Kenya, A Political History: The Colonial Period.* London: Oxford University Press.

Benson, G. P. 1995. "Ideological Politics versus Biblical Hermeneutics: Kenya's Protestant Churches and the Nyayo State." In Hansen and Twaddle 1995, 177–199.

Berger, Peter L., ed. 1999. *The Desecularization of the World: Resurgent Religion and World Politics.* Grand Rapids: Wm. B. Eerdmans; and Washington, D.C.: The Ethics and Public Policy Center.

Bhebe, Ngwabi. 1999. *The ZAPU and ZANU Guerrilla Warfare and the Evangelical Lutheran Church in Zimbabwe.* Gweru, Zimbabwe: Mambo.

Bhebe, Ngwabi, and Terence Ranger, 2001. *The Historical Dimensions of Democracy and Human Rights in Zimbabwe.* Vol. 1, *Pre-colonial and Colonial Legacies.* Harare: University of Zimbabwe.

Bhengu, Nicholas. 1974. "Evangelism in Townships." In *I Will Heal Their Land,* ed. Michael Cassidy. Pietermaritzburg: Africa Enterprise.

Biber, Charles. 1992. *Cent ans au Mozambique. Le parcours d'une minorité.* 2nd ed. Lausanne: Editions du Soc.

Bratton, Michael, and Nicolas van de Walle. 1997. *Democratic Experiments in Africa: Regime Transitions in Comparative Perspective.* New York: Cambridge University Press.

Bull, Mutumba Mainga. 2002. "Gender Dimensions of Multiparty Politics: Elections 2001 in Zambia." Presented at the International Conference on the Political Process in Zambia 2001, Norway.

Butselaar, Jan van. 1984. *Africains, Missionaires et Colonialistes: Les Origines de l'Église Presbytérienne du Mozambique (Mission Suice), 1880–1896.* Leiden: E. J. Brill.

Bwala, Inuwa. 2000. "Kaduna Riots: Mass Burial for Victims." *The Punch* (Ikeja, Nigeria), May 26, pp. 1–9.

CAN (Christian Association of Nigeria). 1989. *Leadership in Nigeria (to Date): An Analysis.* Kaduna: CAN Publicity, Northern Zone.

CAN (Christian Association of Nigeria), Kano Branch. 1982. "30 October 1982 Kano Religious Disturbance Memorandum." Presented to the Datti Ahamed Religious Disturbances Panel, Kano State Government, December 22.

CAN (Christian Association of Nigeria), Plateau State. 2001. "Memorandum Presented to the Commission of Inquiry into the Crisis in Jos from 7–12 September 2001."

Cassidy, Michael. 1989. *The Passing Summer: A South African Pilgrimage in the Politics of Love.* London: Hodder and Stoughton.

———. 1991. *The Politics of Love: Choosing the Christian Way in a Changing South Africa.* London: Hodder and Stoughton.

Catholic Commission for Justice and Peace. 1998. *State of the Nation: A Comprehensive Statement on the Current Situation in Zambia by the Catholic Commission for Justice and Peace.* Lusaka: Catholic Commission for Justice and Peace.

Chanda, Donald, ed. 1993. *Democracy in Zambia: Key Speeches of President Chiluba, 1991–92.* Lusaka, Zambia: Africa Press Trust.

Chidester, David. 1992. *Religions of South Africa.* London: Routledge.

Chidester, David, Chirevo Kwenda, Robert Petty, Judy Tobler, and Darrel Wratten. 1997. *African Traditional Religion in South Africa: An Annotated Bibliography.* Westport, Conn.: Greenwood Press.

Chikane, Frank. 1988. *No Life of My Own: An Autobiography.* Braamfontein, South Africa: Skotaville.

Chikulo, Bornwell. 1996. "Presidential and Parliamentary Elections in the Third Republic: 1991–1994." In *Democracy in Zambia: Challenges for the Third Republic,* ed. Owen Sichone and Bornwell Chikulo. Harare, Zimbabwe: SAPES Books.

Chiluba, Frederick J. T. 1995. *Democracy: The Challenge of Change.* Lusaka, Zambia: Multimedia Publications.

Chingota, Felix L. 2001. "The Pastoral Letter of the Church of Central Africa and the Democratization Process in Malawi." Presented at the International Conference on Interrogating the New Political Culture in Southern Africa, Harare.

Chitando, Ezra. 2001. "For We Have Heard for Ourselves? A Critical Review of T. Ranger's Portrayal of Christianity as an Aspect of African Identity." Festschrift workshop. Reprinted in *Studia Historiae Ecclesiasticae* 28 (1): 218–234.

Church of Nigeria, Anglican Communion, Province III. 2001. "Communique of the Meeting of Church of Nigeria (Anglican Communion) Province III, Held at the Cathedral Church of St. John Jimeta, Yola–Adamawa State, 24–26 January 2001."

Clarke, Peter. 1988. "Islamic Reform in Contemporary Nigeria: Methods and Aims." *Third World Quarterly* 10 (2): 519–538.

Coleman, Simon. 2000. *The Globalisation of Charismatic Christianity: Spreading the Gospel of Prosperity.* Cambridge: Cambridge University Press.

Comaroff, Jean. 1985. *Body of Power, Spirit of Resistance: The Culture and History of a South African People.* Chicago: The University of Chicago Press.

Comaroff, Jean, and John L. Comaroff. 1991. *Of Revelation and Revolution.* Vol 1, *Christianity, Colonialism and Consciousness in South Africa.* Chicago: University of Chicago Press.

———. 1997. *Of Revelation and Revolution.* Vol. 2, *The Dialectics of Modernity on a South African Frontier.* Chicago: University of Chicago Press.

Crehan, Kate. 1999. "The Rules of the Game: The Political Location of Women in Northwestern Zambia." In Hyslop 1999, 139–151.

Cruz e Silva, Teresa. 1992. "Igrejas Protestantes no Sul de Moçambique e Nacionalismo: o caso da 'Missão Suiça' (1940–1974)." *Estudos Moçambicanos* (Maputo), 10: 19–39.

———. 1996. "Protestant Churches and the Formation of Political Consciousness in Southern Mozambique (1930–1974): The Case of the Swiss Mission." Ph.D. dissertation. University of Bradford.

———. 2000a. "Identidades étnicas como fenómenos agregadores num espaço social urbano: os casos da Mafalala e Chinhambanine." In *Racismo, etnicidade e poder: um estudo em cinco cidades de Moçambique,* ed. Carlos Serra, 195–208. Maputo, Mozambique: Livraria Universitária, Universidade Eduardo Mondlane.

———. 2000b. "As redes de solidariedade como intervenientes na resolução de litígios: o caso da Mafalala." In *Conflito e Transformação Social: uma paisagem das justiças em Moçambique,* ed. Boaventura Sousa Santos and J. Carlos Trindade, 427–450. Maputo/Coimbra, Mozambique: CEA/CES.

———. 2001a. *Protestant Churches and the Formation of Political Consciousness in Southern Mozambique (1930–1974).* Basel, Switzerland: P. Schelettwein Publishing.

———. 2001b. *Igrejas Protestantes e Consciência Política no Sul de Moçambique: o caso da Missão Suiça (1930–1974).* Colecção Identidades, 12. Maputo, Mozambique: Promédia.

Dahl, Robert, A. 1971. *Polyarchy: Participation and Opposition.* New Haven and London: Yale University Press.

———. 1989. *Democracy and Its Critics.* New Haven and London: Yale University Press.

Dale, Penny. 2003a. "From TV Evangelist to Zambia's Vice President." BBC News, June 2. Accessed at http://news.bbc.co.uk/2/hi/africa/2956122.stm.

———. 2003b. "Zambians split over woman leader." BBC News, May 2. Accessed at http://news.bbc.co.uk/2/hi/africa/2991931.stm.

Daneel, Marthinus L. 1970a. *God of the Matopo Hills: An Essay on the Mwari Cult in Rhodesia.* The Hague: Mouton Press.

———. 1970b. *Zionism and Faith Healing in Rhodesia: Aspects of African Independent Churches.* The Hague: Mouton Press.

———. 1971. *Old and New in Southern Shona Independent Churches.* Vol. 1, *Background and Rise of the Major Movements.* The Hague: Mouton Press.

de Gruchy, John W. 1991. "From Cottesloe to Rustenburg and Beyond: The Rustenburg Conference in Historical Perspective." *Journal of Theology for Southern Africa* 74 (March): 21–34.

———. 1995. *Christianity and Democracy.* Cambridge: Cambridge University Press.

Diamond, Larry, and Marc F. Plattner, eds. 1994. *Nationalism, Ethnic Conflict, and Democracy.* Baltimore: The John Hopkins University Press.

———. 1996. *The Global Resurgence of Democracy.* 2nd ed. Baltimore: The Johns Hopkins University Press.

———. 1999. *Democratization in Africa.* Baltimore: The Johns Hopkins University Press.

Dickson, Kwesi A. 1995. "The Church and the Quest for Democracy in Ghana." In Gifford 1995, 261–275.

Diko, M. n.d. *A Man with a Vision and a Mission: The Life and Ministry of Nicholas Bhekninkosi H. Bhengu.* Unpublished.

Dillon-Malone, Clive. 1978. *The Korsten Basket Makers: A Study of the Masowe Apostles, An Indigenous African Religious Movement.* Manchester: University of Manchester Press.

Dubb, Allie A. 1976. *Community of the Saved: An African Revivalist Church in the East Cape.* Johannesburg: Witwatersrand University Press.

ECWA General Secretary. 1999. *"The Position of ECWA on the Infamous Proclamation of Sharia Law in Zamfara State."* Position paper of the Evangelical Church of West Africa, released at the end of the General Church Council of ECWA in Nigeria, at the ECWA Headquarters, Jos, Plateau State, October 20–22.

Engelke, Matthew. 2002. "Live and Direct: History, Ritual, and Biblical Authority in an African Christian Church." Ph.D. dissertation. University of Virginia, Charlottesville, Virginia.

Falola, Toyin. 1997. "Christian Radicalism and Nigerian Politics." In *Dilemmas of Democracy in Nigeria*, ed. Paul A. Beckett and Crawford Young, 265–282. Rochester, N.Y.: University of Rochester.

Fasholé-Luke, Edward, Richard Gray, Adrian Hastings, and Godwin Tasie, eds. 1978. *Christianity in Independent Africa*. Bloomington, Ind.: Indiana University Press.

Ferreira, L. C. 1987. *Igreja Ministerial em Moçambique, caminhos de hoje e amanhã*. Lisboa.

Figueira, Mário. 1972. *Seitas Religiosas em Moçambique*. Lourenço Marques, Mozambique. Mimeo.

Freitas, Afonso Ivens Ferraz de. 1956–1957. *Seitas Religiosas Gentílicas*. 4 vols. Lourenço Marques, Mozambique. Mimeo.

FRELIMO. 1978. *Conferência do Departamento do Trabalho Ideológico*. Maputo: Instituto Nacional do Livro e do Disco.

———. 1983. *Consolidemos aquilo que nos une: reunião da direcção do Partido e do Estado com representantes das confissões religiosas, 14 a 17 de Dezembro de 1982*. Maputo: INLD.

Freston, Paul. 2001. *Evangelicals and Politics in Asia, Africa, and Latin America*. Cambridge: Cambridge University Press.

Gaitskell, Deborah. 1999. "Hot Meetings and Hard Kraals: African Biblewomen in Transvaal Methodism, 1924–60." Paper presented at the African Studies Association (ASA) Meeting, Nashville, Tenn., November 6–10.

Gangwari, John U. 2000. "The Role of Religion in Politics: The Middle Belt Perspective." Presented to the Federal Government Panel on the Review of the 1999 Constitution of the Federal Republic of Nigeria, University of Jos, Jos, Nigeria, January 9–10, 2001.

Gifford, Paul. 1988. *The New Crusaders: Christianity and the New Right in Southern Africa*. London: Pluto Press.

———. 1990. *Christianity: To Save or Enslave?* Harare, Zimbabwe: Ecumenical Documentation and Information Centre of Eastern and Southern Africa (EDICESA).

———, ed. 1993. *New Dimensions in African Christianity*. Ibadan, Nigeria: Sefer.

———, ed. 1995. *The Christian Churches and the Democratisation of Africa*. Leiden: E. J. Brill.

———. 1998. *African Christianity: Its Public Role*. Bloomington: Indiana University Press.

Gitari, David. 1996. *In Season and Out of Season: Sermons to a Nation*. London: Regnum.

Githiga, Gideon. 1997. *The Church as a Bulwark against Extremism*. Oxford: Open University/Oxford Centre for Mission Studies.

———. 2001. *The Church as the Bulwark against Authoritarianism: Development of Church-State Relations in Kenya, with Particular Reference to the Years After Political Independence 1963–1992*. Oxford: Regnum.

Gonçalves, José Julio. 1960. *Protestantismo em África*. Vol. 2. Estudos de Ciências Políticas e Sociais 39. Lisbon: Junta de Investigações do Ultramar, Centro de Estudos Políticos e Sociais.

Hale, Frederick. 1993. "Coming to Terms with Evangelicals and Apartheid." *Journal of Theology for Southern Africa* 84 (September).

Hamalengwa, Munyonzwe. 1992. *Class Struggles in Zambia, 1889–1989, and the Fall of Kenneth Kaunda, 1990–1991*. Lanham. Md.: University Press of America.

Hanlon, Joseph. 1991. *Mozambique: Who Calls the Shots?* London: James Currey.

Hansen, Holger Bernt, and Michael Twaddle, eds. 1995. *Religion and Politics in East Africa: The Period Since Independence*. London: James Currey.

Hansson, Gurli. 1991. *The Rise of Vashandiri: The Ruwadzano Movement in the Lutheran Church in Zimbabwe*. Uppsala: Swedish Institute of Missionary Research.

Harries, Patrick. 2001. "Missionaries, Marxists and Magic: Power and the Politics of Literacy in South-east Africa." *Journal of Southern African Studies* 27 (3): 405–427.

Hastings, Adrian. 1979. *A History of African Christianity, 1950–1975*. Cambridge: Cambridge University Press.

———. 1991. "Politics and Religion in Southern Africa." In Moyser 1991, 162–188.

———. 1995. "The Churches and Democracy: Reviewing a Relationship." In Gifford 1995, 36–46.

Haynes, Jeff. 1996. *Religion and Politics in Africa*. London: Zed Books.

Helgesson, Alf. 1994. *Church, State and People in Mozambique: An Historical Study with Special Emphasis on Methodist Developments in the Inhambane Region*. Uppsala: University of Uppsala.

Hendriks, J., and J. Erasmus. 2001. "Interpreting the New Religious Landscape in Post-apartheid South Africa." *Journal of Theology for Southern Africa* 109 (March): 41–65.

Hinfelaar, Marja. 2001. *Respectable and Responsible Women: Methodist and Roman Catholic Women's Organizations in Harare, Zimbabwe (1919–1985)*. Zoetermeer, Netherlands: Boekencentrum.

Hogben, S. J., and A. H. M. Kirk-Greene. 1966. *The Emirates of Northern Nigeria: A Preliminary Survey of their Historical Traditions*. London: Oxford University Press.

Honwana, Alcinda M. R. M. 1996. "Spiritual Agency and Self-renewal in Southern Mozambique." Ph.D. dissertation. University of London, School of Oriental and African Studies.

Horowitz, Donald L. 1994. "Democracy in Divided Societies." In Diamond and Plattner 1994, 35–55.

Huntington, Samuel P. 1991. *The Third Wave: Democratization in Late Twentieth Century*. Norman: University of Oklahoma Press.

Hutchinson, Mark, and Ogbu Kalu, eds. 1998. *A Global Faith: Essays on Evangelicalism and Globalization*. Sydney: Centre for the Study of Australian Christianity, Robert Menzies College, Macquarie University.

Hunwick, John. 1992. "An African Case Study of Political Islam: Nigeria." *The Annals of the American Academy of Political and Social Science* 524 (November): 143–155.

Hyslop, Jonathan, ed. 1999. *African Democracy in the Era of Globalization*. Johannesburg: Witwatersrand University Press.

Ibrahim, Saka. 2000. "Sharia Zamfara Governor Told to Comply with FG's Directive." *The Punch* (Ikeja, Nigeria), March 14, p. 9.

———. 2001. "Sharia Is Supreme—Sani." *The Punch* (Ikeja, Nigeria), April 2.

Ifidon, Ehimika A. 1996. "Citizenship, Statehood, and the Problem of Democratization in Nigeria." *Africa Development* 21 (4): 93–106.

Ilesanmi, Simeon. O. 1995. "Recent Theories of Religion and Politics in Nigeria." *Journal of Church and State* 37 (2): 309–327.

Imo, Cyril O. 1995. *Religion and the Unity of the Nigerian Nation.* Stockholm: Almqvist and Wiksell International.

INE (Instituto Nacional de Estatística, Mozambique). 1999. *II Recenseamento Geral da População e Habitação 1997: Indicadores Sócio-demográficos, Niassa; Nampula; Maputo cidade; Maputo Província; Zambézia; Tete; Sofala; Manica; Cabo Delgado; Gaza e Inhambane.* Maputo, Mozambique: Instituto Nacional de Estatística.

Jeater, Diana. 1993. *Marriage, Perversion, and Power: The Construction of Moral Discourse in Southern Rhodesia 1894–1930.* Oxford: Clarendon Press.

Jenkins, Philip. 2002. *The Next Christendom: The Coming of Global Christianity.* New York: Oxford University Press.

Johns, Sheridan. 1972. *From Protest to Challenge: A Documentary History of African Politics in South Africa 1882–1964,* ed. Thomas Karis and Gwendolen M. Carter. Vol. 1, *Protest and Hope 1882–1934.* Stanford, Calif.: Hoover Institution Press.

Johnstone, Patrick. 2001. *Operation World.* 6th ed. Cumbria, UK: Paternoster Publishing.

Joseph, Richard. 1993. "The Christian Churches and Democracy in Contemporary Africa." In *Christianity and Democracy in Global Context,* ed. John Witte, Jr. Boulder, Colo.: Westview.

Jowitt, Ken. 1991. "The New World Disorder." *Journal of Democracy* 2 (1).

Kadoma Conference. 2003. "Zimbabwe in Transition—Challenges for the Churches—Kadoma Conference Communiqué." Meeting of Fifty-nine Christian Denominations in Kadoma, Zimbabwe, September 25.

Kamwambe, G. T. Ngubola. 1991. *Frederick Chiluba: Is He Riding a Tide of Fortune?* Lusaka, Zambia.

Karanja, John K. 1999. *Founding an African Faith: Kikuyu Anglican Christianity 1900–1945.* Nairobi: Uzima Press.

Karis, Thomas, and Gwendolen M. Carter, eds. 1972–1977. *From Protest to Challenge: A Documentary History of African Politics in South Africa 1882–1964.* Vols. 1–4. Stanford, Calif.: Hoover Institution Press.

Kastfelt, Niels. 1994. *Religion and Politics in Nigeria: A Study in Middle Belt Christianity.* London: British Academic Press.

Kenya Domestic Opposition Programme (K-DOP). 2003. *When Kenyans Spoke: 2002 General Elections Report.* Nairobi.

Kileff, Clive, and Margaret Kileff. 1979. "The Masowe Vapostori of Seki: Utopianism and Tradition in an African Church." In *The New Religions in Africa,* ed. Bennetta Jules-Rosette, 151–167. Norwood, N.J.: Ablex Publishing.

Kinoti, George. 1994. *Hope for Africa and What the Christians Can Do.* Nairobi: African Institute for Scientific Research and Development (AISRED).

Kinoti, George, and Peter Kimuyu, eds. 1997. *Vision for a Bright Africa: Facing the Challenge of Development.* Nairobi: African Institute for Scientific Research and Development (AISRED).

Kinoti, Hannah W., and John M. Waliggo, eds. 1997. *The Bible in African Christianity: Essays in Biblical Theology.* Nairobi: Acton Publishers.

Kukah, Matthew Hassan. 1993. *Religion, Politics and Power in Northern Nigeria.* Ibadan, Nigeria: Spectrum Books Ltd.

Kumo, Suleiman. 1972. "The Organisation and Procedure of Sharia Courts in Northern Nigeria." Ph.D. dissertation. University of London, School of Oriental and African Studies.

Kurewa, John Wesley Zwomunondiita. 2000. *Preaching and Cultural Identity: Proclaiming the Gospel in Africa.* Nashville: Abingdon Press.

Kwashi, Benjamin A. 2000. "The Bishop's Charge." Delivered to the Third Session on Friday in St. Peters Anglican Church, Bukuru, Jos, Nigeria. Self-published.

Laakso, Liisa. 1999. "Voting Without Choosing: State Making and Elections in Zimbabwe." *Acta Politica* 11. University of Helsinki, Department of Political Science.

Lafargue, Jérôme. 1996. "Presidential Power and Christian Churches in Zambia: Between Mutual Seduction and Rivalry." IFRA (Institut Français de Recherche en Afrique) Working Paper Series.

Lester, Toby. 2002. "Oh Gods!" *The Atlantic Monthly,* February. Accessed at http://www.theatlantic.com/doc/200202/lester.

Lienhardt, R. Godfrey. 1982. "The Dinka and Catholicism." In *Religious Organization and Religious Experience,* ed. John Davis. ASA (Association of Social Anthropologists) Monographs, 21. London and New York: Academic Press.

Lopes, Carlos. 1996. "The Africanisation of Democracy." *African Journal of Political Science* 1 (2): 139–153.

Mahmud, Abdulmalik Bappa. 1988. *A Brief History of Shari'ah in the Defunct Northern Nigeria.* Jos, Nigeria: Jos University Press.

Maier, Karl. 2000. *This House Has Fallen: Midnight in Nigeria.* New York: PublicAffairs.

Makumbe, John. 1998. *Development and Democracy in Zimbabwe: Constraints of Decentralization.* Harare, Zimbabwe: SAPES Books.

Manhanga, Trevor. 2003. "Zimbabwe: A Land of Hope and Promise. Critical Reflections on the Potential for Settlement." Address before a Stakeholders Conference on Dialogue and Transition, Harare, Zimbabwe, July 5.

Marshall, Ruth. 1991. "Power in the Name of Jesus." *Review of African Political Economy* 52: 21–37.

———. 1993. "Power in the Name of Jesus: Social Transformation and Pentecostalism in Western Nigeria Revisited." In *Legitimacy and the State in Twentieth-Century Africa: Essays in Honour of A. H. M. Kirk-Greene,* ed. Terence Ranger and Olufemi Vaughan, 213–246. London: Macmillan, in association with St. Antony's College, Oxford.

———. 1995. " 'God Is Not a Democrat': Pentecostalism and Democratisation in Nigeria." In Gifford 1995, 239–260.

Martin, David. 1999. "The Evangelical Protestant Upsurge and Its Political Implications." In Berger 1999, 37–49.

———. 2002. *Pentecostalism: The World Their Parish.* Oxford: Blackwell.

Maududi, Sayyid Abul A'la. 1967. *Islamic Way of Life.* Riya .n: Presidency of Islamic Research, Ifta and Propagation.

Maxwell, David. 1995. "The Church and Democratisation in Africa: The Case of Zimbabwe." In Gifford 1995, 108–129.

———. 1998. " 'Delivered from the Spirit of Poverty?' Pentecostalism, Prosperity and Modernity in Zimbabwe." *Journal of Religion in Africa,* 28 (3): 350–373.

———. 1999. *Christians and Chiefs in Zimbabwe: A Social History of the Hwesa People c.1870s–1990s.* Edinburgh: Edinburgh University Press for the International African Institute, London; Westport, Conn.: Praeger.

———. 2000. " 'Catch the Cockerel Before Dawn': Pentecostalism and Politics in Post-colonial Zimbabwe." *Africa: Journal of the International African Institute* 70 (2): 249–277.

———. 2001. " 'Sacred History, Social History': Traditions and Texts in the Making of a Southern African Transnational Religious Movement." *Comparative Studies in Society and History* 43 (3): 502–524.

———, ed., with Ingrid Lawrie. 2002. *Christianity and the African Imagination: Essays in Honour of Adrian Hastings.* Studies of Religion in Africa, 23. Leiden: Brill.

———. 2007. *African Gifts of the Spirit: Pentecostalism and the Rise of a Zimbabwean Transnational Religious Movement.* Oxford: James Currey; Athens, Ohio: Ohio University Press; Harare, Zimbabwe: Weaver Press.

Mazrui, Ali. 1991. "Africa and Other Civilizations: Conquest and Counterconquest." In *Africa in World Politics: Post-Cold War Challenges,* ed. John W. Harbeson and Donald Rothchild. Boulder, Colo.: Westview Press.

Mbikusita-Lewanika, Inonge. 1997. "The Role of Christian Women in Multi-party Politics." In Mbugua 1997.

———. 1998. "Facing the Challenges of Politics." In Nalumango and Sifuniso 1998.

Mbugua, Judy, ed. 1994. *Our Time Has Come: African Christian Women Address the Issues of Today.* Grand Rapids, Mich.: Baker Book House.

———. 1997. *Making a Difference: Christian Women and Politics.* Nairobi: Association of Evangelicals in Africa.

McCulloch, Jock. 2000. *Black Peril, White Virtue: Sexual Crime in Southern Rhodesia, 1902–1935.* Bloomington: Indiana University Press.

Meneses, Maria Paula Gutierrez. 2004. " 'Quando não há problemas, estamos de boa saúde, sem azar nem nada': para uma concepção emancipatória da saúde e das medicinas." In *Semear outras soluções: Os caminhos da biodiversidade e dos conhecimentos rivais,* ed. Boaventura de Sousa Santos. Colecção Reinventar a Emancipação Social: Para Novos Manifestos. Porto, Portugal: Edições Afrontamento.

Meyer, Birgit. 1998. "The Power of Money: Politics, Occult Forces, and Pentecostalism in Ghana." *African Studies Review* 41(3): 15–37.

———. 1999. *Translating the Devil: Religion and Modernity among the Ewe in Ghana.* Edinburgh: Edinburgh University Press for the International African Institute.

Mihyo, Paschal. 1995. "Against Overwhelming Odds: The Zambian Trade Union Movement." In *Globalization and Third World Trade Unions,* ed. Henk Thomas. London: Zed Books.

Ministério do Plano e Finanças. 1996. *Moçambique: Panorama Demográfico e sócio-económico.* Maputo, Mozambique: Direcção Nacional de Estatística.

Mitchell, Gordon, Nokuzola Mndende, Isabel Apawo Phiri, and Janet Stonier. 1993. *The End of the Tunnel: Religious Education for Non-racial South Africa.* Cape Town: University of Cape Town Press.

Moi, Daniel T. Arap. 1986. *Kenya African Nationalism: Nyayo Philosophy and Principles.* Nairobi: Macmillan Publishers.

Morier-Genoud, Eric. 1996. "Of God and Caesar: The Relation Between Christian Churches and the State in Post-colonial Mozambique, 1974–1981." *Le Fait Missionaire* (Lausanne, Switzerland) 3 (September).

———. 1998. "Ya-t-il une spécificité protestante au Mozambique? Discours du pouvoir post-colonial et Histoire des Églises Chrétiennes." *Lusotopie* (Paris) 407–420.

Moyser, George, ed. 1991. *Politics and Religion in the Modern World.* London and New York: Routledge.

Moyser, George. 1991. "Politics and Religion in the Modern World: An Overview." In Moyser 1991, 1–27.

Mukonyora, Isabel. 1997. "Christian Orthodoxy and Ecumenism." *The Ecumenical Review* (World Council of Churches) 49 (4): 451–456.

———. 1998a. "The Complementarity of Male and Female Imagery in Theological Language: A Study of the Valentian and Masowe Theological Systems." Ph.D. dissertation. University of Oxford, U.K.

———. 1998b. "The Dramatization of Life and Death by Johane Masowe." *Zambezia: The Journal of Humanities of the University of Zimbabwe* 25 (2): 192–207.

———. 1999. "Women and Ecology in Shona Religion." *Word and World* (St Paul, Minn.: Luther Seminary) 19 (3): 276–284.

———. 2000a. "The Dramatisation of Life and Death by Johane Masowe." *Swedish Missiological Themes (SMT)* 88 (3): 409–430.

———. 2000b/2001a. "Marginality and Protest in the Sacred Wilderness: The Role of Women in Shaping the Masowe Thought Pattern." *Southern African Feminist Review (SAFERE)* 4 (2) and 5 (1): 1–21.

———. 2001b. "The Identity of African Christians." Review of *A History of the Church in Africa*, by Bengt Sundkler and Christopher Steed. *H-Net: Humanities and Social Sciences Online.* Accessed at http://www.h-net.org.

———. 2005. "Masowe Wilderness Apostles." In *Encyclopedia of Religion and Nature*, ed. Bron R. Taylor and Jeffrey Kaplan, 1054–1056. London and New York: Thoemmes Continuum.

———. 2007. *Wandering a Gendered Wilderness: Suffering and Healing in an African Initiated Church.* New York: Peter Lang; Zomba, Malawi: Kachere Press.

Mukonyora, Isabel, James L. Cox, and Frans J. Verstraelen. eds. 1992. *Rewriting the Bible: The Real Issues: Perspectives from within Biblical and Religious Studies in Zimbabwe.* Gweru, Zimbabwe: Mambo Press.

Murray, Jocelyn. 1974. *The Kikuyu Female Circumcision Controversy with Special Reference to the Church Missionary Society's Sphere of Influence.* Ph.D. dissertation, University of California, Los Angeles.

Mutua, Makau W. 1999. "Returning to My Roots: African 'Religions' and the State." In *Proselytization and Communal Self-Determination in Africa*, ed. Abdullahi An-Na'im, 169–190. Maryknoll, N.Y.: Orbis Books.

Nalumango, Mbuyu, and Monde Sifuniso, eds. 1998. *Women Power in Politics*. Lusaka, Zambia: Zambia Women Writers Association.

Ngunyi, Mutahi G. 1995. "Religious Institutions and Political Liberalisation in Kenya." In *Markets, Civil Society and Democracy in Kenya*, ed. Peter Gibbon, 121–177. Uppsala, Sweden: Nordiska Afrikainstitutet.

Nguru, Godfrey. 2002. "Islam and the Constitution Making Process in Kenya: The Case of Kadhi Courts." World Mission Briefings, Oxford Centre for Mission Studies, April.

Nherere, Pearson, and Marina D'Engelbronner-Kolf, eds. 1993. *The Institutionalisation of Human Rights in Southern Africa*. Copenhagen: Nordic Human Rights Publications.

Nyong'o, Peter Anyang', ed. 1987. *Popular Struggles for Democracy in Africa*. London: Zed Books.

Nzongola-Ntalaja, Georges. 1997. "The State and Democracy in Africa." In Nzongola-Ntalaja and Lee 1997.

Nzongola-Ntalaja, Georges, and Margaret C. Lee. *The State and Democracy in Africa*. Harare, Zimbabwe: African Association of Political Science.

Obasanjo, Olusegun. 2000. "Address by His Excellency President Olusegun Obasanjo, On the Occasion of the Formal Signing Into Law of the Corrupt Practices and Other Related Offences Act 2000," Abuja, Nigeria, June 13. Accessed at http://www.nigerianembassy.nl/Presidents.htm.

Obateru, Taye. 2000. "Middle-Belt Set to Get Out Northern Group." *Vanguard*, July 20, p. 1.

O'Dea, Thomas F. 1966. *The Sociology of Religion*. Englewood Cliffs, N.J.: Prentice-Hall.

Ofori-Amankwah, Emmanuel H. 1986. *Criminal Law in the Northern States of Nigeria*. Zaria, Nigeria: Gaskiya Corporation.

Ojewale, Olu. 2000. "Our Conditions for One Nigeria—Southern Governors Take United Stand on Sharia." *Newswatch* (Ikeja, Nigeria), October 23.

Okullu, Henry. 1974. *Church and Politics in East Africa*. Nairobi: Uzima.

———. 1997. *Quest for Justice: An Autobiography of Bishop John Henry Okullu*. Kisumu, Kenya: Shalom Publishers.

Onaiyakan, John. 1989–1990. "The Strategies for Islamic Expansion in Nigeria and Christian Response—Notes and Reflections." *Bulletin of Ecumenical Theology* (Enugu, Nigeria) 2 (2)–3 (1).

Onome, Osifor-Whiskey. 2000. "Shagari's Biblical Goodness." *Tell: Nigeria's Independent Weekly* (Ikeja, Nigeria), March 20, p. 3.

Ostien, Philip. 2000. " 'Islamic Criminal Law': What It Means in Zamfara and Niger States." *Journal of Public and Private Law* 4 (1): 1–18.

Panter-Brink, Keith. 1994. "Prospects for Democracy in Zambia." *Government and Opposition* 29 (2): 231–247.

Peel, J. D. Y. 2000. *Religious Encounter and the Making of the Yoruba*. Bloomington: Indiana University Press.

Pereira, F. 1999. *Particularidades da dinâmica do conflito armado no distrito do Alto Molócue, 1982–1992: violência armada e guerra mágica*. B.A. dissertation. Maputo: Faculdade de Letras, Universidade Eduardo Mondlane.

Petersen, Robin M. 1995. "Time, Resistance, and Reconstruction: Rethinking Kairos Theory." Ph.D. dissertation. University of Chicago.

Philpott, Graham. 1993. *Jesus Is Tricky and God Is Undemocratic. The Kin-dom of God in Amawoti*. Pietermaritzburg, South Africa: Cluster Publications.

Phiri, Isabel Apawo. 1997. *Women, Presbyterianism and Patriarchy: Religious Experience of Chewa Women in Central Malawi*. Kachere Monograph 4. Blantyre, Malawi: Christian Literature Association in Malawi.

Pobee, Joseph S., and Gabriel Ositelu. 1998. *African Initiatives in Christianity: The Growth, Gifts and Diversities of Indigenous African Churches—A Challenge to the Ecumenical Movement*. Geneva: World Council of Churches Publications.

Purvis, John Stanley. 1962. *Dictionary of Ecclesiastical Terms*. London: Thomas Nelson and Sons Ltd.

Putnam, Robert. 1993. *Making Democracy Work: Civic Traditions in Modern Italy*. New Jersey: Princeton University Press.

———. 2000. *Bowling Alone: The Collapse and Revival of American Community*. New York: Simon and Schuster.

Raison-Jourde, Françoise. 1995. "The Madagascan Churches in the Political Arena and Their Contribution to the Change of the Regime 1990–1993." In Gifford 1995, 292–301.

Ranger, Terence O. 1978. "The Churches, the Nationalist State and African Religion." In Fasholé-Luke et al. 1978, 479–502.

———. 1986. "Religious Movements and Politics in Sub-Saharan Africa." *African Studies Review* 29 (2): 1–69.

———. 1995. "Conference Summary and Conclusion." In Gifford 1995, 14–35.

———. 1999. "Taking on the Missionary's Task: African Spirituality and the Mission Churches of Manicaland in the 1930s." *Journal of Religion in Africa* 29 (2): 175–205.

———. 2002. "The Zimbabwe Elections: A Personal Experience." *Transformation* 19 (3).

———, ed. 2003. *The Historical Dimensions of Democracy and Human Rights in Zimbabwe*. Vol. 2, *Nationalism, Democracy, and Human Rights*. Harare: University of Zimbabwe.

———. 2004. "Nationalist Historiography, Patriotic History, and the History of the Nation: The Struggle over the Past in Zimbabwe." *Journal of Southern African Studies* 30 (2): 215–234.

Ranger, Terence, and Mark Ncube. 1995. "Religion in the Guerrilla War: The Case of Southern Matabeleland." In *Society in Zimbabwe's Liberation War*, ed. Ngwabi Bhebe and Terence Ranger. Harare: University of Zimbabwe Publications.

Remmer, Karen. 1986. "Exclusionary Democracy." *Studies in Comparative International Development* 20 (Winter): 64–85.

Retief, Frank. 1994. *Tragedy to Triumph: A Christian Response to Trials and Sufferings*. Milton Keynes, U.K.: Nelson Word Publishing.

———. 1997. "The Truth and Reconciliation Commission Faith Community Hearings." East London, November 17–19. Unpublished.

Retief, Malcolm Wilhelm. 1958. *William Murray of Nyasaland*. Lovedale, South Africa: Lovedale Press.

Roesch, Otto. 1994. "The Politics of the Aftermath: Peasant Options in Mozambique." In Eduardo Mondlane Foundation, *Elections in Mozambique*. Seminar presentation, Amsterdam. Also published in Southern Africa Report 9 (3): 16–19.

Ross, Kenneth R., ed. 1996. *God, People, and Power in Malawi: Democratization in Theological Perspective*. Kachere Monograph 3. Blantyre, Malawi: Christian Literature Association in Malawi.

Rotberg, Robert I. 2000. "Africa's Mess, Mugabe's Mayhem." *Foreign Affairs* 79 (5): 47–61.

Sachikonye, Lloyd, ed. 1995. *Democracy, Civil Society, and the State: Social Movements in Southern Africa*. Harare, Zimbabwe: SAPES Books.

Sanneh, Lamin. 1994. "Translatability in Islam and in Christianity in Africa: A Thematic Approach." In *Religion in Africa: Experience and Expression*, ed. Thomas D. Blakely, Walter E. A. van Beek, and Dennis L. Thomson, 22–45. London: James Currey; Portsmouth, N.H.: Heinemann.

———. 1996. *Piety and Power: Muslims and Christians in West Africa*. Maryknoll, N.Y.: Orbis.

———. 2001. "A Resurgent Church in a Troubled Continent: Review Essay of Bengt Sundkler's History of the Church in Africa." *International Bulletin of Missionary Research* 25 (3): 113–118.

———. 2003. "Shari'ah Sanctions as Secular Grace? A Nigerian Islamic Debate and an Intellectual Response." *Transformation* 20 (4): 232–244.

Schoffeleers, Matthew. 1999. *In Search of Truth and Justice: Confrontation between Church and State in Malawi 1960–1994*. Kachere Book No. 8. Blantyre, Malawi: Christian Literature Association in Malawi.

Selolwane, Onalenna Doo. 1997. "Gender and Democracy in Botswana: Women's Struggle for Equality and Political Participation." In Nzongola-Ntalaja and Lee 1997.

———. 2006. "Gendered Spaces in Party Politics in Southern Africa: Progress and Regress since Beijing 1995." United Nations Research Institute for Social Development (UNRISD) Occasional Paper 13. Accessed at www.unrisd.org/publications/opgp13.

Sengulane, Denis. 1994. *Vitória sem vencidos: a história do processo de paz para Moçambique do ponto de vista do Conselho Cristão de Moçambique*. Maputo, Mozambique: CCM.

Serra, Carlos, ed. 1999. *Eleitorado Incapturável*. Maputo, Mozambique: Livraria Universitária, Universidade Eduardo Mondlane.

Shah, Timothy. 2000. *Proceedings of the Africa Regional Workshop*. INFEMIT Research Project on Evangelical Christianity and Political Democracy in the Third World. Harare, Zimbabwe.

Sichone, Owen B. 1999. "The Sacred and the Obscene: Personal Notes on Political Ritual, Poverty, and Democracy in Zambia." In Hyslop 1999, 152–166.

Singh, David Emmanuel. 2000. "Abu al-Al Mawdudi's Political Theory: Some Ideas for Muslim–Christian Relations." *Transformation* 17 (1): 6–14.

Smith, Edwin W. 1928. *The Way of the White Fields in Rhodesia: A Survey of Christian Enterprise in Northern and Southern Rhodesia*. London: World Dominion Press.

Sogge, David, ed. 1997. *Moçambique: Perspectivas sobre a ajuda e o sector civil.* Amsterdam: Frans Beijaard.

Solidarity Peace Trust, Zimbabwe and South Africa. 2003. "National Youth Service Training—'Shaping Youths in a Truly Zimbabwean Manner': An Overview of Youth Militia Training and Activities in Zimbabwe, October 2000–August 2003." Report dated September 5. Accessed at http://www.reliefweb.int/library/documents/2003/spt-zim-5sep.pdf.

Southall, Roger. 1999. "The 1999 Elections: Consolidating Democracy or Foreshadowing Decline?" *Indicator South Africa* 16 (1).

Spittler, Russell P. 1994. "Are Pentecostals and Charismatics Fundamentalists? A Review of American Uses of These Categories." In *Charismatic Christianity as a Global Culture*, ed. Karla Poewe, 103–116. Columbia, S.C.: University of South Carolina Press.

Steele, Ron, and Ray McCauley. 1996. *Power and Passion: Fulfilling God's Destiny for the Nation.* Cape Town: Struik Christian Books.

Sundkler, Bengt. G. M. 1961a. *Bantu Prophets in South Africa.* 2nd ed. London and New York: Oxford University Press.

———. 1961b. "The Concept of Christianity in the African Independent Churches." *African Studies* 20, 4: 203–213.

———. 1976. *Zulu Zion and Some Swazi Zionists.* London and New York: Oxford University Press.

Takaya, Bala. 1989–1990. "The Foundations of Religious Tolerance in Nigeria." *Bulletin of Ecumenical Theory* 2 (2)–3 (1).

Thompson, Edward P. 1964. *The Making of the English Working Class.* New York: Pantheon Books. (Published in the United Kingdom in 1963.)

Throup, David, and Charles Hornsby. 1998. *Multi-Party Politics in Kenya: The Kenyatta and Moi States and the Triumph of the System in the 1992 Election.* Oxford: James Currey.

Tomori, Pascal. 1991. *Anthony Obebunmi Okogie: The People's Bishop.* Lagos, Nigeria: Self-published.

Transparency International. 2005. *Transparency International Annual Report 2005.* Berlin. Accessed at http://www.transparency.org/publications/annual_report.

Turaki, Yusuf. 2000. "The Socio-political Implication of Sharia for Christian in Nigeria." Presented at a seminar in Kaduna organized by the Christian Association of Nigeria (CAN), January 29.

Turner, Harold W. 1978. "Patterns of Ministry and Structure Within Independent Churches." In Fasholé-Luke et al. 1978, 44–59.

Tutu, Desmond. 1995. "Identity Crisis." In Gifford 1995, 95–97.

Ugbolue, Henry. 2000. "Atiku in Trouble—Booed in Mecca." *The News*, 2 April 2, pp. 15–18.

Umar, Muhammad Sani. 1993. "Changing Islamic Identity in Nigeria from the 1960s to the 1980s: From Sufism to Anti-Sufism." In *Muslim Identity and Social Change in Sub-Saharan Africa*, ed. Louis Brenner, 154–178. London: Hurst and Co.

UNDP (United Nations Development Program). 1999. *Mozambique—Peace and Economic Growth: Opportunities for Human Development.* Mozambique National Human Development Report 1998. Maputo, Mozambique: UNDP.

van de Walle, Nicolas. 2001. *African Economies and the Politics of Permanent Crisis, 1979–1999*. Cambridge: Cambridge University Press.

van der Veer, Peter, ed. 1996. *Conversion to Modernities: The Globalization of Christianity*. London and New York: Routledge.

van Dijk, Rijk. 1992. "Young Puritan Preachers in Post-independence Malawi." *Africa* 62 (2): 159–181.

van Rooden, Peter. 1996. "Nineteenth-Century Representations of Missionary Conversion and the Transformation of Western Christianity." In van der Veer 1996, 65–87.

Venter, Dawid. 1999. "Globalization and the Cultural Effects of the World-Economy in a Semiperiphery: The Emergence of African Indigenous Churches in South Africa." *Journal of World-Systems Research* 5 (1): 104–126.

Vines, Alex. 1991. *Renamo: Terrorism in Mozambique*. London: Centre for Southern African Studies, University of York, in association with James Currey; Bloomington, Ind.: Indiana University Press.

Vines, Alex, and Ken Wilson. 1995. "Churches and the Peace Process in Mozambique." In Gifford 1995, 130–147.

von Doepp, Peter. 1998. "The Kingdom Beyond Zasintha: Churches and Political Life in Malawi's Post-authoritarian Era." In *Democratization in Malawi: A Stocktaking*, ed. Kings M. Phiri and Kenneth R. Ross. Kachere Books, No. 4. Blantyre, Malawi: Christian Literature Association in Malawi.

Walker, David. 1994. " 'Evangelicals and Apartheid' Revisited." *Journal of Theology for Southern Africa* 89 (December).

Walls, Andrew F. 1996. *The Missionary Movement in Christian History: Studies in the Transmission of Faith*. New York: Orbis Books and Edinburgh: T & T Clark.

Walshe, Peter. 1995. "Christianity and Democratisation in South Africa: The Prophetic Voice Within Phlegmatic Churches." In Gifford 1995, 74–94.

Wambugu, Njeru. 1997. "Why AICs Must Speak Out." *Baragumu*. Organization of African Instituted Churches, Research and Communication Services, Nairobi, Kenya.

Watt, Peter. 1992. *From Africa's Soil: The Story of the Assemblies of God in Southern Africa*. Cape Town: Struik Christian Books.

Weinrich, A. K. H. 1982. *African Marriage in Zimbabwe and the Impact of Christianity*. Gweru, Zimbabwe: Mambo Press.

Werbner, Richard. 1985. "The Argument of Images: From Zion to the Wilderness in African Churches." In *Theoretical Explorations in African Religion*, ed. Wim van Binsbergen and Matthew Schoffeleers, 253–286. London: Routledge & Kegan Paul.

———, ed. 1998. *Memory and the Postcolony: African Anthropology and the Critique of Power*. London: Zed Books.

West, Gerald O. 1999. *The Academy of the Poor: Towards a Dialogical Reading of the Bible*. Sheffield: Sheffield Academic Press.

West, Gerald O., and Musa W. Dube, eds. 2000. *The Bible in Africa: Transactions, Trajectories, and Trends*. Leiden: Brill.

Westerlund, David. 1992. "Secularism, Civil Religion or Islam? Islamic Revivalism and the National Question in Nigeria." In *Religion, State and Society in*

Contemporary Africa: Nigeria, Sudan, South Africa, Zaire and Mozambique, ed. Austin Metumara Ahanotu, 71–101. New York: Peter Lang.

Wilson, Ken B. 1992a. "Cults of Violence and Counter-violence in Mozambique." *Journal of Southern African Studies* 18 (3): 527–582.

———. 1992b. *Internally Displaced, Refugees and Returnees from and in Mozambique.* Swedish International Development Authority (SIDA) Studies on Emergencies and Disaster Relief, No. 1. Uppsala, Sweden : Nordiska Afrikainstitutet.

Wimbush, Vincent L., ed. 2000. *African Americans and the Bible: Sacred Texts and Social Textures.* New York: Continuum.

Wolffe, John, ed. 2002. *Global Religious Movements in Regional Context.* Aldershot, U.K.: Ashgate Publishing.

Woodberry, Robert D. 1999. "Religion and Democratization: Explaining a Robust Empirical Relationship." Presented at the annual meeting of the Religious Research Association, Boston, Mass., November 1999.

Xundu, C. M. 1988. "The Congress of the People Campaign and an Overall View of the Freedom Charter." In *The Freedom Charter and the Future*, ed. James A. Polley. Cape Town: Institute for a Democratic Alternative for South Africa (IDASA).

Zakaria, Fareed. 2003. *The Future of Freedom: Illiberal Democracy at Home and Abroad.* New York: W. W. Norton.

Index